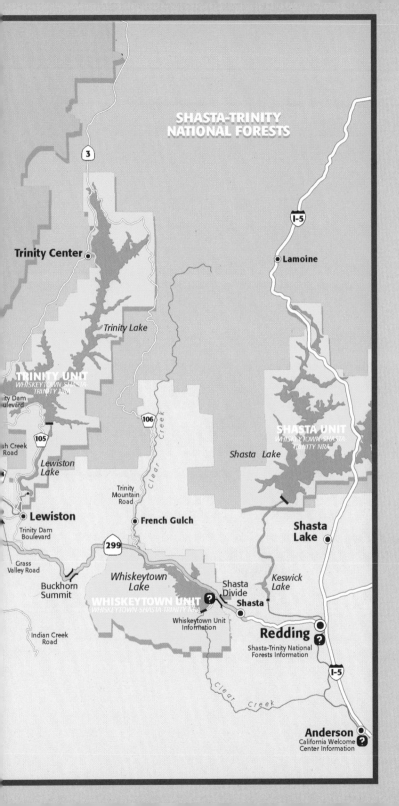

SHASTA-TRINITY NATIONAL FORESTS

3

I-5

Trinity Center

Lamoine

Trinity Lake

TRINITY UNIT
WHISKEYTOWN-SHASTA TRINITY NRA

106

ty Dam
ulevard

105

Shasta Lake

h Creek
Road

Lewiston
Lake

SHASTA UNIT
WHISKEYTOWN-SHASTA TRINITY NRA

Trinity
Mountain
Road

Shasta Lake

Clear Creek

Lewiston

French Gulch

Trinity Dam
Boulevard

Shasta
Lake

299

Keswick
Lake

Grass
Valley
Road

Whiskeytown
Lake

Shasta
Divide

Buckhorn
Summit

WHISKEYTOWN UNIT
WHISKEYTOWN SHASTA-TRINITY NRA

Shasta

Whiskeytown Unit
Information

Indian Creek
Road

Redding

Shasta-Trinity National
Forests Information

I-5

Clear Creek

Anderson
California Welcome
Center Information

S0-AFZ-471

Legend

TRINITY SCENIC BYWAY
Highway 299 • Blue Lake to Old Shasta

N
W — E
S

0   5   10   15   20 miles

〰️ Trinity Scenic Byway

Highway Summit

(299) State Highway Sign

Rivers and Creeks

Other Roads and Highways

[I-5] Interstate Freeway Sign

● ◉ ○ Cities and Towns

(101) Federal Highway Sign

🔥 Fire Lookout

⬡ Forest Highway Sign

❓ Tourist Information

(204) Primary Forest Route Sign

[5N13] Secondary Forest Route Sign

Traveling the Trinity Highway

Lowell "Ben" Bennion & Jerry Rohde
Principal Editors & Authors

Robin Stocum   *Chief Photographer*
Margaret W. Pearce   *Map Editor*
Riley Quarles   *Creative Guidance*

Kim T. Griswell & Gisela Rohde   *Associate Editors*
Mark Rounds *Associate Photographer* Charlie Villyard *Graphic Designer*
Skip Cody, Karen Mino Faukner, & Michael S. Meadows   *Cartographers*
Scores of Humboldt State University Students   *Associate Authors*

 MountainHome Books

Library of Congress Catalogue Number: 00-091768.
   ISBN number: 0-9640261-2-0
Manufactured by McNaughton & Gunn, Inc., Saline, MI
Published by **MountainHome Books**
First printing: November, 2000
Second printing: April, 2001

Colophon: Body text in Aldine 401 BT, sidebar text in Humanist 777 Light BT, body titles in Cooper Black Headline BT, sidebar headlines in Windsor BT; layout produced in Adobe PageMaker 6.5 *Plus* and Adobe Photoshop 5.0 LE.

Disclaimer: The information contained in this book is intended to provide users with an enhanced, safe touring experience. To the extent possible, the authors have identified potential hazards and have urged prudence and caution when visiting the areas described herein. The authors, publisher, sponsors, and copyright holder assume no responsibility for injuries, damage to equipment or goods, or other problems that readers of this book may encounter while traveling in the Highway 299 corridor and its surroundings, and this book is provided with this understanding acknowledged and accepted by the reader.

Notice: This project is made possible with a Rural Community Assistance Grant from the United States Department of Agriculture (USDA) Forest Service. USDA prohibits discrimination on the basis of race, color, national origin, sex, religion, age, disability, political affiliation and familial status.

MountainHome Books
1901 Arthur Road
McKinleyville, CA 95519
(707) 839-0078
gjrohde@reninet.com

Meet the Road Crew of Traveling the Trinity Highway:

Ben Bennion – coauthored *Sanpete Scenes: A Guide to Utah's Heart* in 1987. *Traveling the Trinity* caps a 35-year teaching career. He recently retired from Humboldt State University and moved to Salt Lake City to start a new life as a writer.

Jerry Rohde – has written three previous guidebooks with his wife, Gisela. He is a Past-President of the Humboldt County Historical Society, a part-time public school teacher, and an occasional Humboldt State University instructor.

Robin Stocum – is a Eureka native who lives in a restored miner's cabin in the Trinities with his wife, Eileen, and a friendly ringtail. His award-winning photos of outdoor scenes are shot with an antique camera that uses 4x 5-inch film.

Margaret W. Pearce – joined Humboldt State University in 1998 as an Assistant Professor of Geography. She has since used a National Science Foundation grant to create *Kosmos*—a state-of-the-art computer cartography lab.

Riley Quarles – as the Coordinator of the Courseware Development Center at Humboldt State University, Riley helps faculty generate CD-ROMs and websites for classroom use. For many years he lived in Trinity County.

Kim T. Griswell – has M.A.'s from Humboldt State University in Literature and in Teaching Writing. She currently works as a Book Development Manager for The Education Center, Inc. in Greensboro, North Carolina.

Gisela Rohde – besides publishing guidebooks with her husband, Jerry, Gisela gives presentations and conducts tours pertaining to natural history. She is also Serials Manager at the Humboldt State University Library.

Stan "Skip" Cody – graduated in 1995 from Humboldt State University in Geography. He currently applies his cartographic skills as an Applications Programmer for Thomas Brothers Maps in Irvine, California.

Karen Mino Faukner – earned a B.A. in Geography at Humboldt State University in 1999. Since then she has advanced to a position as GIS Technician/Cartographer at CH2M in Redding, California.

Michael S. Meadows – plans to graduate from Humboldt State University in 2002 with a major in Geography and a minor in Geology. On the side he has become proficient in making both maps and sushi, a rare combination.

Mark Rounds – graduated from Humboldt State University in 1995 with a major in Geography and a near minor in Photography. Mark now works in Santa Fe, New Mexico for the Santa Fe Southern railroad and as a freelance phtographer.

Charlie Villyard – is an Art major at Humboldt State University who plans to graduate in 2001. He has developed a strong interest in multimedia design and intends to specialize in book design and layout.

Table of Contents

Foreword

"An unsung land will die" is an often-stated Australian belief. As if in response to this creed, a community of writers composed of several score students and two professors from Humboldt State University produced this book. It is the exploration of a region and its history, a region situated along an astonishingly beautiful stretch of highway, river, and ocean in Northwestern California. The project began in a Geography class called "Writing about American Places," with students taking field trips to points along the Trinity Highway, then writing up their notes.

The idea for a book emerged, and students began to integrate their interviews with old-timers, their library research, and their field observations. The little towns along the Scenic Byway served as subjects for the chapters, and the highway itself became an organizing vehicle for the text. The book took a long time to complete. What transpired was a kind of literary relay, with one group researching and writing on an area until the semester ended, and then passing on their unfinished but vital work to the next set of student researchers and writers, who carried the project forward until the end of their term. The relay continued semester after semester, year after year.

The writings grew in number and improved in quality. Every new class and every new set of students approached their subjects with new excitement. They conducted research on families, uncovered the histories of buildings, described the flora and fauna of the land, and presented the stories and legends of various peoples—Native Americans, White Americans, French, English, Chinese, Irish, Portuguese—who inhabited the Shasta-Trinity-Humboldt region over time. In their writings, students penetrated layers of geographical, natural, and human history until each place was unveiled in many of its particulars.

Guiding these students in their research and field trips, and providing the continuity necessary between the various classes and writers, were Professors Ben Bennion and Jerry Rohde. Ben and Jerry's inspiring leadership evoked improved writing from every young participant, allowing the project to grow. Most important, their editing and revisions brought coherence, art, and vitality to the text, so that, finally, it became what it is: a colorful, comprehensive, and memorable record of a place and time which are emblematic of the evolution of the American West.

The dedication of Professors Bennion and Rohde to their students, whom they took on— one by one—as apprentices and co-authors, must be emphasized. Seldom do undergraduates enjoy such an opportunity to work with published authors and to write under such careful and caring direction. Unlike most students in college writing classes, these young people wrote for real purposes, for a real audience, under the guidance of experienced hands. This book is a testimony to the finest of teaching and learning.

Traveling the Trinity Highway captures the spirits of the land as well as the spirits of our ancestors. In reading it, one experiences the birth pangs of a little town called Weaverville and the death throes of the Wiyot tribe on Indian Island, near the city of Eureka. One relives the conflict of cultures and customs in stories about the Chinese in Shasta, Trinity, and Humboldt counties. One marvels at the endurance of people who survived floods, fires, and violent fights with agonizing regularity.

There are many ways to read a book like this. It is geography, history, myth, biography, and architecture. It is a study of the process by which a so-called wilderness surrendered to a mobile civilization. It is a handbook for exploring towns and studying landscapes, for reading maps and photos, for learning about the rocks, plants, and waters that are the backdrop for human drama. It is a dialogue of the past with the present, of old voices with new voices. The whole of the book lets one see, hear, breathe, and taste the Shasta end of the Sacramento Valley, the Trinity River and its little towns, the California Pacific and its northernmost ports. It is hoped that this book will have a lasting effect, not only in memorializing this marvelous and still mysterious region, but in teaching us to be ever more conscious of our own particular place, wherever that may be.

—Karen A. Carlton, Dean,
Humboldt State University

Preface

The term *Trinity* generally refers to three closely related things, most often to a trio of gods. However, California's Trinity River got its name from an early but erroneous assumption that it emptied into the Pacific at Trinidad Bay. Since then several other important places in Northern California have received the same *toponym*: notably the alps that separate the Trinity from the Klamath River, a forest, a lake, and the 140-mile highway that connects the Central Valley and the North Coast. The road from Redding to Arcata took its name from the county at its center, which counts as many black-and-white mileposts as Shasta and Humboldt counties combined.

These three counties form a tenuous trinity whose most tangible connection is Highway 299. This vital corridor may carry more traffic than many scenic byways, especially in the summer when residents of the foggy North Coast move inland for more sun while Central Valley dwellers head west for relief from the heat. But both sets of travelers, as they cross the four summits between the valley and the coast, have long recognized the scenic splendors of the up-and-down region. In 1993 the United States Forest Service's Shasta-Trinity National Forest and Six Rivers National Forest acted on that perception by recommending and securing "Scenic Byway" status for Highway 299 West.

To make travelers more aware of the Trinity Corridor's attractions, the Forest Service's Big Bar Ranger District, halfway along the highway, teamed up with two other groups to create another unusual trinity. Led by the Trinity County Chamber of Commerce, towns along the road formed a Trinity Scenic Byway Association (TSBA) to promote interest in the region. The third member of the team, Humboldt State University (HSU) in Arcata, became involved simply through serendipity. On a Labor Day weekend (1990), Geography Professor Ben Bennion hiked Granite Peak in the Trinity Alps. After traveling part of Highway 3 (already a Scenic Byway), he completed a Forest Service Customer Survey Card about the route and its brochure and recommended a similar guide for Highway 299. Eighteen months later the survey card reached the desk of Virginia Beres, a Big Bar ranger, who informed Bennion of the Forest Service's and TSBA's plans. Together they proposed publication of both a brochure and a guidebook based on essays drafted by students in Bennion's place-writing classes—a project endorsed by all three sponsors and funded largely by the Forest Service.

A prize-winning *Trinity Scenic Byway* flier appeared in 1994, but given its broader scope, the book has taken almost as long to complete as the rugged South Fork-North Fork stretch of the highway did. From fall 1992 until Bennion's retirement (spring 1999), scores of students signed up for Trinity-related courses to prepare papers for publication. Alas, these would-be authors and their teacher soon realized that quality writing requires frequent revision. One semester-long class did not allow enough time to probe a place in depth or revise a report more than twice.

To assist with the requisite rewriting and revising, "Dr. B." hired three professionals—guidebook authors Jerry & Gisela Rohde and Kim T. Griswell, a Master's candidate in English. Their writing and editing raised the standards originally set for the book by Ben. Students listed as co-authors may be surprised to see how much the four editors' red pens have pruned and changed their prose. (We have added our names to theirs so they'll know whom to credit or blame for the edits.) Students cited as contributors played a vital role as researchers in creating rough drafts for what Dean Karen Carlton's perceptive *Foreword* terms a "literary relay."

The same sort of upgrading affected the visuals prepared by the first group of graphic artists. Thanks to HSU's new Kosmos cartography lab and Professor Margaret Pearce, Karen M. Faukner and Michael S. Meadows could refine Stan "Skip" Cody's original maps. On one of many Trinity fieldtrips, Bennion met a fine photographer named Robin Stocum, who was much better equipped than student Mark Rounds to reprint old photos and develop new ones. Trinity Scenic Byway Association leader Dale Lackey began the design and layout of the book but had to withdraw for health reasons. At that crucial juncture (August 1999), Jerry & Gisela Rohde replaced him on PageMaker. We later secured the aid of

HSU's Courseware Development Center Director Riley Quarles and Designer Charlie Villyard in preparing the book for publication.

In the course of producing this portrait of the Trinity Highway, we have come to feel as fortunate as the legendary princes of Serendip. When they traveled, "they were always making discoveries, by accidents and sagacity, of things which they were not in quest of…" (*The American Heritage Dictionary*, 3ᵈ ed., p. 1647). We think the unforeseen changes in the long evolution of the book have improved its quality. Giving the book more of a "Ben & Jerry" flavor than originally planned has enabled us to blend various writing styles into what we hope readers will regard as a satisfying taste of a fascinating byway. (We also hope some of you share our fondness for wordplay).

Ben & Jerry's superb team has created a unique guidebook, one designed to cultivate what HSU publicist Tim Sims terms "an affinity for the Trinities"—not just the mountains and rivers but many of the sites and landscapes tied to this scenic byway. We have anchored the towns strung out along the corridor in the context of their changing connections with each other. Integrated with the text are some 150 illustrations, selected to help readers visualize the people and places we have highlighted. The inclusion of many older images underscores the countless changes wrought by fires, floods, and an American fondness for the most modern fashions.

We have prepared this guide for all Trinity Highway travelers, even armchair types, but especially for *topophiles*, those who love to stop and explore a particular town, trail, river, or ruin. Following the bird's-eye view of the salient features of the Trinity Corridor, the guide is divided into six regions. Since the geographical sequence proceeds east to west, travelers coming from the opposite direction will need to read the regional chapters and their sub-sections in reverse order. We regret this inconvenience but could not avoid the problem. The book has a landscape, or horizontal, format to fit the highway itself and features six orientation maps, all drawn at the same scale, opposite each regional chapter's table of contents. We have included larger-scale maps for the seven towns chosen for "customized" tours. Dedicated place-lovers may wish to secure more detailed maps and guides in advance of making a Trinity trip.

In pursuing the lures of Highway 299 that piqued our interest the most, we soon discovered the truth of an axiom expressed by two lifelong Trinity residents. One observed that "History here is not an exercise in documenting fact. Legends, fanciful tales, and less-than-factual memories embellish much of the oral and written history of this region." The other Trinitarian, referring to a local historian who liked to stretch his stories, made the same point more succinctly: "He drew a long bow." Among our sources we often found contradictory versions of a given incident like the China Slide of 1890. Should we present both accounts, accept one as more reliable than the other, or search for yet another? Ultimately we had to make many such judgment calls, especially in creating the anecdotes, often framed as sidebars, that we used to enliven our place descriptions and interpretations. We have tried to report our findings accurately but accept responsibility for any errors (fie!) that have crept into the volume.

Finally, we want to thank the many people who have assisted us in "Traveling the Trinity Highway" countless times. On the acknowledgements page, we list our student contributors and then, in east-west order, the people who have provided information, critiques, and permissions. At the end we identify the written sources we found most valuable.

All local informants still know far more about their particular places than we, as outsiders, have learned over the past eight years. They may even agree to guide you around their locales, if you can catch them at a convenient time. Perhaps our overview will encourage these experts to examine more closely the people and places bound together by the Trinity Highway and spur regional scholars to write more comprehensive histories of the tri-county corridor.

Fortunately for topophiles, this scenic byway has not attracted tourists en masse, so even at the most frequented sites or on the most popular trails, Trinity travelers seldom have to contend with crowds. Thanks to their remote and rugged nature, Northern California's various "Trinities"—whether highway, river, mountains, or forest—disperse their residents and visitors because they contain such an array of appealing places.

Happy traveling along, on, in, and through the Trinities!

—Ben & Jerry

Acknowledgements & Sources

Student Contributors:

Student writers who contributed were: Jennifer Ackerman, Paul Amaral, Lesley Atlansky, John Barco, Charlie Bennett, James Black, Justin Byrne, William Carlson, Nicole Cosentino, Stephanie Coultas, Wesley Crawford, Daniel "Joe" Dacus, Brian Dowd, Richard England, Carter Fleming, Amy Gibbard, Kevin Gibbs, Robert Gjestland, Brent Goudreau, Kain Hanschke, Christian Harlow, Scott Hermann, Graham Hill, Mark Hoerl, James Hopson, Conrad Huygen, James "Jay" Johnston, Brian Knott, Suzan Logwood, Catherine McCluskey, Susan Nash, Joshua Nolan, Anders Olsen, Robert Pekari, Cari Pogan, Christopher Rhodes, John Slanika, Bill Smith, Erich Sommer, Chris Stone, Blake Thomas, Neal Wagner, Monty Walker, Will Warto, Benjamin Weinberg, Donald Wilson, Timothy Williams, Suzanne York.

Providers of Assistance & Information:

We are indebted to many institutions and individuals for their help. In Redding, Duane Lyon, Public Affairs Officer, Shasta-Trinity National Forest, has given the book unstinting support and the editors remarkably free rein. Ken DeCamp, Forest Service Visual Information Specialist, produced the fine inside cover map and critiqued the French Gulch section. Dr. Winfield Henn, head of the Forest Service's Heritage Resource Program, and Bureau of Land Management archaeologist Eric Ritter unearthed valuable documents for us.

At the Shasta Historical Society in Redding, Diane Kathleen and her volunteer staff found photos, maps, and other key sources for Chapter II. Judge Richard B. Eaton granted several students interviews and then read what they wrote with a critical eye. Linda Cooper, Jack Frost, and Winnie Yeung at Shasta State Historic Park helped us tap their Museum's fine collections. Staff of the National Park Service's Whiskeytown Unit, notably Carol Jandrall and Wendy Janssen, provided critical information and insights. In French Gulch we interviewed Andy Bouchard, Judy and David Brinton, Don Carlson, Bernice Fox, Henry Feutrier, and Gene and Marie Nixon.

No one assisted Ben & Jerry's team more than the Weaverville Museum's friendly and efficient staff. They took their cue from the Museum's manager, Hal Goodyear, who never refused any of many requests. Weaverites whom we interviewed included Irl Everest, Pat Hicks, Greg Lowden, Steve Mackay, Henry Meckel, Pat and Blaine Menning, Diane and Joe Mercier, Leonard and Scott Morris, and Herb Woods. The Trinity County Library's staff in Weaverville cheerfully offered their help. Pat Mortensen, Trinity County Grants Administrator, served as an efficient liaison for the final critical year of the project.

Elsewhere in Trinity County, Susan Shepherd and Jim Smith of Junction City, Kim McLaughlin of Rigdzin Ling, and Harold Rodgers of Slattery Gulch provided essential information. Charley Fitch's Big Bar Ranger District staff, particularly Virginia Beres and Gay Berrien, helped us greatly. Lee Carpenter introduced us to Burnt Ranch, and Danny and Marie Ammon and Dena Magdalen oriented us to their South Fork/Salyer homeland.

In the Willow Creek/Hoopa area we relied heavily upon Stephen Paine, Elsie and Richard Ricklefs, Max and Marc Rowley, Bill Skoonberg, and Margaret Wooden. The Humboldt County Historical Society staff, especially Matina Kilkenny, graciously shared their expertise, as did Jean Leavitt (Blue Lake), Tom Richardson (Korbel), Cam Appleton, Michael Behney, Brousse Brizard, Tom Gage, Susie Van Kirk, and Dick Wild (all of Arcata), Ray Hillman and Arlene Hartin (both of Eureka), and Jim Chezem (Redwood Creek). The many docents at the Humboldt County Library's Humboldt Room were always willing to offer their help. At Humboldt State University (HSU) we turned often to the staff of *its* Humboldt Room—Joan Berman, Edie Butler, and Erich Schimps. Tom Mendenhall frequently provided computer assistance. We received material and moral support from college deans Lee Bowker, Mark Rocha, and Karen Carlton (an unusually fine facilitator). Vice-President Don Christensen provided enrichment grants through the HSU Foundation for two writing workshops that allowed students to interact with Karen Carlton (as an English professor) and distinguished place writer Page Stegner. The HSU Geography Department gave Bennion great latitude in scheduling Trinity-related classes.

We extend special thanks to our patient, if gently prodding wives, to whom we dedicate this guidebook. For years they had good reason to wonder if they would ever see any light at the end of the long highway.

Selected Sources:

Architectural Resources Group. *Eureka: An Architectural View*. Eureka: Eureka Heritage Society, 1987.

Boggs, Mae H. B., Compiler. *My Playhouse Was A Concord Coach*. Oakland, CA: Howell North Press, 1942.

Carr, John. *Pioneer Days in California*. Eureka, CA: Times Publishing Co., 1891.

Cox, Isaac. *The Annals of Trinity County*. Eugene, OR: Harold C. Holmes, 1940.

Eastwood, Alice. "From Redding to the Snow-Clad Peaks of Trinity County." *Sierra Club Bulletin* IV, no. 1 (Jan. 1902): 39–52.

——. "Trees and Shrubs of Trinity County." *Sierra Club Bulletin* IV, no. 1 (Jan. 1902): 53–58.

Fountain, Susie Baker. "Papers." Photocopy. (Available in the Humboldt County and Humboldt State University libraries.)

Fountain, Susie Baker. "The Story of Blue Lake." (Available in the Humboldt State University Library.)

Giffen, Helen S. *Man of Destiny: Pierson Barton Reading*. Redding, CA: Shasta Historical Society, 1985.

Heizer, Robert F. *Handbook of North American Indians*, Vol. 8. Washington, D.C.: Smithsonian Institution, 1978.

Huntington, C. A. "Autobiography." Photocopy. (Available at the Humboldt County Historical Society.)

Jones, Alice Goen. *Flowers and Trees of the Trinity Alps*. Weaverville, CA: Trinity County Historical Society, 1986.

——, ed. *Trinity County Historic Sites*. Weaverville, CA: Trinity County Historical Society, 1981.

Jorstadt, W. O. "George." *Behind the Wild River: A Search for a Better Way to Live*. Lewiston, CA: Trinity, 1995.

La Grange, Clémentine de. *From the Known to the Unknown; The Memoirs of Baroness de La Grange, 1892–1894*. Translated from French by Thomas Buckley, PhD. Weaverville, CA: Trinity County Historical Society, 2000.

Linkhart, Luther, and Michael White. *The Trinity Alps: A Hiking and Backpacking Guide*. 3d ed. Berkeley: Wilderness Press, 1994.

Meckel, Henry. "From Whom We Are Descended." Photocopy.

White, Katherine A. *A Yankee Trader in the Gold Rush: The Letters of Franklin A. Buck*. Boston/New York City: Houghton Mifflin Co., 1930.

Wilutis, Richard. "The History of the Trinity Highway: A Study in Transportation Dynamics." Master's thesis, Humboldt State University, 1990.

History clipping and pamphlet file collections at: Humboldt County Library, Eureka; Humboldt County Historical Society; Humboldt State University Library; Trinity County Historical Society History Center; Trinity County Library, Weaverville.

Newspapers: *Arcata Union, Blue Lake Advocate, Humboldt Times, Redding Record-Searchlight, Trinity Journal*.

Periodicals: *The Covered Wagon, The Humboldt Historian, Trinity*.

Acronyms for Photo Credits:

BLM – Blue Lake Museum
CHPW – *California Highways and Public Works*
HCHS – Humboldt County Historical Society
HSSA – Historic Sites Society of Arcata
HSU – HSU Library
RRS – *Redding Record-Searchlight*
SHS – Shasta Historical Society
SSHP – Shasta State Historic Park
STC – Simpson Timber Company
TCHS – Trinity County Historical Society
WCCFM – Willow Creek/China Flat Museum
WNRA – Whiskeytown National Recreation Area

Color Photo/Map Credits:

Key: BB: Ben Bennion; KD: Ken DeCamp; GR: Gisela Rohde; JR: Jerry Rohde; MR: Mark Rounds; RS: Robin Stocum; CV: Charlie Villyard; JW: Judy Walton.

Front cover: RS; back cover, clockwise from upper left: RS, BB, RS, BB; inside cover map: KD, CV; color collage, 1st page: 1. GR, 2. GR, 3. BB, 4. RS, 5. MR, 6. JR, 7. RS; color collage, 2nd and 3rd pages: 1. JR, 2. MR, 3. JR, 4. RS, 5. RS, 6. RS, 7. RS, 8. BB, 9. RS, 10. RS, 11. MR; color collage, 4th page: 1. JR, 2. BB, 3. JW, 4. BB, 5. MR.

Mount Shasta, snow-mantled monument of Northern California, seems to float above the trackside weeds near, appropriately, the Siskiyou County town of Weed. The 14,162-foot pinnacle acts as an intermittent beacon for the Trinity corridor, even for planes hovering over Humboldt Bay. (Robin Stocum photo)

I: A Bird's-Eye View of a Serpentine Highway

Trails & Tribulations: Rough Routes From Redding & the Redwoods

As Hilton McDonald was bringing the mail from Burnt Ranch to Junction City last Wednesday, just as he reached Pelletreau Point the pack mule stumbled and fell off the trail, rolling 200 feet down into the Trinity River. The mule was killed but floated out. All the mail was recovered except the locked sack containing letters and valuables. This is the first time that we remember that the mail has been lost on that route.

— *Blue Lake Advocate*, May 10, 1913

McDonald was not, however, the first to have trouble traversing the trails of the Trinity. Packers, travelers, and other mail carriers had endured such difficulties since the 1850s, when whites began making their way to the gold diggings along the river and its tributaries. Rich but remote, the region defied easy access, so that McDonald found himself following the same routes and using the same mode of travel as had his predecessors for more than 60 years. By the time of his mishap, railroads and highways had penetrated most of the state, but it would take another decade before the river gorge grudgingly saw its first road, the original version of the Trinity Highway.

Whites found travel in Trinity country troublesome from the start. Jedediah Smith led a party of trappers, mules, and horses through the territory in 1828; it took them an entire month to cross the mountains northwest of Red Bluff before they finally reached the Hoopa Valley. The Josiah Gregg Party had, if anything, a more trying time of it 21 years later when they pushed west from the Trinity diggings toward the ocean, crossing a series of heartbreakingly steep ridges and then plodding through the nearly impenetrable redwood forest as they neared the coast. Had the golden, riverside riches of the Trinity not beckoned, few subsequent travelers would have been bold enough to attempt the return trip.

But gold was there in abundance, discovered less than six months after the great Mother Lode rush of 1848. The new strike drew streams of miners, merchants, and mule packers into the mountains and canyons of the Trinity region, and soon a series of routes offered passage inland from the coast. Trails departed Rohnerville (near Fortuna), Eureka, and Union (now Arcata)—all bound for the mining camps, all fraught with such perils as aggrieved Indians, poor pathways, blizzards, and floods.

Most of the Trinity trails went somewhat south of the present highway, crossing through hill and ridge country that offered easier going than following the rugged river and stream canyons. In 1887 a more northerly route finally opened from Charlie Berry's place on Redwood Creek eastward to Willow Creek. The first part of the trail, which had been built by Berry him-

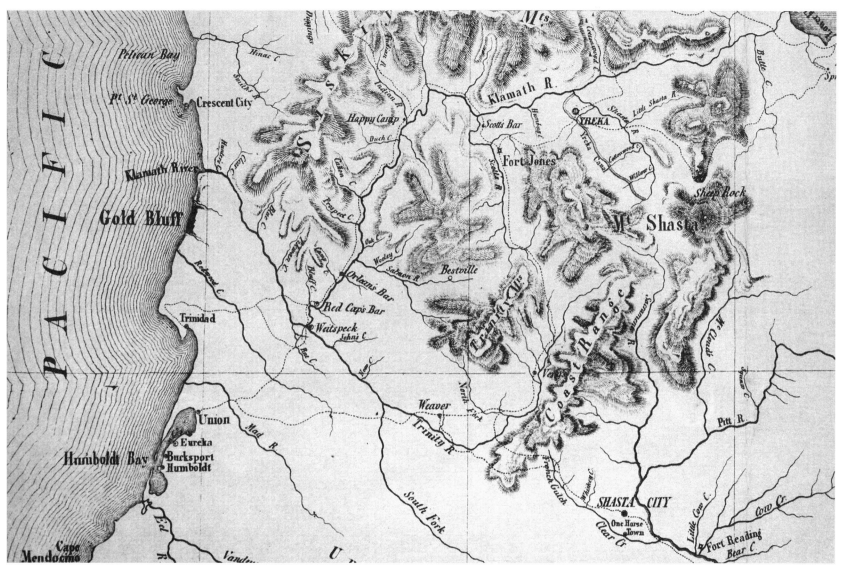

Part of perhaps the first "Map of Lower Oregon and Upper California," published by Thomas Tennent, 1853. Note Weaver's (Weaverville) location midway between the supply centers of coastal Union (Arcata) and inland Shasta City (Shasta). (SHS map)

self, was grandly called a "road" but hardly deserved the description; it was reportedly "constructed on the cheapest ground with no regard as to grade or elevation. In some of the steepest places the grade exceeds 30%, which would be a good slope for a house roof." Wagoners had to add two horses to their usual five-horse team when making the climb.

The more westerly stretch of the Arcata–Willow Creek route was in better shape; it was gravel-covered roadway all the way to Bald Mountain, a grass-topped peak lying along the Mad River–Redwood Creek divide; Brizard & Co., which operated several general stores in the inland area, maintained a warehouse on the flank of the mountain. Brizard shipped supplies by rail from the company's main store in Arcata to a branch store in Blue Lake, whence the goods were transferred to wagons for the journey past Korbel, up the mountain through Angel's Ranch, and on to the warehouse. In dry weather the wagons could continue to Hoopa or Willow Creek, but when rain turned the ungraveled sections of road to mud, the merchandise was repacked onto mules for the final part of the trip.

Overall, travel and transport were easier when approaching the Trinity region from the east. William Spencer Lowden completed the Buckhorn (Grass Valley) Toll Road in the late 1850s, crossing Buckhorn Summit and building an astounding 150 bridges along the route.

(*See sidebar, below.*) When the first stage from Shasta came over the road in late April 1858, it was met and escorted into Weaverville by a collection of citizens in buggies and on horseback, along with the town's German brass band. "There was," reported the *Trinity Journal*, "a performance on the Independence balcony by the band [that] ended the demonstration in honor of one great step in the progression of improvement." Three years later, Charles Camden built a shorter and easier toll road from Shasta that connected with the eastern end of Lowden's road at the Tower House. A full-fledged thoroughfare now connected Weaverville with Shasta, which was strategically situated on the Sacramento to Portland stage line.

Roadbuilders' Reprise

To say that roadbuilding ran in the Lowden family is an understatement; it absolutely galloped. When William Spencer Lowden began his 24°-mile toll road in 1857, he commenced more than a century of continuous Lowden-related road activity in Northern California. Inspired by William Spencer, the next three generations of Lowdens crafted the region's highways and turnpikes, until the local roadmaps were filled with their work.

William Spencer was not content with his first roadway, even though at the time it was considered "the finest in the state." Within a few years he had joined with James Hoadley and W. L. Fox to create the Lewiston Turnpike, a 14-mile toll road that linked Whiskeytown and Lewiston and served as a wet-weather alternate to Lowden's Buckhorn route.

William Spencer's sons, Hank and William Jefferson, continued their father's work by operating the Buckhorn toll franchise until it expired in 1912. That same year, one of William Jefferson's offspring, Spence, took up the flame by joining the California Division of Highways. As an engineer, he helped design all the major routes along the state's spine—the Sierra Nevada—including highways 395 and 209. At age 63, Spence died at his desk, an engineer to the end.

Spence's brother, Perry Sr., was yet another Lowden highwayman. Perry kept to low ground, working on route 70 in the Feather River Canyon and on 299 along the Trinity, where he helped extend his grandfather's road of almost a hundred years earlier.

Perry Jr. followed the family tradition into the fourth generation by also becoming a state highway engineer. He proudly noted that while the course of his great-grandfather's toll road "has been modified in some places, we are still using the route he carved out over Buckhorn Summit."

Perhaps the early Lowdens did their work too well. The state is now crisscrossed with a near-sufficiency of roadways, leaving so little challenge for modern-day highway engineers that none of the latest crop of Lowdens—Perry Jr.'s kids—has chosen to follow in their busy forebears' routefinding, roadbuilding footsteps.

Mexican packers with their loaded mule train in Blue Lake. Such trains supplied A. Brizard's chain of general merchandise stores, located in the outlying areas of Humboldt, southern Del Norte, and western Trinity counties. Note Brizard's "Emporium" at right rear. (HCHS photo)

A four-span mule team hauls freight from Redding across the Trinity above Lewiston, c. 1910. (C. E. Goodyear photo)

The Buckhorn Toll Road's "one great step" was followed by a series of stumbles. A pair of great road-thwarting ridgelines stood between the coast and the Trinity River, while the way west of Weaverville was blocked by bulky, mineral-rich Oregon Mountain. Worse yet was the canyon of the Trinity itself, whose steep slopes and rocky gorge defied anything but the roughest of trails. Work crews gnawed and nibbled at the terrain, trying to build a through road from inland valley to coast, but for decades a thin trail served as the only link.

Yet the roadbuilders persisted, and from both ends they gradually pushed their way toward the center of the route. A road out of Weaverville was cut through the La Grange Mine operation on the west side of Oregon Mountain; the mine closed in 1918, and about a decade later the road was rerouted over the tailings themselves. Sharply inclined and twisting, the roadbed was littered with what locals called "Ford eggs"—rocks that motorists had placed behind the wheels of their Model A's when they stalled on the steep climb.

From the west, work crews contracted to build sections of the roads to Hoopa and Willow Creek. It was slow, demanding work. The first step was to clear any trees and rocks out of the proposed route, using dynamite when necessary. Then came the initial roadbed cut, made with a 400-pound, horse-drawn plow; if the slope was too steep for horses, the cut had to be widened by pick and shovel. Next was more horse work, this time with a V-bladed scraper that pushed the loosened dirt over the outside bank. The plow and scraper then alternated until the roadbed was extended to its full width. Even these minimally mechanized operations were eschewed by some roadbuilders; one contractor, the Charlie Moon family of Redwood Creek, built their entire half-mile section of 12-foot-wide road using only picks, shovels, wheelbarrows, and great determination.

In time the road crews reached Willow Creek and pushed east, following the main Trinity until they reached its confluence with the South Fork. There, construction stopped; wagons could go no farther, so their cargoes were unloaded, ferried across the South Fork, and then packed onto mules (the same old story) for the lengthy last leg of the upriver journey. (*See sidebar, next page.*)

Far to the east, the road over Oregon Mountain had been extended along the north side of

Hennessey's High Road Hiatus

The trails that satisfied most of the river's hardy residents were not, for John Hennessey, adequate for his aging mother. She and her husband had located long ago above Burnt Ranch and Maria Hennessey, now a widow, had grown old on the family homestead. In the meantime her son John had grown rich, making a killing in the Nevada mines. In 1905 he decided that Maria should have easier traveling to the coast. Hennessey accordingly retained his brother-in-law, the surveyor for Sutter County, to lay out a road from the South Fork Trinity to the family ranch and bankrolled $10,000 to build it.

Construction of the 12-mile route proved more difficult than anticipated, and Hennessey poured more dollars into the project as his workmen chipped away at an unyielding stretch of rock. Then the panic of 1907 hit; financiers across the country saw their fortunes fall apart. If Hennessey felt the pinch at first, he didn't show it; work on the road (and debits to his bank account) continued. By May 1909, nine miles of the route were finished, and the local paper announced that the "remaining three miles will undoubtedly be built this summer."

The paper was wrong. Hennessey had already spent more than $50,000 on the project, and his reserves were running low. Late in the previous year he had offered to give the state both the unfinished road and a bonus of $5,000 if they would build the last stretch. The highway department, however, wanted a lower-elevation route to Burnt Ranch that followed the Trinity River, and Hennessey's high road, bound for the family homestead, went over Hennessey Ridge instead. The offer was refused.

Hennessey's Road remained only three-fourths built. John died, and later his mother, still unable to reach town by wagon, also passed away. When a road at last reached the Hennessey place, it was an entirely different one that came up the Burnt Ranch side of the ridge from the new highway. Years later, the CCC finally finished the nearly forgotten ridge-crossing road, and it can be traveled today as a Forest Service backcountry route.

The road still bears John Hennessey's name. Yet despite his best efforts, it never bore his mother.

Feeding time: John Hennesssey with a pair of bear cubs.
(TCHS photo, gift of Lowrie Gifford)

the river from Junction City as far as North Fork (Helena), but this still left the remote 40-mile stretch between the south and north forks of the Trinity with only pack and mail trails for travel.

For years those forty miles between the North Fork and South Fork remained roadless. Construction along rock-studded cliffs, as John Hennessey had discovered, was time-consuming and expensive. To make matters worse, state highway officials, in an ill-founded attempt to economize, had selected a more southerly route as the first "lateral" connecting the North Coast with the Sacramento Valley. The course they chose began near Fortuna, ran east up the Van Duzen River, and then zigzagged over the mountains to Red Bluff; it had the advantage of utilizing a section of preexisting road, but it never came close to the Trinity County seat of Weaverville or to the many towns that lay along the river. Completed in 1912, it languished in limbo, traced more often across a map than driven in an auto.

This southerly road, which became Highway 36, preempted state funding for a Trinity lateral. The only boost the northern route received was a $50,000 federal allocation from the Forest Service, which saw the road as vital to the development (chiefly through logging) of the Trinity National Forest.

But merchants and motorists, businessmen and boosters all agitated for a roadway along the river, and the state at last began work to link Arcata and Redding with a through highway.

With handbuilding still the order of the day, the state economized by recruiting convicts from San Quentin and Folsom prisons to do much of the work. As the crews hacked and blasted their way along the rocky riverside slopes, locals still took to the pack trails for their supplies. Many of the mid-river residents kept their own string of mules for this purpose; every spring and fall the Pattison, Trimble, and Waldorff families each took a train of eight to twelve animals to Korbel, the closest source of cheap provisions. Picking their way over the trails, the mules averaged about 20 miles a day, which meant overnight stops at or near Hyampom, Grouse Mountain, and High Prairie both coming and going. At Korbel, the redoubtable

Trinity River Highway construction crew challenged by the New River Bluffs, Burnt Ranch area, c. 1918. (WCCFM photo)

High Praise for the New Highway

While driving the just-completed roadway, one motorist was transported to poetic heights as he passed through the river's deep gorge. Writing to the *Blue Lake Advocate*, words gushed from his pen like water tumbling down the Trinity, as he told of traveling

...up the Trinity River over the new Highway, sometimes 1200 feet or more above the water, with its long snake like tail cut through the solid rock; the deep, dark shadowy canyons, and precipitous walls, garnished as it were with forests of fir and pine and in the open space yellow and purple flowers in profusion, and way down below you, so far the sense of distance seems to thrill, even to the extent of fear in some, you see small mountain streams emerging out of a green canopy, the small cataracts, riffles and falls showing silver in the sunlight, and the deep pools a blue, so intense in color...

Yet if such marvels were now available to an adventurous motorist, another aspect of the canyon had been lost. The packers and their animals, after a reign of almost 75 years, were now gone, and no longer could another observer write:

There is something very pleasing and picturesque in the sight of a large packtrain of mules quietly descending a hill, as each one intelligently examines the trail, and moves carefully, step by step, on the steep and dangerous declivity, as though he suspected danger to himself or injury to the pack committed to his care.

Now it was left to trucks and buses to transport the pump organs, cook stoves, and children that the mules had, for so many decades, so carefully carried.

mules were each loaded with up to 300 pounds of goods—coal oil in five-gallon cans, flour in 50-pound sacks, crackers, sugar, salt, coffee—with three sacks lashed to each side of every animal. The Pattisons alone packed in 1,200 pounds of flour on every trip, by itself a four-or-more-mule load.

The mule trains moved more than foodstuffs. In 1917, a music lover on the middle Trinity packed a pump organ between Helena and Big Bar, making the nine-mile trip in four hours. Earlier cargoes on other routes were even more impressive: a 600-pound millstone conveyed by a single mule between Shasta and Weaverville in 1855; a cast iron, six-hole cook stove that went from Helena all the way to Burnt Ranch; a quarter-ton engine transported to a North Fork placer mine; and various small children, who were loaded into accommodating wooden boxes that were then lashed to the mules' saddles and carried 25 miles along the narrow trail above the North Fork.

Mule packing dwindled as roads replaced the trails. Brizard & Co. ran its last pack train in 1919, but some far-removed residents held out longer. Only in 1924 did apple ranchers in Zenia, situated in remote southwestern Trinity County, finally abandon the trails; they'd found an innovative and inexpensive way to ship their produce to Weaverville—send it by *parcel post*. The fruit was first trucked to the Northwestern Pacific Railroad, which ran through the southwestern corner of the county; from there the ambulant apples went by rail south to Santa Rosa and then east and north to Redding, where they were again loaded onto trucks and taken the last leg along the new highway. It required a looping trip of 460 miles to reach a destination only 76 miles away by trail, but the economics were compelling: packing cost 2½¢ per pound while the postal service charge for transporting the same weight was only a penny.

By then, the ends of the river roadway had been linked. (*See sidebar, above.*) Although there were still some rough stretches to be smoothed out, the semi-completed Trinity Highway was dedicated at Salyer in August 1923. Five hundred participants packed the community hall,

Temporary detour trestle over debris channel at Oregon Gulch, 1934;
debris courtesy of the La Grange Mine. (SHS photo)

dancing the evening away to music supplied by—whom else?—the Highway Orchestra.

The Salyer celebrators were somewhat premature in their festivities, for the new roadway was a fragile creation, at the mercy of many of the forces that plagued the trails of an earlier day. By December 1924, a temporary bridge at Don Juan Point went down the river when hit by winter floods; the only crossing left along the middle Trinity was a suspension bridge at Big Bar that had been shipped in a few years earlier by—of course—parcel post, and which accommodated nothing larger than mules.

Thus the highway was hardly finished before it saw a series of repairs and refinements. The Oregon Mountain section, that of the mine tailings and Ford eggs, was an obvious obstacle to easy travel, but improving it required removing the top of the mountain to lessen the grade. The road equipment of the day was inadequate for the task, so some enterprising individual thought up an alternative—why not use mining technology to do the job? It seemed a stroke of engineering genius—the defunct La Grange Mine, once a huge hydraulic operation, had already washed away part of the mountain, and

the mine's "monitor" nozzles and some of its water ditches were still usable. After securing an agreement with the mine company, the facilities were repaired and prepared, and in February 1934, two huge nozzles went to work. During the wet seasons of the next five years the monitors relentlessly tore at the hillslope, assisted once by a 42-ton dynamite blast after they stalled on bedrock. When the hydraulic work was finished, nearly 11 million cubic yards of the mountain had been washed away, and the highway had—for less than a twentieth of the regular roadbuilding expense—a gentler grade.

But the project had another cost, for the highway hydraulic work achieved what the La Grange Mine never managed—the complete removal of a section of the ridgetop. The mighty monitors carved a gaping wound that is still unhealed more than 50 years later, a gray gash of slumping hillslope that refuses to grow plants and keeps sliding onto the highway. Even today, the crumbling countryside continues to pay the bill for the roadbuilders' egregious engineering experiment.

Other segments of the highway were improved as funds became available, but the process was agonizingly slow; only in 1962 was the last oil and gravel section of the roadway paved with asphalt. A major modernization east of Blue Lake, begun in 1969, improved driving conditions but eliminated one of the most memorable stretches of the old highway, the long awaited but oh so slow to arrive Lord-Ellis Road. (*See sidebar, next page.*)

The "Lord Help Us" Finally Got Helped

It seemed like an excellent idea when someone first suggested it—why not build a new road on a more direct route between Blue Lake and the ridge to the east? It would save distance and avoid the higher elevation of the existing Bald Mountain route, where the snows in winter could reach a depth of ten feet. A petition was circulated, and the first two signers—William Lord, a mule packer, and Edward Ellis, who worked for Brizard & Co.—gave their names to the project. Soon, and for very good reason, the proposed Lord-Ellis Road was called the "Lord Help Us" instead.

The route was first considered in 1891. Four years later, construction began on a trail along the future roadbed; less than the petitioners envisioned, it was nevertheless a start. Two more years passed, the route was resurveyed, but still no sign of any road appeared. Another year and—progress!—County Supervisor S. F. Pine had a bridge constructed across the route's main stream, the North Fork Mad River. A presumably hopeful sign, but it was followed by no further activity, prompting a complaint two years later (it was now 1900) that

> …there has never been a vehicle of any kind, not even a wheelbarrow, that passed over [the bridge] for the reason that there was no need to get to it. The worst feature of the matter is that the land on which the bridge now stands is owned by the Bank of Arcata and Humboldt County has no right of way over it.

So the bridge stood in disconnected disuse, straddling the North Fork, while weary travelers plodded along the old ridgetop route that lay to the south. As time passed the automobile came into its own, and agitation to build the road again increased. In 1912 the *Blue Lake Advocate* broke years of silence to announce glumly that "[m]any are wondering if the Lord-Ellis Road will ever be built."

Then came a see-saw of events: 1913 found a new survey of the route "just about complete," but the following year brought tidings that the county grand jury opposed building the road. Nonetheless, in 1915 officials began to purchase rights of way through the Northern Lumber Company's holdings. Then, in 1916, came news both good and bad: contractor Thomas Englehart of Eureka was busy clearing three miles of roadway in May, but a fire destroyed Supervisor Pine's yet-to-be-used bridge.

Undaunted, the roadbuilders redoubled their efforts. When all the 1918 contract bids came in too high, the county continued construction on a day-by-day basis. The final section of road, which went down Green Point toward Redwood Creek, was handbuilt by a crew of Greek workers. In August 1921, the 14-mile road was finished, a mere 30 years after Lord, Ellis, and their hopeful cohorts had first petitioned for it.

Nowadays, if the weather is agreeable and the traffic light, time-conscious Trinity travelers can speed from Arcata to Redding in something close to three hours. If they drive that quickly, however, they'll have little chance to more than glimpse the route's many roadside spectacles—sparkling waterfalls, high climbing forests of pines and oaks, dark cliffs that rise like windowless walls from the rocky river gorge. They might miss entirely a series of subtler sights whose importance would, in any event, not be readily apparent—the winding, forest-obscured ribbon of pavement that was once the Lord–Ellis Road; the faint indentation, on the gorge's far hillside, where the Big Bar bound mules once trod; an oddly angled bridge, dated 1923, reposing in forlorn decay below the current highway. These images are pieces of a picture no longer whole, parts of a place, or series of places, that have receded far into the past.

They seemingly serve little purpose, other than to remind us of what once was and to hint at how things became what they are now; they are seldom appreciated by those of us who pass by in our air-conditioned cars and 4WD trucks, but if Hilton McDonald or one of his ilk were to again come up the canyons, bound for the mines before dark, he would pause and respectfully lift his hat, for he would know their true significance.

Heavily loaded logging truck crosses North Fork Mad River, having just descended from Lord-Ellis Summit, c. 1950. (CHPW photo)

Early Inhabitants: Tribes of the Trinity Territory

The remote and rugged region now called northwestern California has long been known for its abundant resources—titanic timberlands that cover the countryside like a green blanket, rushing rivers that could easily water much of the state, mountainsides loded with gold and other precious minerals—but one facet of the area's great wealth is usually ignored: the numerous Native American cultures that long coexisted here before the arrival of the whites.

Nowhere else on the continent did so many tribes inhabit such a small space, and, possibly, nowhere else was life so generous and so secure. Here the native peoples had the best of two worlds, for it was in the watersheds of the Trinity, the Mad, and other nearby rivers that the salmon-rich fisheries of the Pacific Northwest mingled with the acorn-abundant oak woodlands of California. Here, too, the thick forests, swift streams, and steep mountainslopes combined to create protected confines that allowed the various tribes to dwell in relatively isolated safety, seldom coming into conflict with their neighbors.

In this rough-hewn, river-cut terrain, many tribes or bands claimed an entire drainage system as homeland, the larger groups sometimes spilling over into a neighboring watershed, the smaller ones perhaps sharing a single canyon. The area that later became Humboldt County contained at least 13 different tribes, while in the open lands to the east, nine distinct groups of the more widespread Wintus covered much of today's Trinity and Shasta counties. In between, the tiny Chimariko and Tlohomtahhoi tribes occupied the area's most daunting terrains, the Trinity River's gorge region and the remote fastness of the upper New River.

For centuries these early inhabitants lived in harmony with the land, and, for the most part, at peace with one another. Nearly everything they needed for survival was close at hand: game animals supplemented fish in their diets, while berries, nuts, and bulbs were added to the ubiquitous acorns. Hides and plant fibers provided clothing, just as stone, wood, and bone were crafted into tools. Near the coast, pit houses were made of redwood slabs; inland,

structures were built from bark and cedar slabs. Only a few hard-to-get items were obtained by trade with other tribes. In addition, the Indians honored ceremonies, beliefs, and customs that were old past remembering, and which had fulfilled the needs of generations of people. For a long while life was stable and prosperous.

All that changed in the 1850s with the arrival of the whites. Gold strikes in the Trinity and Salmon mountains brought a flood of miners, packers, and merchants into the tribes' territories, tearing apart the land and terrifying the native peoples. It was an influx that included the extreme elements of white "civilization." As one early anthropologist put it,

> …during the early mining days in California, there were gathered together some of the wildest, most reckless, savage, and dangerous men ever collected in a similar area anywhere in the world.

For the Indians, this sudden onslaught of immigrants was a disaster beyond imagining. Miners ripped up canyons and gulches and filled the rivers with silt, ruining the salmon runs and rendering the water unfit to drink. To provide food for the new populace, ranchers ran cattle on traditional hunting grounds, driving away what deer and elk weren't shot. Packers led long mule trains through tribal lands, and their animals grazed the grasslands that once offered the Native Americans edible bulbs. Settlements sprang up where most convenient, often on sites long occupied by Indian villages. The various tribes soon found themselves pushed off their land and deprived of their sources of sustenance. (*See sidebar, below.*)

The results were tragic but predictable. Some Indians resisted, ambushing pack trains and burning the ranches of recently arrived settlers; other tribes were more accommodating, moving to less desirable areas. Either way, they were assaulted and abused by the whites. Native American men were frequently shot on sight, women raped or forcibly taken as partners, and children captured and sold as slaves;

entire villages and encampments were attacked by surprise and the inhabitants massacred. Many of the surviving Indians ended up on newly established and badly run reservations that were poorly supplied and rife with disease. For some 15 years open conflict continued, until nearly all the native people had either been killed or subdued.

The coming of peace did not end the persecution. Decades of discrimination and indifference, some of it institutionalized by the federal government, followed. Several tribes, their numbers small to begin with, ceased to exist, while others were assimilated by larger groups. Local Indians found they had lost not only most of their land but also much of their culture.

Yet with remarkable resiliency, many Native Americans maintained portions of their identity as they gradually overcame the obstacles of living in a white-dominated world. Traditional skills and beliefs are today still honored and preserved by part of the Indian populace, and

tribal governments act, with increasing effectiveness, to assert their peoples' rights. Despite nearly a century and a half of destruction and disruption, the descendants of the early inhabitants have endured.

Eight tribes had their homelands along or near the route of the Trinity Highway. From east to west they are:

The Wintus

The Wintus occupied territory in what is now the easternmost section of the scenic byway. One of their tribal bands was situated in the Redding-Shasta area, another around French Gulch, a third on the upper Trinity River, and a fourth in the vicinity of Hayfork. Five other groups lived to the east.

Traditional Wintu life was centered around permanent villages, each of which contained anywhere from four or five bark houses to as many as several dozen; medium- to large-size

A Wintu Woman Speaks:

The White people never cared for land or deer or bear.

When we Indians kill meat, we eat it all up. When we dig roots we make little holes. When we build houses, we make little holes. When we burn grass for grasshoppers, we don't ruin things. We shake down acorns and pinenuts. We don't chop down the trees. We only use dead wood. But the White people plow up the ground, pull down the trees, kill everything. The tree says, "Don't, I am sore. Don't hurt me." But they chop it down and cut it up. The spirit of the land hates them. They blast out trees and stir it up to its depths. They saw up the trees. That hurts them. The Indians never hurt anything, but the White people destroy all. They blast rocks and scatter them on the ground. The rock says, "Don't. You are hurting me." But the white people pay no attention. When the Indians use rocks, they take little round ones for their cooking....How can the spirit of the earth like the White man?...Everywhere the White man has touched it, it is sore. (*Touch the Earth*, p.15)

villages usually had a semi-subterranean earth lodge that served as a sort of men's club. At the village of Nomkenteau (located in Watson Gulch), Chief Taika persuaded his people to spend two years constructing such a lodge, after which all the nearby Wintus were invited to a multi-day celebration of feasting, dancing, and gambling.

The main event at such gatherings was gambling. Two teams would play "big wood," wherein a dealer concealed a stick in a bundle of grass, manipulated the objects, and then waited for members of the opposing team to guess which hand held the bundle. A single game could last anywhere from 24 to 48 hours, during which time the men "gladly" staked all their valuables on the outcome of the contest.

Names, for the Wintus, were like personal property, and could be inherited by children upon their parents' death. A person might choose to abandon his or her name and give it to a child; in other cases, a nickname might be adopted to reflect someone's peculiar characteristics. Among the more evocative Wintu names were: Xonostet—"dried-up one," Sedimseli—"leads coyote by the hand," Xupusbuli—"war mountain," Lulikanalmet—"varicolored flower woman," and Kahitcarau—"windy flat."

During the warm months the Wintus established temporary hunting and gathering camps. Here they collected various berries and bulbs, hazel and buckeye nuts, and several types of acorns, favoring those from the California black oak. Deer, black bears, and rabbits were the most popular game foods and chinook salmon the favorite fish. According to George Redding, an early-day white observer, the Wintus

> …have, in all that relates to their supply of food, a knowledge of the natural history of their immediate vicinity that seems wonderful. No fish or crustacean of the river, no reptile, no animal or bird, nor tree or plant but has a name; and every child is taught these names, and given the knowledge of what can be used as food and what would be injurious.

The Wintus were a large tribe by regional standards, numbering perhaps 14,000 people in the late 1840s. Then the whites arrived; by 1850 they had established Shasta County, and soon thereafter the destruction of the Wintus began. The newcomers provided a "friendship feast" for the Indians and poisoned the food, killing about 100 of the Trinity group; a similar tactic claimed another 45 from the McCloud area. In 1851, at the town of Old Shasta, settlers reportedly burned the Wintu council meeting house and massacred some 300 members of the tribe. Near Hayfork, in Trinity County, white vigilantes surprised another band of nearly 300 Wintus at Bridge Gulch, murdering all but three or four. Other attacks followed; when not killed outright, the Wintus "were hunted down, captured, and forcibly marched to the coastal reservations."

Decades of trauma took their toll. By 1910, less than 400 Wintus remained, still struggling against prejudice; not until 1928 were their children accepted into public schools. Dams on the Trinity and Sacramento rivers subsequently flooded valleys long occupied by the Wintus, dispersing "the last large concentrations" of the tribe. Today, the Wintus are spread across the country, with only small enclaves occupying traditional lands.

The Chimarikos

West of the Wintus, Chimariko territory ran along a canyon-bound stretch of the Trinity River, extending downstream from Big Bar to near the mouth of the South Fork. The tiny tribe, which probably numbered only some 250 people, occupied a half-dozen or so villages at hospitable locations on flats near the riverside or, farther westward, on benchlands above the rock-strewn gorge. At one time the Chimarikos probably also ranged south toward Hayfork and Hyampom.

Each village, in addition to its dwellings, had a single sweathouse; both types of structure were circular and covered with a layer of earth placed on top of madrone bark. The largest village was Cutamtace. In the early 1850s, soon after the first whites reached the area, the community came under attack. Some horses had disappeared from an upriver French Canadian mining camp and, without pausing to investigate, the miners set out to punish the inhabitants of Cutamtace:

> Starting out heavily armed as Canadian trappers always are, they reached the outskirts of the village under suspicion before daybreak, surrounded it, and set the huts on fire. Then, hiding in the underbrush, they shot the Indians as they ran from the flaming huts. The women and children alone were spared and managed to escape.

> When a count was made fourteen victims were found lying on the ground.

From that day forward the spot was known as Burnt Ranch.

Another of the villages, Hotinakcohota, at Cedar Flat, saw its site soon appropriated by the miners who swarmed into the river canyon. In May 1863, the store there was attacked by a band of about 40 Indians. The raid was probably led by Puyelyalli, a Chimariko from Big Flat, who inspired his oppressed tribe to stage a temporarily successful resistance. The miners quickly rallied, however, and soon the Indians "were hunted to the death, shot down one by one, massacred in groups, driven over precipices," until "[i]n the summer of 1871 it was commonly said that there was not an Indian left." The few remaining Chimarikos had fled downriver to the Hupas or over the Trinity Mountains to the Salmon River and Scott Valley. "After an exile of many years, the survivors, then numbering only some half-dozen, struggled back to their old homes." By 1906, when anthropologist Roland Dixon visited the area, he found only two reputedly full-blooded Chimarikos left; he studied their nearly extinct language, learning a phrase that sadly summed up the tribe's condition: "*tcaxawintinda tcigule*"—"we are all old."

The Tlohomtahhois

The identity of the tribe (or tribes) that inhabited the remote and rugged New River drainage remains a subject of confusion and controversy 150 years after the white invasion of their homeland. A group called the New River Shasta is sometimes assigned to the area above the forks of the New, while the Chimarikos are often credited with controlling the river's lower stretches. The first ethnographer to study the area, Stephen Powers, claimed that a tiny tribe called the Chimalakwe had resided in the region at the time of the white arrival but within 15 years had become extinct.

In the 1920s, however, C. Hart Merriam, probably the foremost authority on California Indian geography, located and interviewed a man he believed was the last surviving member of this "extinct" tribe, Saxey Kidd. Merriam learned from Kidd that as a small child his parents and the rest of his people had been annihilated by the gold seekers that had rushed into the New River country. Kidd, who had been born on the upper stretch of the river, was taken to live with the Hupas and had later spent time with the Chimarikos. He spoke both of these languages but had forgotten most of his own. Eventually, Kidd recalled some 35 words of the language he'd last heard as a young boy, including the name for his tribe—Tlohomtahhoi.

According to Merriam, the domain of Kidd's tribe included the entire New River drainage, from the Trinity River on the south to the Trinity-Salmon divide on the north. His assertions were contested almost immediately by other Indian scholars and such challenges continue to this day, with current Tsnungwe activists claiming Kidd as their own. The full story of the New River Indians will never be known, but C. Hart Merriam, in his interviews with Saxey Kidd, apparently learned what little was left to tell.

The Tsnungwes

Downriver from the Chimarikos lived a branch of the Hupa tribe called the Tsnungwes, or South Fork Hupas. There is some uncertainty about the boundaries of the area they occupied, but their territory centered on the confluence of the Trinity and South Fork Trinity rivers and probably extended some distance up the South Fork. Of their nine or so villages, by far the largest and most important was Hlel-Din—"the place where the rivers come together"—at the mouth of the South Fork; it served as the tribe's religious and political center and may have contained upwards of 500 people. Goods from distant locations were brought to Hlel-Din and traded; they included dentalia from Washington, obsidian from the Modoc Plateau, and redwood canoes from the coast. In this cosmopolitan community many of the Tsnungwes were multilingual, often speaking Chimariko, Wintu, Whilkut, Wiyot, and Hupa in addition to their own language. One Hupa historian terms the Tsnungwe "the group most closely related to the Hupa."

An important Tsnungwe ritual was the Flower Dance, held as a young woman's coming-of-age ceremony. All the residents from her own village attended, along with many people from outlying villages; the meetings between young people at these gatherings sometimes led to matrimony.

The earliest white account of the Tsnungwes comes from L. K. Wood, who, as part of the Gregg Party, traveled through the tribe's territory in 1849:

> We came suddenly upon an Indian Rancheria…As soon as they saw us, men, women and children fled in the wildest confusion…leaving everything behind them…They had never seen a white man nor had they received any intelligence of our coming; and to them thus suddenly brought into contact with a race of beings so totally different in color, dress, and appearance from any they had ever seen is attributable the fear they betrayed.

All too soon the Tsnungwes' fear proved justified, as the tribe was compelled to join neighboring Indians in defending their homeland from encroaching settlers and miners. While the men were off fighting, many of the women and children attempted to hide in the

Hupa leader Captain John, in traditional dress, with plank house in background. (HSU photo)

New River area; some were captured and taken to the Hoopa Valley. Most of the surviving Tsnungwes eventually found themselves on the new reservation established at Hoopa in 1864.

By then, the village of Hlel-Din no longer existed. Whites had appropriated the area, setting up a flour mill and a ferry and commencing to mine. When some of the Tsnungwes left the Hoopa reservation in the 1880s, they relocated in their old territory along the South Fork Trinity, upstream from the site of Hlel-Din. Today, much of the property along the lower part of the river belongs to their descendants.

Contemporary Tsnungwes are working for federal recognition as a tribe; they have joined with the Nor-El-Muk band of Wintus from the Hayfork area in a pact of mutual support for their respective recognition efforts. The Tsnungwes have also established programs to both preserve and reinstitute elements of the Tsnungwe culture, binding together a part of what was torn asunder some 140 years ago.

The Hupas

Lying along the lower end of the Trinity River is the land of the Hupa tribe. Numbering perhaps 1,500 people in 1850, the Hupas exercised a force far beyond their size, apparently controlling not only their own stretch of river but also exerting influence in the surrounding areas to the east, south, and west. Stephen Powers, who visited the region in the early 1870s, declaimed: "They are the Romans of Northern California in their valor and their wide-reaching dominions; they are the French in the extended diffusion of their language."

By the time of Powers's visit, white attacks had decimated most of the local tribes and

Hupa Indians gather at the Hoopa Valley Indian Reservation. The names of the tribe and the valley, which are pronounced identically, have different transliterations. (HSU photo)

fort to improve conditions for the tribe. Billy Beckwith became a leader of the cause; in 1891 he wrote to a local newspaper, imploring sympathetic whites to support the Hupas:

> ...a promise was made to the Indian, "You shall have the Hoopa Valley for your home," and they have been waiting all these years to have the land set apart...and become citizens. When will the white man give us our land and good men teach us and not bad men such as we have now?...Shall we ever get justice done to us? We have waited now thirty years. We have been kept in wicked hands, no one to teach us good things, only wicked things. Many here died, others are suffering now. Is this my treatment at the hand of my white brother for all my good will and deeds toward him?

Despite Beckwith's eloquent plea, there was little immediate "justice" for his people; finally, in 1933, they were allowed to establish a tribal council, which then conducted business for the Hupas. Over the ensuing years, the council has extended its authority, bolstered by legal precedents that recognized the sovereignty of Indian tribes. By the 1980s, the Hupas had so increased their power that tribal police officers successfully turned away employees of the California Department of Food and Agriculture who attempted to enter the reservation to conduct a controversial pest eradication program.

In pre-white times, several villages occupied the banks of the Trinity River in what is now called the Hoopa Valley. Chief among these

driven them off much of their land, but he found the Hupas still occupying their original territory. To maintain their homeland, the Hupas had first tried non-belligerence; finally, when pushed too far by white attacks, they resorted to combat, joining with neighboring tribes in a fierce resistance that forced many settlers out of the area. In 1864 the Indians, still undefeated, agreed to a peace treaty that established a twelve-mile square, centered in the Hoopa Valley, as a reservation.

Corruption and indifference marked much of the new reservation's early administration, and individual Hupas began a continuing ef-

were Takimildiñ, the "Place of the Acorn Feast," and Medildiñ, the tribe's largest community. Each village family owned a *xonta*, a pit house made of cedar planks. Here they cooked, ate, and kept their belongings; it was also where the women slept. The men slept and worked in a separate structure, the *taikyuw*, or sweathouse.

Notable among the Hupas' crafts is their basketry. Women traditionally begin the baskets with a foundation of hazel shoots; for loosely twined containers they then add roots of alder, willow, cottonwood, and wild grape, while tighter woven work features roots of gray pine, ponderosa pine, lowland spruce, or coastal redwood. Designs are made with the white tips of beargrass, the black stems of maidenhair fern, and the dead fronds of giant chain ferns that have turned reddish brown. Oregon grape roots and lichen provide yellow dyes, while alder bark furnishes a red-brown coloring.

In earlier days, the men also created notable craft works. Each year, after the summer rains, they constructed a fish dam on the Trinity for the fall salmon runs, alternating its location between Medildiñ and Takimildiñ. The men first embedded a series of poles, each split to form a V-shape, across the river; they then built a walkway along the top of the dam, added horizontal oak poles and woven mats, sealed the bottom with branches and stones, and finally placed fishing platforms below it. Salmon migrating upriver were stopped by the dam and easily caught from the platforms. Like the women's basketry, the men's work was as beautiful as it was functional.

The Hupas, along with other nearby tribes, regularly conducted two "world renewal" rituals, the Jumping Dance and the White Deerskin Dance. On occasion, they staged another impressive event, a peace-making ceremony used to terminate hostilities between two warring factions. After agreeing to a settlement, a meeting place was selected,

…and on the appointed day both sides appeared in full force. The payments were received in a solemn reconciliation dance which was very similar to the incitement and victory dances [used during the hostilities]. Two opposing lines of armed men began to dance 100 to 150 yards apart and gradually danced closer and closer until they shook hands. They then passed through each other's line and went to the campfires to eat and the payments by each side were actually handed over. The intermediary did not let the parties stay together too long, lest fighting break out again.…The women stood by prepared to prevent fighting; they were armed with sticks or clubs to strike down the bows of the men, and if scuffling did occur, they seized and held the arms of the combatants.

The Chilulas & the Whilkuts

Except for a short Yurok-controlled stretch near its mouth, Redwood Creek was divided into two tribal territories, the Chilulas claiming the northern, lower section of the stream canyon and its nearby hillsides and the Whilkuts (or Whilklits) occupying the upper drainage to the south.

The tribes were closely related; both spoke a variety of the Athabascan language group, as did their Hupa kin to the east. The Hupas apparently felt a closer affinity with the Chilulas, whom they permitted to participate in their ceremonies; the Whilkuts, on the other hand, could attend Hupa dances but only watch.

Although both the Chilulas and the Whilkuts fished in Redwood Creek and its tributaries, they were better known for their hunting. They drew on this skill extensively during the so-called "Indian Wars" of the 1850s and 1860s, when, with the support of the Hupas, they drove every white settler from both the Bald Hills and Redwood Creek.

Much of the Chilula section of Redwood Creek was dominated by the stream's namesake tree species, and the tribe in fact called themselves "the people within the redwood trees." They spent much of their time, however, not in the narrow, conifer-filled depths of the northern canyon, but on the sunny hillslopes of the Bald Hills, where they gathered acorns, collected bulbs, and hunted vast herds of elk. Farther south, between Lacks Creek and Minor Creek, the valley opened out, and here the Chilulas established a string of streamside villages.

The Chilula-Whilkut boundary was probably about four miles north of today's High-

A band of Redwood Creek Indians, probably Whilkuts, possibly Chilulas. Note the conical brush house at rear right. (HCHS photo)

way 299 bridge. From there, Whilkut land ran south up the remainder of Redwood Creek; the tribe also spilled over into the North Fork Mad River drainage and part of the Mad's Main Fork, south of Blue Lake. A large Whilkut village, T'chil-kahn´-ting, was located on Captain Flat, a short distance north of the Chezem Road bridge across Redwood Creek.

The Chilulas lived in rectangular redwood plank houses that resembled those of the Tolowas and Yuroks. Whilkut dwellings, while of the same shape, were made of bark slabs instead of planks and lacked a fire pit. Unlike their neighbors to the north, the Whilkuts built a round ceremonial structure similar to the dance houses of central Californian tribes.

After fiercely resisting the entry of white settlers and packers into their homelands, both tribes joined with their Hupa allies in the peace settlement of 1864; almost all of the Chilulas and Whilkuts then moved onto the Hoopa reservation. There, the Chilulas were easily assimilated into the Hupa tribe, but the process was more difficult for the Whilkuts, and many eventually drifted back to their home territory. In 1972 only an estimated 20 to 25 Whilkuts remained. Much earlier, the Chilulas had, in the words of one anthropologist, "ceased to exist as a separate people."

The Wiyots

Southwest of the Chilulas and Whilkuts was the domain of the Wiyots, who occupied the coastal region along the lower Mad and Eel rivers and around Humboldt Bay. It was these areas where the first white arrivals chose to settle, and the Wiyots suffered terribly as a result. In February 1860, a series of vigilante attacks on three Wiyot villages killed as many as 300 men, women, and children in a single night. Many massacre survivors were displaced from their homes and dispossessed of their lands. By 1910, only about 150 Wiyots remained.

Culturally, the Wiyots were somewhat isolated from other Indians of the region. Most of the nearby tribes spoke a type of Athabascan that differed greatly from the Algonquian-based language of the Wiyots. Although the Yuroks, neighbors to the north, spoke a distantly related tongue, the two tribes were never close. One scholar has deemed the Wiyots "a people with a style entirely different from the Yurok." Their creation myths, according to the same source, "are without parallel in Northwestern California."

As might thus be expected, the Wiyots had difficulties with other tribes. In the late 1840s, raiding mountain Indians nearly exterminated the Wiyots living near present-day Blue Lake; white settlers who arrived in the area a few years later reported seeing 30 to 40 graves of the victims. The North Fork Mad River, which rises east of Blue Lake, appears to have been claimed at different times by both the Wiyots and the Whilkuts, and the raid may have resulted from a territorial dispute. Soon, however, the Whilkuts and their allies would welcome the protective seclusion of their more remote ridges and valleys to the east, for the Wiyots were nearly defenseless when whites attacked them on the unprotected coastal plain.

Yet the tribe survived the white onslaught, if barely, and today Wiyots occupy a recently established reservation atop Table Bluff, just south of Humboldt Bay, while also claiming land at Blue Lake. Still evident at the boundary of the tribe's traditional territory is the Indian Arrow Tree, a dead, broken-topped redwood on the mountainside above Korbel. (*Note: for directions to the tree, see page 216.*) For centuries the tree stood beside a trail used by the Wiyots and the Whilkuts, and members of both tribes would leave arrows, spears, and green boughs in its bark as they walked by; in later times it became a landmark beyond which no mountain Indian would travel. Dead for perhaps a century or more and now devoid of its arrows, the tree's scarred, fire-darkened trunk still stands, an emblem of survival that recalls the many Indians who once passed this way…and that waits for those whose time to pass has not yet come.

*Before you go over the snow-mountain
   to the north,
Downhill to the north,
Oh, do look back at me.*

—Wintu love song

The Trinity Highway's Varicolored Vegetation

Stretching from dry, sunbaked Redding to coastally cool and damp Arcata, the Trinity Scenic Byway passes through a progression of plant communities, each the result of a particular combination of temperature, precipitation, soil, and sunlight. En route, the drought-resistant plants of the inland chaparral sector gradually give way to the moisture-loving forest species found at and close to the redwood coast. At least nine roughly defined botanical regions are traversed by the highway, inviting the inquiring observer to note the distinctive attributes of each.

Chaparral

Representative area: *Whiskeytown Lake*

Principal trees and shrubs: *whiteleaf manzanita, gray pine, knobcone pine, ponderosa pine, yerba santa, California black oak*

Hot, dry summers dictate plant development in the chaparral region. The relentless heat forces many chaparral residents to create a waxy coating on their leaves, which slows the evapo-ration of much-needed moisture. Shallow soils with few nutrients prod the plants' shallow roots to search for scarce food and water, while frequent fires have forced an adaptive strategy of reproduction by heat-released seeds. Only the most stubborn species survive the rigors of the chaparral zone.

For example, the cones of the knobcone pine cleave tightly against the tree's branches until a conflagration consumes the area; only then will the cones open, releasing their seeds onto the barren, charred ground. The faded, gray-green needles of the gray pine are emblematic of its dry environment, while the tree's characteristic divided trunk and scraggly foliage bespeak the rigors of survival in inhospitable habitat—steep, rocky slopes that contain little moisture and few nutrients. Surprisingly, the seeds of this often-stressed tree are high in both protein and fat content, and they thus served as a food source for various Indian tribes. In chaparral areas with better soils, the California black oak prevails, its acorns providing another Indian edible. Also of use was yerba santa, a medium-size shrub that grows on dry hillsides; its resin combated respiratory problems, purified the blood, and reduced fevers. The early-day Spanish fathers, who learned of these uses from the California Indians, subsequently bestowed upon the plant its common name, which means "holy weed."

Low-Elevation Ponderosa Pine Forest

Representative area: *south-facing slopes below 2,000 feet on the east-side grade to Buckhorn Summit*

Principal trees and shrubs: *ponderosa pine, California black oak, Douglas-fir, western redbud, California buckeye, bigleaf maple, Pacific dogwood, poison oak*

Most old-growth stands of ponderosa pine have disappeared due to logging, leaving a regenerating forest less than 120 years old. As new trees begin to cover desolate ground, their shade actually inhibits the sprouting of new ponderosas, inviting other species into the habitat. Two kinds of brush predominate in this area: western redbud and California buckeye; both grow on warm sites such as south-facing slopes. Redbud bursts forth in spring with clusters of dazzling purple-pink blossoms before clothing itself in a more subdued summer covering of soft green, heart-shaped leaves. Buckeye begins with a darker green foliage, followed by large, spectacular white flower spikes that may reach ten inches in length and that protrude from the leaf mass like the prickles of some giant hedgehog.

A colorful companion tree is the Pacific dogwood, found in moist, shaded sectors of this habitat. The creamy white flowers that adorn it in spring are replaced by bright red berries. Poisonous to humans, the berries provide an important source of calcium and fat for wildlife, while the rest of the tree—bark, leaves, seeds, twigs, and flowers—is also consumed by birds and mammals. In fall, the dogwood's leaves turn a variety of harmonious hues, from burgundy red to watermelon pink to honey orange to pale yellow.

Also attractive in autumn are the leaves of poison oak, a shrub or vine best known for its irritating effect on the skin of most humans. Arraying themselves in groupings of three, the oft-lamented leaves tint yellow, pink, and scarlet in fall, providing a winsome warning to "look but do not touch."

Mid-Elevation Douglas-fir Forest

Representative area: *north- and east-facing slopes above 2,000 feet on the east grade to Buckhorn Summit*

Principal trees and shrubs: *Douglas-fir, ponderosa pine, sugar pine, California black oak, buckbrush, Pacific madrone, tanoak, bigleaf maple, poison oak, greenleaf manzanita, white fir, chinquapin*

The cooler temperatures of this shaded, higher-elevation zone create a markedly different plant community from that on the lower, sunnier slopes of Buckhorn Summit. With its cones dangling—pinelike—downward, Douglas-fir frequently dominates the area; not a true fir (whose cones rise upward from the limbs), it grows best in areas of high light intensity, so that it often populates sites cleared by landslides or fires. The tree attains its greatest size in moist locations, growing up to eight feet in diameter and over 200 feet tall in some regions of the Pacific Northwest.

Sugar pine gains its common name from the sweet resin released when the wood is cut or burned. Also known as the "king of pines," the species is one of the largest and most magnificent of the conifers. It grows scattered on poor soil sites and/or mixes with other evergreens rather than forming true stands. While Douglas-fir is now considered a standard building material, early settlers often preferred sugar pine, rendering its wood into not only houses but also fences, sluice boxes, bridges, and tunnel supports. Indians preferred consumption to construction, eating both the sugar pine's resin and seeds.

Oregon White Oak Woodland

Representative area: *hillside across Trinity River at Douglas City turnoff*

Principal trees and shrubs: *Oregon white oak, ponderosa pine, Douglas-fir, California black oak, Pacific madrone, canyon live oak*

White oak woodlands are found on south- and west-facing slopes in inland valleys; the species prefers moist settings but can, when necessary, adapt to drought. Conifers frequently compete with oaks, and local Native Americans would therefore burn selected areas to eliminate unwanted evergreens and preserve their source of acorns. Oregon white oak is the only native oak of British Columbia and Washington; its range extends southward through its namesake state and into Northern California. The white oak's wood has long been used for furnituremaking, shipbuilding, and cabinetwork; its sweet tasting acorns were traditionally eaten by the local Indian tribes and are found attractive by many animals.

Pine-Oak Woodland

Representative area: *north side of highway at Big Bar ranger station*

Principal trees and shrubs: *canyon live oak, gray pine, ponderosa pine, western redbud, Pacific madrone, poison oak, whiteleaf manzanita, buckbrush*

The signature tree of this community is the canyon live oak, which mingles with Douglas-fir on gently sloping hills but stands alone on steeper slopes, clinging to the canyonsides with its rock-clasping roots while spreading its enormous, contorted limbs over the tilted terrain. The canyon live oak actually adapts to several settings, changing its stature accordingly—it appears as anything from a straight-trunked, medium-size tree to a low, spreading shrub. To see one looming large in the night, its dark shape etched by the moonlight, is to understand why the Druids held oaks sacred.

Mixed Evergreen Forest

Representative area: *Burnt Ranch*

Principal trees and shrubs: *tanoak, Pacific madrone, California black oak, canyon live oak, bigleaf maple, sugar pine, ponderosa pine, Douglas-fir, chinquapin, poison oak.*

Mild, moist sites welcome this community of vulnerable vegetation, which is often threatened by fires and logging. Pacific madrone is a distinctive species here, its brown outer bark mottled where it has peeled to expose a delicate, reddish-hued inner layer. Madrone prefers the drier patches of recently disturbed areas, while tanoak likes locations with more shade. The slow growing tanoak is often dwarfed by the towering Douglas-fir, but a mature stand is a sight to behold—tall, stout-trunked trees, rising like oversized alders into the forest canopy, where they contend with the conifers for primacy. The tanoak once was cut extensively for its tannin-rich bark, which was sent to leather works in the Bay Area before the advent of synthetic tanning agents. Like the Douglas-fir, the tanoak is misnamed. Although it possesses the acorn of the oak, its flowers resemble those of the chestnut, and it actually belongs to the beech family. Its acorns were eaten by local Indians.

Coniferous Woodlands

Representative area: *Willow Creek to Berry Summit*

Principal trees and shrubs: *Douglas-fir, Pacific madrone, tanoak, bigleaf maple, red alder, greenleaf manzanita, thimbleberry, coyote brush*

Coastal influences are apparent in this transition zone, which encompasses much cutover countryside. Red alder, a graceful, gray-trunked deciduous tree, thrives on recently logged or burned land where moisture is abundant. Alders are beneficial colonizers, fixing nitrogen in the earth, increasing organic material, and lessening the density of the soil while increasing its acidity. In years past, red alder was considered a "pest" species by silviculturalists, who doused it with herbicides; more enlightened tree managers now cultivate it as an essential component of a regenerating forest.

Prairies & Oak Woodlands

Representative area: *Berry Summit to Redwood Creek*

Principal trees and shrubs: *Oregon white oak, California black oak*

The region's two deciduous oaks form fringes along ridgeslope grasslands, the rounded forms of their foliage harmonizing with the gently swelling hillsides. Local Indians maintained the prairies by controlled burning; later, sheep and cattle ranchers also kept the grasslands free of encroaching conifers to maintain rangeland for their stock. In this setting the California black oak, usually a consort of more dominant trees, rises to prominence. In spring, its tiny leaves unfold a delicate pink, gradually turning to pale green before reaching a deep, verdant summer luster. The leaves yellow in autumn, often gradating into golds and browns before falling to carpet the grass. Winter finds the black oak a ghostly gray silhouette, a grove of them spread like a darkling fog upon some distant, sere brown hillslope.

Redwood Forest

Representative area: *Lord-Ellis Summit to the coast*

Principal trees and shrubs: *coast redwood, Douglas-fir, red alder, Pacific madrone, tanoak, blueblossom, snowbrush, thimbleberry*

In the cool, wet environment west of the Lord-Ellis ridgeline, the coast redwood surmounts its surroundings, creating a thick forest of tall timber that rises from the canyon bottoms to blanket the mountainsides. Other conifers fill secondary niches in the forest, while red alder and blueblossom often cover cutover sites. Most of the redwoods visible from the highway are second- or even third-growth, mere striplings compared to their mighty ancestors that fell a century or so ago to the logger's ax. Still, this younger generation gives a hint of what came before—trees that reached 300 feet or more skyward, with diameters that often measured 15 to 20 feet. Trees that, undisturbed by man, would easily live five hundred or even a thousand years or more. Now, to feel the forest's full effect, viewers must content themselves with a long-distance perspective, where acres of young redwoods array themselves along the canyon, their spindly trunks concealed by a nearly unbroken mass of dark green foliage.

Where logging is recent, cutblocks are often covered in spring with the light green leaves of red alder or with the cloudlike bloom of blueblossom, a colonizing ceanothus that perfumes the air with its sweet, heady scent. In fall, an occasional golden flame bursts from the dark forest where a solitary bigleaf maple tints its leaves. Even in their diminished condition, however, redwoods remain the rulers of the coastal forests.

Flowering Plants Found Along the Highway

Among the wildflowers and flowering shrubs that grow along Highway 299 are the following; other species are located (and listed) on the various hikes and side trips.

alumroot
baby blue eyes, white
blue dicks
blueblossom
buckbrush
buckeye, California
buttercup (various species)
coltsfoot, western

delphinium, red
dogwood, Pacific
fairybell, Hooker's
false Solomon's seal, fat
fiddleneck
hound's tongue, western
Indian warrior
jewel flower, mountain
lewisia, Siskiyou
lupine (various species)
monkeyflower, chickweed
mule ears, narrow-leaved

ookow
paintbrush (various species)
phlox, showy
popcorn flower
poppy, California
redbud, western
sanicle, purple
saxifrage, Merten's
soap plant
triteleia (various species)
violet, two-spot
waterleaf (various species)

Wondrous Waterway: Reflections on the Trinity River

Trinity River is a cold nymph of the hills.

—Benjamin P. Avery (1871)

To the Indians who lived along its banks, the river was waterway, barrier, and source of sustenance. Their canoes would carry them through its safer stretches, but elsewhere the unyielding rocks and churning rapids prevented any traffic. Moreover, the canyon that the Trinity had cut was a sunderance so great that travelers sought routes that kept them far above the water, descending only when necessity compelled them to risk crossing it. Yet the formidable could by turns be fruitful, for the same stream that could sweep a canoeman to his death would bring forth great runs of fish that were prized so highly as food.

The Yuroks, who lived where the river ended, called its lower reaches the "Hupo" or "Hupa," and gave the tribe who dwelt beside it the same name. Farther upstream, where it ran through canyon and gorge, the Chimariko people called it "Tcitra" or "Chiti," depending on which ears heard the word.

When whites tried their own hand at naming it, they bungled badly, relying on the briefest of impressions rather than any sense born of long relationship. Jedediah Smith ominously referred to it as the "Indian Scalp" when he drove a herd of mules and horses through its drainage in 1828; seventeen years later, Pierson B. Reading entered its upper reaches and abruptly (and erroneously) christened it the Trinity, without bothering to confirm his belief that the river met the sea at its namesake, Trinidad Bay.

Subsequent explorers eventually determined that the Trinity in fact never reached the ocean; diverted from its westward rush by an impenetrable ridgeline, the river turned north to meet the larger Klamath at the Yurok village of Weitchpec. From there the mingled waters coursed northwesterly to the coast, finally flowing into the Pacific far above Trinidad.

But Reading's mistakenly chosen name endured, spreading like an infectious geographic bacillus to soon also claim both a mountain range and a county. Most of those who had influence in the matter were miners, anyway, and they no doubt approved of the presumed blessing that using the waters of the Trinity might confer on their work.

It was Reading himself who first discovered gold on the river in 1848, and the subsequent rush of fortune-seekers crowded the banks of the Trinity and its tributaries for miles throughout the mountains. Soon the free-rushing river became slave to the miners, its water first used to wash the ore-bearing rock through sluice boxes and then to blast it from the hillsides with huge hydraulic nozzles.

Slave and also victim, for the river, lately pure mountain snowmelt, carried with it a contaminated load of mining slurry after its use. The Chimarikos saw the Chiti turn from clear to cloudy and challenged the miners over the change. The newcomers responded by hunting the Indians to near extinction, thereby teaching them "that they must not presume to discuss with American miners the proper color for the water in the Trinity River."

For more than ten years the gold-seekers continued their wasting work before the river answered. In the winter of 1861–62 a great storm struck, its warm rain washing over the land in torrents. Weaverville blacksmith John Carr witnessed the result:

> When the river was at or near its highest, one could see floating down parts of mills, sluice-boxes, miners' cabins, water-wheels, hen-coops, parts of bridges, bales of hay, household furniture, sawed lumber, old logs, huge spruce and pine trees that had withstood former storms for hundreds of years—all rushing down that mad stream on their way to the boundless ocean. From the head of settlement to the mouth of the Trinity River, for a distance of one hundred and fifty miles, everything was swept to destruction....The labor of hundreds of men, and their savings of years, invested in bridges, mines and ranches, were all swept away.

The Trinity was to remain untamed, and always a risk, until the middle of the next century, when a new need at last brought it under control; mining had long ceased to rule the state, but agriculture, for just as long ascendant, accomplished what the hydraulickers never did—subdue and nearly still the river on its journey to the sea. Trinity Dam, built during the 1960s, impounded the upper river, readying most of its water for removal to the thirsty croplands of the Central Valley and slowing the remnant flow to at times hardly more than a trickle.

First damned by destructive mining practices and then dammed by the Bureau of Reclamation, the Trinity today is a far cry from its former self. Hydraulicked, dredged, and diverted, the river has seen its once-magnificent salmon and steelhead runs steadily dwindle as the passing decades bring continued distress to their habitat. Today, supporters of a rejuvenated Trinity strive to gain approval of increased flows, which might return the river and its inhabitants to a measure of their former glory.

Far up the drainage, behind its imprisoning curtain of concrete, the water is waiting.

The Trinity Along the Highway

The Trinity River Highway derives it name—and much of its most spectacular scenery—from that stretch of its route (roughly between Junction City and Cedar Flat) where river and roadway run so close together that at times they appear about to touch. Earlier travelers seemed intent on keeping their distance from the stream; the Indian trail that the packers later followed stayed near the ridgetops high above, descending (at places such as Big Bar) only when it needed to cross the water. The original highway, completed in the 1920s, dropped closer to the river but still remained safely aloof. Its tracings are still visible, at intervals, above the current road.

If today's highway runs a lower course than its predecessor, so does the river; deprived of 80 percent of its water by the demands of hydropower and high-powered agriculture, the Trinity now moistens only the very bottom of the canyon it cut, leaving Route 299 high and dry above it even during heavy storms and spring runoff. But while the river does not reach the roadway with its water, it does wash over it with manifest charms: fishing holes that still glint with salmon and steelhead, enough gold to tempt a few diehard mini-dredgers, and the requisite rocks and riffles for rafters and their ilk. Moreover, the mountain scenery spreads its mantle across the canyon's dramatic contours with arresting ease—stands of gray pine and white oak rising from riverside to ridgetop, their foliage covering the slopes like a softly rising fog; rocky points that jut resistantly toward the roadway as the river grudgingly bends to the demands of geology; the springtime splash of pink atop a river rock that announces the arrival of the showy stepflower (*Lewisia cotyledon*), or the coming out of its colorful companion, the cerise bloomed western redbud (*Cercis occidentalis*), that annually (and all too briefly) bursts forth by the roadside.

Here along the highway, the heart of the river still beats.

A New Angle on Fishing the Trinity

The harvest moon, full in the pre-dawn sky, illuminates the glassy smooth river. Stars twinkle above as the first traces of a rosy autumn sunrise begin to emerge from behind the Trinity Alps, pushing through the dense mist that cascades over the ridgelines and fills the mountain crevices. The crisp air is sharp with the scent of decaying madrone, oak, and bay leaves and the mossy smell of the river itself. Two bald eagles fly, single file, up the canyon voicing their unmistakable morning cries. The gravel settles underfoot as I shift my weight from foot to foot in an effort to stay warm. My movement causes a few pebbles to trickle down the embankment, spilling into the black water of the placid pool I intend to fish. Aside from the kittering of the eagles and the tinkling of the pebbles falling into the river, all is quiet.

I am abruptly snapped out of my dreamy state by a tremendous boil surging up from the depths not six feet from where I stand, a wake-up call that sends a shiver down my spine and jumpstarts me into action. My first cast lands right where intended and I brace with antici-pation. The weight taps bottom twice and then I feel nothing. To many folks nothing is nothing to get excited about, but for a Trinity River fisherman who knows the nature of a light-biting chinook, a little nothing can mean a whole lot of something. I set the hook as hard as my light drift rod will allow and confront my first chinook of the day. She fights, as many Trinity River kings do, with slow headshakes until the situation becomes clear, and then she's off to the races with reel-smoking runs and dogged persistence, never rising from the depths until the last moment when the battle ends. The only difference between this king and the others I had caught that week was that she jumped twice and was mint bright, as if she had just come in from the ocean, although this spot was nearly 100 miles from salt water. As I inspected my prize I found not a single nick or abrasion on her and admired her perfectly formed fins. This was clearly a wild fish and, judging by her prime condition, she had a long way to go before reaching her destination. I felt she must be one of the rare native stock that spawn in the tribu-taries of the Trinity ranges, just starting her long journey home. I thanked her for the dance and sent her on her way, as I do all native fish.

Trinity River king (or chinook) salmon are not large by most people's standards: 8-18 pounds is normal with the average being around 10 pounds. Anything over 25 pounds is considered a monster, and a king over 35 pounds is a real trophy. In the fall, jack salmon (those under 24 inches, usually immature males) ascend the river in large schools and are often aggressive, providing great sport on light tackle. Sometimes the jacks act like a school of hungry piranhas. They frequently will follow a lure right up to the bank, taking quick nips at it until one of them gets the hook. This can be a frustrating sight when they aren't in a biting mood but are willing to follow the lure, inches away.

Kings are schooling fish, and if one is seen then there should be more in the area or on the way. One thing I love about Trinity salmon is their frequent habit of rolling on or just below the surface, leaving a highly visible wake or boil and no doubt as to their whereabouts. A good way to find a likely fishing spot is to check out a number of places until rolling fish are spotted. If you find active salmon, be ready for a hookup on the first cast, as kings have excellent eyesight, and if they are going to bite they usually waste no time in doing so.

Pacific salmon are not physically capable of eating once they enter fresh water, and there is much debate as to why they would even strike a lure, but they certainly do, although hot-and-cold best describes the way river salmon react to lures. One minute they will attack everything in sight and the next . . . nothing, sometimes for hours on end, until the next feeding frenzy begins. The exception is that first cast when anything is possible, and most fishermen are caught with their pants down!

The steelhead of the Trinity watershed are also on the small side. They generally run from 3-8 pounds, with a 12-pounder considered big and one in the 15-pound range a trophy. The Trinity also gets a good run of "half-pounder" steelhead, immature fish that go up river as if to spawn and then turn around and head back to sea for another year or two before returning as adult steelhead. These "steelies" are aggressive and take flies and spinners with a jolting strike. What the half-pounder steelhead lack in size they make up for in fight. They are some of the punchiest fighters I have ever battled, and they frequently jump and run so fast it's difficult to keep up with them as they race around the pool. With the exception of winter fish go-ing back to sea after spawning and the half-pounders, most Trinity steelhead travel alone or in pairs, which means if you catch one, don't waste time fishing that spot afterward. Even if they did travel in schools, it probably would be best to move on because they go so crazy when hooked that any fish in the pool will most likely be spooked. Look for steelhead in shallow riffles and runs with moderate to fast current. They usually aren't found in deep slow pools, but may be in the tailout of the pool or at the top in the faster water.

A small run of sea-run brown trout occurs in the Trinity. They are occasionally caught when fishing for steelhead in the upper sections of the river. The browns provide a real surprise when landed, for they fight like an adult king but are the size of a steelhead, leaving one to wonder just what is on the end of the line.

Coho or silver salmon run in the late fall, but they are on the endangered species list and anglers should not target them. The silvers are found in the same places as the kings, deep pools and runs with moderate to slow flows. If a fish with white gums and a deeply hooked jaw is landed, it probably is a coho and must be re-leased promptly without removing it from the water. The penalties are steep, so take no chances.

The standard baits and rigs for salmon and steelhead can be as simple or as complex as one desires, from a worm on a hook to a fancy slid-ing bobber rig complete with slip knots, bear-ing beads, weights, and swivels. The rig itself probably is not as important as how it is pre-sented, and whether it is being presented to aggressive fish, though certain types of rigs will work best in certain types of water.

Probably the most standard rig seen on the river is the tried and true sliding bottom drift-ing setup, used anywhere there is enough cur-rent to get the weight to slowly tap along the bottom as it drifts downstream. Sliding bobber rigs can be very effective in the slow pools, and they bring back memories of fishing the farm pond for bluegill and bass, but these quickly fade after the hook is set and a rampaging chinook takes the place of a pint-sized panfish. The last important technique is the use of arti-ficial lures, specifically when targeting bright and aggressive fish. Spinners, wobbling spoons, and diving plugs are the most commonly used lures for the salmon. Steelhead will take all these lures as well as small jigs and flies.

Worms, shrimp, or roe (fish eggs) are the best baits for steelhead, and roe and tuna balls are the best for kings. Tuna balls? Yes, but only on the Trinity have I ever seen these things work. I have always felt that what is on the hook is not as important as how it is presented. I might add that, on a bet to prove my point, I caught a beautiful king on a piece of salami from my sandwich. Tuna balls are simply oil-packed tuna wrapped in Moline (mesh netting) and tied off with a piece of elastic thread. Often in clear water a drift bobber like a corkie, cheater, or spin and glow will do the trick better than any-thing else, probably because they don't spook the fish like a chunk of bait or a flashy lure. In upcoming seasons bait fishing may be restricted or outlawed.

After one gets acquainted with the river, the fish, and the methods used to catch them, the next step is to gain some local knowledge regarding the habits of these fish: where and when they can be found in certain sections of the river. The best way to gain this type of knowledge would be to spend several seasons fishing the river, observing its habits, and talking to others who love the river and have given close attention to run timings. The next best thing is to read the following section on the run timing of Trinity fish by a person who has been lucky enough to get to know the river intimately. These suggestions are based on observations and questions that began at the age of eight when I hooked and lost (rod, reel, and all) my first steelhead on the New River, recently closed to save the remaining steelhead. Generally the runs are predictable to within a week or two.

Winter
(December-March)

If the powerful winter storms hold off, or if the precipitation falls as snow, some quality winter steelhead fishing can be had in December and January anywhere the water has more than a few feet of visibility. The South Fork of the Trinity is the first to dump mud into the river. Next in line is the New River, which enters just

above Grays Falls. If the Trinity is still dirty farther upstream, then fish the North Fork or Canyon Creek confluence pools, as these tributaries rarely go off-color, and steelhead often congregate in the clear water that pours into the main channel.

The frigid water of winter requires special techniques if one expects any success. Getting the slowest presentation possible without hanging up on the bottom is critical because in cold water steelhead are lethargic and not willing to move very far for bait or a lure. Cured roe com-

An unusually icy Trinity in winter. (Robin Stocum photo)

bined with a brightly colored drift bobber and a small piece of highly visible yarn tied to the shank of the hook are the best bet. Large silver-plated spinners retrieved slowly also work well. They should be fished with a weight setup to keep the lure near the bottom and to get the slowest presentation possible. Winter is when the lunkers run in the Trinity, but go in early before the river blows out for the season.

Most of the late winter fishery occurs in the river above Cedar Flat. The most popular drifts are in the sections from Lewiston to Junction City, if the water is clear enough. If the river is off-color, but not totally blown out, one may find good fishing at the tributary confluences where clean water pours in and creates a clear pocket in the muddy main stem. If the river clears by late March, there should be some good fishing downstream for steelhead that have already spawned and are returning to the ocean. These downstreamers, or run-backs, are hungry and feed very aggressively. Many folks claim they would rather catch one 4-pound spring steelie than 10 larger run-backs. Pound for pound, they are the hardest fighting steelhead I have encountered.

Spring/Summer (late May-August)

By late May the water has slowed down from spring snowmelt conditions and approached prime condition for fishing. In high water years the river may have an opaque, greenish-blue color that from a distance appears cloudy. Don't let this keep you off the river. If the water isn't too high or swift, you may find that the fish bite quite well.

Spring steelhead are found throughout the river and, unlike their fall- and summer-run cousins, occupy many different types of water, not just swift water and deep tailouts. The first spring chinook salmon (known as springers) are always encountered in the lower river between the Tish Tang campground and Hoopa sometime in early May. Most folks pursue these lower-river kings from drift boats, using diving plugs and bait plainers to fish the water directly downstream of the boat. The river below the South Fork is open all year, so this is where the first springers are caught. The head of the run will usually reach as far as Grays Falls by late May. The springers move through the lower river quickly, and one must be at the right place at the right time to act.

June is the month of the springer. Bright silver king salmon and summer-run steelhead can be found from the mouth of the Trinity at Weitchpec to the confluence with the North Fork and beyond. This is perhaps the best month to experience the beauty of the Trinity River: cool mornings, hot afternoons, challenging fishing, and a clean river to swim in when temperatures rise. Bring the sunglasses, sunscreen, floppy sun hat, and lots of water. Fish in the mornings and evenings when the heat is tolerable and the fish are active.

This is also prime time for the highway section of the Trinity from Junction City to Cedar Flat. One can either float the river in a raft in search of rolling salmon or, for those less inclined to get wet, take one of the many highway turnouts above the river. In this section the bright kings seem to prefer deep pools and runs with flow, while the dark ones (fish that have been in the river a while and are preparing to spawn) usually favor the deepest pools with little or no flow. If your purpose is to catch a fish to eat, leave the darkies alone and fish the faster water.

If you fish the fast water in search of a bright king, you may also have the good fortune to tangle with a summer-run steelhead. You won't have to ask what has attached itself to the end of your line, as the summer-runs jump high and frequently try spinning cartwheels to dislodge the hook.

The spring chinook run continues in the first half of July, but most of the action occurs above Cedar Flat. Dark salmon are much more common and are often quite visible in the low, clear summer flows. The hot weather and warm water cause the fish to become less active, so most of the fishing is best when the sun is off the water. During the heat of the day the kings will seek out the coldest water they can find, at the bottom of the deepest pools and in the fast water at the base of heavy rapids. Two good places to witness the salmon leaping rapids are Grays Falls (just upstream of Hawkins Bar) and Hell's Hole above Big Flat.

Summer steelhead are still present as well, but many have already ascended their spawning tributaries by mid-July and provide only incidental catches. There are still plenty of fish in the far upper river, but most are preparing to spawn and are suitable only for sport.

Fall (September-November)

Early September is when the first good fall chinook fishing begins in the lower river below Willow Creek, with the best action between Hoopa and Weitchpec. Limited fishing opportunities occur as far upstream as Grays Falls.

By late September good fishing can be found up to, and above, the South Fork confluence. By this time the head of the run is usually somewhere between Willow Creek and Hawkins Bar. The lower river can be hot at this time as the run stretches from the middle river to the mouth, with fresh kings pouring into the lower Klamath on every high tide through late October.

By early October every pool in the lower river has chinook, and the run of fall steelhead is increasing. Fishing in the area above Cedar Flat turns on at this time, and fresh kings can be found clear up to Junction City, with the early fish even farther upstream. October is another prime month to fish the Trinity. Unless early fall rains raise the flow, the Trinity will be low and clear, calling for light tackle, thin line, and small baits or lures.

By late October the whole river is alive with king, coho, and steelhead, and any place from Weitchpec to the Lewiston Dam can be good if a school of aggressive fish is found. Steelhead are in many of the riffles and tailouts throughout the river, and there are at least a few salmon in every pool. During low fall flows, a freshet of rain or a frosty night will make both the salmon and steelhead ready to bite the following day if the temperature drops a bit.

Early November is still pretty good for kings along the middle river, but for the best action head for the upper river and look for kings stacked up below rapids and in deep pools. The main concentrations of kings will be above Big Bar at this time. Steelhead are another story. Their run peaks in November throughout the river, providing great sport on light tackle. Late November sees the end of the fall chinook run. The steelhead run is still going strong with fall-run fish in the upper river and the larger, brighter winter-run fish filling the lower river with every fresh rainfall. With a few dry days between storms the river remains fishable until the first storms of winter slam into the coast and blow it out.

The Trinity River remains a fine fishing stream with good runs of both hatchery and native fish. The runs since 1995 have improved, but the preceding drought years had a heavy impact on the river. Let's not forget this as we set the hook on yet another wild chinook, or as we debate keeping a limit of fish when one or two would feed the whole family. Coho salmon is a federally listed endangered species, but the steelhead and the chinook salmon seem likely to escape that status on the Trinity, if only because of the effects of the Lewiston Lake Hatchery. To lose salmon fishing would eliminate an integral element of the area's sense of place. Concerned sport fishers should act responsibly by releasing native fish and keeping only as many hatchery fish as needed. The greatest thrill comes in catching the fish and feeling their ancient power telegraphed to our fingertips through a strand of fishing line.

Geologic Knots & Mining Nodes

Earth scientists refer to the Klamath Mountains, the tortured region through which Highway 299 runs, as a "knot" because it ties together several geologic provinces of extremely complex origin. To the south and west are the Coast Ranges, ridges of former seafloor sediments scraped up by the advance of the North American Plate. To the north and east looms the higher Cascade Range, a chain of volcanoes that stretches from Mount Lassen north to the Canadian border. Tucked away between these two long chains stand the saw-toothed Trinity Alps. The Great Valley Province—the wide trough containing the Sacramento and San Joaquin valleys—meets the Klamath Mountains near Redding, where the Trinity Highway begins twisting its way through some 140 miles of traumatized topography.

The Klamaths are called "knotty" not just for their tangled geology. The rugged terrain has made most of the region fairly inaccessible. In addition, the same rains that nurture the mountains' thick forests have obscured much of the rock with dense vegetation and deep soils, much to many geologists' dismay. Nevertheless, road cuts and mineshafts provide at least a partial picture of the region's geologic history.

The rocks of the Klamaths are a hodgepodge of former islands that drifted into North America, by the process of plate tectonics, some 225 million years ago. The collisions brought molten rock from the earth's mantle to its crust. Where this magma reached the surface, volcanoes grew—towering Hoods, Shastas, and Rainiers. Where the molten material cooled before breaking the crust, granite masses known as batholiths, similar to those found in the Sierra Nevada, formed. Then, perhaps 100 million years ago, the northern end of the Sierra broke off and gradually moved to the west, becoming, in the process, the Klamaths. When this tumultuous era finally ended, a long period of erosion by water and ice sculpted the uplifted land into spectacular peaks, sharp ridges, and deep valleys.

Tiny amounts of gold in large quantities of ore were concentrated in the hot waters circulating through the rock surrounding the cooling batholiths. These waters, under tremendous pressure from the heat of the magma, were injected into cracks and fissures. When they cooled, the minerals hardened into quartz veins ranging in width from a fraction of an inch to ten feet. When erosion wore the rock away, as it did during a long quiet period in the Klamaths, it deposited gold at the bottom of streambeds lined with gravel and sand. As the streams eroded downward, they left remnant beds behind on the hills. These old terraces often contain large deposits of placer gold—the very type sought and found by Pierson Reading (and hordes of other miners) along tributaries of the upper Sacramento and Trinity rivers within months of his friend and former employer John Sutter's more famous find in the Sierra Nevada.

Individuals or small groups could work the placer deposits using inexpensive implements. Although 49ers employed the familiar pan as a prospecting tool, they soon adopted larger-scale methods to increase their return. They worked the old terraces by running diverted water through the gravel beds. This system of sluicing separated the gold by washing away the lighter sand and gravel.

By the 1860s, placer miners had their eyes on slopes far above the creeks and rivers, but they needed to get more water to wash larger volumes of gravel after the richest deposits gave out. By channeling this most vital resource through flumes far from the source streams and forcing it through a giant nozzle, often called a "monitor," companies could run (and ruin) entire hillsides through their sluices and extract substantial sums of gold.

In the Sierra Nevada this method of hydraulic mining washed so much sediment onto Central Valley farms that the state banned its use by the 1880s. Since the Trinity system drains directly into the Pacific, hydraulic mining remained legal in the Klamaths until the 1960s. Although the monitors extracted much wealth from the placers, they were not very efficient. A lot of the gold washed right through the sluices, winding up at the bottom of the rivers.

Until about 1900, Trinity miners had developed no easy way to extract this "wasted" gold from the riverbeds. Then they imported dredges from the placer mines of the Mother Lode. These floating "factories" scooped out tons of sand, cobble, and gravel, sorted and washed it in sluices to collect the gold, and then deposited the tailings along the riverbanks.

Two main types of dredges worked the waters of the Trinity region. The first and largest was a self-contained unit known as the bucket-line dredge. In its operation an endless string of buckets scooped material off the river bottom and dumped it onto a revolving screen at the front of the dredge. Oversized rocks dropped onto the stacker belt, which piled the tailings into long arcs as it moved back and forth. Finer material fell into the sluices, where the gold was recovered. Because of their size, bucket-line dredges could be used only along stretches of river wide enough to afford ample room to maneuver.

Smaller streams, such as Reading's Creek, Brown's Creek, Weaver Creek, and narrow sections of the Trinity, could not accommodate the large bucket-line dredges and were left nearly untouched until the 1930s, when a more portable dredging system was developed. Called the dragline dredge, it consisted of a floating gravel-washing plant (the "boat") and a crawler-type crane (the "dragline") that had a long cable with a drag bucket attached to its end. The dragline "walked" along the streambank ahead of the boat, digging out gold-bearing gravel and depositing it in the boat's hopper. A rotary screen on the boat separated the finer gravel from

As seen in this pre-1910 photo, the three monitors at the Union Hill Mine first drove gravel into a bedrock ditch; the ambulant alluvium then flowed through a tunnel to the Trinity River. (C. E. Goodyear photo)

larger rocks. The gravel fell into sluices and moved through the gold recovery process while the rocks were carried out to the tailing piles. The dragline's action of feeding gravel into the boat gave the dredge its nickname: "doodlebug."

Soon after discovering gold, miners traced placers to their rock-bound places of origin, called lodes. Since lode mining required expensive equipment to drill shafts and separate the gold from the rock, companies, rather than individuals, had to work the quartz veins. The earliest such mine, the Washington near French Gulch, opened in 1852. The French Gulch district proved to be one of the richest in the Klamaths, with five different mines each producing more than a million dollars worth of gold. One of the largest granitic bodies, the Shasta Bally Batholith, had pushed into the area south of French Gulch 130,000,000 years ago, introducing quartz seams and veins.

Successful lode mines also operated in the Trinity's neighboring tributaries of North Fork and Canyon Creek. Miners probed veins formed at the collision of an island arc with the edge of the continent. Granite batholiths—now exposed as the serrated peaks and ridges of the Trinity Alps—rose to the north of this mining region, providing a source of heat for the formation of the lodes. A third lucrative mining district developed farther west around another huge batholith—Ironside Mountain. The lode gold of the New River mining district was forced into existing rock when this batholith rose during the formation of the Coast Ranges

The Junction City Mining Company dredge rearranges some Trinity topography. (TCHS photo)

about 170,000,000 years ago.

West of Redding the Trinity Highway provides a splendid cross-section of the underlying geologic structure of the Klamath Province in a series of road cuts. Except for the batholiths, the ages of rocks seen along the road become younger toward the west, reflecting the successive additions of land to North America from Pacific islands.

The ancient rocks of the eastern Klamath—best seen along the edges of Whiskeytown Lake—have been highly altered from their origins as seafloor sediments and volcanic lava flows. Here and there, however, distinct parallel beds appear, all angling down and east—evidence as to how plate tectonics can reshape the horizontal beds of sedimentary rock.

West of the Tower House-French Gulch turnoff, Highway 299 spirals up through the granitic rock of the Shasta Bally Batholith. At first glance, it looks nothing like the sparkling salt-and-pepper formations familiar to Yosemite Valley visitors. Instead, the exposed Shasta Bally is a cream-colored, crumbling rock that resembles sandstone more than granite. Abundant rainfall and mild temperatures are responsible for its appearance, allowing for deep weathering of the surface rock. As water seeps

The Paymaster Mine, c. 1905. The wood-burning mill, foreground, is now on the premises of the J. J. "Jake" Jackson Museum in Weaverville, where it is fired up for special occasions. (TCHS photo)

into tiny cracks between individual crystals, chemical reactions weaken the softer minerals. With its internal structure removed, the rock disintegrates into a soft sandy soil. West of Buckhorn Summit, by contrast, a few fresh outcrops of granite reminiscent of the Sierra Nevada appear along the road.

Ten miles west of the summit, the highway passes through a high cut that exposes sand and gravel. Though far from any major stream, these rocks are rounded like those on a river-bed. This sediment collected on a swampy plain 25,000,000 years ago, as the Klamaths were carved and dissected by erosion. In spite of its age, the gravel here poses a hazard to the high-way by frequently tumbling down. The chain-link fence placed to contain the falling rock provides one more example of the conflicts be-tween geologic and human time scales.

Oregon Mountain and Gulch, between Weaverville and Junction City, present another prime illustration of time scales converging. The deep gullies were not created by eons of rains, but by the hydraulic monitors of the La Grange Mine a century ago. The relentless "gi-ants" stripped away much of the land surface, leaving a ravaged terrain that is only recently regaining a covering of trees and grasses.

The mounds of rock between Junction City and Helena are reminders of the dredging that took place along this section of the Trinity. The dredges drastically altered the riverbed, depos-iting heavier gravels on top of lighter sands and silts. These inversions made it more difficult for the river, once damming reduced its flow, to move downstream. The fields of arc-shaped deposits along the banks bear witness of where the big bucket-line dredges were at work.

Along its relatively level stretch, from Junction City to Cedar Flat, the Trinity Highway passes through rock from the series of islands that accumulated on the Pacific shores of North America 200,000,000 years ago. This material has been highly altered by the heat and pressure of ancient collisions, but some parallel beds are evident—all dipping eastward. Among many other rock types, limestone and marble occur in pockets scattered throughout the area.

Three miles west of Hayden Flat, the road passes into the Ironside Mountain Batholith, which stretches along a 40-mile north-south axis from Orleans to Hayfork. Old Ironside is merely one outcrop of this mass of granite, but it towers directly over the mouth of New River. Its sides, like the faces of the never-ending road cuts in the Trinity Gorge, are streaked with rust from the weathering of iron-rich minerals in the granite. Resistant granite in the river has created turbulent rapids as the water has tried to cut through the rock.

After rupturing many old river terraces between Hawkins Bar and Willow Creek, Highway 299 finally enters the rock of the last island to hit North America. The younger, less altered material mainly displays oceanic sediment. The beds seen in the cuts are parallel, though seldom horizontal or even straight. Instead, the black and dark gray rock has twisted into fan-

A westward-bound motorist on the Trinity Highway speeds past Oregon Mountain debris clogging Oregon Gulch. (SHS photo)

tastic shapes due to the relentless force of the slow, grinding collision.

Berry Summit marks the western edge of the Klamath Mountains and the eastern end of the Coast Ranges. The latter are arranged in long parallel ridges separated by muddy coastal rivers. This summit passes over South Fork Mountain, a continuous north-south ridge that stretches for 90 miles. Most rocks of the Coast Ranges are relatively soft and therefore easily eroded. As a result, the road cut material has

weathered rapidly, obscuring much of its structure. From Berry Summit to Arcata, soft rock and heavy vegetation combine to confound attempts to study the roadside geology. Travelers can finally relax along the broad sweep of Humboldt Bay's eastern shore as they motor from Arcata to Eureka, where the lofty has become low, the rugged has relented, and the Klamath Knot has at last loosened.

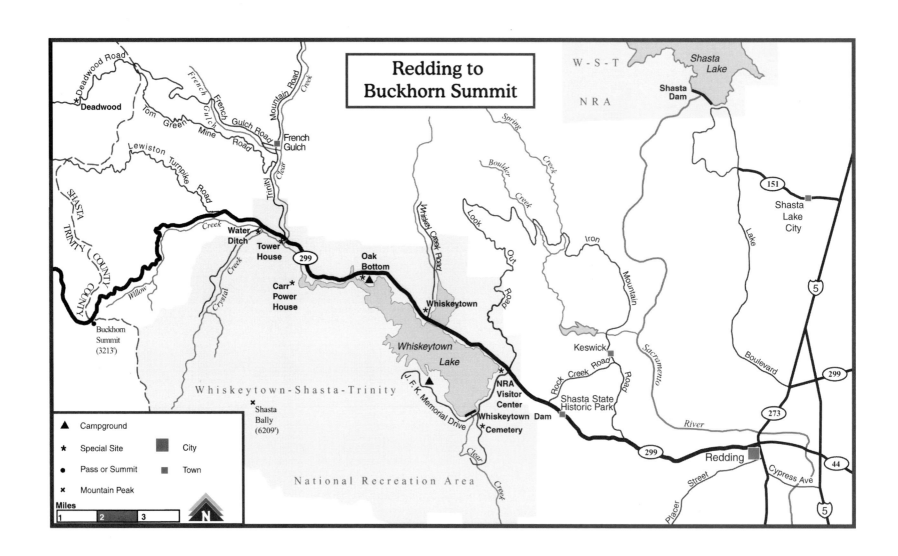

Redding to Buckhorn Summit

Deadwood Road

Deadwood

Tom Green Mine Road

French Gulch Road

Mountain Road

Creek

French Gulch

Lewiston Turnpike Road

SHASTA TRINITY COUNTY

Creek

Water Ditch

Tower House

299

Carr Power House

Crystal

Oak Bottom

Whiskeytown

W - S - T

NRA

Shasta Lake

Shasta Dam

Spring Creek

Boulder Creek

151

Shasta Lake City

Look Out Road

Iron Mountain Road

Whiskey Creek Road

Buckhorn Summit (3213')

Willow

Whiskeytown Lake

J. F. K. Memorial Drive

Keswick

Sacramento

5

299

Whiskeytown-Shasta-Trinity

Shasta Bally (6209')

NRA Visitor Center

Whiskeytown Dam

Cemetery

Clear

Creek

Rock Creek Road

Shasta State Historic Park

River

Boulevard

273

National Recreation Area

299

Redding

Placer Street

Cypress Ave

44

5

Legend:

▲ Campground

★ Special Site

● Pass or Summit

✖ Mountain Peak

City (shaded)

Town (square)

Miles
1 2 3

N

38

II. Bucking up for Buckhorn Summit

1. A Primer for Reading Redding: Crossroads of the North Valley
   Steve Gibson & Ben Bennion

2. "Sweet Shasta Town": Rustic Relic of Dry Diggings   *Gregory Coit, Daniel Lane, & Ben Bennion*

3. Turning a Clear Creek Into a Whiskey(town) Lake   *Gavin Hoban & Ben Bennion*

4. French Gulch: A Still Glimmering Gold Town   *Liz Ames & Ben Bennion*

A Primer for Reading Redding: Crossroads of the North Valley

> Redding is a good service station town, because when people get here their bladders are full and their tanks are empty.
>
> — Redding oil businessman

With 80,000 residents spread far in every direction, Redding dwarfs all other Trinity Scenic Byway towns—even the cities at the opposite end of the Byway. While Eureka has its well-defined Old Town and Arcata its Plaza, Redding lacks a clear center in spite of its location as a natural cradle of convergence. The city straddles the Sacramento River at the northern end of the Central Valley, yet it has never functioned as a river town because it lies about 30 miles above the head of steamboat navigation (located at the older and more compact town of Red Bluff). Redding began, in 1872, as the northern terminus of the California and Oregon Railroad. Once it bridged the river and wrested the county seat from Shasta, the newly incorporated town rapidly became an *entrepôt*—

a trade hub that the local *Searchlight* (Feb. 22, 1898) dubbed the "Distributing Center of Northern California."

In its early decades Redding had a clearly delimited half-mile square center bounded by North, South, East, and West streets. The "Official Map" of 1890 labeled a large rectangle within that area as the "Rail Road Reservation." California and Oregon streets lined the east and west sides, respectively, of the railroad station. They, in turn, were paralleled by Market and Court streets—an apparent attempt to keep politics and commerce a safe distance from the trains (and from each other). The street names running from south to north began with Sacramento and ended at Shasta, with Placer, Yuba, Butte, and Tehama sandwiched between them in that order. Many California geography students will recognize the significance of those six county names, but they may not sense the distinction between *Redding* and *Reading*—two toponyms pronounced the same as *red*. (*See sidebar, page 42.*)

From the beginning, Redding's city seems to have faced north toward Mt. Shasta rather than east toward a closer and lower Lassen Peak, perhaps because the railroad—and later US 99 and I-5—kept the town turned that way. In any case, the rail town and auto city has found its official logo well beyond its boundaries by converting "Shasta" into a trinity of images—mountain, lake, and dam. Redding's new City Hall displays the three Shastas prominently both inside and outside the main entrance. (Long before the dam and lake appeared in 1938–45, the upper Sacramento Valley had enough aesthetic appeal to generate a proposal in Yreka—derived from *I-eka*, an Indian name for Mt. Shasta—for a large national park bisected by 75 miles of C&O track.) Redding's turning outward for its icons may reflect the difficulty any auto-dependent crossroads city has in finding an internal identity. As local historian Jean Beauchamp observed as early as 1973, the "downtown is now graced with a hybrid of concrete, wood and plastic that disguises the few remaining buildings that once gave Redding its character." For its centennial the city

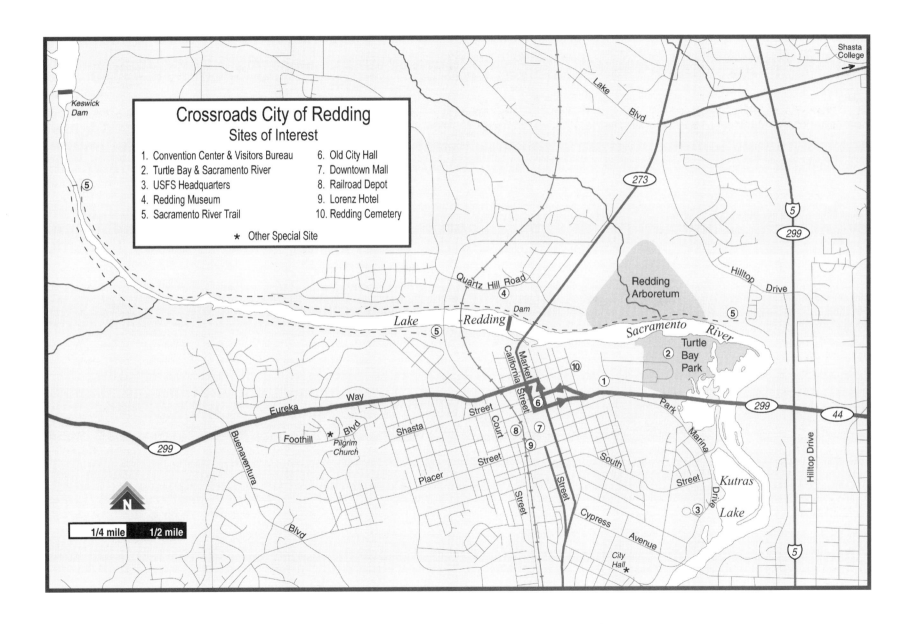

Crossroads City of Redding
Sites of Interest

1. Convention Center & Visitors Bureau
2. Turtle Bay & Sacramento River
3. USFS Headquarters
4. Redding Museum
5. Sacramento River Trail

6. Old City Hall
7. Downtown Mall
8. Railroad Depot
9. Lorenz Hotel
10. Redding Cemetery

★ Other Special Site

Shasta College

Keswick Dam

Lake Blvd

273

5

299

Quartz Hill Road

Redding Arboretum

Hilltop Drive

Lake

Redding

Dam

Sacramento River

Turtle Bay Park

California Street

Market

Eureka Way

Street

Court

Park

Marina

299

44

Buenaventura

Foothill Blvd

★ Pilgrim Church

Shasta Street

Street

South Street

Hilltop Drive

Placer Street

Street

Kutras Lake

Cypress Avenue

City Hall ★

Blvd

N

1/4 mile   1/2 mile

5

tried to preserve some of the old center within an enclosed shopping area along Market Street, but the new mall proved less than magnetic.

Recently Redding has turned to the Sacramento running through it to develop a sizable riverfront park as a focal area. And its 1998 General Plan calls for a higher skyline (up to 100 feet) to make the downtown more visible and attractive. The largest city of the North Central Valley clearly intends to make itself much more than a pit stop and a convenient base for exploring the Shasta Cascade region that surrounds it. Neither its size nor its roughly rectangular road grid—formed by Highways 273 and 299, I-5, and Cypress Ave.—should deter travelers from exploring the place and finding such unexpected gems as the final (and unfinished) church designed by Frank Lloyd Wright (located on Foothill Blvd.). Its emphasis on triangles, epitomizing the Trinity, may have special appeal for Scenic Byway pilgrims.

A reading of Redding's or any city's distinctive features does require some sort of geographical-historical primer. The original site, known as "Poverty Bend," held no particular resource attraction apart from its "fine view of the surrounding country, and the ground be-

What's in a Place Name Anyway?

The C&O Railroad Company thought it appropriate to name this new town after its general land agent Benjamin B. Redding, a distinguished citizen of Sacramento. Many Shasta County residents, however, considered it more fitting to honor their most prominent pioneer, Major Pierson B. Reading. In 1844 he had secured from the Mexican government a "Rancho San Buenaventura" that reached from Cottonwood Creek past "Poverty Bend" (the future site of Redding) along the western side of the Sacramento River. A Shasta Assemblyman persuaded the California legislature to pass a bill (1874) changing the spelling of the town's name from *Redding* to *Reading*, but six years later another legislator had the state repeal the act—much to the company's (and presumably Mr. Redding's) satisfaction.

Rancher Reading, had he still been alive, probably wouldn't have cared, for his name already appeared on the state map in several places that must have meant more to him than another new rail town. Soon after the discovery of gold at Coloma in 1848, Reading visited his friend and former employer John Sutter. He returned from the Mother Lode to prospect, with the aid of Wintu Indians living on his ranch, the Shasta foothills and Trinity Mountains. First near the lower end of Clear Creek, not far from his adobe home, and then a few months later along the upper Trinity, Reading's group panned out sizable sums of gold on both streams—80,000 dollars in just six weeks at the latter site. Such success triggered a second and often overlooked rush of 49ers. A rough bunch of miners from Oregon jumped his Trinity claims and derided him for hiring Indians, but his name stuck to each of two river bars and a creek. (Both of these bars have monuments marking the sites of his spring/fall 1848 discoveries.)

After being routed from his "diggings," Reading returned with his Wintu to ranching and other enterprises. One of them involved trying to extend the head of navigation northward from Red Bluff and included the selection of a site at the mouth of Clear Creek for a town named Reading. The plan came to naught, but the locale now lies at the southern end of Redding and close to the city's only Indian rancheria. The tiny enclave symbolizes the fate of the Wintu, who served as a "friendly" labor force for the Major and whom he "befriended" to the extent that a master-servant relationship allowed. He admitted as early as 1851 that "Indian troubles arise in the first place from aggressions made by the Whites." The several hundred Wintu living on his estate must have died off rapidly—probably from disease more than aggression—for in 1862 his wife reported the presence of "two or three hundred men on our place, mostly Chinamen...."

While Redding has no streets named after Pierson B. Reading, unless one counts Buenaventura Boulevard, the city honored him during the 1943 centennial of his arrival in California by having a peak in Lassen Volcanic National Park named after him. He hiked to the top of Lassen Peak in 1864 with the first woman (an artist) to make the ascent. That same year he and a partner by the name of Bumpass began mining sulfur in the hot springs area far below Reading Peak. Benjamin Redding, on the other hand, had to settle for having just one place named after him.

Map of Redding, c. 1890, centered on train depot. Note the single bridge spanning the "distant" Sacramento River and the ruled "square" along North, East, South, and West streets. (SHS map)

ing studded with wide spreading and beautiful oaks." And in summer, before air-conditioning, it often turned into a hellhole, with temperatures soaring above 100 degrees, because of the "dead-air pocket" created by the North Valley's microclimate. In selecting a town site, the railroad surveyors were more concerned with grade and terrain, and their supervisors were not ready in 1872 for the costly challenge of cutting a line through the rugged Siskiyou Mountains to the Oregon border and beyond. Keeping the northern terminus in Redding before extending the rails to Ashland (and Port-

land) by 1887 gave the town time to take advantage of its depot function at the expense of Shasta and other settlements. As the *Yreka Journal* correctly predicted (June 26, 1872): "The railroad will bring a string of new towns right up through the middle of the State, and the old mining towns will look down upon them from their mountain eyries [aeries] with an ill concealed envy and jealousy. The railroad cannot go to them, and they cannot go to the railroad."

Even with the capture of regional trade and the county seat, Redding grew more slowly than expected. The 1890 census recorded only 2,500

residents, thanks to the general decline in the county's mining economy, frequent fires in the town's business district, and the expulsion of a large Chinese population four years earlier. After a "rousing anti-Chinese meeting," a committee of leading citizens gave the "Celestials" an ultimatum, and "they left like an army breaking camp, some going to San Francisco, others to China, and the rest scattering throughout the County and State."

Beginning in the 1890s, a copper boom—ironically centered on *Iron* Mountain northwest of Redding—replaced gold mining as a major source of economic growth. Nearby Keswick, nicknamed "Copper City," soon had several stores "and saloons galore." One timber man supplied the Mountain Copper Company's smelters and roasters with 500 or 600 cords of wood per month. Mining practices despoiled the surrounding hills and ruined crops to such an extent that the smelters were eventually forced to shut down. At a much later date the Environmental Protection Agency designated the Iron Mountain Mine as a Superfund cleanup site. The closing of the copper mine and some of the area's large lumber mills, even before the onset of the Great Depression, made "Poverty Flat" once again an apt name for Redding, which had long since lost most of its oaks to construction.

The Central Valley Project, centered on the colossal Shasta Dam, generated a new boom in the North Valley on the eve of World War II. Construction of the dam doubled the size of Redding to nearly 10,000 and spawned new towns such as Central Valley, Project City, and Summit City (all incorporated in 1993 under the more appealing name of Shasta Lake). As the lake itself filled, workers began moving into the area to fill new demands for labor. Many of the CVP workers found jobs after 1945 in a revitalized timber industry while others gravitated to a gradually growing service sector that increasingly emphasized outstanding medical facilities and marine activities. The latter centered on the three units that by 1965 comprised the Whiskeytown-Shasta-Trinity National Recre-

ation Area, all within easy reach of Redding.

As late as 1970, the crossroads of the North Valley still had fewer than 20,000 people. But its population has increased by almost another 20,000 each decade since then, a trend projected to continue until at least 2020. This rate of growth suggests that the city has finally fully capitalized on its cradle of convergence position at the head of California's huge Central Valley. Besides making the Sacramento River more central and the Downtown more magnetic, planners will try to transform North Market Street into a visitor-friendly corridor

that links the city's two logical focal areas. If they succeed, the street may yet live up to its "Miracle Mile" nickname. While waiting for these grand plans to materialize, take an independent reading of "Bridge City" by visiting one or more of the ten sites briefly described below in whatever order suits your fancy. They are grouped into two equal sets—one centered on the river, the other on the downtown.

1. The **Redding Convention and Visitors Bureau,** just off the first exit (Auditorium Drive) on Highway 299 west toward downtown Redding, provides the standard informa-

Pierson B. Reading's daughter Alice, left, and a friend view the crumbling right wing of his Buenaventura Adobe, located near the mouth of Cottonwood Creek, in the 1930s. (SHS photo)

tion sought by travelers plus an artistic guide to "Redding's Historic Architecture" that features three self-guided tours (only one suited to walking). Best of all, the Convention Center puts one right on…

2. The **Sacramento River and Turtle Bay,** the hub of a projected riverine parkway between Shasta Dam and the City of Anderson. Boaters can put in at the Posse Grounds ramp on the north side of the Center and drift a few miles down to the Bonnyview Bridge ramp or take a few hours and go all the way to Red Bluff. In lieu of white water, the river offers good-sized trout, a mixed oak savanna and riparian forest, and somewhat cooler vistas of the valley. Turtle Bay Park swarms with young people rather than turtles, attracted by a 200-acre arboretum, a spectacular seasonal butterfly sanctuary, and a popular Paul Bunyan's Forest Camp. A harp-shaped pedestrian bridge will soon span the river and integrate the park. With its single sundial spire and graceful plaza, the bridge may yet become the internal icon that Redding has long lacked.

3. Opposite the exit to Turtle Bay is Park Marina Drive; it leads to the **United States Forest Service's Shasta-Trinity Headquarters** (2400 Washington Ave.). The district office provides the latest maps and information for not only the far-flung Shasta-Trinity National Forest but also for the units of the National Recreation Area it administers. The Forest Service has mounted a magnificent exhibit of the upper Sacramento region's transportation history (the first of four rotating displays) at the California Welcome Center, located next to Anderson's outlet stores off of I-5 south of Redding.

4. The **Redding Museum of Art and History** and the **Carter House Natural Science Museum** (in Caldwell Park off of Quartz Hill Rd.) also belong to the Turtle Bay complex. They have small but outstanding collections. The former often prepares exhibits that highlight the history and cultural landscape of the Shasta County end of the Trinity Scenic Byway while the latter features frequent "Animal Discovery" times. **Diestelhorst Bridge**, easily reached from Caldwell Park, dates back to 1914, when it replaced Reid's Ferry. George and Caroline Diestelhorst, "market farmers" from the German territory of Hannover, acquired an 83-acre parcel on the south side of the river in 1859, and the next year Ed Reid—a farmer on the opposite side—got the ferry license. A new road bridge across Redding Lake opened in 1997, parallel to the venerable Diestelhorst, which is now reserved for pedestrian use. In earlier days, Redding youngsters flocked to the older bridge, where they jumped from swinging ropes into their favorite "Swimming Hole."

5. The original six-mile **Sacramento River Trail**, begins and ends at the Diestelhorst, following both sides of the river as far west as the stress-ribbon foot bridge below Keswick Dam. A recent 1.7-mile extension on the north bank takes walkers, joggers, and bicyclists along the edge of Redding's fine Arboretum and into Turtle Bay Park (when the new bridge is completed). The harnessed river's level is now regulated by engineers' formulas for irrigation and hydroelectric power generation rather than by the vagaries of the seasons. The salmon that once churned these waters seldom reach Redding or their spawning beds due to damming and related activities. By contrast, for centuries prior to the 1840s, about 5,000 Wintu camped in wickiups along the river's big Redding bend each autumn to spear and smoke countless fish. The trail's new connection with Turtle Bay and the park's traditional Wintu Bark House bring the history of this river bend full circle.

6. Redding's **"Old City Hall"** (1313 Market Street), built in 1907 in Romanesque Revival style, contrasts architecturally with the Streamline Moderne **Fire House** constructed behind it in 1939. The city outgrew its hall years ago but fortunately decided to convert it into an art gallery and a theater instead of razing it.

7. The **Downtown Redding Mall** preserves a few historic buildings underneath a covered superstructure. Its creators did not anticipate the appeal of the larger suburban shopping centers that sprang up along Hilltop Road and elsewhere. The old city mall now seems half-deserted, but it offers ample space to the Shasta County Historical Society (open daily, 9:00 A.M.–4:00 P.M.) for its valuable collections and exhibits and its efforts to retain a remnant of Redding's rapidly disappearing past.

8. The **Railroad Depot** has undergone a major transformation of its own in recent years.

While both freight and passenger trains still stop daily, the area now functions more visibly as a bus terminal.

9. Among the several stately hotels that surrounded Redding's railroad depot at the turn of the century, the most prominent one still standing is the **Lorenz Hotel** (1509 Yuba Street). Built with Trinity mining money by Susan Lorenz, this cinnabar red Beaux Art-Renaissance Revival building has housed senior citizens since 1978. Every Thursday night in summer, in the park behind the old hotel and the new Kennett-Diamond Brewery, Redding stages a lively Market Fest as part of its "Discover Downtown" promotion.

10. The **Redding Cemetery**, at the eastern dead end of Eureka Way, occupies a bluff that brings us back to the Sacramento River. It is the only site near the downtown area that provides a partial vista of the city. Through the memorial park's leafy canopy you can glimpse the great river below, Lassen Peak to the east, Mount Shasta to the north, the Trinities to the west, and the open valley to the south. Closer at hand, you can scan the gravestones for the names of some of the former residents of Old Shasta—first stop on the Scenic Byway proper.

Chester Mullen, a "Carpenter with a Camera," snapped this Market Street shot sometime before 1915. It features the "Big Store" of McCormick Saeltzer Co., left, and both horse- and motor-powered vehicles. (SHS photo)

"Sweet Shasta Town": Rustic Relic of Dry Diggings

From Shasta town to Redding town
The ground is torn by miners, dead;
The Manzanita, rank and red,
Drops dusty berries up and down
Their grass-grown trails. Their silent mines
Are wrapped in Chapparal and vines;
Yet one gray miner still sits down
'Twixt Redding and sweet Shasta town…
That great graveyard of hopes! Of men
Who sought for hidden veins of gold:
Of young men dead suddenly grown old—
Of old men dead, despairing when
The gold was just within their hold!
That storied land, whereon the light
Of other days gleams faintly still:
Somelike the halo of a hill
That lifts above the fading night;
That warm, red, rich and human land
That flesh-red soil, that warm red sand,
Where one gray miner still sits down!
'Twixt Redding and sweet Shasta town.

—Joaquin Miller

In Redding, Highway 299 West begins, fittingly, as Eureka Street. The road rises rapidly into what Joaquin Miller called the *Piedmont* or foothills of the Trinity Mountains. But before the air temperature has cooled down more than a few degrees, the ruins of Old Shasta loom on the horizon. Only five miles from and 500 feet above Redding, they stand as a haunting reminder of a gold rush town that had all but died by 1930. Any real appreciation of this rustic relic, blurred by the wide highway and heavy traffic that run and whiz through it, requires at least a brief journey into its past. Such a trip can take different routes, but ideally all of them ought to start at the old Courthouse (and Jail) that now serves as the Visitor Center of the Shasta State Historic Park. If time permits, after a visit to this newly remodeled Museum, stroll around town with the official "Brief History and Tour Guide" in hand or, if it's not available, let us brief you with our own similar version. (The Shasta Historical Society's 1999 *Covered Wagon* outlines a longer itinerary that pinpoints nearly 30 sites between Shasta, Redding, and the lower end of Clear Creek.)

Whichever guide you choose, try to imagine the town in its prime as Shasta County's largest and most important city. That era lasted from 1851, when "miners burned down the Wintu council meeting house and massacred about 300 of the people" and replaced Reading's ranch as the county seat, until at least 1872 and the rise of Redding, which hastened Shasta's decline and demise. This mining camp became the county's leading town because it combined the advantages of both site and situation. Its original name of Reading's Springs, based on the "pure and unfailing waters" found there by Major Reading while trapping, signifies its first physical attraction, even if Mt. Shasta, an "imperial" peak in Miller's eyes, ultimately imposed its name on the infant town.

The fact that the "mines on every side" [of the city] are rich and extensive" underlines the site's central location relative to the dry diggings found everywhere between French Gulch and Reading's Buenaventura on the upper Sacramento. The miners grew even richer once they formed a company that dug the 40-mile Clear Creek Ditch to divert water to the deposits

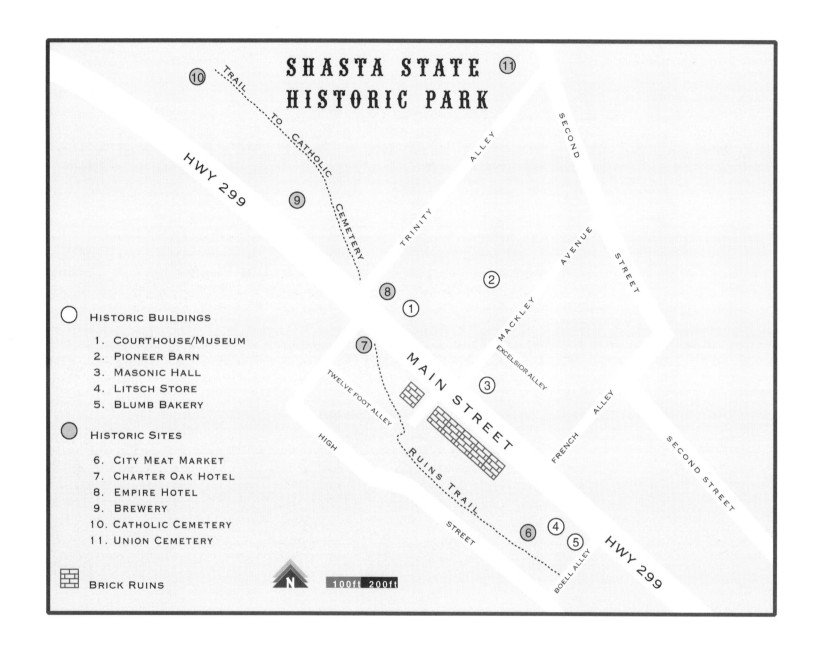

SHASTA STATE HISTORIC PARK

HWY 299

TRAIL TO CATHOLIC CEMETERY

TRINITY ALLEY

SECOND STREET

AVENUE

MACKLEY

EXCELSIOR ALLEY

FRENCH ALLEY

SECOND STREET

MAIN STREET

TWELVE FOOT ALLEY

HIGH STREET

RUINS TRAIL

BOELL ALLEY

HWY 299

○ HISTORIC BUILDINGS

1. COURTHOUSE/MUSEUM
2. PIONEER BARN
3. MASONIC HALL
4. LITSCH STORE
5. BLUMB BAKERY

● HISTORIC SITES

6. CITY MEAT MARKET
7. CHARTER OAK HOTEL
8. EMPIRE HOTEL
9. BREWERY
10. CATHOLIC CEMETERY
11. UNION CEMETERY

▦ BRICK RUINS

N

100ft 200ft

found south of Shasta in such fine-sounding places as Horsetown and Muletown.

Even before completion of the ditch in 1855, Shasta City had emerged as the "head of *whoa* navigation," where "wagons [and horses] stop and packing [the mules] commences." Packers and others engaged in supplying miners profited greatly during boom seasons. For instance, in the fall of 1854 the *Shasta Courier* reported that "stages arrive crowded every day." The paper figured that more than 2,000 mules "are now employed in packing from this place to the various towns and mining localities north [and] west of us"—including Yreka (reached via French Gulch) and Weaverville. With each mule carrying an average load of 200 pounds, this amounted to about 100 tons per week. A team of packers could make up to $2,000 a trip.

Merchants in turn benefited from supplying the mule drivers. While working on his books early one morning, William Robbins heard a knock at his store door. A local packer eager to hit the trail bought $3,000 in supplies before Robbins even had a chance to think about fixing breakfast.

As miners "placered with more or less success" all the streams entering the Sacramento River from the west, nothing but fires or floods—when "every little gulch ran a river of water"—could slow down the boom of the first decade. "Shasta in Ashes" cried the *Courier* headline of June 18, 1853, after windswept flames wiped out the city's business district in half an hour. Even with losses estimated at $500,000,

five weeks later the paper could claim: "There is a freshness and uniformity about the buildings, which, together with the broad and well graded street, gives it a business-like air particularly pleasing. Shasta is altogether a better built and more convenient and comfortable town than it ever was before the fire. Building is still going forward with California rapidity." The

city graded Main Street, widened it from 60 to 110 feet (or 90 from "awning to awning"), and then began rebuilding with locally manufactured brick. Adding heavy iron shutters and covering the roofs with dirt supposedly made the buildings more fireproof, although some were still gutted by a bad fire in 1878.

After "going down hill like the other min-

Until the early 1900s Shasta City was the center of "Whoa! Navigation" for Shasta County. Here, traffic is heavy in front of Craddock Stables, located next to the Masonic Hall. (SSHP photo)

ing towns" in the 1860s, Shasta "looks dull." But it still carried on a good deal of business as a stagecoach hub and kept hoping that the California and Oregon Railroad would somehow restore "the former prosperity of the town." Within two weeks of the arrival of the first train in Redding, County Judge C. C. Bush of Shasta opened a branch store in the new town. Others soon followed him eastward, often taking their bricks with them, so that by 1880 nearly as many people lived in Redding as in Shasta.

The 1870 census provides a picture of the

Shasta, 1870, from the Catholic cemetery. Note the many frame structures that complement the brick buildings. (SSHP photo)

town while still near its prime, before businessmen began to desert it for more promising prospects at Redding and elsewhere. That same year Colonel William Magee first surveyed Shasta's property boundaries. His large-scale map, when tied to the census schedules—which listed the value of each owner's land and personal property, makes it possible to form at least some impressions of the town's population.

Males and miners stand out among the 924 people recorded by Samuel Gilbert, but not as much as one might expect. The male-female ratio of 2:1 had dropped considerably from a decade or two earlier. Omitting the all-male Chinese population (more than 10 percent of the men), the ratio was only 3:2. Miners clearly made up the leading occupation, but overall they were outnumbered by the diverse trades that supported them in myriad ways.

The population's varied origins mirrored the wide range of occupations, yet certain states and countries jump out from among the birthplaces listed: Missouri, New York, Ohio, Germany, Ireland, China. Only the Chinese had their own neighborhood, a little "Hong Kong" located on the southeast edge of town but missing from Magee's map, even though a few of them owned and operated businesses that catered to their countrymen. Over half of Shasta's population turned out in "scorching hot weather" for the town's 4th of July celebration in 1870, held in a pine grove on a hill above High Street. But the whites were unwilling to socialize with the Chinese, Indians, or blacks. "After the Caucasians had appeased their appetites, the colored population had a 'lay out.'" The Chinese had a separate school and temple, a Joss House not unlike the one that survived in Weaverville.

Any census, of course, leaves out the large number who moved into or out of town between the censuses or those who happened to be away for an extended period. Two such people who remained attached to Shasta were Joaquin Miller and Mae Boggs. (*See sidebar, next page.*)

Shasta's first Court House and Jail, "one of

Joaquin and Mae

Born near the Ohio-Indiana border in "a covered wagon pointed west" in 1841 or 1842, Cincinnatus Hiner Miller seemed destined to end up in California or Oregon. His "Quakerlike father" tried both business and teaching in Cincinnati but tired of each and turned to farming farther west—first across central Indiana and Illinois, then all the way to the Willamette Valley of Oregon. Content with their wooded sheep farm near Coburg, Hiner's gentle parents could not deter him from heading for the Klamath gold fields. There in 1855 before he turned 15, "miners invaded the area around Castle Rock [or Crags], polluted the streams, and assaulted the Wintu, who tried in vain to protect their land." Miller was badly wounded in the conflict by an arrow, but a Shasta Indian woman nursed him back to health. For the next few years, he lived in several places among both whites and Native Americans—working cattle on Reading's ranch, digging for gold, and "always scribbling poetry." (Only after Hiner had gained fame as a poet in the Bay Area did an-

other writer rename him Joaquin.) The place he liked best was Mountain Joe's cabin on the McCloud River below the peak whose alpenglow he saw as "The Autograph of God."

Because Joaquin had lived for awhile with an Indian woman, he became known as a "squaw man." In the summer of 1859 he was apprehended for allegedly stealing a horse after his own mount had given out. His captors placed him in the poorly built jail on the hill above Shasta City. He escaped with the aid of an Indian friend, possibly his mistress, but he always maintained his innocence—later insisting he stole a mule, not a horse. Miller based much of his fiction on Shasta County fact, but in time "his fiction became fact" in the minds of local storytellers. Whatever actually happened in the horse-stealing incident, he had alienated many whites by aiding the Wintu. His attitude put him in a no-win situation, prompting him to return to Oregon, where he enrolled in a law school.

In 1886, after an absence of some 25 years, Joaquin returned to Shasta City. While there he went out on his hotel porch after a rainstorm and saw the "same splendid moon" and "the wondrous stars! Large and glittering as the great glittering nuggets we used to gather from the gulches in the days of old [or gold?]."

Although not "born and cradled

on wheels," Mae Bacon—20 years younger than Heiner Miller—could claim a Concord (made-in-New Hampshire) stagecoach as her playhouse. She and her widowed mother left the Mississippi River town of Louisiana, Missouri, in 1871 and traveled to Shasta City by rail, steamboat, and stagecoach. They chose that city as their destination because Bacon's bachelor uncle, Williamson L. Smith, superintended a stage line between there and Jacksonville, Oregon. Uncle Williamson shrewdly built a stagecoach barn near Redding's new depot just before the first train arrived. He and the Bacons rode on the engine's cowcatcher as it entered the station, and Miss Mae, of course, jumped off first.

She attended schools in Shasta and Yreka but landed her first job in Redding as a clerk with McCormick, Saeltzer & Co. through family connections. (McCormick had bought out his partner C. C. Bush and gone into business with Dr. Louis Wellendorff, Mrs. Bacon's brother-in-law, and Rudolph Saeltzer, Wellendorff's nephew.) Mae and her mother bounced back and forth between Redding and San Francisco, where other Bacon children lived. Soon after her mother's death in 1900, Mae married a mining investor named Boggs. After her Uncle Williamson died in 1902 and she inherited his share of McCormick,

Saeltzer & Co., the Boggses decided to build a home on San Francisco's Nob Hill. (When the 1906 earthquake destroyed their home, they were the first to rebuild, with a house imported from Seattle.)

In San Francisco, Boggs became prominent as a suffragist and a supporter of many major civic causes. Like Joaquin Miller, she had no occasion to return to Shasta County for more than a quarter of a century. When she did, in 1930, and saw the shabby state of his "sweet Shasta town," Boggs started a campaign to preserve it as a Pioneer Park and to place plaques in honor of her heroes—the stagecoach drivers! Over ten years time she also compiled a ten-pound collection of 19th-century newspaper clippings and documents, publishing it under the title *My Playhouse Was a Concord Stagecoach*. In 1950 the state finally endorsed her dream by restoring the courthouse and creating Shasta State Historic Park. Two rooms just inside the Museum were set aside to house part of her remarkable collection of California books and paintings. The latter represent artists who worked in the Golden State during her 100-year life and include a few fine local landscapes, which, along with the Museum's old maps and photos, make it much easier to visualize Old Shasta.

In the mid-1930s a young Richard B. Eaton showed Mae Boggs the Wellendorff Store ruins upon her return to Old Shasta after a 30-year absence. (SSHP photo)

the very best wooden structures" anywhere, cost only about $5,000 to build in 1854, but a fire the following year destroyed it. County offices found temporary accommodations in the Charter Oak Hotel across the street but had to wait until 1861 for completion of a new courthouse for $25,000 and had to settle for brick instead of marble. The main hotels and stores tended to crowd along that part of town closest to the seat of government.

Walking along the Ruins Trail above Main Street (and below High) will reinforce the panoramic images viewed in the Museum, which now houses colorful "Jailbird Jake" downstairs. As you wander through town and perhaps out to one of the town's three surviving cemeteries, test your sense of Shasta by playing a game of "Place Chase." (*See sidebar, next page.*)

Most visitors to Old Shasta leave without ever strolling to the edges of town and inspecting the Union, Catholic, and/or (farther away, on Muletown Road) Masonic cemeteries. Burial grounds often repeat in miniature form some of the general features of a given town or society. The small areas set apart for the remains of Native Americans, Chinese, Jews (around the Pioneer Baby Grave west of town), and paupers have become all but invisible in the landscape. The three surviving cemeteries, with aging headstones spread out over shaded hills, took care of the dominant white population of Christian background. In many instances these graves reveal not only the diverse birthplaces of those who lived here, but also the ages and even the causes of their deaths. Most striking is the large number of people who died young, whether of mining injuries, childhood diseases, or while giving birth. Old Shasta, too, experienced its own premature death, thanks to Redding and the railroad, but at least the remarkable Mae Boggs managed to "resurrect" it as a State Historic Park, enabling it to escape the fate of the Whiskeytown area—our next destination.

Judge Richard B. Eaton, some 60 years later, conducting a tour of Old Shasta. (Mark Rounds photo)

Old Shasta Place Chase

Match each number (1-10) on the Shasta map with the clue below (A-I) that best describes it.

A. Which of the historic buildings looks most out of place, as if it did not belong in Old Shasta?

B. Which of the sites was most likely operated in 1870 by a German named Simon Maltzer?

C. Which of the historic buildings still serves as the meeting place of the "Oldest Chartered Lodge" of its kind in California?

D. Which of the historic buildings belonged to the same family for the longest period?

E. Which store among the Brick Ruins housed a company run by three partners—one in San Francisco, a second in Sacramento, and the third (missing from the company's name) in Shasta?

F. On which street of Old Shasta did the *Hotel Français*, operated by Mary A. Tapie, most likely stand?

G. On which historic sites were Shasta's "most distinguished" and "most beautiful" hotels located?

H. The 1870 Shasta census listed Charles Boell, age 54, as a Bavarian-born "Saloon Keeper," but the historic building he owned at the time functioned as a business now more likely to serve bread than beer, namely the store known as?

I. Which cemetery most likely contains the graves of Shasta's Bavarians and Madame Tapie?

If you have identified all ten places correctly, then you qualify as a superior place-chaser and should dash down to Blumb's Bakery or Litsch's Store for a treat as tasty as a dish of Ben and Jerry's ice cream.

Turning a Clear Creek Into a Whiskey(town) Lake

A few miles up and over the steep "Shasta Divide" take us from the rustic ruins of Old Shasta to the watery remains of Old Whiskeytown. Some 120 feet beneath the surface of Whiskeytown Lake, under the bridge with the "no diving or jumping" sign, lies the lake's namesake. The placid scene of sailboats and shrubby hills is best viewed from our first stop—the Visitor Center Overlook off Highway 299 atop the divide. This panorama gives no hint of the area's history, yet the flooded flats, gulches, and ridges that flank the highway were once home to hundreds of people. Only by scanning an old aerial photo or the accompanying 1944 "topo" can we visualize, however dimly, the pre-lake landscape.

Judging by some of the map's place names close to Whiskey Creek, the gold craze started by Pierson B. Reading drove at least one mule and an ox mad and made murderers out of two or more miners. At Mad Mule Gulch seven men took out $10,000 worth of gold in just 15 days, and in Mad Ox Gulch someone found a nugget that weighed 81 ounces. A few miners in the Clear Creek dry diggings averaged $50 per day, but most struggled to survive on their paltry gleanings and often had to cope with illness, injury, or the worst kind of deprivation—no whiskey!

Local folklore claims that one day a mule laden with a barrel of whiskey moved down a steep grade near the confluence of Clear Creek and two of its tributaries. Upon catching sight of the eagerly awaited spirits, several thirsty miners rushed to the site but spooked the mule. The barrel fell into the water and burst open. The men immediately jumped in after it and lapped up as much of the whiskey as they could. Naturally, both the mining camp and the stream were soon christened Whisky Creek (so as not to be confused with nearby Brandy Creek); as the place grew, it became known as Whiskytown (later spelled with an "e").

Located too close to a booming Shasta City, its population increased slowly. In spite of being overshadowed by the county's political and economic center, Whiskeytown still served as a popular stopover for argonauts, offering them the essentials—a hotel, saloon, store, post office, and even a church. The last two frowned on Whiskeytown as a proper name, but eventually it won out over competing toponyms such as Schilling, Mt. Shasta, Blair, and Stella.

Even in its heyday, c. 1855, fewer than 200 people resided in the town itself. However, more than a thousand, mostly men, lived in the larger voting district, with Chinese miners forming a sizable percentage despite the discrimination they encountered. The so-called "Celestials" weathered mixed treatment by the whites, ranging from passive tolerance to overt discrimination. A merchant named Qui Chin had enough means to pay $5,100 for title to the Oak Bottom House about two miles west of Whiskeytown, but whites shunned his hotel/saloon and many of his countrymen moved elsewhere, forcing him to sell out for only $300.

Both Whiskeytown and Oak Bottom found themselves on the turnpike constructed in the 1850s to connect Shasta City with towns farther west and north. Those who profited most from the traffic were two men who secured the site where the roads to French Gulch and Weaverville intersected. Within six months of the Gregg Party's exhausting trip from Rich Bar (on the Trinity's East Fork) to Humboldt Bay in late 1849, Charles Camden and Levi Tower met on a ship sailing from San Francisco to Union (Arcata) and made a similar trek overland in reverse sequence. They founded no town in what is now the Tower House Historic District west of Whiskeytown, but the brothers-in-law (after Camden married Tower's sister) prospered in different ways and to varying degrees. Camden collected road tolls and developed mines and sawmills, while Tower, until his untimely death in 1865, operated the most popular hotel on the toll road.

Most Clear Creek settlements shrank in size after the railroad reached Redding and Shasta lost the county seat. None of them except French Gulch benefited directly from the quartz mines that developed in the Trinity Mountains. During the Great Depression, Whiskeytown barely supported a handful of small-scale mines and "snipers"—one-man operations. Surprisingly, the old town still had about 200 inhabitants when the Trinity River Diversion to the Central Valley began in 1959. This project impounded enough water to fill three sizable reservoirs. After being collected in Trinity (formerly Clair Engle) and Lewiston lakes, the "green gold" flows through an 11-mile tunnel to the Carr Powerhouse at the western end of Whiskeytown Lake. There, a mile or so past Oak Bottom, the bright silver chutes or penstocks, clearly visible from the highway, hum as the water tumbles to the lake.

Just before the filling of the reservoir began, in 1963, contractors moved the building that housed the old town's store (now vacant) and post office to their present site, a quarter mile north of Highway 299 just west of Whiskey Creek Bridge. They relocated the cemetery to a shady slope below the Clair A. Hill Whiskeytown Dam. On September 28, some 10,000 people gathered to hear President John F. Kennedy's dedication speech. In a nostalgic christening of sorts, a local miner tossed a whiskey barrel over the dam.

Since 1965, the National Park Service has administered the Whiskeytown Unit of the Whiskeytown-Shasta-Trinity National Recreation Area. (For some reason, the other two

The shaded Tower House, pictured here c. 1910, was a pleasantly cool and popular stage stop for travelers between Redding and Weaverville. It advertised "secure stables" for horses and mules. (SHS photo)

units were assigned to the Forest Service.) The park now attracts approximately one million visitors a year, mainly between May and October. Recreation enthusiasts flock to the lake-centered region for a wide range of reasons. The Visitor Center, open seven days a week (though hours vary with the season), provides a wide selection of brochures, books, and maps related

Charles Camden, who came to California from Liverpool, England via Lima, Peru. (NPS Whiskeytown Unit photo)

to the Whiskeytown unit's recreational, educational, and restoration activities. It also features fine interpretive exhibits pertaining to the area's early inhabitants—the Wintu Indians—and its gold rush history. In addition, many of the NRA's programs and projects focus not on the lake but on the extensive backcountry.

Whiskeytown visitors whose time is limited should consider taking a short hike or drive to get a broader sense of the new place created by the damming of Clear Creek. Just below the Visitor Center is the Shasta Divide Nature Trail, a self-guided .6-mile loop that starts on the south side of the parking lot and drops down to the lakeshore. Besides seeing a fair sample of the area's trees and shrubs, one can also get a closer view of the unusual "water curtain" designed to move cooler lake water into the Sacramento River for the benefit of spawning salmon. Throughout the Whiskeytown NRA many other short-to-moderate length trails beckon bikers, hikers, joggers, or horseback riders. The backcountry's 39,000 acres also include more than 50 miles of dirt and gravel roads, some open only to 4-wheel-drive vehicles. (Ask Visitor Center personnel for a trail/road map of the area and for current weather conditions.) Whiskeytown has two year-round campgrounds: Oak Bottom and Brandy Creek. The former offers RV and tent camping, the latter limits camping to self-contained RVs. Travelers not equipped or inclined to camp will probably want to seek accommodations in the Redding area or French Gulch.

To see the Kennedy Memorial and the long Whiskeytown Dam, turn right after driving 1.6 miles south past the Visitor Center. With the press of a button, you can listen to a recorded excerpt of President Kennedy's dam dedication speech. Backtrack across the dam and turn right for a short distance (1.2 miles), if you want to observe compelling evidence of old Whiskeytown's ability to survive its inundation. To the left lies the liveliest, most colorful cemetery on or near the Scenic Byway. The variety of headstone styles and the myriad decorations combine with the setting to make one think that even the deceased residents of Whiskeytown must have as much kick left in them as a spooked mule. Either the old burg won't die, still allowing new burials at the graveyard, or it doesn't want us to forget its fate.

The 8-mile drive from the Visitor Center to the Tower House Historic District offers many vistas of the lake but few safe turnouts. At 2.5 miles past the Whiskeytown Post Office turnoff, one can turn left and drive down to the inviting Oak Bottom marina to sample the modern boating scene. There a large Irish family long operated a productive farm after a decade of prospecting in French Gulch.

Another 2.5-mile drive brings us to the Tower House-French Gulch junction. Ironically, given the name of the historic district, nothing remains of Levi Tower's large hotel, which burned to the ground in 1919, and only a few trees from its orchards. Charles Camden's "cottage in the garden," on the other hand, has stood since 1852 (and has a painting that depicts the crossroads in its prime). Prospering from his multiple enterprises, the hard-working Camden wasted little time in enlarging his dwelling to its present size. He also upgraded the road to Shasta City and "much improved" the bridge across Clear Creek by covering it "with substantial siding and a good shingle roof," making it the best span in the county. After designating the area a historic district in 1974, the National Park Service restored the house but declined to rebuild the bridge.

The park's budget permits only Sunday afternoon tours of the Camden home twice a month during the summer. However, five mounted exterior exhibits make it easy to explore the Tower-Camden environs without a ranger. On a loop trail of less than a mile, one can visit Tower's grave; follow a now-dry ditch once used for mining and irrigation; pass the house and barn built for a caretaker after 1900 (because the Camdens moved to Oakland); and look at the abandoned El Dorado Mine—a hard-luck venture. A longer and steeper semi-loop trail leads through the thick mixed forest that enshrouds Mill Creek above the mine.

A shorter and easier trail follows the Crystal Creek water ditch built by Camden in 1885–88 and restored by the Park Service in 1999. "As soon as the flumes were in I was prepared to mine with much greater advantage and success, besides selling water to the others," Camden shrewdly concluded in his autobiog-

Once freight teams left Shasta City for Whiskeytown or French Gulch, they had to negotiate the steep and, at the time, much more winding road over the Shasta Divide. (SHS photo)

raphy. From the level, mile-long trail, lined with glowing tiger lilies in spring, one can look down on Crystal Creek, which drains much of Shasta Bally. To reach this cool oasis, turn left on Crystal Creek Road about one-half mile west of Clear Creek, and pull into the parking area, left, just up the road.

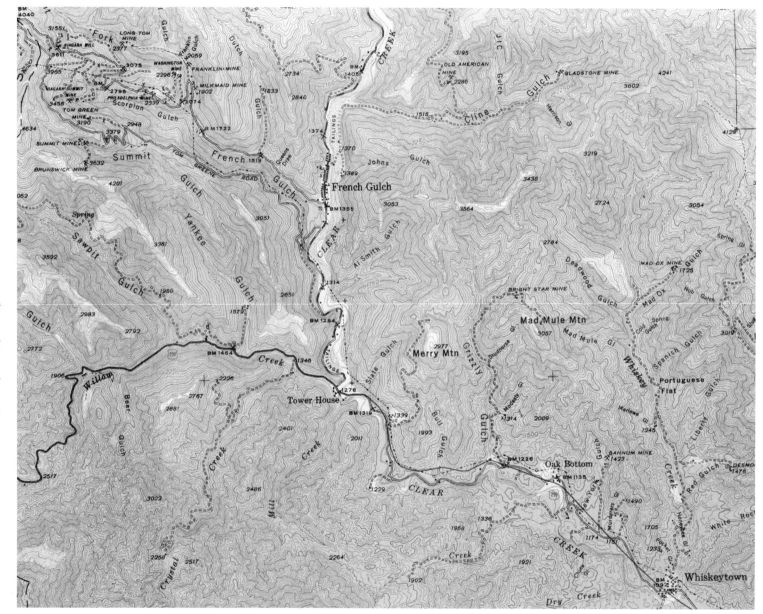

This 1944 USGS map displays many of the mines and towns that attracted fortune-seekers to the Whiskeytown-French Gulch area for almost a century before the damming of Clear Creek.

58

French Gulch:
A Still Glimmering Gold Town

Across Highway 299 from the Tower House Historic District, several signs compete for attention. Half-hidden behind the jumble is one that urges travelers to "Visit Historic French Gulch"—just three miles north on paved, two-lane Trinity Mountain Road. Unlike Old Shasta and the Tower House district, the town hasn't any museum or preserved ruins, but its long Main Street includes a few Gold Rush architectural gems that have received state or national recognition. Longevity alone should accord French Gulch *historic* status, since no other town featured in this guidebook has remained tied to mining so long.

Spawned by the Shasta-Trinity Gold Rush in 1849, a mining camp manned by French Canadians from Oregon sprang up where Dutch (for *Deutsch* or German) Gulch Creek joins French Gulch Creek. Named for the latter stream, the camp kept its name even after it was moved, five years later, to a lower, more level and lucrative site along Clear Creek. The new location was so loaded with placer deposits that creek claims were limited to ten feet per miner.

A railroad surveyor who later stopped at French Gulch while traveling from Eureka to Shasta remarked: "As many as a hundred men were engaged in digging and washing gold when we passed. The amount of gold seemed undiminishable!" Strategically situated on the western branch of the California-Oregon Stage Road, French Gulch soon became the main supplier of goods and services for mines along Clear Creek and west to the Trinity Divide. Because of the incredibly high density of gold found between the creek and the divide, two parallel roads were constructed westward to connect the town with the maze of mines evident as late as 1944 on the French Gulch Quadrangle map (*see opposite page*).

The large number of "Gulches" shown on that map reflects more than the rugged topography of the Trinity Mountains. The term *gulch* refers to any "deep, steep-sided gully," "with or without a stream" (*Dictionary of the American West*, p. 157). But since gold veins often occurred in such ravines, "*gulching*" became synonymous with mining. Certainly miners' diggings made

many a Shasta-Trinity gulch even deeper and steeper than nature had. Those who spend a night or two in French Gulch will conclude that Clear Creek occupies a gully so deep and steep as to rule out the viewing of any sunsets or sunrises.

Miners in gulches, of course, kept their eyes and noses not on the sky but glued to the ground. With keen senses of sight and smell, they had no need for geologists to spy or sniff the gold they sought. Dr. Thompson Plumb, for example, noticed the singular odor of arsenic after driving a "bull-prick" bar into some gold-bearing quartz at the site named the Highland Mine. Another early miner, Frank Wheeler, used the same method to find the vein that became the Summit Mine.

Until 1898, the French Gulch District "yielded more mineral value in a given time, than any other similar and equal area in the northern part of the State," according to the Redding *Searchlight's* Mining Edition. Many miners left the declining placers in the 1860s, but "the less aggressive" or more persevering

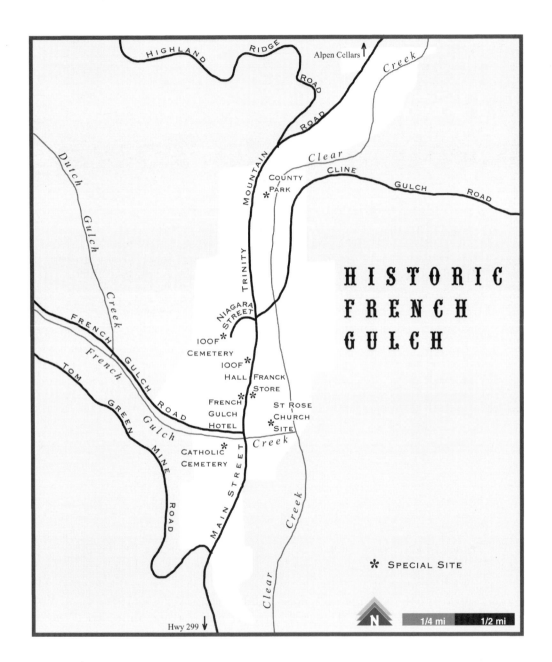

HIGHLAND RIDGE ROAD

Alpen Cellars ↑

Clear Creek

Dutch Gulch Creek

Mountain ROAD

Clear CLINE GULCH ROAD

County Park *

TRINITY

NIAGARA STREET

HISTORIC FRENCH GULCH

IOOF *
CEMETERY
IOOF *
HALL FRANCK STORE

FRENCH GULCH ROAD

FRENCH GULCH HOTEL *

ST ROSE CHURCH SITE *

CATHOLIC CEMETERY *

FRENCH GULCH MINE ROAD

TOM GREEN

Creek

MAIN STREET

Clear Creek

* SPECIAL SITE

N   1/4 mi   1/2 mi

Hwy 299 ↓

Chinese took over. By 1870 they comprised nearly half of the district's population. The discovery of new fields along the upper Trinity and the development of improved techniques to rework old sources kept the town thriving. Only after the railroad connected Oregon and California in 1887 did the western side of the Portland-Sacramento Stage Road finally lose out to the eastern (Redding-Yreka) line. French Gulch declined but never quite died despite the rise of Redding.

The area now numbers nearly 500 residents and stretches out for about a mile along Main Street. In 1990, the census-taker counted twice as many people living outside of town as inside, most of them scattered along Clear Creek or the gulches that drain into it. The first glimpse of French Gulch may startle visitors, since mobile homes sited atop tailings dredged up between the world wars hardly fit the standard image of a mining town. The tailings and trailers have erased any sign of French Gulch's long abandoned Chinatown (and Madame Klondike's brothel). But once the road crosses the narrow bridge over French Gulch Creek, the scene changes from a suburban trailer park to a semi-rural setting. Irrigation ditches line both sides of Main Street to keep the grass and gardens green and the shade trees growing during the long warm summers.

St. Rose's petite Catholic Church, formerly located at the confluence of French Gulch and Clear Creeks, used to catch the eye until an arsonist torched it in 1998. Its bright white steeple rose high, as if reaching for the mountains that tower over the town. French Gulch apparently never had enough faithful Catholics among its French, German, and Irish miners to warrant a resident priest, but they erected a makeshift church anyway in 1855, only to see it decay and eventually fall. They probably would not have rebuilt it, except for the generosity of Rose Anna McDonald—co-owner of the Brown Bear Mine near Deadwood (on the western side of the Trinity Mountains). She donated both land and money for the new church, which was erected in 1898 and dedicated to her patron saint, St. Rose of Lima, Peru. Although the church was no longer used for services and seldom opened for any purpose, the local Progress Club restored it in the 1980s as a reminder of French Gulch's Catholic community. Most of the faithful moved away or simply "retired" across the road and creek to the cemetery that overlooks the town high above the south end. Protestant residents never bothered to build a chapel, content to hold church in the schoolhouse.

Saloons, which once numbered five, probably commanded a more central position than churches in French Gulch. The two that have survived face each other across the lower part of Main Street, where one can watch or join the small but fairly steady stream of patrons who move back and forth on weekends (Thursday-Saturday) between the big French Gulch Hotel and the little E. Franck Bar. The size of the fines levied by the bartenders against anyone

French Gulch as it was on August 14, 1909, looking north from the Catholic cemetery. St. Rose Church, lower right, and the school, upper center, are prominent buildings. (SSHP photo)

caught cursing matches the relative size of the two friendly rivals—two bits for Franck's spittoon, five bucks for the inn.

The hotel in its present form dates back to the late 1880s, when an Irishman named Feeney enlarged the building to house travelers and stockmen driving their herds of sheep and cattle from winter pastures in the Central Valley to summer pastures in the Trinity Mountains and Alps. The Feeney Hotel had to compete with Harrison Fox's older Empire Hotel as a boarding house, but both benefited from Shasta County's copper mining boom at misnamed Iron Mountain from 1896–1919. The smelt-

ers there bought French Gulch quartz for just two dollars a ton to serve as a flux in the second phase of copper smelting. They credited the mine owners with the value of any gold gleaned from the operation and, in effect, created yet another boom in the region.

When the Empire Hotel faced bankruptcy during the Great Depression, Feeney's youngest daughter, Arleta F. Woll, bought it from a bank. After moving the Empire's big bar—shipped from England via Cape Horn—to her hotel, she had her ex-rival's inn razed. The huge mirror above the bar did not crack during the move but at a later time, when the owner's twelve-year-old son supposedly threw a sack of coins at her (and missed!) because he could not get her to stop drinking and take him home. Another version of the story, from an alleged eyewitness, claims the son (in his 20s) simply got mad at his mom one afternoon and threw a whiskey glass at the mirror before leaving the bar.

The Feeney Hotel has gone through so many owners and changes since the 1940s—including the new but old name—that little of its original decor, apart from the old bar, cracked mirror, and tongue-and-groove interior wall surfacing, remains. But that is more than enough to justify its place on the National Historic Register. Recent owners have converted it into a bed and breakfast inn and, in the process, reduced the original 36 boarding rooms to 8 (plus quarters for the innkeepers) and named them Miss Lillie, Captain Jack, etc. The hotel is open nightly most of the year (March-December) and offers dinner Thursday-Saturday and on Sunday, brunch. Their salads never include miner's lettuce, but for a group of hungry HSU students who had just toured the Washington Mine and Stamp Mill in 1994, they served steaming bowls of miner's stew. (*See current chef Andrew Bouchard's version of the recipe, sidebar below.*)

Outwardly, the French Gulch Hotel overshadows the bar across the street, partly because the latter long functioned as just one section of E. Franck & Co.'s Store of "Miners' Supplies and General Merchandise." Established in 1854 and rebuilt of native stone after an 1867 fire, the store has been run by the founding Franck families (German, *not* French) ever since. Bernice Englebright moved into French Gulch with her mobile family as a teenager in 1928, but she married a grandson of Harrison Fox (whose mother was a Franck) and stayed, never to move again. Soon after her husband's death (1979), this "Foxy" grandma raised many an eyebrow, she frankly admitted, by closing the Franck store but keeping the bar open three nights a week.

Anyone who frequents the bar should focus their attention, at least briefly, not on the dollar bills pinned to the ceiling, but on the Franck/Fox heirlooms and historic photos that compete with cover girls for space on the walls. The bar offers much more than a cold beer and a good game of pool, namely, the nearest semblance of a French Gulch museum. If not busy

French Gulch Miner's Stew

(Courtesy of Certified Chef Andrew Bouchard, French Gulch Hotel)

2 pounds lean beef, cubed into 1-inch pieces
1 gallon beef stock
1 15-ounce can tomato sauce
8 large carrots peeled and cut into large pieces
3 medium onions, diced large
1 whole celery (8 or more stalks, including the yellow tender leaves)
1 pound tan roux (equal parts clear melted butter and regular white flour, blended well to a very thick peanut butter texture and then cooked in oven at 350° for 30-45 minutes)
¼ cup Worcestershire sauce
3 Tbs Kitchen Bouquet

2 tbs ground white pepper
2 Tbs salt

In a large, heavy stock pot (16 quarts or bigger), heat one cup of canola oil until hot, add lightly floured beef cubes, and brown well in pot on high heat, stirring often. Discard oil, return beef to pot, heat to high temperature, add 1-2 cups of beef stock, and deglaze the meaty brown pieces stuck to the pot by stirring constantly. Add onions, carrots, celery, salt, pepper, Kitchen Bouquet, Worcestshire sauce, tomato sauce, and remainder of beef stock. Heat to almost boiling and begin adding the roux, blending well with a big, heavy whisk. (*Note: the roux thickens slowly, so do not add too much at a time; if it turns too thick, thin with water.*) Whip the stew well to eliminate any lumps of roux. Simmer for 90 minutes, slowly stirring the bottom of the pot with a long spoon and continuing to whip. Cook until meat is tender. Serve with warm cornbread or biscuits.

Serves: 20 normal eaters or 10 empty miners.

A quintet of quaffers line up at Clint Watson's Bar while it was still in the Empire Hotel. Later the Feeney family moved it to their new hotel up the street. (SSHP photo)

pinning dollar bills to the ceiling, Bernice's son-in-law bartender can tell visitors about the Franck brothers, who moved from Mannheim, Germany, to Missouri in 1846 and from there to Whiskeytown and French Gulch in the early 1850s. They, like many other immigrants, found merchandising preferable to mining, but often after first finding gold.

After leaving the bar, take a look at the oldest house in town, just north of the old store, where Fredrick Anton Franck and his wife raised their twelve children. If it's not dark, visit some of the Francks themselves—buried in the town's main cemetery, half-hidden on the hill off of Niagara Street (west of Main Street). On the way to the cemetery, pause for a glance at a gleaming white building whose height and rectangular proportions make it seem oversized in this town. It belongs to Lodge No. 75 of the Independent Order of Odd Fellows (IOOF), chartered in 1858. The local chapters (including a Rebekah Lodge) of this benevolent and fraternal society still meet in their second-floor chambers, but their numbers and influence have dwindled in the past century. The ground floor serves as a meeting place for a variety of town socials. The building dates from 1913, when its members donated $7500 to replace a structure just one-third the size of the hall constructed in 1886–87 for $1500.

Just beyond the IOOF Hall, on the same side of the street, is the busiest place in town. Since the closing of the French Gulch General Store, the Post Office serves more than ever as the town's main gossip center. Here one can listen in on local conversations and mail postcards before heading to the north end of town and the French Gulch County Park. Framed by thickets of blackberry bushes, the park occupies a long acre next to Clear Creek. Although it belongs to the county, the town has paid someone to maintain it for as long as anyone can remember. For locals, it provides a favorite place for picnicking, fishing, or swimming. Those wading into the cool, clear waters of the river-sized creek should keep their eyes open for flashes of sparkling gold. If none appear, then watch the tailings beside the stream. The sun still tints them, reminders of the many miners (and dredging machines) that literally left no stone unturned in the never-ending search for wealth. Their success has kept "the Gulch" alive much longer than most mining towns of Northern California, and the historic place they have created will clearly outlive the last mine, which closed in 1997.

That judgment seems valid in view of the town's belief that progress should include preservation. A 1993 Bureau of Land Management-National Park Service plan to establish an Off-Highway Vehicle staging area one mile south of French Gulch provoked strong opposition from a "community [that] cherishes the...historical nature of their tranquil hamlet, and recognizes its responsibility to preserve it for its heirs." Instead of endorsing the plan, they recommended that the government consider restoring the Coggins Mill that occupied the proposed staging area from 1946 until the 1960s. A more likely compromise is the planned construction of a long trail north from French Gulch to picturesque Castle Crags State Park.

Upon concluding their stay in French Gulch, visitors may wish to depart by any of three routes:

1. A return southward along Trinity Mountain Road (which is called "Main Street" in town) leads back to Highway 299, whence the standard Trinity tour can be continued.

2. By heading west on French Gulch Road from the middle of town, excursionists will encounter long-defunct Deadwood and still-living Lewiston. About four miles from French Gulch the gravel road passes the historic Wash-

French-born Henry Feutrier, the suave and savvy late manager of the Washington Mine. He died inside the mine in 1994. (Mark Rounds photo)

ington Mine and Stamp Mill. (**Warning:** *this rugged, winding route over the Trinity Mountains can present driving difficulties. Check locally for current road conditions.*)

3. A northern departure follows Main Street through town, whereupon its name reverts to Trinity Mountain Road. Circuitous, partly gravelled and partly paved, the route passes through much scenic, mountainous terrain before meeting Highway 3 north of Trinity Lake. From there, excursionists can proceed southwestward on Highway 3 to its junction with Highway 299 in Weaverville and then resume their Trinity trip. Two features besides the lake make this byway a tempting choice. Alpen Cellars, located ten miles east of Highway 3 on the East Fork of the Trinity, welcomes anyone interested in seeing how a small family winery can succeed in such a remote mountain setting. Keith Groves, who received his degree in enology at Fresno State in 1984, wondered if grapes would grow in a high (2,600 feet) mountain valley. He discovered that the East Fork's microclimate would indeed nurture "early maturing vinifera grapes such as White Riesling, Gewurztraminer, Chardonnay and Pinot Noir" and then recruited his retired parents to assist in the operation. The Groves' wines have won an astounding number of prizes. If, after tasting any of the Alpen Cellars varieties, you prudently decide against driving any long distance on the same day, merely continue to the junction with Highway 3, where you can check out (and check into) the historic Carrville Inn (rebuilt

in 1918 after fire destroyed the original hotel). For half a century the hamlet here functioned as a major stop on the California-Oregon Stage Road. (***Warning:*** *the trip from French Gulch to Highway 3 is lengthy, challenging, and hard on passenger cars; check locally for current conditions. A quicker and easier approach to the route's highliglights is to take Highway 3 from Weaverville to Carrville, there turn east on Eastside Road, and continue on to Alpen Cellars.*)

A hearty serving of Miner's Stew should fortify anyone about to buck (or buckle) up for the twisting climb from Tower House to Buckhorn Summit—the highest of four summits crossed by the Trinity Highway. This 11-mile stretch, notably the upper half, may remind skiers and drivers of a slalom course, but imagine what it was like long ago—even when sitting in "the two best places on a huge cart, with benches for seats, called a 'stage.'" In late March of 1893, Baron and Madame de La Grange, two French aristocrats, had traveled in such a stage for several hours from Redding before stopping "at a primitive but exquisitely clean little hotel in French Gulch for a scrumptious meal." Three days and 30 miles later the baroness expressed great relief upon reaching Weaverville, after being "jolted, thrown from one side to the other, when we weren't hanging on for dear life to the frame of this salad shaker." She did not describe the route taken by her cart nor the other stops made, but they may have spent one night at the no longer extant Buckhorn Station, four miles past the summit. The *Trinity Journal* (May 31, 1862) described it as "the half-way house between Weaverville and Tower's." (In keeping with the mountain's name, the hotel had antlers hanging on every wall.)

The La Granges, of course, made the jolting journey 35 years after William Lowden first constructed the spiraling 24°-mile road from Tower House to Weaverville, at a cost of about $30,000. Shasta-Trinity residents complained as much about the condition of their roads as the affluent French couple accustomed to finer modes of travel. Coaches did not even attempt to cross over Buckhorn Mountain (renamed Hoadley Peaks) in the winter. So newspapers always noted the start of a new travel year. "For the first time this season, the [Weaverville and Shasta] stage rolled in on Monday [April 26, 1866]. It is an institution which travelers can appreciate, and is a welcome change from the winter mode of travel in the mountains."

Because Lowden's wagon road crossed so many bridges, which often washed out along Grass Valley Creek west of the Shasta-Trinity line, Lowden himself, J. F. Hoadley, and others sponsored the building of a more direct road via Lewiston and Rush Creek. Completed in 1866, it became known as the Lewiston Turnpike. The following year the *Shasta Courier* reported that "All the Trinity travel now passes over the Lewiston road, the grade on the old route, in many places, being entirely destroyed." The new route proved challenging enough, judging by a later (1881) report carried by a Redding paper. "Up the steeps and around the curves the stage progresses until the top of the mountain is reached and a change of horses made, then down, down, down to Lewiston." A few miles farther the coach crossed the Trinity at Lowden's bridge and ranch, changed horses again, then rode "over Brown[s] mountain backward and forward to Weaverville." After completing the ride, the writer drew the right conclusion: "Trinity county seems to be composed altogether of mountains with here and there a basin."

Deciding just where to construct roads through the mountains of Trinity County always proved both problematic and political. Ironically, Highway 299 followed the more difficult route over Buckhorn while the easier Lewiston turnpike no longer carries through traffic. On many maps Lewiston looks like a little Redding, with half a dozen different roads converging upon it. Two of them parallel each other quite closely to connect the Scenic Byway directly with this tiny but picturesque gateway to the Trinity Alps. If you miss the first Lewiston turnoff, take the second.

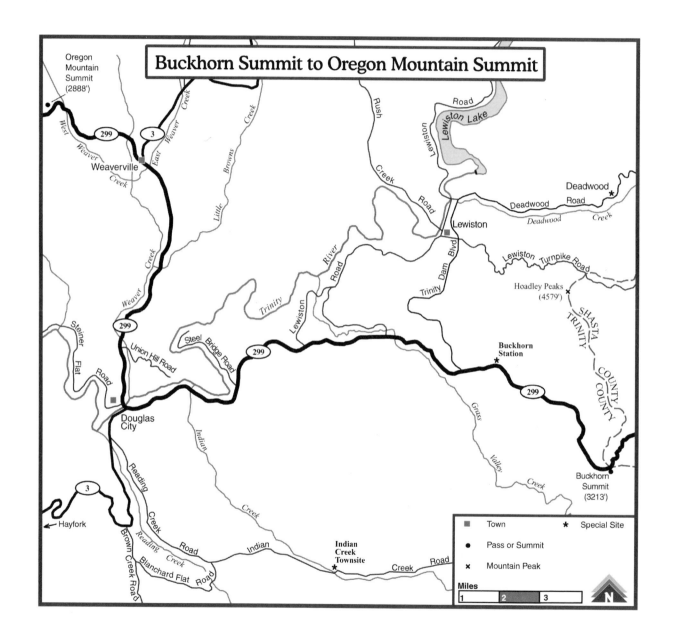

Buckhorn Summit to Oregon Mountain Summit

Oregon Mountain Summit (2888')

299

3

West Weaver Creek

East Weaver Creek

Weaverville

Browns Creek

Little Creek

Weaver Creek

299

Steiner Flat Road

Union Hill Road

Steel Bridge Road

299

Weaver Creek

Rush Creek

Creek Road

Lewiston Lake

Road

Deadwood

Deadwood Road

Deadwood Creek

Lewiston

Lewiston Turnpike Road

Trinity River

Lewiston Road

Trinity Dam Blvd

Hoadley Peaks (4579')

SHASTA TRINITY COUNTY COUNTY

Buckhorn Station

299

Douglas City

Indian Creek

Creek

Grass Valley Creek

Buckhorn Summit (3213')

3

Reading Creek Road

Hayfork

Brown Creek Road

Reading Creek

Blanchard Flat Road

Indian Creek Road

Indian Creek Townsite

Creek Road

	Town		Special Site
	Pass or Summit		
	Mountain Peak		

Miles
1   2   3

N

66

III. Basins Wedged Between Mountains

Little Lewiston: Gateway to the Trinity Lakes

When was the last time you whistled while working? One Lewiston pioneer's livelihood, indeed his very life, depended on it. On a hot summer day in 1856, G. A. Wirzen sat down under a tree to escape the heat, only to feel a rapid rise in his pulse rate. Next to him lay a rattlesnake! Reacting quickly but quietly, the cool Swede did what came naturally—he whistled. To his amazement, the coiled rattler raised its head and undulated back and forth, cobra-like, as if entranced. Wirzen kept whistling as the snake quivered and rolled over to a prone position. Only then did he dare pick it up and carry it home for further observation.

From farmer to charmer, the "Whistling Wizard" took to the road with a 15-rattlesnake entourage. They performed before packed houses in Weaverville, Shasta, and elsewhere. "The snakes have...become so docile, that they will crawl around the neck of their master, lick his lips and cheeks, and sleep like good-natured pets in his bosom." Or so claimed the *Trinity Journal*.

The Lewiston area no longer has any snake charmers. Since Wirzen's time all kinds of characters have passed through this charming place, but relatively few have found it alluring enough to stay very long. Nestled in a once fertile basin along the upper Trinity, the county's third largest town (after Weaverville and Hayfork)—with close to 1,500 residents—lies less than 15 minutes north of Highway 299 or east of Highway 3. Trinity Dam Boulevard, Old Lewiston Road, and Rush Creek Road give the eastern heart of the county easy and ample access to Lewiston (and vice-versa). Before completion of the Trinity Dam (1961), older turnpikes also converged on this centrally located crossroads.

From its founding, this way station served as both a base and a gateway for Trinity gold-seekers. Where the present old steel bridge has stood sentinel since 1900, Tom Palmer started a ferry service in 1851. He named the place Lewis Town after an orphan lad (Frank Lewis) whom he had befriended in Colorado. Palmer turned this Trinity crossing over to Lewis when he moved farther upstream to manage another ferry that he established just below the original

Trinity Center. Tom maintained his interest in young Frank's welfare, supposedly setting aside five Porter Ale bottles filled with gold dust as an inheritance for him. Alas, the dusty "pale ale" disappeared with Palmer's untimely death.

A toll bridge, operated by Olney Phillips as early as 1854, soon replaced the ferry service at Lewis Town. A series of bridges eventually gave way to the steel bridge designed and built by Olney's son "Cap" in 1900. The bridge, restored and rededicated in 1999, has maintained its position as Lewiston's leading landmark. No other Trinity County bridge has managed to survive the river's floods for a full century.

And no other town seems to have tied itself quite so tightly to the Trinity River. The one-lane bridge not only conveys traffic, it connects the roads that converge at the center of town. From the west or Rush Creek side of the span, one can best see the small section of Lewiston that has survived as a "historic district."

The narrow bridge draws the eye directly to one of the town's two key gathering places—the Paulsen Store, clad with shiplap siding.

Originally started in 1860, it changed hands several times before Jacob and Louisa Paulsen, who already operated a store and hotel on their ranch at the mouth of Rush Creek, acquired ownership at the turn of the century. Selling everything from domestics to dynamite, the business attracted everybody. Here one could tell the weather just by watching the walking but aging weather vanes. When it was warm enough outside, they sat on captains' chairs under the locust trees to chat or doze. When the temperature cooled down, they turned tail—chairs in tow—and headed for the comfort of the wood stove, where they likely heard stories about the exploits of one of the county's prominent pioneers. (*See sidebar, next page.*)

Nowadays just a few bucks will buy anyone a fine time at the annual Lewiston "Peddler's Faire" in early June. Only then does little Lewiston come close to showing as much life as it did a century or more ago during its heyday as a gold town, when miners, merchants, and stagecoaches crowded its rutted streets. Now merrymakers, artists, and artisans peddle their crafts and collectibles on paved roads.

Visitors can sit where the pioneers did in front of the Paulsen store with basically the same two options. Step inside and browse around or stay outside beneath the veranda (instead of the locust trees) and try to resist any of many tantalizing aromas: corn-on-the-cob, popcorn, Indian tacos, barbecued chicken, and steaks. Either venue provides an inviting way to begin exploring the town or the upper Trin-

ity Valley. Gain both memories and memorabilia of a bygone era while chatting with some of the locals who struggle to keep the town and its legacies alive.

Two doors north of the Paulsen store stands the old town's other main rendezvous—the

venerable hotel. It now functions as a restaurant/bar for "bait-dunkers," but it long housed many of the sourdoughs that stopped in Lewiston on the hot and dusty *or* cold and icy— but always bumpy—ride aboard the Shasta-Weaverville stagecoach. For 25 cents a meal and

Built in 1900, the steel-trussed main span of the durable Lewiston Bridge had round steel casing piers to support it. The wooden approaches and deck were replaced with steel in 1932. (C. E. Goodyear photo)

William Lowden's Fast Feats

After an inauspicious debut as a 19-year-old 49er from western Illinois, William Spencer Lowden made his start in the Lewiston area. Two years of mining at sundry Trinity-Klamath sites netted him enough money to lay out a 160-acre ranch four miles downstream from the town at the mouth of Grass Valley Creek. When his parents and siblings joined him, they expanded the size of the Lowden farm fourfold.

Best known as a road-builder and surveyor, young Will gained his initial fame as an express rider. In the summer of 1854, the *Shasta Courier* pointed out that "The expressmen have recently been enjoying some very good sport, on Fridays, in riding down the road to meet the stage [at Bell's Clear Creek Bridge], and then, with the latest pacers, racing back to our office." On September 9, the paper noted that Mr. Brastow, of Adams & Co.'s Express, made the trip from Red Bluff to Shasta (40 miles) in 2 hrs. and 40 min., using five horses. William Lowden, riding eight different animals for Cram, Rogers & Co.'s Express, rode from Shasta to Weaverville "in the unprecedented time of 2 hrs. and 47 min.: [the same] distance over a very hard mountain road."

Just before Christmas that year, Lowden & Co. completed an 800-foot bridge across the Trinity at the family's Grass Valley ranch, perhaps in part to improve his record-breaking times. Right after New Year's, 1855, he rode "the greatest race of my life." The *Courier's* account of his times and distances is a bit confusing, but apparently he delivered a file of state papers—including a special message from President Franklin Pierce—all the way from San Francisco. He covered the 60 miles from Tehama to Shasta in 3 hrs. and 37 min. Then he pushed on to Weaverville, "having made the entire distance of 100 miles [from Tehama], during a severe storm, and breaking the trail through two feet of snow over Trinity Mountain, in the unprecedented time of 9 hrs. and 47 min....If any Expressmen, in any other portion of the State, have beat this time, we would like to know it." His January time was clearly slower than his September clocking, but the newspaper must have figured that road and weather conditions made the winter trip "unprecedented."

In the long run, Lowden's fast rides proved less important than his graded wagon roads in putting

Lewiston's First Congregational Church, built in 1895 for a mere $750. (Robin Stocum photo)

Lewiston on most Shasta-Trinity travelers' maps. Moreover, while the races gained him fame, the roads earned him far more income.

The Lowdens built both a hotel and a toll bridge at their ranch. The tolls alone netted as much as $400 per month. For awhile William also owned a pack train of 60 mules, which could gross him $2,400 for a three-day trip from Colusa, on the Sacramento River, to Weaverville.

25 cents a bed, prospectors gathered at such oases to wet their collective whistles and whet each other's appetite for gold.

The old "downtown" area, including the schoolhouse and church that rise above it on Old Lewiston Road, has taken on a more antiquated appearance since the construction of the dams on the Trinity. The resultant building and recreation boom revived the area by creating a new and larger town on the ridge above old Lewiston. The two sections seem like two different worlds in spite of their proximity and physical interaction, if only because they represent two contrasting centuries.

Due to its smaller size, Lewiston has long had difficulty competing with more distant Weaverville as a gateway to Trinity and Lewiston lakes and the eastern end of the Trinity Alps. Highway 3, a less busy scenic byway than 299, passes just 10 miles northwest of Lewiston via Rush Creek Road. When full, Trinity Lake boasts 145 miles of shoreline; just downstream, Lewiston Lake channels and diverts much of the Trinity's water to the Central Valley via Whiskeytown Lake. Below the Lewiston Dam one can fly fish the river as far down as the town or else watch the fish in the hatchery that was built to offset the loss of spawning habitat above the dam.

Several old towns along the upper Trinity met their watery waterloo with the construction of the reservoirs. Trinity Center survived only because its citizens insisted on moving as much of the town as they could to higher ground. That task must have seemed easier than the earlier challenge of dredging up the riverbed to unearth gold. Vestiges of that mining era linger all along the upper river, but one can also sense signs of regeneration, especially after comparing present scenes with old photographs taken from the same vantage points.

Highway 3 and the Trinity Lakes offer two different kinds of recreational worlds. The jagged peaks, only one of which (just barely) juts above the 9,000-foot mark, beckon backpackers while the lakeshores invite the water

Lewiston's Country Store, complete with gravity flow gasoline pump and ice-cooled Coca-Cola® case, was long operated by the Jacob Paulsen family. (Mark Rounds photo)

The Trinity Dredge Company operated on the river several miles above Lewiston from 1912 to 1940. (TCHS photo)

and sun worshipers. Some visitors may want to experience both worlds; little Lewiston serves as a congenial gateway for either kind of getaway, with overnight accommodations available in both uptown and downtown.

Backcountry Byway: Indian Creek

Hidden among the hills southeast of Douglas City, an all-but-forgotten region of historic mines and ranches reposes in near total neglect, known only to its few residents and a handful of Trinity locals with long memories. Yet many modern-day riches remain here for the plant lover or history buff, all situated on secluded side roads just minutes from the bustle of Highway 299. The trip makes an ideal half-day jaunt from Weaverville or a relaxing diversion for tourists willing to briefly depart the highway.

Westbound motorists receive a prelude to the excursion when they cross the Indian Creek Bridge at milepost 59.71 of Highway 299. A row of sycamores at the Indian Creek Lodge, right, stands sentinel at the approach to the bridge. To the left, a trailer park marks the creek's debouchure as it leaves the southern hills. Situated several miles upstream was a once-bustling but now long-vanished mining camp; here, along the highwayside, a scattering of homes and businesses comprises the contemporary Indian Creek community.

The side trip begins a mile and a half west of the creek crossing at the junction of Highway 3 and Highway 299, just east of Douglas City and the adjacent Trinity River bridge. Turning left onto Highway 3, our way follows the river briefly before bending left into a side canyon. At 0.9 mile the route turns left onto Reading's Creek Road (one lane, paved), just past the turnoff for Marshall Ranch Road. We proceed gradually up the hillside through a forest of pines, oaks, firs, and madrones; Reading's Creek lies far downslope to the right. Splashes of springtime color come at mile 3.4, where red delphinium and narrow-leaved mule ears decorate the roadbanks, and at mile 4.8, where miniature lupine and buckbrush make an appearance.

Just ahead, mile 4.9, the trip turns left onto Indian Creek Road (one lane, at first paved and then gravel). On the hill above the junction is the picturesque, white frame house of the Clement Ranch; the structure dates back to at least the 1860s. The ranch was established in 1855 by New Hampshirite William Clement, who ran cattle, raised hay, and grew produce for the nearby miners; the property remained in the family until 1941. Just east of the junction Indian Creek Road runs past a Clement barn built in 1901.

Our route cuts through the ranch's rangeland amid a scattering of Oregon white oak; at mile 5.2 the roadbed turns to gravel. After a long climb up the hillslope, the road reaches the ridgetop, 6.5 miles, and begins its descent into the valley of Indian Creek. The way soon levels, passing grassy flats speckled with hundred-year-old ponderosa pines; the trees' small size belies their substantial age—they must struggle for sustenance in the scant soil left by mining operations. One such, the Fields Mine, was on the knoll to the right, mile 7.3. Although the mine had closed years earlier, an office building, cookhouse-dining hall, and a large, looming bunkhouse still stood atop the knoll into the 1930s. Water for the Fields's hydraulic nozzles came from a pair of ditches that ran some three miles up the forks of Indian Creek.

At mile 8.1 a sturdy modern bridge spans the creek; the route then climbs slightly and soon makes a wide right turn. To the left is the Indian Creek townsite, still shaded by several black locust trees that have long outlasted the community.

Indian Creek first appeared in the news during the 1851 election, when its populace cast a 36-vote majority for J. W. Denver—enough of a margin to assure him a seat in the state senate. The town's tally was a remarkable achievement, inasmuch as the entire precinct contained no more than three or four voters at the time.

Despite the enthusiasm of the local electors, it took the area a time to develop, but by June 1857, the *Trinity Journal* could report that "miners from every part of the county are flocking in," and that an express service now connected Indian Creek with Weaverville. Over the summer the town "improved wonderfully," so that it came to contain "1 hotel, a market, blacksmith shop, saloon and several dwelling houses." Within two years the bustling burg had added two large stores, another hotel, and a pair of butchers. Among the many miners were a considerable number of Chinese, a situation that did not sit well with one local, who announced, "I don't like to see American and Chinese labor placed on a par. These long-tailed fellows hold many good claims here, and I have no conscientious scruples in driving them off." Such sentiments apparently had little effect, for 20 years later, some 79 Chinese were still listed as living in the area.

Mining continued to maintain the community in the 1860s and 1870s, as town life was enlivened by the balls given at Morris's Indian Creek Hotel. Tickets cost $5.00 for the June 1865 event, which found "about 20 ladies…in attendance, and three times that number of gentlemen," who all "danced to the soul thrilling music of the Douglas City violinist, Jones."

No records remain to account for the community's name; the only mention of Native Americans in the area occurred in 1866, when John McKiernan was reported killed by Indians. Shortly thereafter, "17 well armed and provisioned men left on the avenging errand." The pursuers proceeded into Shasta County, where they murdered "several tame Indians and a Negro" before belatedly determining that McKiernan's attackers had already escaped across the Sacramento River.

By the 1870s it was conceded that the local mines, while "among the richest in the county," were also "about the hardest to work." Areas along the creek bars were often "exceedingly rocky" and situated below the level of the creek, while the gravel beds above the stream were too high to be reached by the water ditches. Quartz mining thus replaced much of the hydraulic activity, with one of the noteworthy newcomers being the Bullychoop Mine high on the upper canyon's hillside.

A summary of the area appeared in the *Journal* in June 1874. It tersely but informatively reported that:

> There are about 100 men, including Chinese, mining in that section and all are doing well. Karsky and company own the trading post and keep it well stocked with all the necessities. Billy Waldorff is in charge. J. B. Siegfried runs the blacksmith shop and Jack Pearson spouts Shakespeare.

Although, as the preceding account indicates, Indian Creek was a nearly complete community, for years it lacked a post office. Finally, in January 1883, this void was filled; unfortunately, the name provided by the postal service was an unintelligible contraction: "Indeek." The resultant indignity was, however, brief. Before the year was out the Postmaster General ordered the Indeek office discontinued and had the community's mail sent henceforth to Douglas City.

The closure signaled a downturn in the town's fortunes. In July 1885, the *Journal* announced that "a ride to this old mining camp on Wednesday last was not productive of anything in the way of interesting local items. A number of old settlers were seen, all of whom complained of dull times.…"

While mining declined, several small-scale ranches endured, run for the most part by four Portuguese families that had made the creek canyon their home. The clans' names—Williams, Rodgers, Joseph, and Frates—are Anglicized versions of the originals, although Freitas Gulch retains that family's original spelling.

By the 1920s the town buildings at Indian Creek sat deserted, and locals in search of companionship gathered at the William Morris House, just across the road. Some of the more isolated residents would trek as much as four miles to sit on Morris's porch, where they would chat while waiting for a chance to take potshots at squirrels on the nearby hillside. (*Note: Bureau of Land Management fence markers indicate both the Indian Creek townsite and the location of the Morris House; much of the remaining property in the canyon is private, and visitors should seek permission before entering any of it.*)

East of the townsite, Indian Creek Road climbs to a low benchland, whence vegetation often obscures views of the streambed. In earlier days, when ranchers still burned their rangeland in the fall, the canyon was much more open. At mile 8.9 the route curves around what was formerly the Manuel Williams House. The hundred-year-old-plus structure originally stood a half mile to the east but was moved to its present location in the 1930s when the family lost their lease on the original house site. Opposite the John Williams Ranch, mile 9.0, left, a large collection of hydraulic mine tailings lies close to the creek. In this vicinity was the home of "Injun-Chinaman," a contrivance of rock walls made from the tailings and covered by a sheet of tin. The local youngsters would amuse themselves by lobbing rocks onto the resounding roof, which invariably brought forth Injun-Chinaman, Chinese sword in hand, Chinese curses pouring from his lips. Despite such depredations, all of Indian Creek's children would awaken each Christmas to find themselves the recipients of small presents, wrapped in red paper for good luck, from the long tormented but always forgiving Injun-Chinaman.

A series of modern dwellings dot the surroundings as the road gradually climbs up the canyon. The tiny Indian Creek cemetery lies just above the road, mile 9.3, right. The Powerhouse/Dan Dedrick House, 10.3 miles, right, marks a junction with the Joseph Gulch Road, left. In the early 1900s a generator was situated in the creek below the house, providing several residences with a weak electric current. The voltage did little more than run a few lights, but in days when many larger communities had no electricity whatsoever, the minuscule effect was magnified by its uniqueness. The building later belonged to miner Dan Dedrick, who had earlier given his name to a small town in Canyon Creek.

The family who gave *its* name to adjacent Joseph Gulch claimed 14 children, all of whom eventually moved away except a solitary son, Frank, who stayed on the ranch until his death. His legacy included three Model T Fords, each of which he deposited in the barn when it stopped running.

Both the Indian Creek Road and the canyon constrict east of the junction; at mile 10.4 a sign accurately proclaims "ROAD NOT MAINTAINED." A conveniently placed turnaround allows motorists to reverse course and retrace their route down through the valley. Those who pause to savor the surrounding scenery will find, in springtime, both redbud and scarlet fritillary blooming beneath a canopy of Oregon white oak and canyon live oak.

(*Note: Intrepid excursionists may continue eastward up the canyon, maneuvering around numerous rocks before reaching Cannonball Flat in another mile and a half. From there a steadily deteriorating road climbs the mountainside, passing the Bullychoop Mine before reaching the ridgetop.*)

Departing the turnaround, the side trip returns down the canyon, reaching Reading's Creek Road at mile 15.9; a left turn takes the route past more of the Clement Ranch to another junction, mile 16.3. The way left leads through the old Wallace Ranch, while our side trip turns right onto Blanchard Flat Road, one lane, paved. After crossing Reading's Creek, the route passes the site of the Blanchard Flat School, 16.7 miles, left; this worthy log structure survives, on display, in the town park at Hayfork. Near the school site are the Blanchard Flat fossil beds, where, in the 1960s, numerous mollusks, cuttle fish, clam shells, and turtle eggs were found in the shale and mudstone formation that runs from here southeastward to Bullychoop Mountain.

Soon Blanchard Flat Road runs out onto a wide, oak-fringed grassland. On the hillside at mile 17.6, left, is a colorful springtime flower congregation that includes western houndstongue, Henderson's shooting star, cream cups, blue dicks, woodland star, Douglas's violet, and dwarf hyperiochiron. Few prairieside plant displays are so accessible or extensive.

Ahead at 17.8 miles is a junction with Brown's Creek Road, two lanes, paved. In the

Union Hill Mine manager C. E. Goodyear took this "self-portrait" in his office about 1909, leaving viewers puzzled as to how he adequately lighted the dim interior for the picture. (C. E. Goodyear photo)

valley to the west lies the Bigelow Ranch, established in 1889 by William Ralph Bigelow, who later became Trinity County Sheriff. A right turn onto Brown's Creek Road soon takes the side trip off the flat and onto the hillside, far above the creek, to a junction with Highway 3, mile 19.4. Another right turn returns us to Highway 299 at mile 22.5 of the side trip.

Diminished Douglas City

Most modern-day 299 travelers pass the hamlet of Douglas City in an eyeblink, giving greater attention to their crossing of the nearby Trinity or, just to the east, the junction with Highway 3 that leads to Hayfork. Were they aware of the area's history, however, they would likely pause at the canyon-bound community, for it occupies an area that in the 1850s and 1860s was a hotbed of mining activity, and, even earlier, was the site of the first Trinity gold strike.

The latter event occurred in July 1848, about a half-mile downriver from where the town is located today. Major Pierson B. Reading, who had recently investigated the gold discovery at Sutter's mill and then made his own finds in the upper Sacramento River Valley on Clear Creek and Cottonwood Creek, came over the Trinity Divide, found a stream, and followed it down to the Trinity. Near the confluence he began prospecting a promising gravel bar. Once again he struck paydirt. Reading returned briefly to his sprawling Rancho Buenaventura (which encompassed present-day Redding), and then returned to his latest mining site with a full expedition—three whites; one member each of the Delaware, Chinook, and Walla Walla tribes; and some 60 Indians from the Sacra-

mento Valley. The party worked for six weeks, their only implements "pan and rocker," and reputedly extracted about $80,000 in gold from the gravel. Then a group of Oregonians arrived; they objected to Reading's choice of (non-white) laborers, drove the workers and their leader off, and promptly took over the operation for themselves. Apparently mistaking the just-departed Indian miners for Hawaiians, the new claimants used a derogatory term for Pacific islanders when they named the alluvial deposit just upriver Kanaka Bar. Although Reading left the area, *his* name remained, attaching itself to both the creek that guided him down to the Trinity and the gold-discovery gravel bar.

So it was that barely half a year after the Mother Lode excitement, the Trinity region had it own "strike." Gold-seekers soon flowed into much of the drainage, rising to a near flood along the section of river near where the original find occurred. It was estimated that "[a]t the height of the gold rush 1,900 miners camped along the three miles of river front west of Douglas City" (the stretch from Kanaka Bar down to Steiner's Flat). Had they all stood at the riverbank simultaneously, a miner would

have appeared, monument-like, every 8½ feet. Feeding the throng were some 13 butcher shops and, in the 1860s, orchardist Henry Lorenz of nearby Steiner's Flat, who once sold $50 worth of home-grown cherries to the fruit-less gold-seekers in a mere half hour.

To allow for sluicing of gravel located above the riverbottom, seven "wheels" were constructed to transport water to the higher reaches of the bars. One such, belonging to Thomas and Company, was 51 feet in diameter. It had 40 paddles, along with 80 buckets that each held 15 gallons of water, and it could be raised up to 22 feet to accommodate the fluctuating height of the river. The great flood of 1861-62 washed out the wheels; few were ever replaced. A ditch system gradually developed in their stead, which, by the 1870s, allowed for hydraulic monitors to supersede the earlier hand mining.

Another contingent of gold diggers congregated just north of Kanaka Bar, occupying Weaver Creek from its nearby confluence with the Trinity all the way upstream to Weaverville. In 1854 some 2,500 to 3,000 Chinese inhabited this area. Judge James Bartlett, a local historian, claimed that "[a]bout the mouth of Weaver Creek were some of the richest placer

Stephen A. Thayer (left), his family, and three friends (rear right) in front of Thayer's store/hotel in Douglas City. (TCHS photo)

saloons (the precise number apparently depending on the sobriety of whoever did the counting), the usual other businesses, and a 40-piece brass band that was "considered the best in the state north of San Francisco." A hotel, built in 1859 by "Old Mother" Hood, was taken over in 1887 by bewhiskered S. I. Thayer, who operated it for 36 years. Thayer had an even longer tenure at the Mason & Thayer store, which he either co-owned or owned outright for 47 years. Only when in his late eighties did he finally retire from both businesses and move to Weaverville, where he died at age 97. An explanation for his appearance, if not his longevity, was provided by "Ripley's Believe It or Not," which proclaimed that Thayer "never owned a razor or a toothbrush in his life."

The summer of 1863 saw Douglas City reacting to a renewal of the white-Indian conflict, which plunged the region into panic. The response, as chronicled by John Carr, proved less than reassuring. (*See sidebar, next page.*)

Late 19th-century Douglas City consisted of the Mason and Thayer store, Thayer's hotel and stage stop, a billiard saloon, barbershop, warehouse, post office, and sundry other businesses, including its own newspaper. Two of the town's leading establishments, the store and hotel, survived the early decades of the new century as the pace of business gradually slowed. Then, in the spring of 1931, an errant spark from the hotel's stove landed on the roof, setting its tinder-dry shingles alight. Sped along by a "brisk wind," the flames soon spread to the store and

grounds ever found in Trinity County."

When Stephen A. Douglas and Abraham Lincoln waged their epic battle for the U. S. Senate in 1858, the residents of Kanaka Bar held a mock election, pledging to rename their town for the winner. As in Illinois, Douglas prevailed (in Kanaka Bar's case by a single vote), and the populace, in a burst of post-electoral enthusi-

asm, proceeded to not only rename but relocate. The community of Douglas City soon rose on the benchland about a quarter-mile east of the lower-lying Kanaka site, the transition doubtless helped along by the winter rages of the Trinity that swept across the riverside bar.

During the early 1860s the newly named "city" claimed three general stores, three to five

some adjacent cottages. By the time the Weaverville fire brigade arrived, "[a]ll that could be done was to remove furniture and household belongings from the doomed buildings."

Douglas City, already so small as to render its name inaccurate, had now shrunk almost to the point of nothingness. Gradually, however, a few new buildings grew from the ample ashes.

The state highway maintenance station, built in 1926 east of the town, added a bit of activity for a few decades until the facility was closed in 1960. Left behind was the 35-foot-tall water tower that housed a 5,000-gallon redwood tank. The tower, now used by the Douglas City Volunteer Fire Department, has become the locale's landmark. Standing sentinel above the diminished, diminutive city, it serves as a symbol of the town's early reliance on water, without which the sluicing and hydraulicking that were the region's mining mainstays could not have occurred. But, as Highway 299 motorists are reminded as they cross the Trinity just east of town, that's now "all water under the bridge." (*See sidebar, next page.*)

When the "Douglas City Rifles" Misfired

In the summer of '63, Douglas City, like nearby Weaverville, formed a militia company to protect its populace from the perceived threat of Indian attack. Commanding the "Rifles" was Captain John Hough, whose services, however, subsequently seemed little needed.

Word soon arrived that Indians were about to burn the Clement (Clemmins' in Carr's account) Ranch, which lay some four miles up the Reading's Creek drainage. The county sheriff, John P. Jones, who had sole authority to call out the troops, was promptly summoned from Weaverville. He arrived near sunset in a two-seated carriage drawn by a pair of white horses, duly accompanied by District Attorney Egbert Allen and David E. Gordon, editor of the *Trinity Journal*. The party promptly set out; in the ensuing darkness Jones found it necessary to light the side-lamps on his buggy, a procedure that some of the soldiers felt substantially reduced their chances for a surprise attack.

At about 11:00 P.M. the troop reached the Clement Ranch, where there were no Indians about, only more darkness. A fusillade of knocking finally succeeded in rousing rancher Clement, who irritably informed his gun-toting guests that for a considerable period of time he had noticed no Indians in the neighborhood. Accordingly, the soldiers bedded down in Clement's corral, having first prepared for their slumbers by nearly draining a demijohn of Weaverville merchant Henry Hocker's best whiskey. Soon the camp grew quiet, only to have its peacefulness pierced by a call for the Sergeant of the Guard. Upon appearing at the source of the sound, that officer (Carr himself) found Sheriff Jones, Editor Gordon, and District Attorney Allen lying alongside each other in the middle of the corral. Carr inquired as to the reason for his summons, to which Sheriff Jones replied, "Sergeant, we want you to furnish us a pillow each. This corral has no soft side to it." To this Carr responded, "All right gentlemen, I suppose you are not particular about what the pillows are made of?" Receiving a "no" for an answer, Carr went off and searched the ranch yard, returning after a time with three large, well-dried "buffalo chips." He then placed one chip under the head of each member of the trio, apologizing that "It is the best I can do for you, gentlemen." To which came the appreciative reply, "It beats hell out of nothing."

Undaunted by their failure to find anyone to fight on the night of their arrival, the Rifles rose at dawn to launch a surprise sortie against a rancheria some half-mile away that was reportedly occupied by a band of Wintu Indians. The soldiers formed into three divisions, surrounded the village (which consisted of some 10 or 12 conical bark lodges), fired a volley, and then charged with fixed bayonets. Upon reaching the rancheria, the bemused militiamen found the members of the other divisions but no Indians. Investigation indicated that the site had been uninhabited for perhaps three or four months.

Having "captured" the village, the Rifles made their way back to Clement's corral, where they learned that Jones, Allen, and Gordon "had retreated in good order to Weaverville before hostilities commenced, taking with them all the commissary stores, if any were left from the previous night." Carr's account, precise in all other particulars, fails to indicate if they also took their "pillows" with them.

Water Over the Bridge

On January 31, 1931, the *Trinity Journal* proudly announced the forthcoming dedication of a new bridge over the Trinity River at Douglas City—the first such ceremony ever held in the county. The article also spelled out the long and frustrating history of efforts to span the river where Weaver Creek joins it (soon after Indian Creek and just before Reading's Creek do). The new bridge would be the fifth— and hopefully the last:

1. The early toll bridge built by two Smith brothers in 1859 was "washed out in the big flood of 1861," which took out every span in the county.

2. Bridge two, completed in early 1862, "lasted until the high waters of 1881 swept it away."

3. Perhaps discouraged by the second loss, Douglas City got by for a decade with a summer footbridge, which had to be rebuilt every year. During the rainy winter months the mail carrier, Tommy Greenleaf, and his buckboard often had to be rowed across the river by two expert boatmen. A second boat towed the two horses.

4. The next span, erected in 1891, lasted until 1906. The newspaper failed to record the cause of its demise, but it was soon replaced—presumably by a better one.

5. The construction of Highway 299 may have prompted the 1931 building of a fifth bridge (counting the footbridges as one). "Now the new one will last probably for all time as modern engineering methods are far ahead of the old and high waters seem a thing of the past."

6. The *Trinity Journal* of January 5, 1956, featured a photo of water "pouring through the [170-foot] gap of Douglas City Bridge caused by the collapse of two sections from the north abutment." So much for *modern* bridges—thanks to the rains that melted an early snowpack soon after the Trinity River Project began!

7. In the wake of the 1955 flood the state installed a temporary bridge until the ruptured one could be repaired. But the old span became increasingly shaky, prompting in 1980 the construction of the present bridge a short distance upstream.

The diversion of much of the Trinity's flow to the Central Valley has lessened the impact of heavy runoffs within the river's drainage. As a result, Douglas City's seventh span rests in relative safety, a soothing situation for a town that has already seen enough water wash over its bridges.

The Douglas City Bridge, probably in its 1906 version. None of the buildings pictured still stand. (TCHS photo)

Unwavering Weaverville: A Consistently Colorful County Seat

In the summer of 1850, three miners—Daniel Bennett, James Howe, and John Weaver—put up a dirt-floored log cabin on the flat near where they were mining. It was the only building in the basin, but it was enough to set them thinking. The men accordingly collected three pine needles and each drew one. Weaver's needle was shortest, and thus the one-house town of "Weaverville" was born.

By February of the following year the little village had grown some, but not much. John Carr came down from the snow-clad mountains to find that Weaverville now consisted of not one, but four cabins, along with a large circular tent. The tent was by far the most active place, for it contained both a gambling house and saloon. After availing himself of the latter, Carr began to learn a bit about Weaverville's brief but boisterous history, discovering that he had just missed one of the town's two public entertainments, a whipping. Hangings were the other, and more frequent, main event.

Some of the punishments resulted from trials duly conducted by the local court, but, as Carr later related in his wonderfully readable *Pioneer Days in California*, "We occasionally had a lynching affair, just to keep the boys' hands in."

At other times, matters never reached either the trial or lynching stage, as with the Fourth of July shootout in 1852 that left Sheriff Will Dixon wounded in the groin and his two assailants, one of them a woman, dead on the floor of their hotel. After this incident, the violence subsided enough that one resident could write reassuringly to his family that:

> Nothing fatal has taken place since my last letter but there have been some awfully close shaves. One man has been shot through the cravat, one through the hat and one in the arm. The Weaverville Hotel has been sacked and fistfights without number have come off, but as nobody has been killed nothing has been done.

—Franklin Buck, September 22, 1852

At the time of Buck's letter, some 3,000 miners were crowded along Weaverville's creekbeds, adding their take to the $20 million in gold already extracted from the glittering gulches. Five Cent Gulch and Ten Cent Gulch were two of the richest panning sites, yielding, respectively, a nickel and a dime to the pan.

Stimulated by the presence of 32 "respectable ladies" in the district, Weaverville that winter held a New Year's Eve ball. Fancy clothes were even scarcer than females, so the few sets of dress coats, white vests, boiled shirts, etc., were worn in rotation—a small group of properly attired men would waltz for an hour or so and then distribute their duds to a new contingent of dancers. Within a few years further refinement had taken hold, so that the town's Fourth of July ball saw many of the miners put, if not their best foot, at least their proper foot forward, having trained for the event by taking a dance class. Only two mishaps, neither of which occurred on the ballroom floor, marred the event:

> Miss Burbank's horse fell...through the bed of an old stream. She went about 15 feet over his head and landed in a soft muddy place, with all her ball fixins' on. Some gents along with her washed off the thickest of the mud and got her in a buggy. Mrs. Todd broke down the seat in a wagon and created considerable confusion as she weighs about 200....Taking it all together...[the ball]...was the greatest affair of its kind here.

Such dignified functions were no more than Weaverville's due as the Trinity County seat. When the Legislature established the state's original 27 counties in February 1850, vast Trinity ran clear to the coast and up to the Oregon border. An election the following year saw inland Weaverville competing with three shipping towns on Humboldt Bay—Eureka, Bucksport, and Union (Arcata)—to become the center of Trinity's government. With their votes thus divided, the coastal merchants proved no match for the miners, and Weaverville gained the honor.

The winter of 1852–53 was of Arctic proportions—a 42-day-long storm left Weaverville buried in snow four to five feet deep, which threatened to collapse any unshoveled roof and left the ravenous residents with little but a large supply of barley to eat. Soon everyone's diet consisted of barley bread, barley mush, and, for variety, barley pancakes, all washed down with "coffee" made from—burnt barley. When a report arrived that a pack train had at last reached nearby Lewiston, much of the town turned out to shovel an eight-mile-long trail to reach the stranded provisions. The sought-for supplies unfortunately consisted mostly of blacksmith's iron and whiskey, which meant that "a few sacks of beans were the only eatables...found on the train."

But come the summer of 1854, blacksmith's iron outdid beans as a prized commodity. Weaverville by then contained a sizable contingent of Chinese miners and shopkeepers; an internecine incident pitted two rival factions, representing Hong Kong and Canton emigrants, against each other in an escalating disagreement. The local blacksmiths were besieged by orders from both sides for the forging of iron pikes, the more lethal the better. John Carr, by now an established smithy, ran his shop "day and night" for three weeks to produce the requisite number of trident points.

His work as armorer finally finished, Carr joined the great gathering of Trinitarians who assembled to watch the duly scheduled conflict. (The battlefield, in Five Cent Gulch, is still the scene of occasional fighting as it now forms part of the grounds of the Weaverville Elementary School.) The Chinese combatants at first seemed reluctant to commence hostilities, whereupon several of the spectators obligingly pelted them with rocks. When the badly outnumbered Canton contingent then saw that a group of whites were holding back some of the Hong Kong soldiery, they seized the opportunity and charged. Their impetus increased when they brought out pistols (heretofore hidden in their jackets) and commenced firing at their confounded opponents. Blacksmith iron was no match for hot lead and the Hong Kong forces fell away in full retreat. The triumphant Cantonese slowed their pursuit only long enough "to jab their long forks in a fallen foe's intestines."

Various accounts claim that anywhere from eight to twenty-seven Chinese were killed in the battle; all observers agree, however, in adding one other fatality to the final total—that of a warmongering white, either a Swede or a Dutchman, who early on fired his pistol into the melee to precipitate more furious fighting and then appropriately dropped over dead himself, the victim of a well-placed bullet fired by a fellow onlooker who was apparently disgusted by the breach in battlefield etiquette.

Fires proved a more regular event than factional fighting. Following a conflagration in 1853 that barbecued much of the business district, the town was rebuilt with widened streets and a set of new structures that boasted such non-flammable features as brick walls, iron shutters, and dirt insulation between ceilings and roofs. The overall improvement was not

Weaverville procession, 1903, probably for the Chinese New Year's celebration. (C. E. Goodyear photo)

immediately apparent, for Weaverville sustained other big blazes in 1855 (two), 1863, 1874, 1897, and a 1905 fire that leveled most of what was then left of Chinatown. Only the brick buildings seemed safe from flame-wrought destruction; of the 22 constructed along Main Street between 1854 and 1859, 20 remained standing a century later.

In the early 1870s Trinity County's mining meteor burned but dimly; Weaverville's population had dropped to some 850, of which about 250 were Chinese. The advent of hydraulic operations then spurred renewed activity, so that by mid-decade the town could claim 1,500 residents. Weaverville nonetheless languished in isolation, connected to the coast by no more than a pack trail and separated from Sacramento by a three-and-a-half-day stage and steamer trip. For all that, the county seat still managed to offer a few amenities, providing the varied products of a brewery, soda bottling works, and cider factory. The cultural events of the centennial year, 1876, included a series of Indian dances performed by members of "the Yuka tribe, who lived beyond Kettenchow," and "a Chinese theatrical company, consisting of twenty male and female artists of more or less renown, including a full band of gongs, drums, cymbals, fiddles, banjos, etc."

The century lengthened, and, in the words of Sharlot Hall, a writer for *Out West*, "the town dropped into a contented dream under the locust trees." Hall observed that it was still dreaming when she visited in 1908:

The little, low brick business-blocks sit along the street, quaint and shabby as old soldiers in the uniform of some forgotten war. The doors and windows are still closed with the big, double iron shutters, heavy and prison-like, rusted and faded to a dingy green; and queer little spiral staircases go up from the edge of the sidewalk to the upper floor, as if indoor space was too valuable to be wasted in stair-room.

Some of the stores have not renewed their shelves since the days when a pinch of gold dust was current "change," and the whip-sawed, hand-planed ceiling is still in place in the oldest hotel. Twice a week the big, brass-belled freight teams pull in up the one long street and the ark-like wagons discharge a varied lading on the sidewalk in front of the little stores. Pack-trains come and go with supplies for the camps beyond reach of wagon-roads, and the buckboard stages come in from the remoter valleys with a few limp mail-sacks on board, and perhaps a box of butter or eggs sent in by some rancher to the town market.

The coming of the stage from Redding is the event of the day; it is the closest link with the world outside, and everybody turns out to watch the passengers climb down and the mail-bags go off. Everybody asks the stage-driver for the news; everybody waits for a possible letter or paper when the mail is sorted, and then the street is suddenly empty and still and dark—the day is over.

At about the time of Hall's account, Weav-

erville briefly roused itself from its rural reverie with the advent of motorized stage service, provided by a lone Stanley Steamer. The much-vaunted vehicle made only a few trips before it burned near Whiskeytown.

"Airmail" delivery was the next attempt at

The Weaverville-Redding stage stands in front of the New York Hotel following a heavy snow. To the left are the Trinity Mercantile and, with its spiral staircase, Clifford Hall. (C. E. Goodyear photo)

modernization. In September 1919, a fire patrol airplane circled town and released a parachute bearing two messages: a letter from Forest Supervisor W. A. Huestis to his wife and a note from the Yreka Chamber of Commerce. It was 19 years before other communications of sufficient import required further air service.

Weaverville continued to revel in its rusticity, so much so that even as late as the 1920s

The Bank Robber Who Received More Than He Took

The stocky, bearded prospector named Davis had attracted little attention during the year or so he'd been in and out of Weaverville. Even on his last day in town, in mid-November 1919, his activities went almost unnoticed when, just before noon, he left the Trinity County Bank with a package under his arm and ambled up to Day's stable; there he obtained his horse, which he then led down a back street before mounting up and riding off on the Lewiston road.

Davis had only just departed town when president C. H. Edwards and clerk Van B. Young returned to their bank. Upon entering the building, they discovered that cashier H. Gray, whom they had left in charge, was nowhere to be found. A persistent rapping sound soon led Edwards and Young to the locked door of the vault, behind which was Gray; Davis had deposited him there at pistol point as collateral on an unauthorized "loan" of $18,000.

Suddenly Davis's name was on everyone's lips—the county's phone lines sang the two syllables as the sheriff's office alerted rural deputies to guard all exit routes from town.

But Davis was nowhere to be found. Although his horse soon turned up about a mile east of Weaverville on the Lewiston road, a week later the *Trinity Journal* could only report that "there is nothing new…regarding the whereabouts of Davis….The officers may be on his trail, or maybe not." Only with the following week's edition did *Journal* readers learn that the sheriffs had conducted a hot pursuit, and with remarkable results.

On the Monday following the robbery, Davis's footprints were found heading into the Trinities up Stuart Fork. Expert trackers traced his route northward over the divide and down into the Salmon River drainage. There, forest rangers phoned rancher George Godfrey to alert him that Davis was headed his way, and Godfrey was ready when a suspicious stranger subsequently showed up.

The rancher had secreted a loaded gun in every room of his house; thus prepared, he easily got the drop on Davis after the robber came inside. Handing his weapon over to his friend, octogenarian Jake Russell, Godfrey then attempted to tie Davis up. All too soon the desperado caught his captor off guard, and, as Godfrey described it:

> We then clinched, and he fought like a wild beast. We wrestled all around the room and he was getting the best of me when I told Jake to help me out. Jake hauled off and hit the fellow over the head, which did not seem to faze him in the least. The blow broke the magazine of the gun. We kept on fighting hand-to-hand until I was all in. I told Jake to shoot him, and Old Jake, true to his word, shot and hit him where he intended to hit him, in the leg. This took the grit out of him and he then gave himself up.

The forest rangers presently arrived and that evening helped Godfrey take the wounded Davis to Forks of Salmon, the nearest town. The following morning, according to Godfrey, "we loaded him on a stage truck and mailed him to Etna."

Later removed to the Siskiyou County seat of Yreka, Davis, alias Ivan Murdoch, admitted that he was actually one Jefferson F. Howell, who had practiced for the Weaverville heist by committing four other robberies over the previous three years. Five days after making his confession, Davis/Murdoch/Howell had his wounded leg amputated.

Follow-up reports indicated that Davis had been too modest with his résumé. His banditry actually began some twenty-five years earlier when he held up a saloon in Utah.

Davis's take, which came to $18,843.18, survived its impromptu trip through the Trinities intact, and soon returned to the safer confines of the bank vault. Davis subsequently suffered his own confinement, at San Quentin Penitentiary, where he had plenty of time to reflect on the effectiveness of rural law enforcement.

cows could be found roaming randomly up and down the town's streets. Come nighttime, some of the less mobile bovines bedded down on the sidewalks.

As the century progressed, Weaverville, its locust-lined streets still shading brick and frame buildings from a bygone era, seemed suspended in time. A reporter from the San Francisco *Call-Bulletin* paid the town a visit in the spring of 1941 and sketched a picture of pastoral peacefulness:

> The houses in Weaverville are all neat and most of them are old. The gardens are beautifully tended. Every house has a front porch, on every porch there's a rocking chair. The lawns are like green velvet and in the yard out back of each house you're apt to see a few horses grazing quietly.

To readers in the City, the scene must have seemed a world away, which is how it apparently appeared to author James Hilton, who reputedly visited the town in the 1930s. One look at the compact community, nestled at the base of the towering Trinities, was enough. Hilton exclaimed, "I've found it. The setting for my story," and Weaverville became the Shangri-La made famous in *Lost Horizon*.

Or so the story goes. The account was taken as gospel by *Trinity Journal* editor William F. Ashbury, who, in 1960, launched a campaign to give the name of Hilton's village to the Trinity County seat. Controversy ensued. Over the next few months Ashbury discovered that the

Weaverville sometime before the 1905 fire that devastated Chinatown, upper right. The Browder House, lower left, was the home of the town's only black (and ex-slave) family. (C. E. Goodyear photo)

power of the press was, in the face of tightly held tradition, decidedly limited. By the following January the abashed editor admitted that his proposal had failed: Weaverville would remain Weaverville and the Trinities would no longer be likened to Tibet.

A more manifest challenge to the town's integrity occurred a few years earlier when a pair of errant truck drivers engaged in an unrequested bit of urban renewal. (*See sidebar, next page.*)

Several years later the Highway Department followed in the terrified truckers' treadmarks by more systematically widening Main Street; instead of battering down buildings, however, the state removed the stately black locust trees that had lined the roadway for decades. The suddenly exposed brick storefronts presented an unappealingly bleak appearance.

Weaverville went into action. Led by Florence Scott Morris, a women's committee planned a beautification and town "paint-up" project, securing the assistance of the W. P. Fuller paint company. In June 1957, hundreds of Weavervillians turned out to literally "paint the town red" (and other harmonizing colors

Runaway Truck 5; Town 2

When Anthony Moreno and Benny Morales left the Cal-Ore mill in Big Bar one March evening in 1950, they had little idea they were about to ride, roughshod, into the annals of Trinity County history. With their truck carrying a stack of 2 x 6 lumber and their trailer loaded with 2 x 12s, the pair was bound for Los Angeles and therefore thought they had a long trip ahead.

It proved somewhat shorter than anticipated.

The rig sped along the highway above the night-dark Trinity River; soon Moreno and Morales zipped past Helena and Junction City. Their heavy cargo slowed them on the grade past the La Grange Mine, but then they were over the Oregon Mountain Summit and on their way down into Weaverville. Moreno, who was driving, prudently applied the brakes to slow the truck's descent.

Nothing happened. The truck soon began to pick up speed. Moreno, worried about saving his engine, started shifting to higher, rather than lower, gears.

The truck roared down the grade and into town, entering the business district at an estimated speed of 70 to 75 miles per hour. Buildings whizzing past them, Moreno and Morales approached the courthouse corner. It was late on a weeknight and Weaverville was fortunately bereft of other traffic.

But not of other objects. At the courthouse, Moreno valiantly tried to turn the truck to the right, hoping to follow the oblique angle of the street. By now, however, the vehicle was charting its own course—one that would lead it into the lobby of the Weaverville Hotel.

Somehow Moreno wrestled the truck away from the building so that they only rode up onto the sidewalk. The trailer, however, proved less compliant, whipping around to smash into the south front edge of the hotel before rearranging additional architecture as it continued southward down the street.

Next to go was the front of Dr. Michelson's office, which the late-staying physician had vacated only moments earlier; then came Henry's Place and the Blaney Building, small frame structures whose fronts "were crushed like matchsticks." The brick Trinity Bakery afforded a more substantial obstacle, but the trailer merely struck it a glancing blow, cracking and distending the building's walls before plowing into the large locust tree that stood outside. The tree proved no match for the trailer; it was torn from the ground, its trunk finally coming to rest some 80 yards down the street.

Now came the Native Sons and Knights of Pythias Hall; its iron spiral staircase was ripped out, the lower portion of its porch wrecked, and its brick front loosened and separated.

So, too, was the trailer at last separated from the truck. The trailer's 2 x 12s were then neatly deposited in front of the Weaverville Drug Store—an unexpected delivery—as most of the trailer finally overturned in the street; the front wheels, still full of energy, continued rolling another 100 yards before they stopped.

Meanwhile, Moreno and Morales were stuck inside the runaway truck, weaving their way wildly through downtown Weaverville. Finally, near the old high school, they rolled to a long-awaited stop.

The evening's events were far from over. Back up Main Street, a small fire broke out in an already battered Henry's Place but was extinguished after burning a bit of wallpaper. Then, some two hours later, the remains of the Native Sons–Knights of Pythias porch collapsed on top of the hall's earlier wreckage. Morning found the lost lumber cargo being converted into barricades to block off the damaged buildings.

Before leaving town, Moreno paid a $25 fine for citations stemming from the accident. A message from the Highway Patrol's Southern California office indicated that the record of Moreno's previous offenses was "too long to send by teletype."

It had, as anyone who surveyed the swath of destruction down Main Street would attest, just grown substantially longer.

---

selected by the committee). Even merchant Moon Lee, who carried rival brand Dutch Boy paint, agreeably colored up his store with Fuller's finest.

One structure that escaped the Morales-Moreno juggernaught was a narrow brick building, constructed by John Carr in 1856 for his blacksmith shop and subsequently used as a saloon. By 1917 it had come to attract bibliophiles rather than bibbers as it commenced over 70 years of service as the Weaverville Library. When heavy trucks passed outside on the street, they did not have the impact of Moreno's vehicle, but they nonetheless attracted attention—the vibration they caused produced a fine dust that drifted down on patrons and books from the ceiling—part of the seven-inch dirt pack placed there as an early method of fire protection. At last tiring of its periodic dustings, the library moved up Main Street in 1991 to its new quarters northwest of the Court House. A "book brigade" of some 600 students, county employees, and other residents passed the library's collection by hand up Main Street from one building to the other.

Had John Carr been there to witness the event, he no doubt would have smiled to see the townfolk still exhibiting striking behavior. Whether shuffling dress ball clothes, shooing sidewalk-seated cattle, or shifting library books, Weaverville's citizens have always delighted in the unusual.

Results of the Moreno-Morales wrecking crew, 1950. (TCHS photo)

Biggest Little Burg on the Trinity Highway

Whether British novelist James Hilton really likened Weaverville to the "Shangri La" of his *Lost Horizon* matters less than the validity accorded this analogy by so many visitors. Whether viewed in its basin setting from a *bally* (Wintu for mountain) or from the Moon Lee Ditch above town, Weaverville resembles a Shangri La more than any other place along the Trinity Highway. The older upper end of Main Street has retained enough of its 19th-century charm to rate National Historic District status and at least a one-day stay. The historic district features a striking blend of cinnabar brick buildings and clapboard houses—the latter often bordered by white picket fences. The center of Main Street, once jammed with the store-home structures of an active Chinese community, now has a spacious air more common to a wooded New England village. To paraphrase one of Jim Augustson's songs from his lively "Gold Country" show at the little Brewery Barn Theater, "If ever there was a Shangri La [along Highway 299], this is [the place]...."

For a small town with no traffic light or highway bypass, as of 2000, Weaverville is difficult to visualize up close—mainly because of its hilly and skewed layout. On a street map it resembles a random tangle of loosely knotted ropes, and for good reason! When William Lowden surveyed it in 1876, he platted it by metes and bounds, with property boundaries defined by natural or human landmarks rather than grid lines. A standard foursquare plat hardly would have fit a place that sprang up as a series of mining camps along the small streams that form Weaver Creek. A reporter for the *Redding Independent* confirmed the town's irregular character five years later: "Weaverville is exclusively a mining town, and evidences of [the] search for the 'precious' can be seen in every direction." "The town...is not laid out with much regularity, but the streets are ornamented with trees, and well watered, keeping them cool and pleasant."

"Weaver's" location may seem strange, since it lies seven or eight miles from the Trinity River (and roughly equidistant from the tiny river towns of Douglas City and Junction City). Yet this still unincorporated "city" of 3,500 serves as the seat of Trinity County and ranks as the biggest burg by far on the Trinity Scenic Byway proper. Of the fewer than 15,000 people who inhabit the corridor, excluding Redding and Arcata/Eureka at either end, roughly a fourth of them live in Weaverville alone. Ironically, it is the only Highway 299 town in the county not located on the Trinity River, a fact deeply rooted in the history of both the highway and the region.

Had we followed the 1860 census-taker and mapped the county's richest gold deposits then, we would have found the majority within Weaver Basin or near the mouth of Weaver (and Reading's) Creek. A Yankee trader and gold-seeker named Franklin Buck described the area as "the best mining country in California as the dirt all pays from the surface in most places." When he arrived in 1852, miners "were seeing about bringing [a "flumed"] Trinity River through this place" via a 28-mile canal costing $250,000. Weaverville failed to bring the river to the basin, but it made every effort to connect itself to the river and the rest of the county and ultimately succeeded. As the region's leading gold producer, the town lost no time in securing the county seat. Much later, it exerted its political clout by overriding a state engineer's endorsement of an all-river highway route that

clined. Ironically, in recent years "Weaver" has become so big that it must pipe some of its water supply from the distant Trinity.

Weaverville's Joss House and its annual Chinese New Year's celebration add even more irony as leading icons of the town's identity.

mining and logging. Yet this burg, in spite of its fewer venerable Victorians, now rivals the "Victorian Village" of Ferndale, in Humboldt County, as a haven for artists. The paucity of architectural gems may be deeply rooted in its not-so-golden past, if we can give Frank Buck's early judgments any credence.

Uptown Weaverville, 1934, before the three small stores, center, were removed for the rerouting of the Trinity Highway past the courthouse, rear right. The "Weekly Trinity Journal" occupied the two-story building to the left, across the street from the Weaverville (formerly Empire) Hotel. (SHS photo)

This is a poor place to make anything but a living; not a merchant here has made anything [1854]…Houses and lots sell here for about $400 [in 1865] and anything worth more very seldom changes hands. Everybody is going away at some time and nobody wants to invest in a good permanent home. "That's what's the matter" in this mining county….The fact is nobody is poor here and nobody very rich. There is no caste and society here and the miner and the man who works [sic] for wages live in just as good houses and eat and drink and wear the same things as the merchant…When a man "makes a raise" as we call getting from ten to forty thousand dollars…, he takes it and leaves…So you see this is the country for a poor man [and a] bad place for a rich man.

would have connected Douglas City and Junction City directly, thus bypassing Weaverville. When built, the highway crossed over Oregon Mountain instead. As the higher and drier county capital burgeoned, all of the river towns—both upstream and downstream—de-

Both appear out of place in the absence of any modern Chinatown but have profound importance as symbols of the town's past. (*See next section, "Weaving Across Weaverville."*) The presence of several art galleries also surprises visitors to a place with an economy long based on

Buck's generalization about there being "no caste and society here" might have applied to most whites, but it certainly did not include the excluded Indian and Chinese populations whose mistreatment he criticized and virtues he touted. A few of his comments about the Chinese deserve citing, if only because they reveal how much one Yankee trader depended on them.

- "John Chinaman (frequently multiplied) is one of my best customers. There are thirty or forty of them and today [Jan. 18, 1853] they have come to town in full force."

- Within the past month (April 1853), "over five hundred Chinamen and as many Americans have arrived here and the cry is 'Lice! Lice!' (rice)."

- "There are three hundred of them on one bar that has been worked out by our people and they are perfectly satisfied if they make two or three dollars per day." (June 5, 1853)

- "We have a Celestial [named Ahyung] for a clerk and he is very successful in trading with his countrymen. These Chinese are the greatest traders in the world. They lay over the genuine Yankee [like me] in buying and selling." (Sept. 18, 1853)

- "I am still in the hog business [Oct. 29, 1859]. Bought another drove here and I am supplying the Chinese butchers and making something."

Buck also acknowledged that "we have all the different characters in the Union," and he was struck by the "vast difference" between, say, New Englanders and Missourians. He had an intense dislike for the Irish but wrote favorably about the Germans—"an institution out here." Their May Day Festival, which lasted three days and two nights, impressed him. "Dancing began at 6, supper at 10, [and] 60 10-gallon kegs of lager beer [were] consumed." The 240-foot circumference of the huge dance hall, meant, he reckoned, that "some of [the] Dutch [or German] Gals waltzed five miles in a night." Ethnic differences no longer characterize the town, but the large number of churches and social clubs implies some degree of diversity.

Weaverville has compensated for its lack of fancy Victorians with a block-long multifaceted museum. No other place along the Trinity Highway has quite equaled this town's efforts to preserve its past. We invite place-lovers who want to investigate Weaver's changing character to: 1) visit the J. J. Jackson Museum; 2) check out the Highland Art Center and the Joss House; 3) stroll along upper Main Street and one or more of its quaint and quiet side streets; 4) hike or bike one of the "Trails Through Time" featured on the map of the splendid "Weaver Basin Trail System"; 5) and, before leaving town, take a romantic ride in a sturdy vehicle to the top of Weaver Bally for sweeping vistas of Weaver Basin and the Trinity Alps.

The Union Hotel (its sign barely visible below and behind the "GARAGE" sign) was owned by mining entrepreneur Peter M. Paulsen, pictured here with his family. (C. E. Goodyear photo)

Weaving Across Weaverville

Many visitors to Weaverville never venture beyond the four blocks of mostly brick buildings located between the J. J. Jackson Museum and the Trinity County Courthouse on Main Street. That's understandable because visits to the three most popular sites—the Museum, Joss House, and Highland Art Center—can easily take an hour or two each. Anyone wanting to see another side of town should wander along Mill, Court, Taylor, or Center streets or walk through one of the three local cemeteries. The Trinity County Historical Society has prepared a fine "Walking Tour of Historic Weaverville" that features 116 sites—too many to inspect closely at one time. For this weave across Weaverville we have highlighted 16 of them along a Mill-Main-Taylor route, a choice based mostly on some of the colorful characters that once owned or occupied them. Apart from the "big three," we have listed them in geographical order, but feel free to "weave" or chart your own way through town.

1. J. J. "Jake" Jackson Museum (508 South Main Street) In 1953, County Treasurer Jake Jackson and a few other local history buffs founded the Trinity County Historical Society, which assumed responsibility for the miscellaneous artifacts then housed in the basement of the Courthouse. A decade later the society began building a museum to hold its growing number of treasures and named it, in 1968, after the man who had regaled Trinitarians with his "Mountaineer" tales and promoted county history for most of his adult life. Since then the museum has gradually expanded its space to illustrate—with periodic demonstrations and workshops—the most important facets of mining in Weaver Basin. The Blacksmith Shop, one of seven that once operated in town, features skilled smithies forging all kinds of tools. The Ditch-tender's Cabin, relocated in 1970 from nearby Munger Gulch, recalls the vital role of water in hydraulic mining. The Stamp Mill, removed from the Paymaster Mine in Eastman Gulch and restored in 1982–84, shows the process of separating gold from its ore. Most recently the Museum has acquired and refurbished a Shasta-Weaverville Stagecoach, which is pulled by a team of horses for the town's biggest annual celebration—the Fourth of July Parade.

Mining exhibits form only a minor part of the old Museum's collection. One finds an amazing array of costumes and firearms—all being watched, as it were, by prominent pioneers whose photos or paintings hang high around the walls of the main floor. Displays in the basement include two old jail cells and beer-brewing equipment used by the Meckel brothers. An attractive gift shop offers sundry publications—including the annual *Trinity*—homemade jams and jellies, and t-shirts.

For serious students of Trinity County happenings, the Museum's biggest attraction is the History Center, constructed in 1994–95 at a cost of $111,000. The historical society more than matched a generous gift from Museum Director Hal Goodyear and his wife Dorothy with contributions from many sources—most notably a donation by Alice Goen Jones from the sale of her *Flowers and Trees of the Trinity Alps*. (The society ended up with a $25,000 surplus which it placed in its Trust Fund.) Jake Jackson would be astonished but delighted to see what one generation of volunteers has accomplished in little Weaverville.

2. Highland Art Center (503 South Main) The center of Weaverville's art community first served as the residence of Reverend A. T. Jackson, minister of the newly finished Trinity Congregational Church next door. He

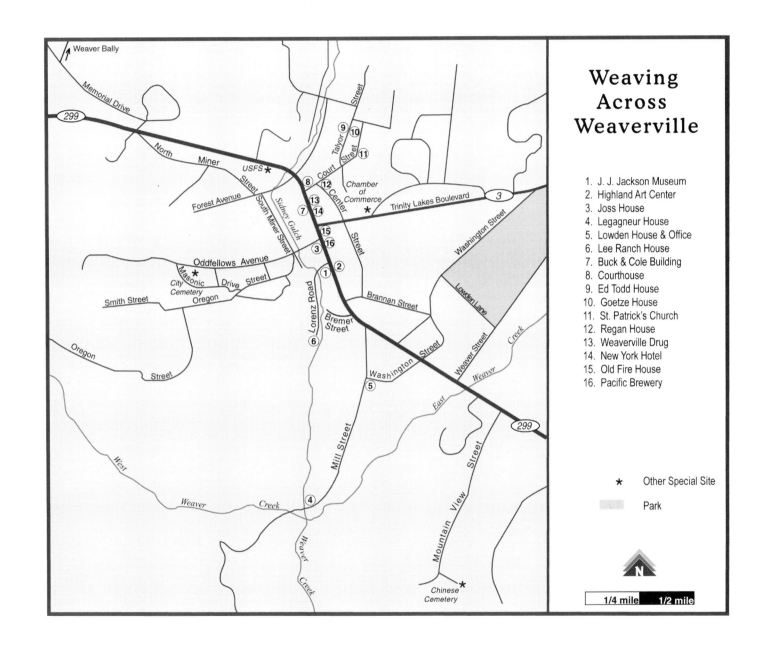

Weaving
Across
Weaverville

1. J. J. Jackson Museum
2. Highland Art Center
3. Joss House
4. Legagneur House
5. Lowden House & Office
6. Lee Ranch House
7. Buck & Cole Building
8. Courthouse
9. Ed Todd House
10. Goetze House
11. St. Patrick's Church
12. Regan House
13. Weaverville Drug
14. New York Hotel
15. Old Fire House
16. Pacific Brewery

★ Other Special Site

▨ Park

1/4 mile   1/2 mile

built the house himself in 1893 and two years later constructed a much larger home down the street for businessman John Whitmore. (The Reverend Jackson, one suspects, prospered more from pounding nails than from preaching sermons.) Helena Meckel of North Fork (renamed Helena in her honor) then acquired this little "white house with green shutters and extensive gardens" that fronted both Main and Center Streets. She moved in after her husband Christian's death in 1904 and soon remodeled and expanded the place. For 30 years she shared her spacious place with niece Annie Young (and her husband Van), and together they made it "the most attractive and best kept residence in Weaverville"—at least in the eyes of her nephew Henry, who boarded with them seasonally in 1917–23. This "town-farm…produced all of the vegetables and fruits needed by the family and most of the hay that fed the cow and calf…." The Youngs maintained the place after Helena's death, and Henry Meckel purchased it in 1953 not long after Aunt Annie died.

Fifteen years later a telephone company owner and his wife bought the property for the express purpose of fostering the fine arts in Trinity County. Gilman and Lucille Snyder set up a non-profit corporation to exhibit the work of local artists who, in turn, could offer instruction in their particular craft—be it drawing, painting, photography, pottery, sculpture, or weaving. Their foundation has converted the old home and its outbuildings into galleries, studios, and instruction space. The Art Center keeps longer hours than the Museum and Joss House and holds receptions for invited artists on the first Friday evening of each month. The center also provides a handy guide to the town's other arts and crafts locations.

The Snyders also envisioned the construction of a performing arts center, designed by a pair of Eureka architects. After 40 years of performing in rented facilities, the Trinity Players, along with other groups, may soon have a small but superior auditorium and an outdoor stage for their presentations—a big addition to Weav-

The relocated and restored Ditch-tender's Cabin, after its move from Munger Gulch to the J. J. "Jake" Jackson Museum grounds in downtown Weaverville. (Robin Stocum photo)

erville's thriving Arts Center.

3. Joss House State Historic Park (Main and Oregon) Weaverville's Chinese Joss House, one of California's few remaining Taoist temples, draws more visitors to Trinity County than any other site save the Museum. *Won Lim Miao*, the Temple of the Forest Beneath the Clouds, stands as the chief survivor and symbol of Weaverville's once sizable Chinatown. After its dedication in 1874, the Joss House, along with the adjoining cabin, served for fully half a century as the spiritual and social locus of Weaver Basin's Chinese community. Its detached location enabled the locust-shaded temple to escape the fire in 1905 that destroyed most of the already shrinking Chinatown. The Chinese end of Main Street extended from the present Museum site past the Pacific Brewery and included 20 percent of the town's population of 600.

The term *joss* applies not only to the temple, but also to any of the deities within it and to the sticks of incense used by Taoists when they worship. The name probably derives from the Portuguese word for god, *deos*, since explorers speaking that language referred to the numerous Taoist temples they saw along the South China coast as "joss houses." According to the *Trinity Journal* of April 18, 1874, locals called the Weaverville temple the "*Josh* House," apparently because "our civilized and Christian people" considered the worship of "our 'Heathen Chinese' population"—with its "constant din" and "disgusting aroma"—so incongruous.

Entering the Joss House is a lot like opening any richly illustrated religious text; it requires much interpretation, best provided by one of the state park's rangers in the absence of a Taoist priest. The temple also makes more sense when viewed in the spirit of *feng shui*, the Chinese art of designing buildings in a site-sensitive way. To the dismay of photographers, the front of the temple faces north, not to avoid the sun but because Sydney Gulch Creek, the site's source of water, flows from that direction.

The closed set of doors inside the main entrance may seem odd, but their purpose is to thwart the entry of evil spirits. Similarly the pair of dragon fish atop the roof are supposed to ward off any fire like the one that razed an earlier temple built behind the present one. Inside the Joss House to the right, a noseless but smiling doorkeeper, a bearded god named Dai Tze, bids visitors welcome. He directs us past the prayer chimney at the center, which draws the smoke away from the burning joss sticks, over to the three altars at the front. Each of them—Mercy, Knowledge, Health (right to left)—has a set of gods or goddesses petitioned by the Chinese to increase their chances of finding fortune in the golden mountains and streams of Trinity County.

The two gods in the center altar—Bok Ai (right) and Kuan Ti—were so important that the Trinity Chinese always celebrated their birthdays. The events featured noisy parades from the Joss House up Odd Fellows Avenue to "schoolhouse hill" (site of the 1878 Grammar School) to an open space safe for the shooting of bombs and firecrackers. The king's umbrella and some of the banners used on "Bomb Days" still adorn the temple walls. Just inside and above the doorway into the community's meeting room are the names, inscribed in wood, of the hundreds of people who contributed to the construction of the Joss House. When disputes arose, the priest tried to resolve them in this small "courtroom" next to his even tinier living quarters.

By 1874, the Chinese comprised close to 40 percent of the population in both Weaverville and Trinity County. They devoted an entire week to the dedication of their new temple, which, the *Trinity Journal* conceded, is "attractively decorated and arranged, and draws crowds of unbelievers," whom the Taoists welcomed with champagne and cigars. Surprisingly, given the 1880s–1890s expulsion of Chinese from Humboldt and Shasta counties, they were never driven out of Trinity County. They escaped that fate, even though most whites viewed them as a "detriment" and as "the direct cause of the burning of Weaverville several times…." "Yankee trader" Frank Buck opined in 1854, when the Chinese threatened to outnumber the Americans, that "they would not be allowed to stay among us" were it not for the sizable sums they paid in mining taxes. Stay they did, longer than anywhere else between Redding and Eureka.

While it may seem incongruous to watch a virtually all-white crowd celebrate the Chinese

New Year in front of the Joss House, as Weaverville has done since 1983, it must make a bemused Dai Tze smile more than ever.

4. Madame Marie Legagneur House (1014 Mill Street) Until Highway 299 finally reached Weaverville, Mill Street functioned as the main road in and out of the south end of town, near where West and East Weaver creeks join. Here, as early as the 1860s, a French woman named Marie Legagneur established a brothel opposite the first stage stop for travelers who had forded the creek. As the gold boom declined, so did Madame's business and health. On a winter day neighbors found her cold and starving and took her to the county hospital—too late to save her life. A century later the "Clampers," the Trinity chapter of *E Clampus Vitus,* placed a plaque at the lower northeast corner of Weaverville's main cemetery to honor her. It reads: "Madam[e] Marie Legagneur 1831–91. In life she gave us a bawdy house; in death she gave us a reflection of our romantic gold rush history." This belated recognition has not stilled Madame Marie's troubled spirit, for the longtime owner of the home that now occupies the site reports recurring signs of Legagneur's ghost: light chains rattle, bedroom doors open, radios turn on, and a glowing figure appears. She apparently means no harm but still laments the agony of her death and perhaps the torching of her home one night, a month after her death.

5. Lowden House and Office (905 Mill Street) One might expect Trinity County's leading surveyor and road builder to have erected a larger and more ornate home. But William Spencer Lowden had this house built in 1890 (after a fire destroyed his first one), in a vernacular style that characterized much of the town he platted after moving here from Lewiston. His business expanded enough to justify construction (1895) of an office with a pyramid hip roof on the Washington Street corner of his large lot. Unkempt vines and rusting

Weaverville's foremost landmark, the Joss House, showing the main entrance to the temple, right, and the door to the attached cabin that served as the social center, left. (Robin Stocum photo)

tin roofs give both home and office a weathered look that belies the once flourishing condition of the Lowden farm with its carefully tended orchards. What other changes can you see after viewing the place through C. E. Goodyear's camera lens a century or so ago?

6. Lee Family Ranch House (end of Lorenz Road, between Joss House and Museum Park) If you stopped at the Moon Lim Lee Rest Area one mile north of Douglas City, you may have read the plaque there that honors Weaverville's most prominent Chinese pioneer family. In 1892, Moon Lee's father, Lim Sue Kin, opened a grocery store in Chinatown that he named Sam Lee—meaning "three waves of prosperity." The business began as a home delivery truck farm at the lower end of (Henry) Lorenz Road, but as it prospered, Lim Sue Kin became known as Sam Lee. By 1918, he could afford to build a shingle-sided ranch house with a veranda porch on a hill above the vegetable gardens (land that is now part of Lee Fong Park). Upon his father's death, four years later, Moon inherited the home and became manager of the store. In 1939, he opened Lee's Supermarket, a much bigger store across Main Street (next to the soon-to-be built Trinity Theatre, recently converted into Meredith Merlo Vineyards).

Moon Lee succeeded as a businessman but also became a respected civic leader. He and his wife Dorothy provided food and credit to many townspeople during hard times, and they strongly promoted restoration of the Joss House as part of the state park system (effec- tive 1956) in much the same way that Mae Boggs saved Old Shasta.

Trinity County acquired the ranch house and surrounding property in 1989 and converted it into a workshop for local artists—wood carvers, quilters, and glass artists among others. The Trinity Arts Council manages the Ranch House and has enhanced it with Lee family artifacts. They also support a folk art gallery, with rotating exhibits, and stage productions at the nearby amphitheater.

7. Buck & Cole Building (222 South Main) The old Buck & Cole store has seen the usual turnover of businesses and occupants since its construction in the 1850s. But it has experienced less structural change than most other brick buildings on Main Street. Thus if the original owners could return to town, they would undoubtedly recognize the structure as theirs, even though the outside spiral staircase was not added until 1860, the year after Cole died and Buck moved out.

On January 18, 1849, in New York City, Franklin Buck boarded a boat captained by John

Surveyor William Spencer Lowden's house and office on Mill Street. The hitching post, center, now stands a short distance away at the Museum, on Main Street. (TCHS photo)

Cole that landed in San Francisco six months later. By 1852, these two "Yankee Trader[s] in the Gold Rush" had worked their way through several businesses from Sacramento to Weaverville, with the younger and unmarried Buck taking time off for a voyage to Hawaii and Tahiti to buy bushels of oranges and potatoes to sell to California miners. According to Buck's book of letters to his older sister in Bucksport, Maine, Weaverville doubled in size during his first year here, counting "fourteen stores, four hotels and four gambling saloons" (with a combined total of "fourteen bar rooms")—all running "in full blast." Cole lived on the second floor above the store after his wife sailed from Maine to rejoin him in 1853. The business survived not only the ups and downs of a seasonal mining economy but also the frequent fires that plagued the town. The partnership dissolved with Cole's death just a few months after Buck returned jubilant from a yearlong trip back home with a new bride named Jennie at his side.

Although they sometimes talked about moving, the Bucks "settled down" for more than seven years in the "New England village" of Weaver as it filled up "with cottages, gardens." They built a new house and farmed an acre of land that included a "cow yard" for their three children. Frank made money by raising hogs and "supplying the Chinese butchers," selling wood (for $8 a cord), and taking over the local "ice business" (fetching the ice from the frozen lake below Weaver Bally). Eventually the Bucks retired to Napa Valley, but only after fi-nally giving up "the idea of ever finding a rich mine or making a fortune in stocks" following a decade-long sojourn in several mining towns of eastern Nevada.

8. Trinity County Courthouse (Main and Court streets) Weaverville, like Shasta City, captured the county seat soon after the Northern California gold rush began. Unlike its eastern neighbor, Trinity County lost little time in constructing a courthouse—a three-story frame structure placed "on the hill at the head of Court Street." Perhaps officials should have taken more care in selecting the site or framing the building. Creaking under the weight of winter snow and wailing when the wind blew, the first courthouse soon became unsafe (and later burned to the ground). In 1865, at the lower end of Court Street (next to the site of John Weaver's first cabin), the county acquired merchant Henry Hocker's much sturdier three-story multi-purpose brick building for gradual conversion into a courthouse. Frequent remodeling has not made the courthouse look any more "courtly," yet it commands more attention now than it did before 1940. At about that time, the rerouting of Highway 299 along Main Street removed three smaller buildings to the west, and a fire razed the grand old Union Hotel to the east (site of the present parking lot). The two events combined to leave the courthouse standing alone along the sweeping bend of upper Main Street. The building's cinnabar color and its long narrow windows (with iron shutters on the front side) accent its austere appearance. Step inside—particularly into the recorder's office (right front), with its walls lined with Lowden land surveys—and you'll know you're standing in one of California's oldest active courthouses.

9. Ed Todd House (312 Taylor Street) Toward the end of Taylor Street, on the western side, stands a model Greek Revival house built in 1880 by the county clerk, who was also a banker/broker and owner of the Weaverville Drug Store. The *Trinity County Historic Sites* volume, the authority on such matters, describes the now run-down home as "a showplace" in its prime. The clerk's widow sold the place to Eliza Todd, who eventually gave it to her son Ed as a wedding gift. One might think only a lumber baron like William Carson of Eureka could afford such a lavish present, but thrifty Eliza from Ireland and her frugal husband William from Scotland had acquired more property than most since their arrival in Weaverville 40 years earlier. She had followed him from San Francisco, taking a steamer to Red Bluff and a stage to Shasta. Fearful of riding a mule, petite (115 lbs.) Eliza walked all the way to Weaver, carrying an 18-month-old child and packing a pair of leather boots she had bought for her husband before leaving. She refused to let a Mexican packer carry the boots for her because she had cached $1,000 worth of gold coin in one and her jewels in the other. While William mined for gold, ran a sawmill, raised cattle, and operated both a meat market and a saloon, Eliza took in washing, milked the cows,

Edith Smallen, a Weaverville octogenarian has lived her entire life, single and married, on Mill Street. Here she has just delivered berries from the local farmers' market to friends who live in the Jacob Flagg home, built in 1876. (Mark Rounds photo)

and gardened.

10. Goetze House (313 Taylor Street)
The Queen Anne home across the street clearly outclasses the Todd House in both size and style, perhaps partly because of their age difference—1897 compared to 1880. Moreover, recent owners have tried to make the stately house look even more Victorian than it did when Henry W. Goetze had it built. One of Weaverville's most successful German immigrants, he arrived as a young man in 1875, almost too late to engage in mining. He rapidly learned, as William Todd already had, how to "mine" other resources as a rancher, butcher, and sawmill operator with extensive Trinity and Shasta holdings. His Grass Valley Creek sawmill furnished the lumber for many a Weaverville home. The Goetzes' son Bill went into business with his father and married Clara "Tody" Boyce, the daughter of a local livery stable owner and stagecoach driver. The couple moved into his parents' home after their marriage and kept it in the family until a widowed Clara entered a rest home in 1981 at age 96.

The younger Goetzes started the Snug Ice Cream Parlor on Main Street in the summer of 1922—a natural outlet for Clara, who specialized in making yummy desserts. Neighbors often saw her riding a horse, reins held between her teeth, with an apple pie in each hand to deliver to some fortunate family. After preparing the apples, handpicked from trees in her yard, and rolling out the crust, she added a special spice in the form of "red-hots."

The Goetze House, 313 Taylor Street, as it appeared near the time of its completion in 1897 by H. W. Goetze, who used lumber from his mill near Buckhorn Mountain. (RRS photo)

For about a decade (1987–96) the Goetze House maintained its reputation for fine foods thanks to an older couple who converted it into a Bed and Breakfast place. They refurbished the home with antiques and old photographs. Dressed in 19th-century fashion, they played the part of the people who once lived there while serving fresh fruit, homemade sausage, and eggs Benedict. One autumn Granny and Papa graciously hosted a writers' workshop for a group of HSU students and shared with them a recipe for **Lemon Curd**—a fine spread for anything from asparagus to French toast:

> Beat 6 eggs in a blender until they are light and fluffy. Mix 2 cups of sugar and 1 cup of fresh lemon juice, adding the mix in small amounts to the eggs. Pour 1 cup of melted butter very slowly into the egg mix while running the blender. Put the lemon curd in a double boiler over boiling water and cook it for 15-20 minutes while it thickens, stirring occasionally. Store it in sterile jars and keep it refrigerated for up to three weeks.

11. St. Patrick's Catholic Church and Cemetery (Court and Church streets)

Weaverville's Catholic Church and Cemetery look down upon Court and Taylor streets from what was originally known as "Graveyard Hill." The first few graves were moved to the public cemetery while miners dug for gold. When the hill failed to yield any nuggets it reclaimed its earlier function well before San Francisco's archbishop arrived in June of 1855 to "confirm some 19 at Weaverville and bless the new church under the name of the Most Holy Trinity [or Godhead] and also the Graveyard. Much attendance & piety, thank God." Fires, however, claimed the church and three subsequent ones built on the same site. The present one dates from 1924 and features an unusual false-front steeple entry adorned with battlements, almost as if it feared another fire.

Most of the cemetery's gravestones face east, making it easier to read the weathered inscriptions in the morning than later in the day. To judge by the legible names, painstakingly compiled by Pat ("I collect facts") Hicks, residents from Ireland (including Eliza Todd) appear to outnumber those from German states, but even France, Croatia, and the Azores are represented. The tilted stones, broken crosses, and rusty wrought-iron fences combine to give the cemetery a certain melancholy.

12. Regan House (217 Court Street) An 1897 fire leveled several homes on the south side of Court Street, all of which were soon replaced with more substantial structures. The architecturally most striking one was built in 1901 by Daniel J. Hall, who had come to Trinity County as a teacher a decade earlier and later won office as District Attorney. After his wife died he sold the house to Horace R. Given, also a teacher-turned-D.A., who lived there for 30 years before selling it to the honorable Edwin J. Regan, yet another D.A. This attorneys' Queen Anne, with its widow's walk, central turret, and gazebo, ranks as Weaverville's most stylish Victorian—a house that in the eyes of an early observer "should stand on a corner instead of in the middle of the block." (The county bought the corner lot at Court Street and Main as a public plaza in 1877 but built no permanent bandstand until the turn of the century. The community restored it for the Bicentennial.)

13. Weaverville Drug Store (219 Main Street) The only building in Weaverville that has not changed its function over the past century and a half began as a "Drug and Book Store," rebuilt in fireproof brick by Dr. H. B. Davison in 1856. It has had many different names and owners, among the latter Louis Wellendorf—described by Frank Buck as "a gay and festive cuss" who "sold all out the other day" [September 1864], apparently because "He was getting altogether too intimate with a certain Secesh family...." (He moved to Shasta and later Redding.) But two families—first the

Two Weaverville walkers pass by the Bowie House, 219 Court Street. (Robin Stocum photo)

Barnickels and then the Hickses (including Mr. Hicks's parents)—have owned the business for more than 50 years each.

The sundry owners have from time to time remodeled the store and changed its sundries, but they have always carried drugs and, except during Prohibition, liquors and wines. Early druggists even "installed a soda fountain for medicinal beverages just inside the entrance" but, alas, had difficulty competing with increasingly popular ice cream parlors. The current owners, the self-styled "Two Hicks," have tried to preserve the flavor of an antique apothecary by hanging gas-light-type fixtures on the high ceiling and by displaying on the top shelves a collection of tools, jars, and glass bottles from earlier eras.

14. New York Hotel (and Saloon) (225-27 South Main) Believe it or not, this hotel—except for its lack of an outside spiral staircase—was once a mirror image of the Buck and Cole Building across the street. For half a century or so it served as the town's main stop for stagecoaches arriving from Shasta County, with the hotel connected to the adjoining Elite Saloon by an archway in 1902. A new owner and a new transportation era resulted in major "modernization" in the early 1930s. Arches were added above the entrance and across the saloon-cum-card room, and both the front and top of the building were squared off—in an attempt to give the 12-room hotel a "Mission" look not unlike that of the much larger Redding Hotel. Since no other Main Street struc-

tures followed suit, at least not in the same style, the New York Hotel became something of an architectural misfit. In the 1990s a group of longtime Weaverites acquired the historic hotel in large part for the purpose of restoring it to some semblance of its former self. It now has its "natural" cinnabar color, a façade sans arches, and antiqued rooms.

15. Old Fire House (307 South Main) After several fires had ravaged Main Street in the 1850s and 1860s, a few Chinese decided to fortify their store-homes by tamping damp red clay—"rammed earth"—reinforced with an occasional oak limb. They added iron doors to their adobes and a foot of soil above the ceiling. The shake roofs might burn, but everything else would escape damage. Four structures in a row survived the Chinatown fires of 1874 and 1905. But only this Old Fire House still stood after a 1977 blaze—probably a result of luck unrelated to the fact that the Weaverville Fire Department had used the old dwelling as its firehouse from 1910 until 1949. The town recognized its importance as a rare example of rammed earth construction and acted to protect its exposed south side and restore its rustic wooden siding façade, even though the building no longer has a function.

16. Pacific Brewery (401 South Main) In 1902, a U.S. Health Bulletin asserted that "During the heated season people need a cooling bracing beverage." According to the same bulletin, a Dr. Amos Gray of New York City had "just completed an unbiased and disinter-

ested analysis into many brands of beer" and concluded "the best to be the beer from Meckel Brothers Brewery of Weaverville." The Pacific Brewery dates from the mid-1850s after Frederick Walter had struck it rich enough in nearby Ten Cent Gulch to fund such an enterprise. A decade or so later he sold his business to the seemingly ubiquitous Henry Lorenz (and several other Germans), who ventured into hydraulic mining in the Red Hill region not long before John and Christian Meckel, brewers at the town of North Fork (Helena), decided to end their partnership. In 1878, John bought the Pacific Brewery from Lorenz and moved his family into a home on Center Street just behind the business. The *Braumeister* advertised in the *Trinity Journal* that he would deliver Meckel beer in five- or ten-gallon kegs, free of charge! After John's death in 1889, his sons changed the company's name to Meckel Brothers Brewery, and they prospered until Prohibition forced them to shut down 30 years later. The building and its equipment remained unused until the 1970s when a Junction City couple bought the brewery, remodeled it into a restaurant, and restored its original name. They also preserved the bar, where folks could buy almost any kind of beer but a Meckel brew. Present patrons probably still wonder how pure and bracing the original beverage was as they eye the ten-gallon keg or 22-ounce brown bottles, which date back to the mellow Meckel years when large locust trees kept the brewery cool.

A Romantic Ride to Weaver Bally

While growing up in Junction City and Weaverville, Henry Meckel kept wanting to see the romantic-sounding glass house that the Forest Service had mounted atop Weaver Bally as a fire lookout in the 1910s. Finally, as a high school freshman, he and a few friends climbed the peak that "hangs" almost a vertical mile above Weaver Basin. Once at the top they asked the lookout if he ever got lonesome. "Oh no," he replied, "I've got chipmunks and deer and at night I watch the trains going up and down the Valley."

Soon after his wedding in the Bay Area, Meckel decided to initiate his bride to Trinity County by treating her to a one-day horseback ride (a 22-mile roundtrip) to the Weaver Bally Lookout. They carried food and mail to the lookout and visited with him at length. She (and he) never forgot that trip, unaccustomed as both of them were to horseback riding.

The Forest Service built a new lookout in 1936 and placed it directly on the peak to improve the view of Trinity Canyon. (The 1936 lookout's cab was airlifted off to the Weaver USFS yard in the mid-1990s after the present lookout was built; plans call for setting up the old cab at the Hayfork Fairgrounds.) Twenty years later the Forest Service combined with the Southern Pacific Land Company to construct a Weaver Bally Road all the way to the top. The panorama of Trinity County's Shangri-La that Weaver Bally provides, even without a glass house, needs no ballyhoo. From the peak one can take a short trail down through stands of pine, fir, and cedar to East Weaver Lake, the town's first icemaker and still an important source of its water.

The "romantic" road is passable for 4WD vehicles in dry weather. After checking route conditions at the Forest Service ranger district office (located on the south side of Highway 299 near the north end of Weaverville), take the Trinity High School turnoff a quarter mile westward. If romantic drives have no appeal, then head up Highway 299 to Oregon Mountain.

Atop Weaver Bally and between his legs, photographer Robin Stocum caught Wally Kibbee— at age 84— showing him how to cross-country ski. (Robin Stocum photo)

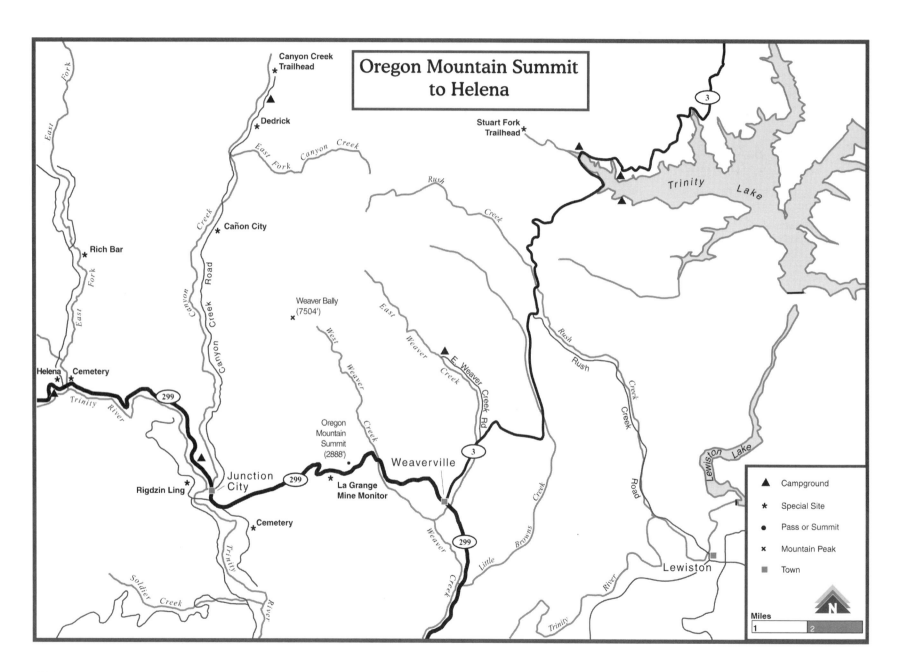

Oregon Mountain Summit to Helena

Canyon Creek Trailhead

Dedrick

East Fork Canyon Creek

Canyon Creek

Rush Creek

Stuart Fork Trailhead

Trinity Lake

3

Cañon City

Canyon Creek Road

Rich Bar

East Fork

East Fork

Weaver Bally (7504')

East Weaver Creek

Rush Creek

Helena

Cemetery

Trinity River

299

West Weaver Creek

E. Weaver Creek

E. Weaver Creek Rd

Rush Creek Road

Lewiston Lake

Oregon Mountain Summit (2888')

Weaver Creek

Weaverville

3

Junction City

299

La Grange Mine Monitor

Rigdzin Ling

Cemetery

Browns Creek

Little Browns

Weaver Creek

299

Lewiston

Soldier Creek

Trinity River

Trinity River

▲ Campground

★ Special Site

● Pass or Summit

✕ Mountain Peak

■ Town

N

Miles
1   2

104

IV. Dropping Down Oregon Gulch to the Trinity River

La Grande La Grange

Just west of Highway 299's Oregon Mountain Summit, a large, orange-brown object reposes in rusty decay by the roadside. Looking somewhat like the nozzle of a giant garden hose, it serves as a monument to Trinity County's hydraulic mining history, the foremost piece of artillery in an arsenal of weapons used to wrest the mineral wealth from the region's retentive landscape. Its story starts more than a century ago, in the alpine mountain fastness many miles to the north…

The snow that fell on Sawtooth Ridge, high in the Trinity Alps, during the winter of 1897–98 began its career much like the snow of any other year, providing a crystalline cover on the craggy line of peaks above the headwaters of the Stuart Fork of the Trinity River. Come spring, it melted, as expected, and flowed down into Upper Lake and Lower Lake, at the head of the Stuart Fork Canyon. There it mingled with the water that had wintered in the lakes and began its journey down canyon, passing through the pastures of Morris Meadows before meeting the flow of a major tributary, Deer Creek.

And here, in mid-April 1898, occurred an event never before experienced in the count-less years of the canyon's existence. Suddenly some of the water no longer continued down the ancient bed of the river, but instead flowed into a channel of fresh-cut wood, soon slowing its pace as it followed the nearly level course of the flume that now ran across the eastern side of the canyon. Only much later, after a run of some nine miles, did the water finally fall, rushing down half of an almost mile-long inverted siphon with force enough to carry it up the other side and into another flume. The water saw sunlight for another mile and a half before moving into the mountainside, churning through a six-by-seven-foot tunnel for more than 8,000 feet. After sixteen more miles of flumes, tunnels, and siphons, the erstwhile snow of Sawtooth Ridge finally reached a temporary resting place—a reservoir near the summit of Oregon Mountain. The trip from the diversion at Deer Creek had taken nine hours.

The stay at the reservoir was brief, for the water's elemental energy was constantly needed to feed the enormous iron nozzles that pointed at the canyonside below. Pushed through these "monitors" by the gravitational force of its drop from the reservoir, the water slammed into the western side of Oregon Mountain, breaking apart and carrying away gold-bearing strata held fast for millennia by a tenacious geologic glue.

On and on the monitors blasted, twenty-four hours a day, with as many as three nozzles attacking the slope at once. If a boulder proved too big for water power, a heavy-duty derrick might remove the rock or a dynamite charge would blast it to bits. Nothing lasted for long; over the next 20 years the monitors and their helpers moved an average of more than a thousand cubic yards of mountainside a day, for a time making the site the largest hydraulic mine in the nation. If there is grandeur in destructive force, then the La Grange Mine was truly *la grande*.

James Ward, an early-day Trinitarian, had seen enough glittering grandeur in the site to mine the mountain at least minimally from the early 1850s to 1872, when he sold out to the Trinity Gold Mining Company, run by Peter M. Paulsen and Orange M. Loveridge of Weaverville. The new owners realized the need for water power to pry loose the paydirt but lacked the funds to make more than a token effort. Little happened until 1893, when a syndicate of French noblemen, led by the Baron Ernest de La Grange, purchased the mine for $250,000.

The Trinity Adventures of Two French Aristocrats

French aristocrats would reap [immense advantages] by expatriating themselves more often.

—Baroness Clémentine de La Grange

In 1884, soon after his return from two years of hunting and trapping in Canada, Baron Ernest de La Grange married a daughter of the Parisian Marquise de Chaumont-Quity. Less than a decade later the adventurous couple decided to "take [their] gold out of the bank...to buy another supply of it...where it lies buried beneath the sand." But they made their fateful decision only after first checking out opportunities in the American West, beginning in Colorado. Accompanied by their two children (ages six and four), a governess, and a coach-man, they crossed a stormy Atlantic in late December of 1892 and caught a train in New York City bound for a still booming Denver. They spent the rest of the winter inspecting a number of mines and ranches within the state.

At first the La Granges leaned toward investing in livestock. Then, for some unspecified reason, "our enthusiasm for ranches has cooled off considerably." Moreover, "As if swept off our feet, we decide in no time at all to go with Mr. Beaudry, a [French] Canadian we met here [in Denver], on a trip to explore mines in Arizona, New Mexico, and California. [He] is well informed about the mining of auriferous quartz and hydraulic placers." Their month-long journey took them from Las Vegas, New Mexico to Weaverville and back to Denver via Los Angeles.

Friends and experts in Colorado advised the baron and his wife to invest in the Ward mine in Oregon Gulch, even though "it will require a lot of time and money." The couple returned to Paris to finalize financing of the project, but by June of 1893, they were back in Weaverville, where Beaudry had rented for them "the prettiest house in the City..., built of wood and set back a bit from the street, with a very rudimentary little wooden fence in front of it...." The baroness figured she could fit four such cottages into their French castle.

The La Granges spent much of their year in Trinity County expanding the Ward mine. They made no changes without first consulting experts and hiring the most qualified people they could recruit—many of them Frenchmen—to take charge of operations. To double the distance of the water ditch, by extending it from Rush Creek to Stuart Fork, the baron went to Paris to secure the support of the new company's stockholders. In his absence, the baroness acted as mine inspector, "riding around the mountains with my little chestnut horse...." To keep closer watch, she "set up a bedroom and a living room for myself in the house at the mine." Early the next year (1894), after "the Company decided to have a house built for us," she herself designed a "sturdy wooden *(continued next page)*

The Baron and Baroness La Grange with an unidentified companion on and beside la grande ditch, 1894. (TCHS photo)

107

...Trinity Adventures

structure" that was erected next to the workers' lodge in less than a month. That home predated the famous mansion or "castle" built for the general manager of the mine after the La Granges returned to France.

Conditions at the La Grange Mine must have offset the advantage of proximity, judging by some of the baroness's observations. The three monitors, she wrote, "sit like big cannons that haven't been loaded yet, aimed at the bedrock." They "are outdoing each other, and the mountain is crumbling and collapsing into a stream of liquid mud that is channeled into the long corridor of the sluice." She feared, quite rightly, that "a little village at the bottom of Oregon Gulch runs the risk of being buried when we run our operation full-scale."

In spite of the improved housing situation, Madame La Grange's hunger for adventure gradually waned. As she admitted, "Staying in this country requires a huge dose of courage: the summer's not too bad, but the winter is a real trial." To make matters worse, the baron-

ess discovered that "Weaverville offers no academic resources," not even for young children like hers. Thus within three months of moving into their new home next to the noisy mine, the expatriates set out for France—never to return to Trinity County.

When the baron died five years later, his father refused to let the baroness take over management of the mine and instead assumed control himself. Decades after her husband's death, she penned an account of their Trinity adventure based on letters she had written from Colorado and California to her sister and an aunt. In January 1998, her grandson, a distinguished French musicologist, visited Weaverville and delighted the Trinity County Historical Society by giving them a copy of her memoir (since translated into English by a Humboldt State University professor and published by the society). His gift also included an album of photos taken along the La Grange Ditch by a San Francisco photographer. The society, in response, surprised Professor Henry-Louis de La Grange by presenting him with a copy of the baron's application for U.S. citizenship, filed in Arapahoe County, Colorado, June 29, 1896. Perhaps the La Granges had further American adventures in mind after all.

Workers pause during construction of the Bridge Camp siphon, where the La Grange water supply crossed Stuart Fork. (TCHS photo)

Five years and another $450,000 later, the Baron began his high-stakes hydraulicking in earnest.

The summer following completion of the Stuart Fork diversion, La Grange and his family paid a visit to their estate near Itazelbrouch, France. From there word reached Trinity County that the Baron had been found dead one September morning, an apparent drowning victim. Only much later was it revealed that he may have committed suicide or been murdered by the husband of a woman with whom he was having an affair.

La Grange's father took over as president of the mining company. In 1901 Pierre Bouery became general manager and soon increased production at the mine. Bouery also busied himself improving his residence, the hillside-clinging "Castle." He installed fireplaces that contained imported tiles, procured stained glass windows, and sent to France for wallpaper. The Castle's wine cellar became famous, as did the dinners its contents accompanied.

In 1905 a group of East Coast capitalists bought controlling interest in the La Grange. They expanded the operation three years later by acquiring the Sweepstakes Mine, which was situated on the south side of Oregon Mountain.

All went well for a decade. Then World War I, in the midst of spreading its devastation across France, extended its impact across the sea to affect remote Trinity County. With workers scarce and materials for maintaining the water diversion more expensive than ever, the mine ceased operation.

New owners assumed control in the late 1920s. They reopened the mine just as the Depression hit and just as soon closed it up again. All remained quiet at the La Grange until 1934, when the whoosh of the monitors again rever-

Excavation of the La Grange Ditch began by harnessing horses to a scraper. "Notice," wrote the Baroness, "the first team, where the driver lifts the two shafts at the back so that the scraper cuts into the soil." (TCHS photo)

*The La Granges, right, survey their 87 workers dining alfresco
at their camp on the ditch site. (TCHS photo)*

berated through the canyon. The object this time was not high grade gravel but a low gradient highway—the nozzles now entered the employ of the state highway department; their assignment: to lower the elevation of Oregon Mountain so that autos could more easily surmount the summit. The monitors did the job, washing another 11,000,000 cubic yards off the top of topography, but a casualty of the operation was the "Castle," the manager's showpiece mansion that perched on the hillside beside the mine. Long disused, and stripped of its furniture and fixtures, the mountainside monument was removed in 1938 during work on the highway project.

The new nozzling more than doubled the debris load that filled the lower reaches of Oregon Gulch. In 1940, the mine owners engaged in a bit of early-day recycling by hydraulicking and dredging the gulch for any retrievable gold. The start of World War II closed the mine for the last time, leaving the La Grange to languish once again.

Today, more than half a century later, the La Grange Mine is little more than a memory. Motorists may pause on their way over Oregon Mountain Summit to peruse the rusting roadside monitor. A short distance down the road, an adventurous spirit may assay the few hundred feet of Castle Road that leads to the unmarked, now-empty site of the mine manager's mountainside mansion. Hikers along the Stuart Fork may wonder at the flume remnants that spread above the trail on the forested hillslope. And, farther up the river canyon, the snow will still fall on Sawtooth Ridge. After it melts, it may make its way to the fields of a Central Valley rice farmer, or it may wash a raft down the Trinity, but it will never again make the nine-hour trip into the waiting maw of a La Grange monitor. The days of Trinity County's grandest, most egregious, hydraulic mine have long since ended.

Ditches to the Riches

The 29-mile-long system of flumes, ditches, tunnels, and siphons that brought the water of Stuart Fork to the La Grange Mine was a masterpiece of late-19th-century engineering. Like many such creations, however, it required constant maintenance. Key to the system was a team of twenty dutiful ditch tenders, housed two to a cabin in ten cabins spaced evenly along the route. Every day the tenders patrolled two miles up and two miles down from their respective cabins, availing themselves of an emergency shack located at midroute when necessary. Each cabin featured a storeroom, stocked prior to winter with six months' food, and a telephone used for twice-daily communication with headquarters.

Some cabins were built directly over the ditch, and by opening a trap door in the floor a ditch tender could retrieve food and other supplies that were conveniently floated down to him. At least once the ditch carried a less convivial cargo—the body of a tender killed in the line of duty.

Modern-day mining enthusiasts

Englishman Ed Blunden, outside his La Grange ditch tender's Cabin No. 3, built in 1901–02 at Munger Gulch. Note ditch, behind Blunden, at lower right. (TCHS photo)

can recall a bit of the ditch tenders' history at two locations. A section of the Weaver Basin trail network north of Weaverville runs beside the remnants of the ditch/flume system that winds around part of Weaver Bally. And in Weaverville itself, an outdoor display at the museum features a reconstruction of ditch tender Ed Blunden's cabin. A visit to either site will rank with the original ditch as a worthwhile diversion.

A Junction, If Not a City

Never a municipality, but always amply fulfilling the rest of its name, Junction City early proved to be a place where everything from wagons and water to mule trains and miners crossed paths and congregated, met and mingled, and otherwise helped make this creekside community what the *Trinity Journal* in 1895 called "the liveliest town in the county." The area's activity was noted as early as 1852, when Isaac Cox came though what was then known as Milltown to cross the Trinity River on John Hocker's ferry. Cox found some 150 to 200 white miners busily at work in the area and about half as many Chinese.

Such a spot was surely a place of promise, and by 1857 the *Journal* was predicting "that Milltown will be the county seat of Trinity before three years, for it is the richest, cleanest, and most central place in the county." In only *two* years the town's status had increased immensely as the Oregon Gulch wagon road and the road to North Fork (Helena) were connected by a route through what now, courtesy of the county Board of Supervisors, bore the tongue-twisting name "Mouth of Canyon Creek." Fortunately the opening of a new post office in 1861 provided a chance for a higher authority to overrule the county's designation, and this the United States Postal Service, mindful of the recent meeting of roads, did by approving "Junction City."

The paint was hardly dry on the new P. O.'s signboard before the great December flood of 1861 wet the town up a bit, washing away anything too close to the unexpectedly expanded Trinity. According to the *Journal* the river at Junction City "became an ocean, spreading from mountain to mountain, sweeping in its furious current farm houses, miners' cabins, mills, men, women and children; in very truth, all that was animate and inanimate." What nature failed to accomplish with its use of water the local miners soon achieved, as the hydraulic nozzles of the Chapman and Given mine began, in 1870, to remove the placer deposits of what then became known as the "Bedrock" area of town (the benchland over which Dutch Creek Road now departs Highway 299).

A year later the boom came not from the water-spewing monitors but from the town's cannon, which had been hauled to the top of Hager and Haas's hill by the local German population. Once there, it was fired until its ammunition ran out (150 shots in all) to celebrate the fall of Paris during the Franco-Prussian War. The popping continued late into the night as Louis Raab donated two baskets of his champagne to the cause, allowing a final firing of a 24-cork salute.

Later that year the still-expansive Raab expanded his mercantile activities by adding a dry-goods department to his grocery business. By then the town's other two merchants also needed to increase their stock, and the 11-year-old Carter House had secured its reputation as a fine hostelry. For all that, Peter Verstegen's "bit-house" was perhaps the most enthusiastically patronized of Junction City's establishments, and it was here that the then-outlandish sum of $116 was won on a single hand of draw poker. With George Grover holding four aces and a nine to beat his opponent's four fours and an eight, it was no wonder the pot grew so large.

Junction City's heyday stretched on through the years, so that on May 20, 1874, the *Journal* was able to report:

A Lively Day. For a small town, Junction City contains a great deal of real life, as witness the following record of last Sunday's doings at that place: The morning hours were enjoyed by the populace in such exhilarating exercises as leapfrog, running, jumping, etc.; singing school at 12:30; Good Templars meeting at 3; preaching at early candlelight; minstrel performance at 8; dance at 11; and at midnight Louis Raab and John Arn were the only sober men in town—so Louis says.

Was it the same *Journal* that less than three months later, on August 1, complained:

> Things Aren't Quite What They Used To Be....Although business is good and money plenty, the old-time life seems to have departed in a good measure. The boys are getting old, like ourself [*sic*], and have settled down to quiet everyday life. The thrilling notes of fife and drum are no more heard, the bloodcurdling Apache war-whoop has fallen into disuse, tricks upon travelers have been abandoned, *leap frog is no more indulged in by the populace...* (emphasis added)

Perhaps the writer was despondent over the loss of Louis Raab's store, which Raab had recently sold. Even so, Peter Verstegen's establishment was still open for business, where he now offered "the best wines, liquors and cigars for one bit." And for the miners, "it had been a good water-season" and things were certainly looking up: "More gold dust will be taken out than in any two previous years."

Hydraulic mining received another boost in 1880, when Albert Hayes bought a stretch of properties on Red Hill, across the river; built a water ditch down Canyon Creek; and then, in a climactic finale, constructed an elaborate, two-towered bridge to transport the water across the Trinity to his new mine.

Come the Fourth of July in 1894 and the Hayes Mine's fortunes momentarily ebbed as its tug-of-war team lost to Junction City's own stalwarts, who, after tugging for three hours, had managed to move the rope in their direction all of 23 inches. Perhaps mourning the loss, Hayes sold the mine that year to a group of French capitalists, who renamed it the Compagnie Française des Placers Hydrauliques de Junction City, which the locals quickly shortened to Cie Fse.

In 1889 a Chinese child playing with matches ignited Junction City's Chinatown, which promptly burned to the ground. Eight years later about one-third of the whites' section of the community conflagrated in spectacular fashion. (*See sidebar, next page.*)

The smoke had barely dissipated before the community was busy rebuilding. Chinatown,

The Cie Fse mine crew, not all of them young, at Junction City, 1897. (TCHS photo)

The Surprise Store's Final Surprise

At two o'clock on a September morning in 1897, Frank Flagg was asleep on the ground floor of the Abrahm & Karsky Company's Surprise Store in Junction City. Upstairs, Ben Abrahm also sweetly slumbered. Twenty minutes later, both men were in the street, Flagg sporting a set of cuts and bruises and Abrahm with "little more on than his night shirt." Their places in the store had been taken by a set of wildly dancing flames.

The alarm soon roused the rest of the town to fight the fire. Although there was no breeze, the recent dry weather had rendered the buildings "like tinder," so that not only was the Surprise Store soon "wrapped in flames," but the Day residence and the Bradbury & Hagelman hotel were also alight. Now the fire crossed Main Street, engulfing the Hutchins and Murphy saloon, Joseph Smith's blacksmith shop, three of Blake & Reed's buildings, and three residences. Just when it appeared that the rest of lower Junction City was about to go, the crew from the Cie Fse Mine arrived, and with their help, the Temperance Hall and the Douglas house were saved. By now, however, a wind had sprung up, and attention turned to the upper end of town. Men climbed to the rooftops with wet blankets and water to douse the "blazing cinders [that] fell in showers." Finally the wind shifted and the danger was over.

In a little over an hour, the fire had reduced Junction City by a third. The Surprise Store was in ashes, but in its last act it had more than lived up to its name.

---

the victim of the earlier fire, had also reestablished itself, and here smoke of a different kind was often in evidence. Warren Gilzean, a youngster at the time, would visit the Chinese section (located near the current post office and store) and observe the men lying on their bunks, pipe in hand, wreathed in opium-scented clouds. Almost without exception each man had a cat perched upon his chest.

The first decade of the new century brought its own devastating fire. This time a heavy wind and the absence of most of the male populace, which was away at the mines, caused about half of the town to burn. Many of the residents had had enough of such inconvenient incinerations; they chose not to rebuild and departed Junction City instead, leaving behind a smoldering monument of charred timbers, twisted water pipes, and assorted debris.

The town's troubles doubled when the Cie Fse Mine then closed, causing another exodus from the community as a large contingent of newly unemployed miners left. The downward turn continued into the next decade, when, in 1919, the Bartlett Hotel burned and the Weaverville Supply Company closed its doors. A further blow was struck, oddly, by the completion of the Trinity River highway in the 1920s, which, by speeding travel, reduced Junction City's importance as a stopover place.

A glimmer of rejuvenation shone in the summer of 1937 when the nearby La Grange and Bergin mines served as locations for *Gold Is Where You Find It*, starring Olivia de Havilland and George Brent. All too soon, though, the film crew returned to Tinseltown, leaving Trinity old-timers to scoff at the moviemakers' inaccurate rendering of mining activities when it subsequently appeared in celluloid.

The following year saw the construction of the second Junction City School; then, according to a commemorative listing of the town's "major events," nothing of consequence occurred for half a century, until 1988, when the old Cie Fse Mine property was purchased for conversion into Rigdzin Ling, a Buddhist retreat and conference center. The completion of the third Junction City School in 1990 dominated the next decade.

Visitors to contemporary Junction City will find a handful of highwayside businesses catering to the needs of tourists and locals, but, except for a rusting hydraulic monitor next to the market, there is little along the main thoroughfare to recall the town's history. A turn onto locust-lined Canyon Creek Road, however, takes us along what was once known as

Main Street past the community's often-photographed icon, the Junction City Hotel. This aging, sagging structure still bears its final name across the top of its false front; below, the galvanized metal porch roof has been bent into a series of serrations that resemble a damaged saw blade. Above the north end of the porch, another faded sign, "B & R Co. Store," attests to the building's earlier service for merchants Blake and Reed. An open front door reveals a litter of old furniture and the detritus of decades of neglect. The sides of the building have settled in drunken disarray, the shiplap siding rising and falling in the undulations that precede eventual collapse. We behold the hotel with a sense of foreboding, realizing that Junction City's last great link to its past perches precariously above the abyss of architectural oblivion.

We have only to glance across the street to see the first manifestations of the town's future. Here the squat blocks of the Fill-More Storage facility rise like oversized, unsettlingly symmetrical tailings piles above the nearby bed of Canyon Creek. The buildings occupy the site of the Bartlett Saloon, where, during the 1900s and 1910s, bartender Fred K. Reed tended to the bibbing needs of travelers, locals, and miners; the latter would in summer migrate down from the mountains for a week or so, staying at the nearby Bartlett Hotel while they placed orders at one of the town's two supply stores and frequented Fred's establishment. But times change, and where Reed once dispersed drunks, Fill-More patrons now deposit trunks.

Junction City, it appears, has come full circle in the near century and a half of its existence: the town now serves as a place to store, rather than extract, valuables. "Gold," as the movie title indicated, "is where you find it." But where it, or its finders, are no longer to be found, the transition from Junction City Hotel to Fill-More Storage is the result.

Junction City side trips from Highway 299:

1. A turn south onto Dutch Creek Road leads past the second Junction City School and across the Trinity River to a junction with Red Hill Road, right, at mile 0.5. A right turn here will bring interested parties to the driveways for Rigdzin Ling, left at 0.1 and 0.3 mile (*see "From Minescape to Mindscape," page 116*).

2. A turn north onto Canyon Creek Road (*see "Canyon Creek Road," page 121*) commences a 13-mile meander into remote mining country that terminates at the Canyon Creek trailhead (*see "Trinity Trailway," page 125*).

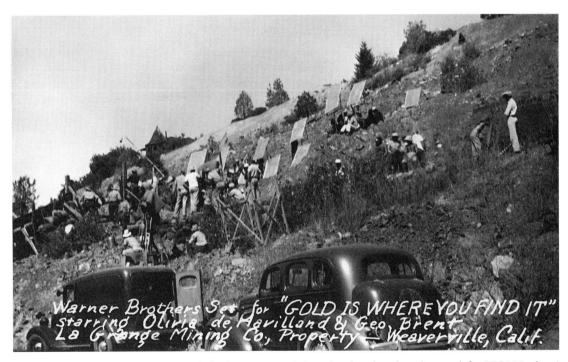

Hollywood comes to the La Grange hillside, setting up below the abandoned castle, rear left. (TCHS photo)

115

From Minescape to Mindscape: Cie Fse vs. Rigdzin Ling

Almost a century after miners of the Cie Fse had disappeared from the scene of Junction City's biggest boom, a Buddhist meditation master appeared in this tranquil town along the Trinity River. His Eminence Chagdud Tulku Rinpoche came in search of land on which he could build a retreat and conference center. He arrived with a few students at a site off Red Hill Road to find a landscape still scarred by the Cie Fse's mining—hills stripped bare to bedrock, gulches further gullied by monitors, and flats piled high with tailings from river dredging. While there, in that unlikely place, Chagdud Rinpoche foresaw the creation of Rigdzin Ling. He and his students could change this "minescape" into a "mindscape" and reclaim some of the region's sublime beauty by creating a Tibetan treasure in Trinity County.

The southwestern or Red Hill side of the Trinity River played a pivotal role in the rise of Junction City. As early as 1867, the *Trinity Journal* observed that "There were more good-paying mining claims in the vicinity of Junction City than any other place in the county." This fact reinforced the town's junction function and made possible its rapid growth in the era of hydraulic mining. Sluicing to wash away the red hills along the Trinity River began in the 1870s, but large-scale operations had to await the arrival of Dr. Albert Hayes, a mining investor from Boston, in the autumn of 1880.

Until then, mines in the area operated without any significant capital from outside sources. Hayes purchased two of the bigger ones and filed several claims along the Red Hill side of the Trinity. After acquiring rights to Canyon Creek water, he had a pipeline constructed to siphon it over the high ridge between the two streams. According to local historian Henry Meckel, "Almost immediately, the Hayes mine became a major engineering project…[with] a great ditch…dug from the top of the mountainous cliffs above Junction City to a dam near Canyon City 8.4 miles from the mouth of the creek." When completed in 1884, this "Great Suspension" bridge stretched 350 feet across the Trinity, carrying Canyon Creek's water with phenomenal pressure to the Red Hill claims.

Within a decade Hayes had 100 men in his employ, but in spite of the mine's apparent success, he sold out in 1894 to some of the same French capitalists who were investing in other Trinity mines, notably the nearby La Grange and the Beaudry (located at Minersville above Lewiston).

La Compagnie Française des Placers Hydrauliques de Junction City—mercifully shortened to Cie Fse—bought the Hayes property and its pipelines for a reported $250,000. Included were 1,200 acres of mining claims, an elaborate network of water ditches, and an assortment of buildings, machines, and livestock. The French Company, not to be outdone by the La Grange, soon invested an additional $200,000 to improve their hydraulic enterprise.

This French-funded mining boom made Junction the "liveliest city" in Trinity County and gave the rowdy town at least a tinge of Parisian culture. Monsieur Edouard Saladin arrived in May 1894 (a year after the La Granges), accompanied by his wife and two young daughters. The *Trinity Journal* described the Cie Fse's overseer as "A civil engineer by profession…[who] stands among the first in France. He has been the head of numerous highly important enterprises." Life for the Saladins in a mining camp so far removed from their aristocratic roots must have been trying, but they responded by building a handsome home and hosting lavish dinners, especially when visited by countrymen. For instance, in the summer of 1895 they held a grand public ball to honor an important stockholder and his party. "The dance took place in a large open building lighted by two arc lights…Music for the dance was provided by a 'full orchestra.' Food and wine were liberally served at a long counter and dancing continued until 4 o'clock in the morning." Sadly, such events lasted only a few years before they were terminated by a family tragedy. (*See sidebar, next page.*)

After the Cie Fse's installation of a new ditch, flume, and piping system, the *Trinity Journal* described Saladin's mine as "one of the largest operations of that kind ever inaugurated in the state." The new ditch ran 11 miles, and the new siphon stretched over a mile in crossing the Trinity River Valley. Each section of iron pipe was hauled in piece by piece from Redding, some weighing as much as 3,340 pounds.

The Cie Fse Mine managed quite well without Saladin for a few years. An electrical lighting system allowed the sluicing of Red Hill to continue at night. But by 1904 profits had dropped enough that the company decided to sell off its properties, mostly in small parcels.

The Cie Fse pipeline and swinging bridge, which crossed the Trinity a half mile downriver from Junction City. It carried water from upper Canyon Creek to the hydraulic mine on Red Hill. (TCHS photo)

Businessmen from San Francisco and Eureka purchased the Cie Fse's water rights and built a power house just two miles downriver from Junction City (just south of Power House Road). For several years the North Mountain Power Company supplied electricity from distant Canyon Creek for Eureka's new streetcars.

As the Cie Fse Mine (and later the La Grange) faded into memory, the Junction City area lapsed into rustic tranquility. But the mine lingered on in the minds of those whose lives were changed by it. The Saladins' eldest daughter returned to Junction City in 1978 (accompanied by her daughter Marguerite) to see where she had spent a few years before her mother's death. Madame Rabout remembered "very little of those days except riding her pony through the hills and going with her father to the mining sites." However, she recognized the fact that "Rowdy mining towns have become quiet rural communities."

Try to imagine her reaction had she crossed the Trinity River bridge at the south end of Junction City, turned right on Red Hill Road, and then seen (on the left side) a sign painted with a dragon marking the entrance to Rigdzin Ling. The dirt drive winds up through pine trees past a rushing creek before reaching an old ranch house that once belonged to a Mrs. Estelle Stevens. The setting of this renamed "Creek House" gives little inkling of the minescape wrought by hydraulic monitors down on the main grounds of Rigdzin Ling.

Directly below Creek House are the main offices of the Chagdud Gonpa Foundation—founded in 1983 by Chagdud Tulku Rinpoche as a center for the study of Vajrayana Buddhism in the American West. The Vajrayana path, as practiced in Tibet and neighboring countries, represents the ultimate thought and intentions of the Buddha. These were the teachings that he gave his most advanced disciples to achieve enlightenment. In transplanting this tradition to the United States, the Foundation first established itself in Cottage Grove, Oregon. When it outgrew that place it purchased 268 acres of Red Hill land, some of it from the estate of the late Estelle Stevens, whose house became the group's primary residence when Chagdud Rinpoche arrived in 1989. Prior to 1959, he had served as the abbot of the original Chagdud Gonpa—a Buddhist monastery founded in 1311 in eastern Tibet. With the Chinese Communists' occupation of his homeland, he fled to India and Nepal, where he helped with the administration of refugee camps. Eventually, with the encouragement of American students of Buddhism, he decided to make the United States his home.

Developing the former Cie Fse property into a Buddhist retreat required the removal of mine tailings and the trucking in of topsoil. The movers created a large flat beneath the pine-

The Saladins' Tragedy

Even as the Cie Fse enlarged and refined its mining operation, the Saladin family moved into a new home—perched on Benjamin Flat above the minty waters of the Trinity. Marguerite herself designed the home and had it landscaped with lovely gardens and locust trees. When she became pregnant again, her mother traveled from France to assist the family. "Notwithstanding the loving care lavished upon her and the scientific attention she received," Marguerite died while giving birth to a third daughter on July 7, 1898. On the same day Madame Saladin passed away, the *Trinity Journal* also reported a fatality from a gunshot wound, a Chinese miner crushed in a slide, a death from tuberculosis, and another due to exhaustion. All were grim reminders of the risks involved in living on a mining frontier, far from the best medical care available.

Monsieur Saladin thought his wife might have survived had they been living in France. His mother-in-law departed heartbroken with her three granddaughters to lay Marguerite's body to rest in the family's homeland. After seeing them off by train in Oakland, Edouard returned to Junction City to conclude business at the mine before making his own departure. As he left, he expressed doubt that he would ever return to Trinity County.

lined red bluffs as a sacred site for Rigdzin Ling. Construction of its centerpiece began soon after Chagdud Rinpoche's arrival. Named for the Buddhist goddess of loving kindness, the Tara House resembles a traditional Tibetan *lha khang*, or "house of the deities," but cost considerations ruled out the building of a larger and more elaborate edifice. The house, completed in 1994, functions as the main conference center; it has a commercial-grade kitchen and rooms for guests. The main hall is decorated with Tibetan designs across the ceiling and often filled with the scent of coconut butter lamps. One wall holds a grand glass case filled with golden-colored statues of the Buddha and sundry deities; offerings are placed on a long shelf below the case. Prayers, accompanied by various instruments, are practiced daily in this room, which also contains texts and liturgies. On the third floor, beneath the pagoda-shaped roof, is Rinpoche's residence.

Northeast of Tara House, members of Chagdud Gonpa are creating a park-like setting for meditation—where a large and elaborate wheel spins 10 times a minute, 24 hours a day, sending out 600 million *mantras* or prayers for world peace. It stands at the center of 8 dome-shaped monuments, or *stupas*, each of them 20 feet high. A stupa houses precious relics and spiritual texts, making it a place where students of Buddhism can find inspiration. The sacred substances within the stupas "have been imbued with prayers on behalf of all living beings, and carry a force of immeasurable benefit for all those with connection to it."

Next to the stupas stands an exquisite statue of Guru Rinpoche, the enlightened master who introduced Buddhism to Tibet. It sits on a lotus pedestal rising from a pond with water streaming from the flower in the four cardinal directions. At night—beneath the pagoda-shaped roof—the statue is lit by a few of the visible lights on the property.

Behind the stupas stands a bank of prayer flags that ripple and roar in the north wind, sending out blessings of enlightened speech. Barely visible from this place of meditation are the often snowcapped tops of the Trinity Alps. Volunteer artists and workers have fashioned this "mindscape" to bring forth the vision of Chagdud Rinpoche and to benefit all who come here to relax and stretch their minds.

Chagdud Gonpa Foundation has set aside specific parts of its property for meditation. Access is restricted to those seeking retreat, often for weeks or months, so they can rest in silent meditation and receive teachings from the resident lama. Sometimes the entire area is off limits to visitors, so anyone wanting to visit Rigdzin Ling should call the administrative office in advance at (530) 623-2714 for permission and directions.

The foundation has reached out to the larger community by donating land for the new Junction City elementary school—located on the same site as the Saladin home—and by offering public lectures on Buddhism to various groups in Trinity County.

This once lunar landscape, made unnatural by the Cie Fse's mining, has since returned to a more natural state wherever it can. Nurtured by the topsoil brought in to cover the bedrock, the lawn that surrounds Tara House is the only place where grass now grows. Swallows congregate here in the spring, while overhead onyx-black ravens fly year round. In the evening, as bright stars pierce the increasing darkness, thousands of frogs chant their own mantras from the ponds beneath the pines.

Making the vision of Rigdzin Ling a reality is an ongoing process. Just beyond the peacock pen near Tara House, a little lake offers swimmers relief from the summer heat. The island at the lake's center will be the site of a temple. With the importing of more soil, gardens will grow fresh vegetables for the kitchen. Once the remaining tailings are hauled away, perhaps fruit trees will again blossom along the banks of the Trinity, as they did before mining companies bought up scattered ranches to sluice and dredge for gold.

Rigdzin Ling has brought to Junction City a non-metallic kind of attraction. The new "gold" sought here is mined through meditation, discipline, and compassion. This remote place once again draws seekers from around the world—this time devotees of Guru Rinpoche and Vajrayana Buddhism. They aim to give life to traditions passed down through generations of Tibetan Buddhists. Their efforts have replaced many of the Red Hill region's receding scars with a mindscape of meditative qualities.

The powerhouse for the North Mountain Power Company, northwest of Junction City. The station, located just east of Highway 299 on Power House Road, was abandoned after the 1955 flood. (TCHS photo)

Canyon Creek Road: Access to the Trinity Alps

Travelers along the Trinity Highway will find their closest access to the Trinity Alps Wilderness via an approach route rich in both mining lore and scenic splendor. Paved Canyon Creek Road runs some 13 miles up the lower part of the streamcourse, passing flower-covered cliffs, mine tailings that stretch like giant molehills, and cabins that cling to the steep canyonsides. Hikers will find the road a pleasing prelude to the charms of the Trinity high country.

Canyon Creek Road departs from Highway 299 in downtown Junction City, running northward beneath a bower of large locust trees. On the right is the picturesquely delapidated former Junction City Hotel.

The route presently exits the community, winding its way up the open canyon; Dalmatian toadflax, California poppy, and lupine line the roadside. On the small flat, mile 1.1, left, the house of miner Dan Dedrick once stood. A scattering of fruit trees recalls the site's one-time appellation: "the Apples." Dedrick and other prospectors established several of the region's most productive mines far up the canyon, and

a town named for him subsequently sprang up near the end of the road. The mining proved so successful that by the late 1890s the Redding *Searchlight* claimed that "[n]o tributary of the Trinity has a richer record than Canyon Creek." By then, the estimated take was some six to ten million dollars. The paper also noted the hold that mining fever had on some of the residents, citing Rollin Smith, 81, who had left his family and job in New York some 45 years earlier and never returned. Still mining, his pet cats his only companions, Smith expected to live past a hundred and to die in the canyon he'd found so captivating.

Power House Road branches left at mile 2.0. The narrow, paved route leads over a low saddle to reach Highway 299 northwest of Junction City. It originally formed part of the first road to Helena and later provided access to the North Mountain Power Company's powerhouse, which transformed Canyon Creek's water into electricity for the faraway city of Eureka.

A wide bend, mile 2.6, rounds Lizard Point, where the recumbent reptiles warm themselves

on the sunny rocks. Ahead on the right are flower-covered cliffs bearing alumroot, monkeyflower, Douglas meadowfoam, and some of Canyon Creek's red delphiniums. On the hillslope across the creek, 2.9 miles, left, is one of two ditches that brought water down the canyon to the Trinity River mines.

"The Steps," which begin at mile 3.0, form a rocky stretch of canyon that in early days thwarted travel along the original road. Later improvements eliminated the difficulty, allowing motorists to focus instead on the profusion of springtime wildflowers that grace the hillside, right. On the lower banks are larkspur, baby blue eyes, and foothill penstemon, while the rocky cliffs feature the tiny naked broomrape and the spectacularly pink Siskiyou lewisia; the latter, in reference to this site, is known locally as "step flower." Vying for attention are a pair of bloom-filled bushes just below the road: chokecherry and redbud. The bankside floral display continues, with butterweed, nemophila, and orange wallflower at mile 3.4. Blue dicks and the striking Kellogg's monkeyflower come

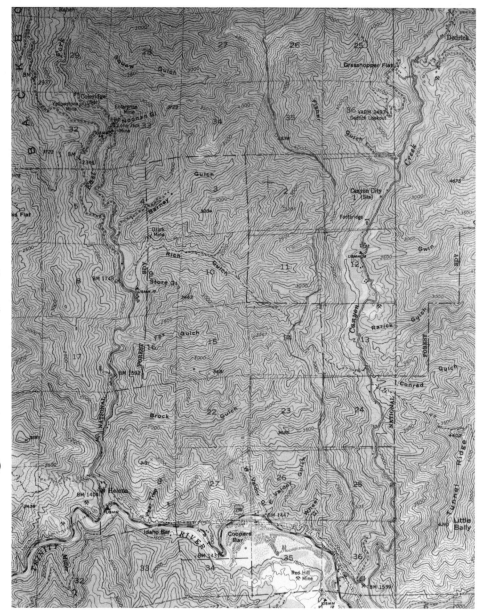

Both Canyon Creek, right, and the North Fork Trinity, left, flow through ore-rich canyons on their way southward to the main Trinity. (USGS map)

next, followed by lupine and white baby blue eyes.

The road climbs Reservoir Hill, 3.9 miles, next to which a dam once impounded water for the lower ditch; canyon live oak joins with mixed conifers as the route leaves the creek. At mile 4.6, left, is the Bluebird Mine "restoration site," now a large expanse of grassy earth. In this vicinity was once the substantial settlement of Pennsylvania Bar, an early-day mining community that in the 1940s was home to writer Ola Sward Peterson; her newspaper column, "Our Gold Mine in the Sky," informed *Trinity Journal* readers of the goings-on in the near-ghost towns of Canyon Creek.

A favorite subject was May Burger and her five French poodles, who lived about a mile upstream. May, then in her sixties, was a former actress who had once appeared with her husband in a performance at Dedrick. There she met miner Jack Burger; years later, she divorced her husband, married Burger, and then divorced him. May found Jack dispensable after he'd turned grocer and "failed" at it for 13 years; he still lived nearby in a little shack and was a frequent guest at dinners. Of her first husband, May allowed that "[h]e had only one fault—wine, women, and gambling."

On a low knoll, mile 7.7, right, is the Cañon City Cemetery, which contains several grave mounds and a single legible marker—for members of the pioneer Gilzean family. Scattered nearby are mountain violet and Oregon grape. A huge, hillside-destroying hole behind the cemetery is a monument to sluicing efforts of an energetic miner named Chris Wolfski.

A collection of fruit trees, mile 8.0, left, covers the grounds of the Guthrie Place, where tenders for the upper ditch lived. To the north is an area once mined extensively by Chinese.

The main section of Cañon City, mile 8.5, is marked by several old buildings, some fruit trees, and a roadside lilac bush. An interpretive sign summarizes the community's history: in the early 1850s the site contained some 800 residents, with a complement of the usual businesses; by 1891 most of the remaining townfolk had relocated upstream at Dedrick, where new gold strikes were in progress. Chronicler Isaac Cox provided a sense of Cañon City's chaotic early days with an accounting of the area's first seven deaths: three resulted from caved-in cliffs, two were suicides, one was a murder, and one (only) came from natural causes.

Canyon Creek Road crosses the stream at mile 8.8, passing the tailings piles of Fisher Gulch. The route now runs along the steep western side of the canyon; across the creek, mile 9.5, right, the scars of extensive hydraulic mining appear among the trees. Grasshopper Flat Road forks left, 10.1 miles, after which the main route begins a descent to Canyon Creek; the bridge crossing, mile 10.5, is noteworthy for the upstream view of the boulder-imbedded gorge. Regaining the east side of the canyon, the road passes East Fork Road, 10.8 miles, right, which leads to several old mines.

The difficult-to-distinguish remnants of

Upper Dedrick, 1904, centered on the tall, gable-ended Gribble Hotel, which had a dance hall upstairs and faced the Dedrick store across the street. (TCHS photo, gift of Leonard Morris)

Dedrick then appear; a monument at mile 11.3, right, describes the town's 50-year (1891–1941) existence. Prominent among Dedrick's long-gone buildings was the three-story Gribble Hotel; its location is now marked by the start of a dirt road that leads up the mountainside to the old Globe Mine. Soon Canyon Creek Road narrows to one lane; after a sharp climb, it passes a large field, 12.2 miles, left, that was the Ackerman Homestead. Dating from 1918, the property featured a garden and hayfield, both watered by a ditch and pipe system that is still visible to the north. A set of concrete steps marks a housesite overlooking the creek.

Ripstein Campground nestles among a stand of conifers and bigleaf maples, mile 12.3, left. The Ackerman ditch cuts through the site, which once also contained the offices and living accommodations for the Chloride-Bailey quartz mill. The campground offers vehicle-accessible and walk-in campsites, the latter scattered among the rocks above the creek.

The road next passes the quartz mill's foundation, 12.5 miles, right; ore from the Chloride and Bailey mines was carried here by an aerial tramway from high on the hillside. Some 19 buckets, each holding a half ton, traveled at 300 feet per minute to reach the 20-stamp mill. This enormous structure covered a great stretch of the slope, each of its eight sections providing a separate step in the milling process. Completed in 1913, the operation had a short life; production dropped during World War I and large-scale activity never resumed.

After climbing steeply, the route ends, mile 13.2, at the parking lot for the Canyon Creek and Bear Creek trailheads. Below the road were the mill and other buildings of the Globe Mine, most traces of which were obliterated by the 1964 flood. The mine itself was situated up the ridgeslope at an elevation of 5,500 feet; its tunnels ran through the mountain from Canyon Creek to Stuart Fork.

Today, the Globe's bustling miners have been replaced by the boot and backpack crowd, who are intent on finding not gold, but the glittering lakes and peaks of the Trinities. Most of the canyon's many mines have long ceased to operate, and the "ghost town of Dedrick" that Ola Sward Peterson found in 1940, "with its darkened, decaying houses," has become ghostlier still. The tailings that litter the streamsides still remain, but they are mere pebbles compared to the great rocks of the high country. In the perspective of the surrounding peaks, the miners' works now seem of small consequence.

The Chloride Mine's 20-stamp quartz mill clings to the cliffside above what is now the Ripstein Campground. (Florence Scott Morris sketch of 1904 photo)

Trinity Trailway: Canyon Creek's Falls & Lakes

Despite their best efforts, travelers along the Trinity River Highway will do no more than catch an occasional, glittering glimpse of the mountain range lying to the north—a peak or jagged ridgeline jutting skyward in snowtopped splendor, soon obscured by a stretch of intervening forest or foothills. The urge then is to change course, approach this alpine grandeur, and behold the greater beauty so strongly promised from afar. Thus enthralled, many tourists soon seek a byway to the beckoning Trinities.

At Junction City, such a route is close at hand. Canyon Creek Road runs some 13 miles northward, reaching one of the most accessible and rewarding entry points into the Trinity Alps Wilderness Area, the Canyon Creek Trailhead. Here, on a bench above the creek, a well-maintained National Forest trail departs a large (but often full) parking area, bound for the Canyon Creek Lakes eight miles ahead.

The path immediately passes a junction with the Bear Creek Trail, right, just before entering the Wilderness Area. A canopy of California black oak, Pacific madrone, Douglas-fir, incense cedar, and ponderosa pine shades the route, which presently cuts along a hillside contour high above Canyon Creek.

Soon the trail bends east, mile 0.3, to reach a crossing of boulder-strewn Bear Creek. In fall the golden leaves of thimbleberry and elk clover combine with the rosy hues of Pacific dogwood to brighten the greenery of five-finger and giant chain ferns.

Climbing from the side canyon, the trail regains the slope above Canyon Creek; the drier soil here hosts imbricated sword fern and Sierra cliffbrake. At mile 1.5 the distinctive leaves of California hazel (fuzzy underneath) and golden chinquapin (dark yellow underneath) diversify the forest foliage. A short path, mile 1.8, left, leads a few yards to an overlook of the creek, where, in autumn, gold-tinted bigleaf maples billow, torchlike, above gray granite boulders in the streambed. Ahead on the main trail is smaller-scale but equally spectacular scenery—the delicate blooms of virgin's bower and crimson columbine.

Mountain ash, snowberry, and blue elderberry then color the trailside a flaglike red, white, and blue with their respective fruits. A junction, mile 3.0, offers a descending spur trail, left, to a camping area. Here long ago a large rockslide buried Canyon Creek, creating the "Sinks," a section of streambed where the water runs underground. A stand of bigleaf maples shades several stone-strewn tent sites.

Bearing right from the junction, the main trail now ascends the canyonside, leveling to pass a lovely, rock-clinging canyon live oak and then offering a view west of the granite-spiked ridgeline. A set of switchbacks, mile 3.4, repeatedly crosses a small side creek that waters paintbrush, lily, delphinium, and other flowers. The route levels and then runs above a pale green pool at the base of Lower Canyon Creek Falls, left, where the stream picturesquely pauses in its cascading descent. After crossing through a carpet of black laurel, the trail reaches a stand of willow, cottonwood, red fir, and white fir, mile 4.2, left. A trio of charming campsites lines the nearby creekside.

Beyond the camping area the trail passes

golden chinquapin, hardhack, and manzanita, while to the right, granite cliffs rise massively up the east side of the canyon. Come fall, the forest here explodes in color—bracken fern, bigleaf maple, and serviceberry tint the landscape various hues of gold and yellow. Despite the canyon's remoteness, such spectacular sights have long drawn an appreciative audience. (*See sidebar, below.*)

Chronicling Canyon Creek

Until nearly the turn of the century, the fastness of Canyon Creek had revealed itself mainly to miners and the local Indians, but neither of these groups publicized much of what they found there. Then, in August 1899, C. Hart Merriam, Chief of the United States Biological Survey, and his assistant, Vernon Bailey, ventured into the Trinities, conducting "a scientific exploration of these little-known mountains." They reported back about "unusual physical features, wildness and grandeur of scenery undreamed of," bringing with them "a small but very interesting collection of plants from the summits of the ridges."

Merriam and Bailey's intriguing account was more than one plant enthusiast could bear. "[I]t seemed as if life would lose its zest if these mountains could not be reached, their rugged peaks climbed, their botanical treasures collected, and their dangers and difficulties overcome," wrote Alice Eastwood, Joint Curator for the California Academy of Sciences and plant pursuer extraordinaire. Eastwood, who had spent many happy months rambling through the rarefied air of Colorado's Rockies, could hardly wait to assay a trip into California's tantalizing Trinities. In July 1901, she happily found herself en route from Redding to the Canyon Creek country, joined by a trio of male hiking companions.

The initial stages of the trip proved difficult, for the party had to hire horses that "were on their last legs and gave us great trouble and delay." The balky beasts plodded the dusty road until "Tom" gave out near Lewiston, where, to everyone's relief, a more resilient mare replaced him. Eastwood's dismay at their dilatory progress was tempered by thrilling views of the roadside vegetation, as she found buckeye and redbud, maples and oaks, "[t]iger lilies that bordered the streams in places, and the bright scarlet California pink [that] peeped from under the shrubs."

The group arrived a day and a half late at Weaverville, and they then had to climb over Oregon Mountain, which "was hot and dusty beyond any place we had passed." At last they reached the cool confines of Canyon Creek, where the travails of their travel were finally forgotten among "the fresh green trees and shrubs."

Now they stopped not because of the horses, but to eat the ripening blackberries and black raspberries, or to note "the colonies of Chinese engaged in placer mining." Here and there they "passed a lonely cabin in which some old miner lived." To Eastwood, "[t]hese men seemed like the driftwood of humanity left behind on the great tide that swept over the country in the days of '49. They were chatty and liked to talk of olden times."

Eastwood's expedition finally reached Dedrick, camping at this "terminus of civilization" for the night. In the morning they passed the Chloride Mine and entered the narrow upper canyon, fording the creek seven times before reaching the upper lake. "Every one was a horror to me," wrote Eastwood of the fords, "but the men roped the animals over without any accidents, and at all except one we found logs on which to cross."

She also found ample scenery to distract her from the dangers— "a succession of most lovely cataracts," and a profusion of "rare and lovely flowers" that ranged "[a]ll through this beautiful cañon." Eastwood filled the remaining pages of her account with a paean to the plantlife, concluding with a listing of over 100 species she identified during the trip.

Nearly a century later, her list remains remarkably current. The heart of the Trinities, first protected as a primitive area and later, in 1984, as a wilderness, has retained much of its earlier appearance. Were Alice Eastwood to return to upper Canyon Creek today, she'd find little has changed, except that a pair of streamside cabins are missing and a higher, drier, hillside trail has replaced her creekbottom route of the seven fords. Still coloring the canyonsides are the mountain ash and snowbrush, the Brewer's oak and bigleaf maple; still standing above the lakes is the rare weeping spruce. Everywhere are familiar friends that Eastwood would again delight in seeing, and that are, delightfully, still there to see.

A large, overhanging rock, mile 4.6, right, bears the blackening of countless campfires; ahead on the left, a stand of tall cottonwoods borders Upper Canyon Creek Meadows. Soon the trail crosses through a thicket of dogwood, black laurel, and mountain alder. After passing a patch of Indian rhubarb near a large, creekside Douglas-fir, the route runs past Brewer's oak and chokecherry. On the hillside above, rectangular masses of concrete-colored granite loom like gigantic World War II bunkers.

At mile 5.8 a spur path, left, leads some 200 yards to the rumbling descent of Middle Canyon Creek Falls, which splashes down a series of water-worn granite terraces. Several switchbacks then bring the main route to a junction, 6.3 miles, with the primitive trail to Boulder Creek Lakes, left.

After two more sets of switchbacks, the main trail passes Upper Canyon Creek Falls, mile 6.9, left, climbs again, and levels to reach a junction at 7.2 miles. To the right is an abandoned route that once led to a dangerous crossing of the outlet to Lower Canyon Creek Lake. The maintained trail branches left, passes through a small grove of snow-stunted aspen and then enters thick forest, bending left to cross the creek on a footlog; nearby are battered sections of rusty pipe, relics from an unsuccessful attempt to siphon water to the North Mountain powerhouse near Junction City. The trail then meanders through thick vegetation, passes a natural enclosure of boulders known variously as Stonehouse or Barton Camp, and then ascends a rocky, open area marked by a series of cairns. At mile 8.0 the route reaches the lower lake, whose emerald liquid lies at the bottom of a dazzling granite bowl. To the east, Sawtooth Peak points a sharply angled incisor skyward; on its far side lies the canyon of the Trinity River's Stuart Fork. Off to the southwest, the bulk of Mount Hilton and its north-running ridgeline hide Papoose Lake, while to the northwest Wedding Cake peak awaits its winter icing of snow. Farther north, Thompson Peak, tallest of the Trinities at 9,002 feet, commands the head of the canyon.

A string of cairns, left, marks the trail as it moves up and around the western side of the water. To the right, several seldom-seen weeping spruce lachrymosely droop their limbs above the lake; this beautiful but reclusive conifer, also known as Brewer spruce, is confined to a few remote areas of northwestern California and southwestern Oregon. At mile 8.4 the route reaches the rocky berm of Upper Canyon Creek Lake. Masses of gray granite run ridgeward to the left; beyond a jagged diagonal of talus, a wall of rock rises above the lake's northwestern shore. To the northeast, hidden in a small cirque, lies remote "L" Lake, reachable by a cross-country scramble up the narrow canyon of its outlet creek. Experienced climbers may accept the challenge of the nearby peaks and be rewarded with spectacular views once they attain the summits. Most scenery seekers will be satisfied with the offerings of the two Canyon Creek lakes, however, knowing they will also reprise the conifer-shaded charms of the return route.

(*Note: Due to heavy use, the Forest Service has instituted a quota system for the Canyon Creek Trail. Persons found without a permit, obtainable at ranger district offices, will be ticketed.*)

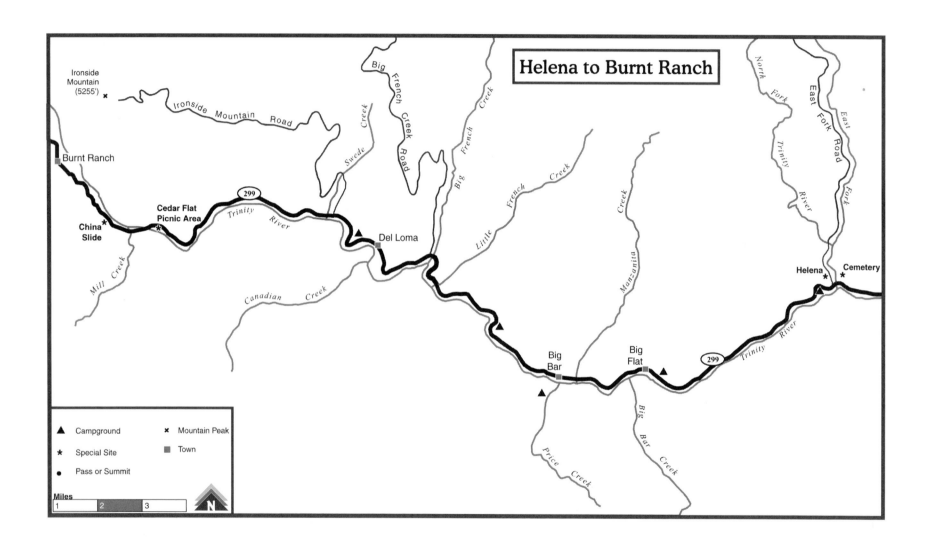

Helena to Burnt Ranch

Ironside Mountain (5255')

Ironside Mountain Road

Big French Creek

North Fork

East Fork Road

Burnt Ranch

299

Swede Creek

Big French Creek Road

Big French Creek

Trinity River

East Fork

Cedar Flat Picnic Area

Trinity River

China Slide

Del Loma

Little French Creek

Manzanita Creek

Mill Creek

Canadian Creek

Helena

Cemetery

Big Bar

Big Flat

299

Trinity River

Price Creek

Big Bar Creek

▲ Campground   ✗ Mountain Peak

★ Special Site   ■ Town

● Pass or Summit

Miles
1   2   3

N

V. Threading Through the Trinity's Bars & Flats

Helena: Ghost of Trinity's North Fork

Some six miles below Junction City (between Valdor Road, right, and Pigeon Point, left), Highway 299 bisects the site of a bygone *Bagdad* (no "h"), memorialized by a small monument on the south side of the road. The sign reads: "on this site once stood the town of 'Bagdad' founded in the year of 1850 by pioneers Craven Lee and David Weed. Peak of population five hundred." Across the road from the monument is the decaying cemetery of a town long known as North Fork but later renamed Helena. Ringed with oak and locust trees and hemmed in by blackberry bushes, the fenced graveyard contains dozens of carved stones and a few wooden markers. The most prominent plot features a row of graves marked with the surname *Schlomer*. In the middle rises the headstone of Harmon Schlomer, "father" not only of his family, but much of the town. Like echoes of the past, these graying graves provide visible anchors to the spirits of the miners and merchants, the blacksmiths and brewers, and their wives and children who once walked this golden ground.

On the opposite side of the river from the cemetery, along *East* Fork Road, lies a broad meadow marked by a few weathered buildings—Trinity County's best claim to a ghost town. As Bagdad faded, even in the midst of heavy mining, North Fork began to bustle as a center of commerce along the western side of the stream. The new burg had a bigger site than Bagdad and, once Harmon Schlomer constructed a toll bridge across the North Fork, it also had a superior situation for tapping the trade routes that converged there until as late as 1931, when a new Highway 299 bridge bypassed fair Helena. (She pronounces her name with a long second "e," and the accent falls on that "le" syllable.)

Nowadays only the gentle rush of water tapdancing on stone breaks the stillness of Helena in spite of its proximity to the busy highway. The North Fork, joined by its East Fork tributary just a mile above the highway, flows like liquid emerald. But beware of the fact that this ghost town is privately owned and overseen by a caretaker who guards his treasure as closely as any miner ever watched his claim. (*Note: be sure to respect all "No Trespassing" signs for everyone's safety and benefit.*)

The detailed map of old Helena in the *Trinity County Historic Sites* book demonstrates how little still stands of the once lively hamlet. The most-photographed building, which greets visitors at the entrance on the right side of the road, served as the Schlomer home and saloon. A short distance north, past the lane that veered east to the old bridge over the North Fork, is the brick domicile that housed the Meckel family and their store. Between his home and Schlomer's, John Meckel built his first brewery 20 years before moving to Weaverville. A bit farther to the left, beneath old walnut trees, are two wooden structures—Schlomer's livery stable and the cottage of a Currie couple (also buried in the cemetery). Blackberry brambles now crowd all of these buildings and the foundations of others, reaching into the porches and walls to help the rains wear them away.

Just as Bagdad owed its brief but exotic life to two men (and many "ladies"), Helena revolved around the long but more sedate lives of the interrelated Schlomer and Meckel families. One cannot understand the contrasting nature of these two hamlets that straddled the North Fork without knowing something about their founders.

The first record of white settlement on this old Chimariko village site comes from John Carr, whose *Pioneer Days of California* recounts his 1851 winter trek over the Salmon Mountains to his long-term place of residence, Weaverville. As Carr and his weary travel companions reached the mouth of the North Fork, they stumbled upon four miners playing cards. The foursome had enough dried meat, beans, and whiskey stashed away in their tent to make Carr and company the outpost's first customers.

Within a year a New England native named Craven Lee filed a claim in Weaverville for the flats on both sides of the North Fork. He and David Weed constructed a boarding place on the east flat that was probably named Bagdad by Lee. Miners traveling down (or up) the Trinity and its North Fork found comfortable lodging at the Lee-Weed place and there shared stories of rich strikes and riotous living. (*See sidebar, below.*)

At one time, Lee had almost 200 acres under cultivation along the lower North Fork, but eventually he had trouble financing his other enterprises and had to sell off most of his land. In 1852, a few years before Lee left Trinity County, John Meckel, who had stopped at Bagdad a year or so earlier, returned to the North Fork, bringing his brother Christian. With their earnings from a Mother Lode mine, they bought some of Lee's land. Eventually they started several thriving businesses: a 50-mule pack train (linked to Shasta City), stores on the

The "Wedding" of Craven Lee

In the early 1850s, gold seemed to flow through the streets of "rowdy, bawdy, lusty" Bagdad, which claimed blacksmith shops, hotels, saloons, and stores. Miners gathered at the Lee-Weed hotel to drink for a spell, spin a few tales, and then gossip about Craven—the town's founder and practical joker who had a reputation for being a "lewd" (an abbreviation of Lee-Weed?) lady's man. When he seemed to "crave" one particular young lady from Big Flat, rumors of matrimony began to fly. His nosy neighbors pestered him so much that he decided to silence them once and for all.

He arranged a trip to Big Bar and the word spread: "Lee is going to get married; be ready to give him a grand shivaree" when he returns. Men gathered from all around, ready to strike up a band in celebration of Craven's nuptials. They grabbed the only musical devices they could put their hands on—scraps of tom-iron found in front of a blacksmith's shop. When Lee arrived that evening and hastily ushered his veiled bride inside, the disappointed crowd surrounded the house and beat out such awful sounds on their makeshift instruments that David Weed, hoping to stop the din, came out and invited them inside for refreshment.

Lee and his bride stayed secluded, so the unruly revelers—more befuddled than ever by drink—threatened to fetch the bride themselves if Craven lacked the courtesy to present her. At last he emerged from a back room and put a finger to his lips: "Be quiet. I will produce my wife forthwith," he promised, but the "bride" he ushered into the room was still veiled. These stubborn frontiersmen smoked and drank the night away, refusing to leave until they could see the woman who had finally tamed Craven Lee. When morning peeped through the curtains, the 30 or so celebrants witnessed the unveiling of Lee's bride at the breakfast table.

"I command you to remove that abominable veil and disclose the face of one whom I have honored to be the wife of Craven Lee," David Weed demanded, turning to the "bride" seated at his side. When the veil at last dropped, the astonished men saw not the pretty face of the young lady from Big Bar, but the bearded face of "Jim, the Packer." Although few later admitted to taking serious part in the wedding serenade that night, Lee, as always, enjoyed his practical joke to the end, insisting that the pile of tom-iron "gongs" be carted back to the smithy's shop where they belonged while he and his "wife" watched.

The handsome but solemn Harmon Schlomer family. (TCHS photo)

East and North forks, a hotel, and a brewery. The Meckels imported a German brewer and then packed his "heady, hearty" beer to the mines in exchange for grains of gold dust to put in their money jars. By the early 1860s, the *Trinity Journal* could assert that "A great quantity of it [North Fork beer] is annually consumed in that section of the county, which accounts for the robust appearance of the populations and their strong Union proclivities."

Harmon Schlomer, after his arrival in 1855 and purchase of more of Lee's land, also prospered—as a blacksmith, bridge-builder, liveryman, and saloonkeeper. Moreover, within a few years he and John Meckel married two Weinheimer sisters, whose parents had emigrated from the same Rhineland village as the Meckels. Brother Christian, still a bachelor at age 40, returned to the family *Heimat* in 1870 to find a bride and soon returned with a lovely 18-year-old named Helena Josephine Hall. The couple later built a hotel north of the Meckel home that became popular up and down the Trinity for its comforts and warm atmosphere or, to use the more expressive German term, *Gemütlichkeit*. The intermarriages of these families gave North Fork a bond and continuity that helped it to survive the devastating flood of 1861 and the subsequent decline of the local mines.

Others were less fortunate. For example, in the winter of 1855-56 Weaverville's lucky-but-never-wealthy Franklin Buck joined Carter Durkee in building (for $3,000) a sawmill in an alternately "Sunny/Snowy/Rainy Hollow" below the confluence of the East and North forks. By summer they had "the saw running day and night" to supply customers "right on the Trinity River" with 100,000 board feet. Their single best client was probably the Chinese company building a flume 440 yards long. A year later Buck rented his half of the mill to Durkee, but the flood of 1861 carried off the entire plant.

The Meckels and Schlomers fared better, even though North Fork no longer ranked "second to Weaverville in point of business," and Isaac Cox could no longer call it the "San Diego of Northern California." By 1878, North Fork's mining operations, and thus its beer sales, had dropped enough to prompt John Meckel's purchase of the Pacific Brewery in Weaverville. His move proved premature, however, for in the mid-1880s a hard rock mining boom hit the East Fork—remarkably close to the starting point of the Gregg Party's epic expedition to the coast. (*See sidebar, page 136.*)

The Meckel brothers launched their first store at Rich Bar or across the East Fork in Store Gulch, near Rich Gulch, where the mines were "rich" enough to keep them in business for about five years. Only then did they retreat to the North Fork and erect a more permanent mercantile. The quartz mines developed north of Rich Bar a generation later proved profitable enough for John Meckel to reopen Schlomer's basement saloon (known as the "Brewery") and for the Meckel hotel to stay in business until the end of the century. In 1891, the Postal Ser-

The "Brewery," where John Meckel established a branch store for his business in the Schlomers' basement. (TCHS photo)

*Helena in the early 1900s: the Curries' cottage and Schlomer's livery stable, right;
Meckel's warehouse and store (with porch), left. (TCHS photo)*

Helena just a few hundred feet off the highway which is to be deplored as it is one of the prettiest spots in the county." By then, of course, most members of the founding Meckel-Schlomer families had either died or moved elsewhere. In 1966, a family from San Jose acquired all of Helena (130 acres) for $50,000. Efforts to restore two of the town's deserted buildings stopped when fire destroyed a hotel (where the phantom fireplace still stands) erected in the early 1930s in place of the Meckel inn.

Until a more preservation-minded person or agency buys the property, the once golden hamlet at the mouth of the North Fork will continue to crumble. Ghostly winds still fan the white locust blossoms, but little remains to mark the passing of this mining crossroads save the few ramshackle buildings, the rustic graveyard, and the fond memories of a few aging survivors. "Being where you had to pitch in and work as a team brought the family together in a way I doubt would happen in the city," a Weaverville centenarian told us with a smile. She and her husband moved from the Bay Area to supervise a newly revived North Fork mine during the Depression. One of their sons has "retired" to run an antique store in Weaverville (catty-corner from the Courthouse), where, when business permits, he's more than happy to share his remarkable memories and mementos of life among the 1930s miners.

Hikers who want to combine signs of mines with an even longer trek into the Trinity Alps

vice established a new post office and renamed it Helena (at husband Christian's suggestion) to avoid confusion with another California community called North Fork, which, ironi-

cally, became known as Korbel two years later.

As the *Trinity Journal* (April 18, 1931) foresaw, the new bridge being surveyed across the North Fork "will leave the pioneer town of

Local Sunday riders stop to pose on the North Fork bridge near Helena, c. 1915. (C. E. Goodyear photo)

than Canyon Creek offers should consider the Hobo Gulch Trail. Half a mile past the Rich Bar turnoff on East Fork Road, head left up the steep 12-mile route that leads to the trailhead and campground. From there many miners and mountaineers have followed an even longer trail to Grizzly Lake and the glistening snowfields that cling to the north face of Thompson Peak—the highest alp in the Trinities.

Rich Bar: Gregg Party Launch Site

To celebrate the sesquicentennial of the Gregg Party expedition from the East Fork to Trinidad and Humboldt bays in late 1849, the two counties' historical societies, the Forest Service, and several local groups dedicated a striking stone monument in a fir-pine grove at Rich Bar. (To reach the site, drive 3.5 miles north of Highway 299 on East Fork Road and take the dirt road that drops down to the right a short distance.) The plaque reads:

This area was the site of some of the earliest mining in the county. Fifty miners worked the bar in 1849. Later operations were extensive. The Klamath and Salmon River trails intersected at the gulch. Knowing the need for a supply route to Humboldt Bay, explorer, pathfinder, scientist Dr. Josiah Gregg, with Lewis K. Wood, on Nov. 5, 1849, led a volunteer party including Thomas Sebring, David A. Buck, J. B. Truesdale, Charles S. Southard, Isaac Willson and James Van Duzen to the coast, reaching the mouth of Little River [below Trinidad] Dec. 13, 1849. The Meckel trading post was established at the gulch in 1852.

It may seem strange that any group of Trinity miners in 1849 would consider cutting a new trade line at least 80 miles long through rough terrain when they could obtain supplies via the already familiar Reading's Springs-Sacramento River route. But as the *Sacramento Transcript* reasoned (Feb. 1, 1851), "Although the Trinity mines are nearer Redding's [sic] Springs by two days' journey than Trinidad Bay, and the road better, yet traders in the interior prefer the latter market on account of being able to make cheaper purchases. Whilst it is necessary to pack or team goods from this point [Sacramento] to Redding's, provisions can be taken in vessels to Trinidad at one-fourth of those rates."

In spite of the rigors of the nearly 40-day trek that this "company of Trinidad adventurers" endured in their *Quest for Qual-A-Wa-Loo* (or Humboldt Bay), all of them except Gregg—who later died of exhaustion near Clear Lake—returned from San Francisco to Humboldt or Trinidad Bay. Many other miners or merchants, notably Levi Tower and Charles Camden, would soon follow their lead in seeking a route across the Coast Ranges to the Klamath-Trinity diggings.

North Fork Trail to Grizzly Lake

Like the canyons it follows deep into the Trinity Alps, the North Fork Trail is a study in extremes: at the upper end, saw-toothed ridges rise majestically above deep valleys and gulches; at the lower end, barren rocks yield to mixed forests and brushy riverside flats. The trail, of course, takes its name from the river that cuts through this varied terrain and vegetation that differ quite markedly from the physiography of parallel Canyon Creek, just a few miles to the east as most crows fly.

The official Forest Service map of the Trinity Alps Wilderness pinpoints the start of the North Fork Trail (12W01) at Hobo Gulch, elevation 3,300 feet. Many of the place names found along the route evoke the region's storied past, beginning with the gulch named after "Hobo Dick"—the "village sot" of Junction City—according to the *Trinity Journal* (July 1, 1937). One summer day around 1900, he headed for the North Fork to visit some cronies at one of the many mines. After goading a hired packer with a mare to the top of Backbone Ridge, Dick "became dazed with the heat and ran top speed all the five miles of trail down to the unnamed gulch where the Backbone and North Fork trails meet." The packer later found him lying at the river's edge with his head submerged in the water. Apparently he had drunk too much water on a hot day. The packer buried him a short distance up the gulch, and the name Hobo [Dick] stuck to the place.

Past Keystone Flat and Backbone Creek the trail leads to a series of miners' cabins or abandoned camps: the Strunce Cabin at Rattlesnake Creek, the Morrison Cabin at Whisky Creek, the restored Jorstad Cabin on Pfeiffer Flat; then through China Gardens; and finally along Specimen Creek to Grizzly Lake. Looming over the lake, Thompson Peak, wizened by millennia of weathering, crowns the Alps.

The 12-mile road to Hobo Gulch begins four miles north of the Helena turnoff, rises sharply to the left and drops steeply as it traverses Backbone Ridge, which separates the North from the East Fork. (**Warning:** *Proceed cautiously, no matter what the season, for the drive presents possible hazards: from fallen rocks or trees in early spring to oncoming traffic, dust, and animals in summer and fall. Winter access is severely limited. At any time of year, inquire about road and trail conditions at the Big Bar Ranger District office before heading into the backcountry.*)

Even veteran backpackers will find the trail to Grizzly Lake long and arduous—a 39-mile roundtrip with substantial elevation gain. The first and shorter half, to Pfeiffer Flat and back, can be hiked in a long day, especially if one stays at the campground tucked in the gulch just below the trailhead. The campsites have toilets and fire pits but no potable water.

The trail gains less than 1,000 feet in elevation over its lower half as it follows the broad valley of the North Fork to Jorstad's Cabin and China Gardens. Along the well-worn path various animals appear amid the abundant vegetation. The bold Steller's jay often heralds the arrival of flatlanders. Numerous tracks indicate that black bears, mountain lions, deer, and smaller mammals also cross the trail. Garter and gopher snakes slither along smooth traces in the dry grasses, while frogs and salamanders prefer moister habitats. Rattlesnakes inhabit both dry and wet environments and deserve the same wide berth you'd give a bear. Spiders and insects, especially the mosquito and horse fly, feed off backpackers and pack animals too weary to swat them away. Home to this diverse fauna is the forest itself. As the elevation gradually increases, dense woodland growth yields to species better adapted to the higher and harsher environment.

The trail reaches a three-way junction, at 0.6 miles, on the north side of Backbone Creek. Follow the middle path and the Papoose Lake sign, but take the high (vs. low) water trail except in late summer or early fall. The "high road" rises quickly above the valley, skirting a series of rock outcroppings. Here the rush of leaves in the scraggly canopy mixes with the constant roar of the North Fork below.

About a mile farther, the upper trail descends gently to join the lower one as it follows the river through a flat sandy flood plain. In summer the dense undergrowth of scrub oak, manzanita, and several kinds of berries scents and colors the riverside flats. Here deep pools reveal the cool, aquamarine waters of the North Fork—ideal sites for dangling sore feet or meditating quietly.

After another mile the trail crosses China Creek (one of several so named in the Trinities) to reach the thick stands of Douglas-fir at China Flat. A short spur, left, leads down to the North Fork, where, in late summer and early fall, a few travel-weary steelhead rest in gold-speckled pools before spawning and returning to the distant Pacific. Nearby boulders provide a sun-dappled perch for a lunch and perhaps a nap.

As the trail traverses China Flat over a series of rocky ledges, several forested peaks rise in the foreground, including Cabin Peak, which once had a fire lookout. Below the crags, the river cuts a deep swath through the sunburned rocks, its narrow banks littered with bleached logs and polished boulders. The trail hugs the cliff side for half a mile before descending abruptly into the shade of Deadhorse Flat, home to a small campsite and riparian vegetation—notably umbrella plant, coltsfoot, and a variety of ferns and grasses.

The three cabins located roughly midway along the lower half of the trail attest to the importance of the North Fork for miners as a major thoroughfare across the relatively low Trinity-Klamath watershed divide. Some four miles from Hobo Gulch, a small rise reveals another verdant area. Downhill to the left, the slumping remains of the Strunce Cabin slowly succumb to the growth of the forest. Joe Strunce immigrated to the United States from Pilsen, Bohemia—famous for its beer—in 1914. A bachelor, amateur botanist, and brewer, generous Joe provided neighbors and passersby with colorful tales of the country and firsthand knowledge of the woods. He also had the only telephone for miles, a Forest Service line linked to Big Bar. (A campsite lies on the other side of the river but is difficult to reach during high water.)

Past Strunce Cabin the trail gently winds its way for half a mile to Rattlesnake Creek Junction. Across the creek is a small camping area at the trailhead to Papoose Lake. A series of switchbacks, past the Grizzly Lake sign to the left, leads away from the flat sandy river soils into a zone of reddish loam. At the top of the incline, trekkers wend their way through the "Zen Garden," a rocky promontory strewn with Buddha-like statues and gnarled pines almost suggestive of bonsai. Two more miles of switchbacks and moderate descents lead to Morrison Cabin, where berries abound—including the deep red globes of gooseberries. The trail continues its last two miles before Jorstad Cabin (*see sidebar, page 140*) along another steep riverside ridge through alternating exposed and forested sections, both home to such plants as ceanothus, penstemon, buckwheat, and lupine.

The trail moves easily away from Jorstad Cabin for about half a mile to Grizzly Creek, a smaller and faster stream that crashes into the North Fork from the east. As the creek's name implies, grizzly bears were once commonplace; now only their smaller black bear cousins remain. After the first crossing of the creek, the path soon passes through a grove of ponderosa pine before entering China Gardens. A small trailside sign indicates that Chinese miners once cultivated a variety of fruit trees, vegetables, and flowers here. They reportedly occupied several sites along Grizzly Creek as well as the North Fork. Some experts surmise that the neatly constructed walls occasionally seen in placer tailings and ponds reflect further evidence of Chinese craftsmanship. The forest has reclaimed the flat, but a bit of snooping may reveal a few old fruit trees and some Asian poppies presumably cultivated for opium.

Beyond China Gardens hikers begin to gain a sense of being deep in the Trinity Alps. Thick-trunked firs give way to thinner cedars and

The Jorstad Cabin at Pfeiffer Flat during an early winter snow. (Dick Wild collection photo)

pines. Turkey buzzards circle overhead in the alpine air above talus-covered peaks on each side of the steep valley. Along the trail signs of mining activity increase. On the right several derelict flumes hang from a cliff once blasted by monitors. A short distance from the confluence of Specimen and Grizzly creeks is the site of a small hydraulic mine named after Fred (or Fritz) Moliter. This Alsatian bachelor reached the area decades after the few dozen prospec-

tors whom Isaac Cox found here in the late 1850s. With his monitor, Moliter worked the mine year-round, returning to Junction City for a few weeks each summer to order supplies, which his burro helped him pack up Backbone Creek to his camp.

A small creek crossing signals a steep climb to the Specimen Creek-Papoose Lake Trail, the first of two major junctions on the upper North Fork Trail. The main path veers sharply to the left and ascends a set of switchbacks before resuming a more level course along an oak-capped ridge of limestone outcroppings. Some 200 feet below, Grizzly Creek has cut a gaping gash into the rock.

A second creek crossing brings hikers to the well-marked junction with the Cecilville Trail (via yet another China Creek), which enters the area from the Salmon River drainage to the northwest. The jagged profile of Sawtooth Ridge juts out to the east between blue sky and green canopy. Just past the Cecilville Junction a few small campsites lie in a shady flat above Grizzly Creek. A demanding set of switchbacks leads to a rock promontory, above which cascades have cut a deep gorge through the sunbaked bedrock. Lined with buckwheat and paintbrush, the trail offers views of the clashing rock and water in the torrent below.

As the trail continues up the narrowing, some would say harrowing, valley, views are obscured by the high walls. Nothing can prepare a hiker for what lies only half a mile ahead: the glare of a snow-filled cirque that overwhelms

George Jorstad's Legacy

Mountain man, miner, writer, and self-styled iconoclast, W. O. "George" Jorstad was born in Dekalb County, Illinois, in 1899 of Swedish immigrants. He traveled widely in his early years before settling in California to work for several newspapers. He first came to the North Fork of the Trinity in 1934 on a short vacation. Many others, mostly miners and livestock graziers, had occupied Pfeiffer Flat long before him. Upon his arrival, the flat had a primitive trough and corral, but their condition suggested that they hadn't been used for years.

George returned to Pfeiffer Flat in 1937, calling it "the most beautiful piece of real estate I'd ever seen...a broad flat along the river, fairly open, set about with giant firs and pines, park-like in appearance, covered with grass growing out of a deep bed of fertile soil. What a find! And there was gold too!" That May he filed his claim in Weaverville and set about building a cabin with the help of long-time friend Bill Harvey, a Brooklyn ribbon clerk.

Jorstad and Harvey built a cabin of durable Douglas-fir from trees that they cut on the far side of the river, floated downstream, and then skidded to the flat by block and tackle. For his floors George chose tiles of hand-shaped cedar. He positioned the cabin and all outbuildings and fences on a north-south axis, basing the decision on his philosophy that it was "proper to build houses four-square with the world."

In 1941, his partner Adzie received a job offer in San Diego; having had her fill of nature one winter when snow nearly buried the cabin, she left Pfeiffer Flat and its iconoclast to accept the position. Initially unsure about what to do, Jorstad soon met a man who owned a ship that needed repair; his reputation as a carpenter made George the prime candidate for the job. He stayed on the windjammer *Kaiulani* for five years, sailing widely around the world while many countries were at war.

Upon returning to the United States, George hurried back to his cabin and found it still in mint condition. He remained there, except for winters, until his health forced him to leave in 1985. Unlike the miners drawn to the North Fork mainly for gold, George had come for a better life. He gave up the comforts of the city to fashion an Eden in the Trinity backcountry. Jorstad summarized his outlook before his death in 1991: "the house is the handiwork of a friend and people who loved each other, in search of a better way to live."

The Forest Service and the Friends of Jorstad have preserved his legacy by restoring the cabin as a Trinity County landmark. Under the stewardship of Dick Wild, a long-time friend and volunteer forest ranger, the cabin and flat retain their function as a way station for youth groups, pack animal enthusiasts, and backpackers. During the warmer months visitors may find Wild at Pfeiffer Flat with his sure-footed mule, Molly. Over a camp-fire, he shares his stories and Dutch-oven-cooked food freely, a tribute to the hospitality once born of necessity in this remote mountain region. Beyond the flicker of fire, in the fluid black of the night, the North Fork offers its own local version of Trinity history.

the landscape of an ancient glacial valley. In the shadow of Thompson Peak and its bone-white polished granite, Grizzly Falls threads its way down 200 feet to the floor of Grizzly Meadows. The fourth feature named Grizzly, the lake cradled in the cirque below the peak, requires a lengthy scramble up a steep talus slope, but the deep blue hue of the water rewards the exertion. Almost 20 miles into the heart of the Trinity Alps Wilderness and a few thousand feet above the North Fork floor, trekkers have reached the end of the trail—exhausted perhaps but happily suspended between earth and sky in this geography of extremes. (For more detailed information on this and other trails in the wilderness area, see Luther Linkhart and Michael White's *The Trinity Alps* [3ᵈ ed., 1994] and Earthwalk Press's *Hiking Map & Guide* [1987]).

Big Flat & Big Bar: Two Tiny Towns

In his 1858 *Annals*, Isaac Cox devoted three pages to describing the course of the Trinity between Helena and Big Flat. The river "for a distance of six miles runs through a canyon inclosed [*sic*] on both sides by mountain ridges upwards of two thousand feet in elevation above the river bed." The "ribbon of a trail," he continued, "wound round the mountain jetties, where, at numerous places, from the river beneath to your stand point, it is five hundred to one thousand feet perpendicular...[;] two cats, or two he-goats, or two spiders cannot travel abreast of one another." Only by walking along a "ribbon" of the old road above the highway at Pigeon Point or by rafting the rapids below can one begin to share Cox's sense of being caught in a six-mile-long chasm. The feeling heightens near Sailor Bar, just before reaching Big Flat, if you stop to turn around and catch a glimpse of snow-capped Alps in the distance.

At first glance, Big Flat and Big Bar seem like inappropriate names for two tiny towns nestled almost side by side along the middle Trinity River, roughly midway between Redding and Arcata. They are anything but big and a mere three miles (and the Skunk Point Group Camp) separate them, which may explain why so many maps omit the smaller, eastern "twin" of Big Flat. Tiny as they are, these sleepy look-alikes offer Trinity travelers the essentials: a post office and a Forest Service ranger district station (both in Big Bar), general stores, a few eateries, laundries, and a number of aging but comfortable cottages. Each place has a Forest Service campground, friendly inhabitants, and easy access to prime fishing, rafting, and swimming sites—all compelling reasons to stop and explore the area.

Neither town, of course, was named for its size, but instead for a big sandbar or terrace created by the Trinity and several creeks in this relatively open stretch of the canyon. The river access turnout just west of Big Flat offers a fine view of an old terrace—a flat formed above the current level when the river flowed at a higher elevation. Here one can also read the plaque placed on a rock in 1997 by the ubiquitous Trinitarian "Clampers" to summarize the history of the "Big Twins," which were first mined in 1849.

The rush came in 1850, when John Weaver & Co. ditched water from Lil' Weaver Creek, now Big Bar Creek, taking out $100,000 in gold at Big Flat. Elizabeth Walton mined here with her husband in 1850. William Warrener in 1854 built the Yankee sawmill, all of wood except for the saw, at Big Bar Creek. In 1855, Warrener built a bridge across the river to connect the Trinity and Humboldt trails. Miners, using 45-foot water wheels, worked Big Flat until the great flood of 1861–62, when water 47 feet above high-water marks swept the river clean of bridges, dams, and wheels.

Within six years of its founding, Big Flat boasted a population of several hundred. Nine of the luckier miners were married; the others vied for the favors of three eligible (and reputedly "fast") women.

The original community of Big Bar occupied a site at the mouth of Big Bar Creek, just a few hundred yards below Big Flat. Somehow the former name floated downstream and

Pipe packers pause in front of George Tinsley's Big Bar trading post, south of Price Creek. The building burned in 1920. (TCHS photo)

snagged itself permanently on bars mined near the mouths of Manzanita, Treloar, and Price creeks. Most of these mining camps didn't last long, and their names also faded away. "Cox's Bar," however, survived as the name of the small elementary school—located on the same site above (and west of) Price Creek since the 1860s. And its namesake, a Major Cox, apparently fared quite well after leaving. He had "kept a store, got rich and departed in 1857." The *Trinity Journal* received a letter from him in 1871 indicating he was living in Illinois and still in good health.

Big Bar's initial claim to fame came from being the first town in Trinity County with a white woman among its pioneer miners. In 1850, Elizabeth Walton's steely nature served her husband well when she prevented a party of Indians from robbing him of $500. The natives apparently decided the money was not worth the risk when his fearless wife confronted them with her commanding voice and...a Colt revolver.

Another early Big Bar character was "Commodore" Line. He prospered by selling property and then persuading the Chinese and other buyers to move on after he had taken their payments. The few with nerve enough to protest pulled up stakes quickly when faced eye-to-muzzle with the Commodore's shotgun. Eventually a deputy arrested him and Line subsequently found himself shipped off to San Quentin.

Big Bar outlived its Waltons, Commodores,

and even the mines largely because of its function as a central crossroads connecting not only the upriver and downriver settlements but also the mountain towns to the south. A trail across the Trinity just west of Price Creek (now a USFS road) passed through Corral Bottom and hooked up with the high ridge Hayfork-Hyampom-Humboldt County route that enabled travelers to bypass the treacherous Trinity Gorge. Perhaps Big Bar's pivotal position on the river also prompted the Shasta-Trinity National Forest to locate a ranger station there in the early 1900s. In any event, its presence gave the town an economic edge over Big Flat.

The station originally occupied an area across the Trinity on the west side of Price Creek, but in 1932, the Forest Service moved its Big Bar operation to its present highway location just east of town. The following year the older site was converted into a camp for a sizable Civil Conservation Corps, which, under Forest Service and United States Army supervision, helped expand the station's compound across the road and for the next few years undertook numerous improvements throughout the Trinity district. In 1934 the CCC built the Price Creek bridge just below the shady campground located along the west bank of the cascading stream. About half a mile beyond the bridge the Price Creek Road passes a small but well-kept cemetery (on the left hand side) and then, after crossing the creek once again, the restored home of pioneer T. B. Price.

Between Big Flat and Big Bar, the placid

river—especially on a warm day—becomes a playground for all kinds of floaters. Both above and below this slow stretch the emerald Trinity often turns white as it passes through a stimulating series of Class I-IV rapids. That must explain why the two towns now display a raft of signs for companies engaged in the booming business of guiding river-runners somewhere between Junction City and Cedar Flat. As a rafting center, Big Flat appears to have the edge over its archrival Big Bar, judging solely by the number of signs that encourage river-running.

Rapids pose only one of the challenges faced by Trinity rafters. Another comes from modern gold miners, drawn to the area by a renewed demand for gold or perhaps just for the adventure of finding it. "Dredgers" still ply the river on the basis of California's 1872 mining law, albeit on a vastly different scale than a century ago. Small machines suck up material from the riverbed, run it through sluices, and then drop it downstream after removing the tiniest particles of gold.

Like all prospectors, these latter-day windfall (or "waterfall"?) seekers guard their underwater claims vigilantly. Mining Trinity gold makes for occasional encounters with the river-runners because the best dredge sites usually lie directly below big rapids where the water slows and deposits gold-bearing sands and gravels. One rafter who had capsized his kayak at the Hell's Hole Rapid reported becoming caught in an eddy current that carried him right up to a dredging machine tethered to the bank.

As he floated near the dredge, a frantic prospector appeared—waving his arms, shaking his head, and shouting: "Don't grab on! Don't grab on!" The sight of the dredger glaring down at him prompted the kayaker to stay in the eddy and ride through the base of the rapid again before trying to climb out of the water. Generally, however, boaters have free run of the "wild and scenic" river. One of them, our expert fisherman (*see Chapter 1, "A New Angle on Fishing the Trinty," page 28*), returns to write as an experienced rafter in the following section.

This Civilian Conservation Corps camp located just south of Price Creek, Big Bar, 1934, housed about 200 workers. (TCHS photo)

Raging Times on the Trinity's Rapids

As our sky-blue river raft floated across the placid green water, I sensed a calm before a storm. At the end of the pool was a sharp horizon line, where the river appears to drop off into space. And drop it does, into a churning chasm, appropriately called "Hell's Hole" or "Dynamite" because of the images it conjures up. Not until our boat was perched on the lip of the rapid did we gain a clear view of what we were plunging into, and from that point on everything seemed to move simultaneously in slow motion and fast forward. Our experienced river guide positioned our boat for the drop, and as we passed the point of no return our craft accelerated. **Booom**...the dynamite exploded, and we all had front row seats.

The cool embrace of the river was a welcome relief from the oppressive heat of the air above. The gleeful squeals of my comrades gave way to an underwater roar, as I was ripped from my raft seat and propelled to the bottom of the river by a downward current. I had entered another world and actually relished the experience. As I bumped the gravel of the river's bottom and began floating to the surface, I opened my eyes to look around and was startled by the sight of salmon racing around the pool, alarmed by the presence of a flailing alien. I was so enchanted that I wanted to stay longer but couldn't because gravity has no influence under water. I bobbed above the water and was pulled aboard as we headed downstream to the next series of rapids.

The Trinity River is a white-water boater's dream; it offers runs ranging from Class I rapids (riffles, small waves, and no obstacles) to Class V cataracts (strong currents, big waves, and boulders)—holes powerful enough to flip or hold boats. The river has rapids to challenge any skill level and good runs for every month of the year, although late spring, summer, and early fall are the best times.

The Trinity has many different faces along its course, from its pristine alpine origins to the free-flowing upper river above Trinity Lake to the deep bedrock canyons of the middle stretch and the wide gravel bars of the lower end. The river also changes with the seasons, from a muddy winter torrent to the low flows of late summer and fall.

In late winter and spring, while the river is still high but relatively stable from snowmelt conditions, challenges await adventurous rafters on the far upper river and in the tributaries. This type of boating is for well-trained individuals only, due to difficult access and tricky navigation through technical rapids. Paddle crews must put the boat exactly where it should be, often a matter of inches. This can be dangerous because the small streams may clog with brush and other debris during high water, creating entrapment hazards as the water drops. Anyone boating during the off-season must know how and when to use a throw bag and be both physically and mentally prepared to take a swim in swift and frigid water. Thick wetsuits, helmets, and high flotation life vests are mandatory. A first trip down any run should be made with a professional river guide, but it is especially important to have one when tackling a small, unfamiliar stream.

As summer flows are dropped to less than

5,000 cubic feet per second (cfs) from Lewiston Dam, the main stem Trinity's most popular runs come into play. The upper ones from Lewiston to the North Fork are good floats for beginning rafters and more experienced canoeists and drift boaters. The section above Canyon Creek is dam controlled. While that means a fairly steady flow, it also cuts off the supply of gravel coming from the headwaters, thus making the channel deeper and more confined. It is so narrow in places that the riparian tree canopy nearly covers the river, creating a feeling of floating through a tunnel of vegetation. The dense cover presents one of the most serious hazards of this section—strainers, trees that have fallen into the river and have water flowing through them; if swimmers get pushed up against one, they may become tangled in the branches and held underwater by the current. If a strainer is sighted downstream, the best thing to do is get out and make sure there is a safe route around it. Because these upper runs are primarily fishing drifts, they get little boating pressure during the middle of the day, when most fishermen are cleaning their catch or preparing for an evening drift.

For a more exciting experience, the popular Pigeon Point run from the North Fork to Big Flat is the top draw. This scenic five-mile run through a bedrock canyon is filled with rapids that are challenging for beginning and intermediate boaters but not too serious if they end up as swimmers. Involuntary swims are frequent in this area, especially at Hell's Hole rapid. This Class III run draws much of the crowd on the river. When someone mentions rafting on the Trinity, most recall this run's biggest rapids—the Slot or "Z" Drop, Hell's Hole, Sailor Bar, Pinball, and Fishtail. The Pigeon Point stretch is a great place to get someone hooked on rafting, because it is exhilarating but not so frightening as to scare a novice away from the sport. Because of its popularity this run often has a festive atmosphere, complete with water fights and beach picnics.

For those who want an intimate river experience and don't mind occasional dunkings, the Pigeon Point run is perfect for inflatable kayaking. Using "rubber duckies," or inflatables, increases the difficulty, but it is the best way to learn a river's currents. One thing to remember is that boaters in duckies get wet, so wearing a thin wetsuit is a good idea, even on a hot sunny day; it's better to be too hot than too cold. I would also recommend a helmet when using a kayak or an unstable boat of any kind, because a head cut could be serious if bathed in dirty river water all day.

The section of river from Big Flat to Hayden Flat is mild with mostly low-class rapids, except for Stayright, below French Creek, which is a tricky II-plus. Beware of Stayright if the water is high, which raises it to a Class IV. This is a great run for beginners, family floats, and adventurous inner-tubers. It is also good for skilled canoeists and beginning-to-intermediate kayakers who feel ready to tackle some whitewater. The stretch below Hayden Flat is more popular with veteran boaters because it's faster and more challenging than the Big Flat-Hayden run but not as difficult as the Pigeon Point float. Most of the rapids here are Class II, with a pair of II-plus drops thrown in for extra excitement. Much of this section flows through a bedrock gorge, a rare occurrence, since most gorges include treacherous rapids that give boaters no chance to sense their sublime beauty.

Speaking of inaccessible gorges, be sure to take out at Cedar Flat, the put-in for one of the most challenging Class V runs in the state—the Burnt Ranch Gorge. This one is for experts only! The hydraulics in the canyon, coupled with many undercut ledges and boulder sieves, make for an unusually dangerous run. The drops come in rapid-fire succession and leave no time for rest. In just eight-and-a-half miles, boaters face four Class V falls and a boulder garden, three Class IV-plus rapids, many IIIs and IVs, and two that change yearly from IV to VI (unrunnable for those who would rather breathe air than water). This stretch is high on the list of "hair-boating" destinations in Northern California, but I recommend it only for those who are well trained, experienced, and in top physical condition. Make this run with a Burnt Ranch veteran, for many moves must be precise and can be learned only with a pro.

Below the gorge, which ends at Grays Falls, the river calms down and becomes ideal for inner-tubing, canoeing, and learning beginning skills. Although not nearly as steep as the Burnt Ranch Gorge, a deep and scenic canyon carries the river for about eight miles before it joins the South Fork. Unless a light boat is carried down the trail to Grays Falls, the best put-in for this run is at the Hawkins Bar day-use area. The stretch from Hawkins Bar to the Kimtu/Big Rock take-out points makes a wonderful one-day run with plenty of time for a picnic on one of many secluded beaches. For a shorter run the South Fork access can serve as a take-out, but keep in mind that boats and gear must be carried up a steep hill to the highway.

Below the South Fork, the Trinity changes dramatically from a narrow canyon river to one with wide gravel bars and a much slower current, until it enters the Tish Tang Gorge above Hoopa Valley. The section between the South Fork and Big Rock has no exciting rapids, but it is a pleasant float and a popular fishing drift in the fall. As the river begins to constrict a few miles below Willow Creek, the next set of challenging rapids makes its presence known with a gentle roar. The most notable ones are Sugar Bowl Falls and T-Bone. Sugar Bowl is not a falls at all, but a re-circulating ledge hole that is quite capable of flipping boats. As long as the hole is avoided there is no problem, but it has claimed a few drift boats, jet sleds, and canoes. I recommend that canoeists and drift boaters scout Sugar Bowl at the beginning of the season, since it changes from year to year. The Big Rock to Tish Tang run makes a great overnight float but can be done in a single day.

Below Tish Tang the Trinity flattens out again as it passes through Hoopa Valley, but it tightens up one final time in the Hoopa Gorge where the rapids rise to Class II. Weitchpec Falls can be tricky and change yearly. This is a Class III rapid and should be scouted by first-timers, especially since it is deep in the gorge with the only access by boat. The take-out is at Weitchpec, across the Klamath from the Trinity confluence; to get there boats must ferry across the Klamath quickly to avoid being washed downstream. This is remote country with private property owners who dislike seeing vehicles on the river bar and don't hesitate to let their owners know. Arrange a shuttle pick-up time at the Weitchpec take-out to avoid leaving your car or truck unattended. What a memorable place to end a Trinity River experience, where its jade green waters spill into the coffee-colored Klamath. The spectacular line where the two rivers meet can be observed from the bridge at Weitchpec. Even in the main stem Klamath the two rivers flow side by side for many miles before finally merging as one on their fifty-mile run to the sea.

White's Bar: Wildlife Viewing Station

The cool riverside woodland of white alder, willow, and bigleaf maple beckons tired but curious travelers to stop and explore the White's Bar picnic area midway between Big Bar and French Bar. One of many old mining sites along the "Bar/Flat" section of the Trinity River scenic corridor, this natural sanctuary contains a cornucopia of wildlife habitats. Five distinct vegetation zones—river, riparian, bar, oak woodland, mixed conifer—converge in an area less than one square mile in size. This remarkable concentration supports many wildlife species, making White's Bar a prime viewing place.

To promote both scientific and public understanding of neotropical migratory birds—songbirds from south of the Tropic of Cancer—the Forest Service operates a bird-banding station here as part of the continental Monitoring Avian Productivity and Survivorship (MAPS) program. Because the Trinity serves as a major migratory corridor within the Klamath Province, banding birds and recording their unique calls and songs help researchers map their regional population patterns.

Moreover, the Forest Service, through its Big Bar Ranger District Office, provides opportunities to learn about these tropical songbirds by offering field trips and talks for local schools and garden clubs. (The station also distributes a free "Wildlife of Trinity River" flyer.)

River Zone

Undeniably the dominant feature of this zone is the Trinity itself. Originating in the tops of the Klamath Mountains, the tributaries of the river swell with snowmelt each spring. These frigid flows constantly reshape the natural landscape, scouring the riverbed and carving out new arrangements of bars, beaches, pools, and riffles.

The dynamic nature of the river environment has spawned various natural adaptations of the wildlife that occupy this alternately severe and benign habitat. The return of steelhead and their chinook and coho cousins during the high river flows of spring coincides with the arrival of their avian predators—the osprey and bald eagle. These birds have adapted to the size of their prey. The hunting prowess of the osprey will impress any birdwatcher. Flying from a perch—usually a tall dead tree—it hovers 50-150 feet above the river before plunging into the water to capture an unlucky fish. As they grasp their slippery victim with their specially adapted talons, they thrust their wings upward and carry their catch to a large stick nest in a nearby snag.

Another remarkable fish-eating bird is the belted kingfisher. Much smaller than the osprey or bald eagle, it uses the same technique of perch and hover hunting to capture its prey. The chatter of this blue and white bird resounds along the river's banks as it flies in defense of its hunting territory.

Patiently stalking an aquatic meal on either side of the Trinity, the great blue heron is perhaps the most regal member of this region's avian community. Its blue-gray plumage blends in with the slate gray rock and dark water of its surroundings. Although it's the largest bird found here, its coloration and wariness camouflage it from casual passersby. When surprised or approached too closely, it ponderously rises into the air, flaunting its 6-8-foot wingspan in dramatic fashion.

On a hot summer day quiet observers may sight a Western pond turtle basking on a warm rock in a protected alcove. This wary reptile retreats into the relative security of the river when bothered. Sometimes seen in groups of three or four, these turtles seem to seek safety in numbers.

The American dipper, or water ouzel, is a common inhabitant of swift-flowing rocky sections of the river in the vicinity of White's Bar. This hyperactive slate gray bird bobs its body like a "Bop" dancer, but its rendition of the 1950s dance has a different purpose. Bobbing apparently helps the ouzel locate aquatic insects in the fast-moving water. Special oil glands and eyelids waterproof the bird's feathers and protect its eyes, allowing it to dive under water and capture prey other birds can't reach.

Although more commonly found in the lower reaches of the Trinity, the occasional appearance of a river otter at White's Bar reveals its fun-loving personality. This playful aquatic mammal seems to enjoy "slipping-n-sliding" down wet muddy riverbanks as much as any kid in summertime.

The common merganser, as its name implies, is the most frequently seen duck on this and many other rivers. In summer, the maroon-headed females chaperone their clutches of 8-10 "ganserlings" along rocky shores of the river. With large feet attached to short legs that are situated far back on the body, the merganser is well adapted for diving after its prey.

Riparian Forest Zone

Early morning visitors to the riparian forest of White's Bar will hear the "Song of the River"—a harmonious blend of sounds orchestrated by dozens of breeding songbirds, singing different but complementary songs. Their seemingly choreographed movements also create a colorful ballet under the forest canopy. Returning from their tropical wintering grounds in Central America and the Caribbean, these birds habitually breed in the insect-rich forests along the Trinity.

Among the most striking birds of this zone are the warblers. These insect-eaters zip through thickets of willow and alder as bright yellow flashes almost too swift for the eye to see. The half dozen warbler species that inhabit White's Bar glean insects from the bark and leaves of trees in addition to snatching them out of mid-air. From the high-pitched staccato trill of the orange-crowned warbler to the sharp, harsh "tsik" of the MacGillivray's warbler, the sounds of this group are among the most varied in the bird world.

One of the largest members of the stout-beaked sparrow family, the black-headed grosbeak forages for insects, seeds, and fruit with its large bill (or *gros beak*). Perhaps the noisiest bird found at White's Bar, its cheerful "eek" or long melodious song echoes through the air. The grosbeak builds sparrow-like cup nests of twigs, plant stems, and rootlets in thickets of alder trees.

Bank swallows nest in the steep, eroded

great blue herons

149

slopes of the Trinity. Friends of all mosquito-haters, they perform gravity-defying acrobatics while capturing a favorite food. Their maneuvers may even catch the eye of the inquisitive raccoon, whose hand-like footprints occasionally appear on White's Bar's sandy beaches. This omnivore has the unusual habit of washing its scavenged food before eating it.

River Bar Zone

Come spring, White's Bar puts on a dazzling display of wildflowers that attract pollinators from far and wide during the short flowering period. Close to the river's edge, a microscopic world of insect larvae teems amid a moist assortment of river rocks and pebbles. Serving as a food base for shorebirds, this ribbon of life sustains healthy populations of killdeer and spotted sandpiper. A few feet beyond the river's edge, the rocky grasslands attract sun-worshiping animals such as the alligator and western fence lizard (the latter also known as "the blue belly").

A piercing "kill-dee" sound signals the presence of the killdeer with its distinctive double breast bands. This wily shorebird feigns injury to lure potential predators away from its nest. The large eyes and rather stout beak of this plover enable it to find and feed upon insects and invertebrates among small rocks on river bars and at the water's edge.

The spotted sandpiper exhibits one of the most unusual social systems in the animal world. Under the right conditions this shorebird practices a polyandrous mating system, with more than one male per female. The female searches out a mate with which to breed. Together they build a nest, but once she lays a clutch of eggs, the mother-to-be departs in search of another mate, leaving the responsibilities of incubating and raising the young to the father. Under optimal conditions, a single female may have five different mates in a single breeding season.

Oak Woodland Zone

Juicy grasses and plants provide black-tail deer, also known as mule deer, with an abundant, high-quality food supply along the Trinity River and in the highland meadows of the Trinity Alps. A springtime visit to a secluded meadow may yield a glimpse of a newborn fawn and her mother bedded down during a warm afternoon. An autumn visit to "big buck country"—the exposed rocky hillside of the river canyon—may allow a close look at the rack of an old buck feeding on herbs in preparation for the annual rut. Physically demanding and sometimes violent, this period of arousal usually occurs during the late fall breeding season when mature males compete for mates.

While far more difficult to spot than the

American dipper, aka water ouzel

mule deer, the mountain lion is one of the Trinity corridor's most fascinating animals. Few people observe this elusive creature in the wild, yet it has probably spotted most visitors to its backcountry haunts. An efficient carnivore, it supplements a diet of black-tail deer (usually the old and sick or young and weak) with smaller mammals such as black-tailed jackrabbits, gray squirrels, California ground squirrels, and dusky-footed wood rats.

Game birds also abound around White's Bar. The California and mountain quails are the most common in the area, often seen foraging for seeds in brushy areas. When surprised, these fast runners generally escape on foot, flying only as a last resort. Forming large coveys during fall and winter, they appear to find safety and warmth in numbers. Although similar in appearance, the Californian's teardrop-shaped head plume distinguishes it from the mountain quail with its long, thin head feather.

Mixed Conifer Forest Zone

Located on the moist slopes of the river corridor, the mixed conifer forest attracts numerous animals. The shady groves of Douglas-fir, incense cedar, tanoak, and madrone offer a cool refuge during hot Trinity summers. Many creatures live almost exclusively in the forest, visiting the river only at night for a drink. Tracks along the soft wet banks signal their passage.

Although seldom or only fleetingly seen in the White's Bar area, the black bear may be spotted lumbering through blackberry thickets in search of a tasty meal. An opportunistic omnivore, it eats both animal and plant food, depending on availability. It knows exactly when and where to harvest seasonal sources. The bear's inquisitive nature may entice it into contact with humans. But due to its strong natural fear of people, all that is usually seen of a black bear is its rear end.

The spotted owl's preference for thickly forested canyons makes it one of the Trinity region's most intriguing birds. As a nocturnal raptor, it feeds on a diet of forest rodents such as the red tree vole and the Northern flying squirrel. From a perch the owl pinpoints the location of its prey with the aid of its disk-shaped face and offset ears. Its adapted wings and sharp talons enable it to swoop down silently and make a fast kill. Spotted owls seek specific nest sites, such as the cavities of broken-top conifers, to raise a pair of young. Very territorial during their breeding period, they use four hesitant, dog-like barks to warn away intruders.

The elusive weasel-like fisher is more often seen (or not seen) in tributary watersheds than in the river corridor. Despite its name, the fisher is not fond of fish. It resembles a cross between the solitary wolverine and the hyperactive pine marten. Its dark brown coat, once sought by fur trappers, effectively disguises the animal as it stalks its prey—porcupine, Douglas squirrel, and blue grouse. A keen observer may spot a fisher sleeping on the limb of a "wolf tree," a twisted conifer that suits it as a resting site. It's best to let a fisher rest, for this raccoon-sized predator deserves its reputation as one of North America's most ferocious animals.

Much more benign, the golden-crowned kinglet belongs to a diverse group of birds that live high in the canopy of the mixed conifer forest. This small insect-eater keeps company with mixed flocks of chickadees, warblers, juncos, brown creepers, and small woodpeckers. Presumably this communal behavior increases the number of eyes and ears available to detect predators and find rich feeding patches. Like a precious jewel attached to a necklace, the kinglet's pendulous nest, constructed of moss, lichen, spider webs, and leaves, hangs from the branch of a conifer.

The middle stretch and both ends of the

spotted owl

151

*golden-crowned
kinglets*

Trinity Scenic Byway lie along major flyways that reflect the region's inherent diversity. Cradled between the dry Central Valley and the wet Pacific Coast, the Scenic Byway's diverse habitats offer a home to myriad animals. The opportunity to observe creatures as different as salmon, shorebirds, or bears on a single trip can enrich the Trinity travel experience. Whether staying for just a few hours or an entire weekend, alert travelers will be surprised by the variety of wildlife found at White's Bar and many other places along or off Highway 299. Imagine how startled a busload of HSU students were when they spotted a lone fisher slinking across a hill above the road to the Washington Mine!

Beyond White's Bar the Trinity continues to veer northwest toward Cedar Flat and the entrance to the Gorge. Little more than a few place names remain to remind us of the miners who briefly occupied a series of bars and flats—Frenchmen, Canadians, Swedes, and others who displaced the native Chimarikos. A Little and a Big French Creek, with a French Bar in between, enter the Trinity two or three miles west of White's Bar. The big one is more likely to catch a traveler's eye because signs point to two trailheads 3 and 13 miles up the dirt road to the north. Both trails, choked with poison oak, will disappoint anyone who has hiked up Canyon Creek or the North Fork.

Trinity River Transition: Del Loma to China Slide

By the time westbound travelers reach diminutive Del Loma, they will have driven most of the "middle" Trinity's stretch of highway. They will have no doubt grown complacently familiar with the cozy confines of the narrow but relatively unintimidating canyon, where pines and oaks cloak the great diagonals that rise from the boulder-strewn riverbed to high ridgelines on either side, and where, nearly within reach, the river's sparkling waters race westward to the sea. Less than ten miles ahead, however, they will encounter China Slide—where the mauled and mangled mountainside marks the start of the thrilling topography of the "lower" Trinity—where the roadway is often etched across rock-faced slopes, where the merely steep becomes nearly perpendicular, and where the charming canyon becomes a vertiginous gorge. No wonder then that in the early days of the Trinity Highway, the "Del Loma decision" confronted coast-bound tourists. Upon learning of what lay ahead—the aforementioned China Slide, a paucity of guardrails, and the cliff-clinging route above the Burnt

Ranch Gorge—trepid travelers would either "turn around, or hire natives to drive their cars to Willow Creek…."

But times change. The highway has improved greatly, and it is no longer necessary to negotiate with Del Loma residents for their chauffeuring services. The one-time turn-around point currently consists of a few houses, an RV park, a store with the almost-inevitable rusting monitor outside, and a row of hillside motor court cottages that appear to date from the first days of the highway. Prior to the early 1850s the area was the site of Cicanma, one of some half-dozen Chimariko villages that lined the river corridor through the tribe's territory. By 1853 whites had taken over and the spot became Taylor's Flat. Taylor soon departed, leaving little but his last name, but the Washington Fluming Company promptly made a greater contribution, constructing a three-mile water race from French Creek. Although the cost of the project caused some of the stockholders to go broke, the flume assured the flat's miners of a water supply, so that when the peripatetic Isaac

Cox visited in 1858 he found a bustling community of "one hotel, three stores, blacksmith and butcher shop, and about fifty miners."

In 1855 whites located a deep cave on the steep hillside above the flat. It was explored for only a half mile of its length, perhaps because of the discovery of "[p]etrified human and animal remains, spread all over the floor, [which] testify that the peril of getting lost is true, and imminent." During the Indian-white conflicts of the 1860s, however, several bands of Chilulas, Whilkuts, and Hupas apparently hid in this and other nearby caves to avoid capture by militia and soldiers.

The Taylor Flat Hydraulic Mine was purchased in 1888 by the North Star Company, which had been digging a tunnel through the rocky point opposite Big French Creek for 11 years. Its purpose was to divert the Trinity, thereby exposing the riverbed for mining. To supplement this effort, the Taylor Flat mine would be worked extensively. The tunnel, which cost the then-whopping sum of $25,000, proved ineffective, and the dissatisfied shareholders soon closed down the Taylor Flat operation, idling "a well-equipped property, including a four-mile ditch and flume and other costly improvements."

With the coming of the Trinity Highway in the 1920s, Mr. and Mrs. James King moved down from the Moliter Mine on Grizzly Creek and opened a stopping place for tourists, fishermen, and hunters. Mrs. King, not liking the name Taylor Flat and perhaps thinking of her mother, Della, began calling the spot Del Loma, which approximates the Spanish for "of the hill." In this place where any hill, even if one were to exist, would be dwarfed by the surrounding mountains, *De la Cueva*—"of the cave"—might have been a more appropriate choice.

Today the cave still serves as an attraction. The Blue Cabins motel will, for a modest fee, grant explorers access via a trail through the motel property. (**Warning: cave exploration can be dangerous.**) Del Loma's other historic enticement, mining, never fully justified its initial promise. As James Bartlett wrote in 1926, the recently renamed flat "had been the scene of many mining revivals since 1858, none of which had lasting success."

Less than a mile west of Del Loma is the Hayden Flat Campground, a Forest Service facility that nestles in the woods directly north of the highway. The campground was built by the Civilian Conservation Corps (CCC) in the 1930s. Across the highway from the campground is easy river access a short distance

The mouth of the Del Loma Cave frames the mountain that may have inspired the renaming of Tayor Flat. (Mark Rounds photo)

downstream.

In another mile is the turnoff for the Ironside Mountain fire lookout. The gravel road first climbs above the Swede and Italian

creek drainages before reaching the lookout, 13 miles from the highway. The view is commanding, especially toward the coast.

The canyon of Swede Creek cuts through

the mountainside north of the highway 0.3 miles ahead. A dirt road climbs beside the creek, whose canyon in fall fills with colorful foliage—the pale yellow of western redbud, the rich gold of bigleaf maple, the pink and red of Pacific dogwood, and the yellow-green of elk clover that stunningly surrounds the deep purple clusters of its fruit. Directly south across the highway is a remnant of the original Swede Creek bridge; by leaning over its railing aspiring ichthyologists can espy a concrete fish ladder in the stream below.

Sandy Bar, 2.5 miles down the highway, was the site of a tragic episode in the Indian-white conflicts of the 1860s. (*See sidebar, below.*)

Some 1.5 miles to the west is a view across the river of the gleaming remnants of the Don Juan Bridge, a suspension contrivance built in 1895 to ease travel along the Trinity River trail. It was removed only recently. For nearly a century it served not only humans and horses but also cattle, pigs, and sheep.

In another 0.3 miles the highway cuts across Don Juan Point. The point and bridge derive

When the Mail Failed to Go Through

In 1863 the mail trail between Fort Gaston, in the Hoopa Valley, and Weaverville ran along the Trinity River. It was always a difficult and dangerous trip, but now, with full-scale fighting between the local Indian tribes and white settlers, it had become even more so.

When mail carrier Walter Van Arman set out from Fort Gaston at 6:00 P.M. on the evening of September 12, he was accordingly accompanied by an escort of two soldiers from Company C, First Battalion Mountaineers. The trio crossed the South Fork Trinity at about 11 o'clock, passing, but not disturbing, Indian camps where the inhabitants were all asleep. By daylight the men were at Burnt Ranch; they then descended to the main Trinity, which they crossed at Cedar Flat. Two miles later, at Sandy Bar, something caught the attention of one of the soldiers, Owen Washington:

As we came in sight of the rocks at that point I told Van Arman the Indians were in there, sure. I knew it just as well then as I did afterwards; I saw them. But Van said they were Chinamen, and we rode on.

Just as we got onto the bar, we got a volley from the rocks, and Terry fell from his mule. He called to me not to leave him, and Van and I jumped off from our mules and ran to him. Another volley and we both got it – Van Arman in the pit of the stomach and I in the right side. Van had held to the bridal rein, so he mounted and rode up the trail, bidding me good-bye as he threw the mail sacks to the ground. Terry was dead. There was nothing for me but to "hoof it," as my mule had fled with Terry's. The Indians kept up their fire as I hobbled away, another shot taking effect in my right thigh. After a hundred yards or more I sat down and tied up my wounds the best I could, for I was bleeding a good deal. About four hundred yards further up the trail I found Van Arman's mule but not Van Arman. Supposing he had gone on, I climbed onto the mule and pushed on to Taylor's Flat. Here I found only some Chinamen the Indians had killed in the morning, and I didn't stop….

Washington then crossed the river, "eluding two Indians who had followed me," and made it to Little Prairie. Here the store and some houses had been burned the day before, and so the wounded soldier had to ride all the way to Cox's Bar, just upriver from Big Bar, before he obtained help.

The following day a party of men headed downriver in search of the other victims of the attack. At the place in the trail where Washington found the mule, they noticed a scrap of paper sticking in a stump. On it was written:

WALTER VAN ARMAN,
Shot by the Indians,
Sept. 16, 1863.

No sign of Van Arman was to be found, only his saddle bags and the unopened mail bags. Terry's body was where Washington had last seen it, but it took three weeks of searching before Van Arman's was located, just a short distance from where he'd left his laconic note. Washington eventually recovered, but his wounds kept him off duty for a year. By then, a treaty had been signed with the Indians, assuring Van Arman's successors of one less danger on their Trinity River rides.

155

The aging concrete span of 1923 Swede Creek bridge (from the original highway) reposes below today's bypassing Scenic Byway, right. (Mark Rounds photo)

many Hailstones in the student body, the school must have had some stormy sessions indeed.

One and a quarter miles past Don Juan Point the highway crosses the Trinity and then passes through Cedar Flat, which Isaac Cox described in 1858 as being "covered with a beautiful grove of cedars." In addition, the flat offered "an enchanting resort for recreative exercise, or rest to the weary laborer, whose fondness of the solemn beauty of nature may enable him to enjoy." No wonder that by then "a thriving village had sprung up" that included a store, hotel, and cabins, all located on the rocky point at the west end of the flat.

But the settlers' village was built upon Hotinakcohota, the Chimariko community that had long existed there until the whites drove the inhabitants off. In May 1863 the Indians decided to temporarily reassert their claim to the land; about 40 of them attacked McCameron's store. A volley of shots brought McCameron and Myers out of the building, running for their lives (successfully, as it turned out) toward Burnt Ranch. The Indians eventually followed, destroying white property as they went, but they tarried long enough to carry off about 3,000 pounds of flour and various other goods and burn the store. Since the sacking of the flat's flour, the site has been a temporary home to mining operations, a convict highway labor camp, and a set of vacationers' rental cabins.

The highway now climbs the southern canyon wall. Below, the Trinity's corridor begins

their names from Don Juan Tiseran, a Spaniard who mined and kept a trading post here in the 1850s. The Don Juan Placer Mine started in 1879 and during the 1890s a rich streak of gold was paying "$60 per day to the man." But the streak played out, and in 1918 Zachariah "Mike" Hailstone and family homesteaded on the point. Mike's wife, the former

Ethel McDonald of Burnt Ranch, was a teacher before her marriage and eventually started a private school on the ranch to instruct her nine children. The school attracted the attention of Ripley's "Believe It or Not" because it "was built by the Hailstone family, was on Hailstone property, [was] taught by Mrs. Hailstone, and all but one of the pupils were Hailstones." With so

forming the constriction that culminates in the Burnt Ranch Gorge. A mile beyond Cedar Flat, Highway 299 passes the gaping geologic wound known as China Slide. Although more than a century has elapsed since the site obtained its name, the unstable slope still discharges the odd rock or boulder and threatens to send more substantial pieces of the topography into the Trinity. In earlier days, riverside residents failed to heed such portents at their peril. (*See sidebar, below.*)

When China Slide Slid

Collins Bar, located near the start of the Burnt Ranch Gorge downriver from Cedar Flat, could never have been considered a hospitable place. To the north, the brooding monolith of Cha-lee-dan Ah-woo, later known as Dixon's Bar Mountain and then as Old Ironsides, darkened the sky as it rose nearly straight up from the river bottom. The ridgeline on the south, though less imposing, was actually more malign; lacking the iron-sided solidity of its northern counterpart, it was but a tool of gravity, all too willing—and, as it turned out—able, to seek a rumbling, slope-shearing repose in the canyon below.

The Chimarikos, who for centuries occupied the area, paid heed to the threat and avoided frequenting the riverbottom. But they were not interested in the glimmer that emanated from the gravels of Collins Bar; those who were—white and Chinese miners—gambled that the rewards were worth the risks.

It was a bet they first lost in 1881, when a portion of the southern slope slid riverward, damming the Trinity for about an hour while entombing an unspecified number of miners in its rock-studded muck. After this, white gold seekers, who had other options, leased the bar to a Chinese mining company.

All went well until the winter of 1889-90. Then Trinity County "witnessed the heaviest rainfall and snow-pack in its history." At Old Denny, far up the New River, the snow lay 14 feet deep. Still, there were no unusual events along the Trinity until the morning of February 3, 1890. At the Don Juan mine the Huestis family was having breakfast when they noticed that the roaring of the nearby river had stopped. Then, as Charles Huestis later recalled:

Mama looked out of the window and said, "My heavens, the water is up around the Jim Bidden cabin across the river." My brother and I laughed for we knew the cabin was at least fifty feet above high water mark. Curiously [*sic*] we looked and sure enough we could see the cabin was afloat....

Wilbur, my brother, said, "By George, a slide in the canyon." We raced out for our boat and pushed it into the river and went down to Cedar Flat using paddles. Phil Morton, who lived there, was sitting on the rock, wet to the skin, for it was raining hard.

Morton's account was that he was sleeping late that morning. He just grabbed a few clothes and waded out the back door. He had a one-inch rope at the barn but it...had already floated away. If he could have had the rope in time he could have tied the house to a tree and saved it. As it was, he watched everything he owned on earth being carried out by the rapidly rising water.

We paddled down to the slide cautiously and then climbed the trail around a turn. There we could see the great raw gash in the mountain side. Never, never will I forget the scene with great blocks of stone, weighing many tons, still breaking loose on the mountain and rolling down.

The water eventually backed up all the way to French Creek, 12 miles up the canyon. In addition to Morton's house at Cedar Flat, Job Hodges's place two miles above Don Juan Point was also washed away, but the worst effects occurred downriver from the slide. According to Wilbur Huestis, when the

...mass of earth slid down into the river bed it displaced water so rapidly that a huge tidal wave rose in front of it and the restriction...of the canyon caused this huge volume of water to rush up the slopes on both sides of the river. The rush of water swept away an old log house which was more than 300 feet above the river at a point more than one-third of a mile downstream from the slide.

The house, at Collins Bar, was normally occupied by five or six Chinese miners, but only two were in it at the time. They were swept to their death by the water, the only casualties of the incident. Thenceforth, the great gouge on the mountain slope was known as China Slide.

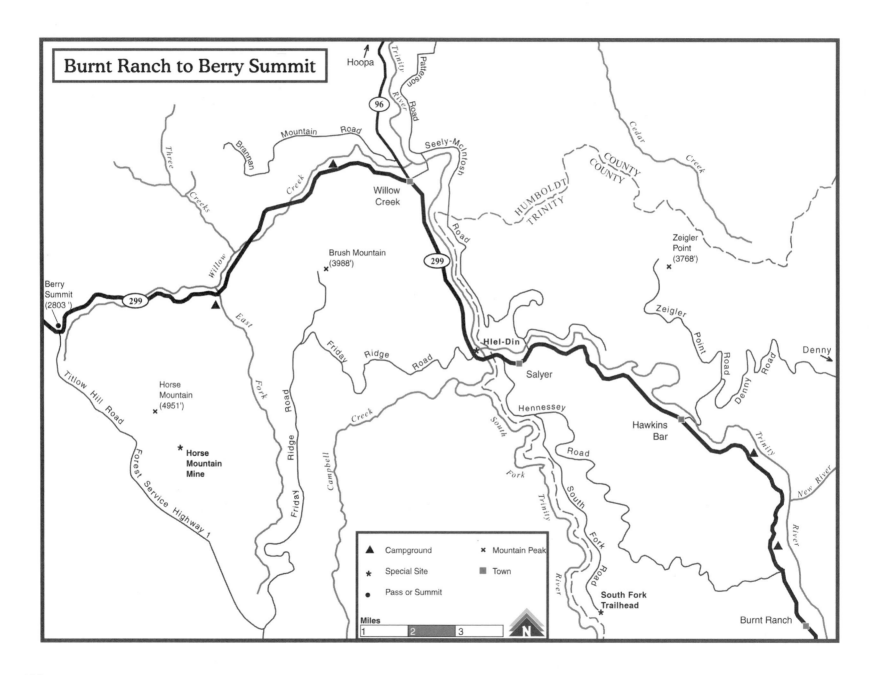

Burnt Ranch to Berry Summit

Hoopa

96

Mountain Road

Three

Creeks

Brannan

Willow Creek

Seely-McIntosh

Trinity River

Patterson Road

Cedar Creek

COUNTY COUNTY

HUMBOLDT TRINITY

Zeigler Point (3768')

Brush Mountain (3988')

299

Road

Berry Summit (2803')

299

Willow

East Fork

Zeigler Point Road

Friday Ridge Road

Hlel-Din

Salyer

Denny

Denny Road

Horse Mountain (4951')

Titlow Hill Road

Horse Mountain Mine

Friday Ridge Road

Campbell Creek

Creek

South Fork

Hennessey

Road

Hawkins Bar

Trinity River

Forest Service Highway 1

South Fork Road

Trinity River

New River

Campground

Mountain Peak

Special Site

Town

Pass or Summit

South Fork Trailhead

Miles

1 2 3

N

Burnt Ranch

VI. Driving Above the Deep Trinity Gorge

Burnt Ranch to Hawkins Bar: Clinging to the Cliffs

As Highway 299 rises above the Trinity past China Slide, it gains far more than altitude. The rhythm of its softly sinuous, nearly level accompaniment of the river is soon replaced by an oscillation between apprehension and awe, as motorists travel across narrow benchlands or along nearly vertical mountainsides while the vanished but not forgotten river rushes through the great gorge far below. To drive this section of roadway even once is to sense the region's uneasy mixture of promise and peril, where beauty and brutality have long coexisted side by side, where the next turn in the trail could bring one to either a pasture of plenty or a disastrous abyss. Today the section from Burnt Ranch to Hawkins Bar is tamer than it once was, but the wonders it now whispers of are still tinged with warning—pass this way with caution…and respect.

Burnt Ranch has earned its name at least thrice. In the early 1850s the Chimariko village that stood there, Cutamtace, was burned and its male inhabitants shot by French-Canadian miners in retaliation for the presumed but never proven theft of some horses. The Chimariko women and children fled the site, leaving it conveniently unoccupied for white settlement. In late 1854 Indians raided the ranch that Clark Durkee had established on the spot, killing or driving off nine mules and two oxen. A company of 20 whites quickly collected. Not pausing to consider that this may have been merely an enactment of the Biblical eye for an eye, they then pursued the raiders to the mouth of Hayfork Creek, killing seven Indians and destroying their village. Not content, the whites also laid waste to several villages along the banks of the South Fork Trinity on their return. Soon, however, another group of seven Indians attacked the ranch but were somehow captured singlehandedly by a Mr. Fish, who kept the saloon there. A council of whites promptly assembled; they decided to release two of the prisoners, giving them 24 hours to bring back a ransom of previously stolen property. When the pair failed to return by the deadline, the five remaining Indians were summarily shot. Four were killed, but the fifth, wounded, managed to escape during the night. According to Trinity chronicler Isaac Cox, who reflected the temper of the times, "necessity and self-preservation obliged the whites to continue killing off the Digger [Indian] superfluity during winter." Those who survived sued for peace, and, after somehow managing to pay Durkee $300 for damages, were granted it.

For a time the area saw no new conflicts, but in 1863 Indians conducted a raid down the Trinity that originated at Cedar Flat. When they reached Durkee's old place, now owned by Winslett and Houck, they set fire to all the buildings at the dairy ranch and stopping place before continuing along the river. The burning of Cutamtace had finally been matched.

The following year many of the area's combatant Indians signed a peace treaty; most of their kinfolk had by then been killed or driven off. After a decade of strife, hostilities at last ceased at Burnt Ranch.

In 1870 Patrick and Maria Hennessey and their family moved onto the Winslett-Houck ranch on the ridgeslope west of the present highway. Daughter Kate Hennessey would travel by horseback with her father up the Trinity en route to Weaverville. Where cliffs obstructed hillside travel they took to the riverbars; in all, the trip took them nearly a week. After they grew up, Kate and her two sisters became "known as good horsewomen…[who] could do most any kind of work called for on a ranch." By her 75th birthday Kate had changed her traveling pursuits. A newspaper article reported that "she thinks nothing about taking a five mile hike over the mountain trail near her home."

Closer to the river, Adam L. McWhorter ranched from 1870 until his death in 1900, when his son-in-law, James McDonald, took over. Two other McDonalds, Royal and Hilton, gained fame in France during World War I when they set a United States Army record by packing a mule in 43 seconds. After his return to Burnt Ranch, Royal faced an even harder task—packing a six-hole cast iron stove in from Helena. Completely stripped, the stove still weighed over 300 pounds, but the mule carried it without mishap until she reached Burnt

Ranch, where an overhanging tree limb caught the top corner of the stove, throwing the animal down on her side. Before McDonald could dismount to help the mule, she had regained her feet and then completed the trip unassisted.

In 1918 Bud and Belle Carpenter, who both came from old-time area families, moved from Willow Creek to Burnt Ranch. After a few years they built a store, but true to the traditions of the locale, it soon burned. It was a bad enough loss for the Carpenters, but worse would come. (*See sidebar, below.*)

When Destinies Dueled at Burnt Ranch

Charles William "Bud" Carpenter and William "Dutch Bill" Herder had only two things in common, a given name that was the same and an early run-in with the law. Their later lives diverged diametrically until one July night on the Trinity Highway, when the pair met—with tragic results.

Carpenter came from a ranching family on the South Fork Trinity. By age 12 he was working as a bell-boy on a Brizard pack train. In his spare time, what there was of it, he taught himself to be a crack shot. He made one shot too many when he killed a deer out of season and the incident was reported. The local game warden, Frank Graham, took young Carpenter to Weaverville, where the boy pled guilty, with reservations, and was fined $25. It was said that warden Graham paid the fine, and later it came out that Bud had shot the deer to prevent a pack of pursuing dogs from further tormenting it.

At 15 Carpenter took up the hazardous occupation of mail carrier. As he grew to manhood he developed a reputation for his teasing and jokes. He married Belle Irving, did some ranching, and eventually moved with his family to set up the Burnt Ranch store. Along the way, he also became a deputy sheriff.

"Dutch Bill" Herder's early life in Oregon was cut from far different cloth. He first made the news when he was arrested for burglary in 1920 while still a teenager. Herder was sentenced to three years in the Oregon penitentiary but was released before his time expired. In 1922 he was convicted of burgling a safe; this time he received a four-year sentence but was then deported to Russia as an "undesirable." Dutch Bill returned from Russia and was rearrested in 1926. His reentry into the United States was a mistake he'd make twice.

On July 8, 1928, Herder, who, despite his extensive arrest record was only 24 years old, drove south from Portland, Oregon, with a pair of other ex-cons, John Bishop, age 44, and "Dutch Pete" Stroff. The latter, at age 52, had three convictions and had spent half his life in prison. Stroff, nothing if not ambitious, had recently considered cracking the safe of the Oregon State Treasury in Salem. Some two years previously the three men had contemplated holding up the Northwestern Pacific passenger train that ran from San Francisco Bay to Humboldt County. The trio was now bound for Eureka.

After they arrived at their destination, a new prospect developed. Learning that Brizard's store in Willow Creek handled considerable money, they drove east on the morning of July 12 to case it out.

En route, the men may have passed Bud Carpenter's son, Lee, who had injured his hand and was on his way to a doctor in Arcata. (*continued next page*)

When Destinies Dueled...

Young Carpenter was no doubt anxious to return to Burnt Ranch, for in three days his father would celebrate his fortieth birthday.

Later that morning, Dutch Pete cased Brizard's store. He watched as store manager (and former game warden) Frank Graham opened a safe to pay a person "some bills over the counter." Stroff had seen all he needed.

At 3:00 A.M. the following morning, Graham, who slept on the premises, was awakened by a strange sound. It was the two Dutches, carrying off the Brizard safe while Bishop kept watch outside. Graham alerted the proprietor of the nearby Willow Creek Hotel, who phoned the Lower Trinity Ranger Station, several miles east on the highway. Just as Ranger Robert Benson received the report, the burglars' car sped past the station. Benson immediately contacted the next point east, Salyer, where a call went out to Bud Carpenter, the Deputy Sheriff at Burnt Ranch. Carpenter enlisted the help of fire guard Oscar Hayward and together the two men waited on the highway by the Carpenters' home.

In about 20 minutes a car sped around the curve by the house. As the vehicle slowed, Carpenter, armed with a 38-caliber revolver, stepped onto the left side running board and ordered the driver, Herder, to halt. Hayward, rifle in hand, jogged along the opposite side of the car as Stroff, seated in the middle of the vehicle, answered that they wouldn't stop. Bishop then jumped out from the passenger's side and walked toward Hayward, saying, "What are you stopping us for? We ain't done nothing." Suddenly he grabbed Hayward's rifle and the two men began a desperate struggle for the weapon. Stroff had leaped out behind Bishop, sawed-off shotgun in hand, and now attempted to draw a bead on Hayward. In the darkness Dutch Pete held his fire for fear of hitting Bishop. Meanwhile, Carpenter held his revolver close to Herder, who himself was armed with an automatic pistol. The two men, who'd led such distant, dissimilar lives, were suddenly facing death a few inches apart. Then Herder grabbed for Carpenter's gun; the deputy, distracted by the fight on the opposite side of the car, was taken by surprise; Herder quickly wrested his weapon away. The night was punctuated by several rapidly fired shots and Carpenter fell to the dirt.

By then Bishop had loosened his grip on Hayward's rifle. The fire lookout brought the gun up and fired; Bishop dropped to the ground. Stroff took off running up the road as Herder gunned the car in the same direction. Hayward fired at the vehicle and then collapsed; one of Dutch Bill's bullets had hit him in the hip. When others arrived on the scene they found three forms in the road. Hayward lay severely wounded; Bishop and Carpenter were dead.

Word of the shootout was phoned ahead to Weaverville, where Sheriff G. H. Bergin ordered roadblocks set up. Soon a car coming from the west was stopped. The driver asked to be taken to the sheriff, where he reported that he was running an errand for his brother at the Junction City power station. His automobile did not match the description of the getaway vehicle and since the time elapsed following the shooting seemed too short for anyone to arrive from Burnt Ranch, he was allowed to continue on his way. Only later did Sheriff Bergin wonder if his decision may have been too hasty.

Soon a posse of more than 75 men—"deputy sheriffs, forest rangers, ranchers, miners, Indians, and others"—was trying to track the murderers. As they searched without success, Bud Carpenter was laid to rest on his own land at Burnt Ranch. More than 250 mourners came to see him buried; "many of them," according to newspaper reports, "had walked forty or fifty miles from their mines and hillside cabins to be present."

On the night of the 16th observers at Burnt Ranch saw a faint light on the far side of the river; they watched as it moved across the face of Ironside Mountain. The fire lookout atop the peak reported seeing the light also, and a search party with bloodhounds set off in pursuit. Their quarry soon threw the dogs off the scent by jumping into the Trinity. Reports the following day had the posse hot on the trail, but still the suspect eluded capture.

Then, late in the morning on July 18th, a disheveled man appeared in the berry patch of George Gaynor's ranch, about ten miles above Salyer on the Trinity's South Fork. The stranger indicated he'd gotten lost while on a fishing trip, and Gaynor told him to keep eating the berries while he went to the cabin to fix something to eat. Once at the house, Gaynor quickly called Sheriff Bergin and then cooked up his entire larder—a pair of fish. About 2:00 P.M. a five-man posse swarmed down on the unsuspecting suspect, who offered no resistance. He was taken not to Weaverville but to the Humboldt County jail in Eureka;
(continued next page)

162

feeling was high in Trinity County and word was out that any suspect taken to its jail was likely to be lynched. In Eureka, teams of interrogators kept at the "lost fisherman" until, after 20 hours, he broke. In the confession that followed they discovered they'd captured Dutch Pete Stroff.

From him they also learned that the man still at large was Dutch Bill Herder, but although reports placed him in both Oregon and Washington, the young gunman eluded capture. Based on his confession, Stroff was soon sentenced to life in prison.

Years passed. Oscar Hayward, who'd nearly lost his life in the shooting, returned to ranching at Burnt Ranch, although he remained partially disabled from his wound. Belle Carpenter, now a widow with five small children, stayed on and opened a boarding house.

The incident was not forgotten. More than four years after the shooting, Humboldt County Undersheriff William C. Cavagnaro sent a picture of Herder to a detective story magazine. In early 1933, a reader of the publication tipped Pennsylvania authorities, who arrested a suspect. Subsequent investigation determined that the man was not Herder.

Then information came from New York City, claiming that Herder, now a ship's engineer, lived there when not at sea. Authorities sent a phony letter to Herder, posted a lookout where he collected his mail, and waited. On April 24, 1933, Dutch Bill came to pick up his letter and was arrested. He was soon sent to California, where he revealed that he had made his way to New York after the shooting and there boarded ship, traveling over the next four years to ports in England, France, Germany, the Free City of Danzig, the Azores, Venezuela, and Mexico.

In late June of 1933 Herder appeared in Trinity County Superior Court and pled guilty to the first-degree murder of Bud Carpenter. He was sentenced to life in prison just a few days before what would have been—had the two men never met on that fateful night at Burnt Ranch—Carpenter's forty-fifth birthday.

A year after Herder's sentencing, a gasoline drum exploded and set fire yet again to Burnt Ranch. This time the combination store and post office, several cabins, and other assorted small buildings were razed. Nineteen additional gasoline drums and (to cap the disaster) a beer truck were also destroyed. The store was rebuilt and a succession of managers ran it for Belle Carpenter until one of her children, Jim, and his wife Mary took over the business in 1950.

For a time local lumber mills added to the area's economy but these operations eventually closed, so that today Burnt Ranch consists of a store and post office (now separate), a school, various year-round and vacation homes, and a Forest Service campground. It has been a long time since the last of the community's several burnings, longer still since two lawmen met three lawbreakers in the night here on the road. Perhaps the sunlight that most summer travelers encounter as they now pass by, which bathes the surroundings in a warming glow, is prophetic of a more peaceful future, when, growing gentler, Burnt Ranch can at last dispel the darkness of its past.

The outskirts of Burnt Ranch are marked by Underwood Mountain Road, left, 1.2 miles west of China Slide, a part-pavement, part-gravel route that rises to the ridgetop on its way south to Hyampom. A stunning view of Ironside Mountain, right, presents itself 0.7 mile later, followed by a junction with Hennessey Road, left, in another 0.7 mile. This historic route (paved at first, then turning to gravel) crosses Hennessey Ridge after passing the site of the Hennessey Ranch, and then descends a verdant, nearly vertical mountainslope to reach South Fork Road in the South Fork Trinity drainage.

Highway 299 then reaches the turnoff, 0.4 mile past Hennessey Road, to the Burnt Ranch Campground, right. The pleasantly wooded, hillside site offers a trail (at the end of its loop road) that traverses three-quarters of a mile of often treacherous mountainslope to reach Burnt Ranch Falls, where the Trinity rushes through a dark, rock-strewn gorge with a force unexpected from a dammed river. In the summer of 1875 Frank Bussell and William Guinn tested the raging waters by, of all things, attempting to navigate *upstream* through the gorge. Launching their newly built boat into the Trinity at the mouth of New River, the thus-imperiled pair grabbed their oars and rowed for all they were worth. Ten days later, the exhausted expeditionists finally reached Cedar Flat, barely five miles from their start. Not surprisingly, Bussell and Guinn left their boat at the flat and returned home by foot, a trip that, over the mountainside trail, took them but half a day.

Just beyond the campground turnoff is the intermittently open Burnt Ranch Store, the third such to occupy the site. The highway then departs the tiny community and soon reaches the stark cliffside above the chasm containing the Bussell-and-Gwinn-thwarting gorge. It was here in the winter of 1910 that 16-year-old mail carrier Frank Irving, brother of Belle Carpenter, was killed when his horse slipped off the trail and fell on him. Irving was bringing the mail down from distant Denny and was forced to make the last stage of his trip in the dark. He was found by his friend, mail contractor William Gray, with the lantern he used for night riding still in his hand.

A pullout, right, 1.4 miles beyond the Burnt Ranch store, is marked by a Six Rivers National Forest sign. Directly to the east, the New and Trinity rivers rumble and tumble to a meeting in the canyon far below. The New, debouching from the narrowest of defiles, drops down a series of rocky rapids to join the Trinity, itself crashing with whitewatered intensity through its own constricted course. Rising with virtual verticality from the two riverbottoms are the monolithic forms of Ironside Mountain, right, and a peak known locally as "Little Ironside" to the left. The ridgeline they would otherwise have formed is cloven from sky to streambed by the knifelike effects of the New. Etched across the lower portion of Little Ironside, the remains of the New River Trail bear silent witness to the terrors of the terrain, which prevented construction of the route until 1914, when brothers John and James Larson completed a suspension bridge a short distance down the Trinity. A picture taken at its opening shows a half-dozen small figures perched like tightrope walkers at one end, with the frothing river swirling past the rocky cliffs in the canyon depths below. To the right of the confluence sits the flat that was once home to Al "Gus" Augustus, a retired logger who occupied the site in the 1970s. Gus reached his 20-acre mining claim via a hand-operated cable car that crossed high above the New to connect with the trail.

The trail and its vertiginous bridge were legendary for the demands they placed on users. One such, a physician from Eureka who owned a share of the Corona Mine far up New River, failed to ever master crossing the bridge. When confronted by the swaying span, he would always drop to his hands and knees and crawl across. His lack of fortitude was more than made up for by a diminutive pack mule, which was charged with carrying a large bathtub all the way to Denny. The tub was "put upside down, mostly over the mule," and rigged to a packsaddle. On the way up the trail the mule, its vision and gait encumbered by its cargo, would often stumble, fall, and land upside down on the trail. Each time the packer would turn the mule over, get it on its feet, and start it up the trail again. "It was said that the mule spent almost as much time in the tub as on its legs," but eventually both the cargo and its carrier made it to Denny.

One mile beyond the overlook is the entrance, right, for Grays Falls Campground, a Forest Service facility set in a woodland notable for its tanoaks, madrones, and bigleaf maples. A wide trail leaves from the end of the picnic area loop road, dropping riverward through elk clover, giant chain fern, wild grape, and assorted wildflowers. The right-hand branch of the route terminates at an overlook of the campground's namesake water feature.

The falls themselves were named for the Gray brothers, William and David, ranchers and miners who lived near the Trinity some distance northwest of the present campground. During the 1860s their ranch site was home to Alex Tinsley's trading post. When the area came under attack during the great Indian raid of 1863, Tinsley was on a packing trip to Red Bluff,

The opening of the New River Trail's Trinity River bridge in 1914 found a half-dozen dedicators defying dizziness from their high perch above the rushing river. (TCHS photo courtesy of Lowrie Gifford)

and his wife and children took refuge at the Winslett and Houck place at Burnt Ranch. The Indians established themselves nearby; Winslett, who at first believed he could keep them at bay, had second thoughts, and, "[a]s night advanced [and] the stillness of death reigned in the Indian camp," Winslett, Mrs. Tinsley, and her children made their way past the war party and reached the Tinsley store. There they secured books, money, and ammunition, barricaded the door with sacks of flour to give the impression that someone was inside, and made for the Trinity. They crossed the river and took the trail to the New River mining camps. After resting there briefly, they crossed the divide into the North Fork Trinity drainage, and finally reached Helena (then called North Fork), "making the perilous trip of 110 miles in less time than it had ever been accomplished by those familiar with the route." There Winslett joined a relief party that hurried downriver, where they found all the buildings at Cedar Flat and Burnt Ranch in ashes. "Through some strange but kindly fate" Tinsley's trading post was still standing, but its entire stock of goods had been appropriated by the raiders.

Hawkins Bar, 1.2 miles beyond the Grays Falls Campground, is the starting point for Denny Road, right. Jere Smith, who had a ranch just north across the river, was famed for his produce, but the lack of road access to the coast hampered his marketing efforts. A report from 1900 noted that Smith:

…will commence gathering the splendid winter fruits grown in his orchards, and feed them to his pork hogs. Last year he fattened a dozen or more pork hogs on the most delicious apples—Baldwin, Smith cider, Rainbo, Newton Pippin, Spitzenberg, Rhode Island greening—because of the impossibility of getting them to the railroad terminus, 45 miles, in marketable condition.

A later generation of agriculturalists are the members of the Colony, "a religious experiment in communal living," which located in 1941 on a nearby flat above the Trinity. Founded by Brother John, a World War I conscientious objector, the original 19-member group had dwindled to four—all elderly—by 1969. Although several new members arrived in the early 1970s, by the mid-1980s the fate of the Colony hung by a heartbeat; the property was on National Forest land, and occupancy was dependent on a lifetime "special use" permit that was valid only so long as at least one of the original colonists remained alive. By then the sole survivor was white-haired Sister Agnes, who maintained a graceful composure for several years until the Forest Service finally negotiated a complicated land swap that transferred ownership to her and her colonial siblings. Extending this happy ending into the present, a revitalized Colony is now involved with a local plumbing company, a ranch, and several other business enterprises.

Hawkins Bar's one nod to history, the private "*Ironside* MUSEUM" on the eastern edge of town, hides its light under the bushel of a "PRIVATE PROPERTY—KEEP OUT" sign that appears to be perpetually in effect. Rusty mining memorabilia stand like forgotten monuments outside the structure, while a glance inside through streaked windows reveals shelves and counters cluttered with bottles, utility line insulators, and an accumulation of other aged objects, all reposing in the obscurity engendered by progressive neglect. The time of New River mining is long past, the erstwhile displays seem to say, and what had once been New has now, after decades of disuse, finally become Old.

Distant Denny

The most isolated region in Trinity County and perhaps in the entire state, the Denny area lies in a forested fastness of mineral-rich mountains that enticed early day gold-seekers to endure the rigors of remoteness for the prospect of a glittering reward. It was, and is, rough country, which attracted, and bred, a rugged people who lived larger than most city-dwelling folk, and who left a legacy of legendary exploits that still excite a century later, when the embers of fading memory fan to flame at the mere mention of the name—Denny.

Denny Road, two-lane and paved, runs northeast from its junction with Highway 299 in Hawkins Bar, dropping to cross the Trinity River at mile 0.2 on the Bill Jackson Bridge. The span was named for a deputy sheriff who, like Bud Carpenter of nearby Burnt Ranch, was "killed in [the] performance of his duties." The road soon switchbacks up the hillside before turning north to briefly run up the canyon of Hawkins Creek. At 1.7 miles the route makes a sharp switchback right and narrows to one lane.

To the west lies the property of the Irving-Wallen Ranch. George Irving mined in the New River area before moving here in 1893 with his wife, Kate, and six children. Seven more children followed over the next 14 years, the last, Annie, arriving just two months before George's death. Kate continued on the ranch without her husband, enduring the additional losses of two sons, Frank and George Jr., who each died in accidents while only teenagers. She also saw another son, Roy, severely injured in an auto wreck and a daughter, Belle, lose her husband, Bud Carpenter, in the 1928 shootout at Burnt Ranch. Just two years after the latter incident the Irving home burned to the ground, but her sons and sons-in-law built her a new house nearby. A young acquaintance, who received a two-pound box of chocolates from her every Christmas, recalled later that "wherever Kate Irving lived, her home was surely a castle for that warm feeling of welcome to friend or stranger [that] prevailed wherever she was."

Bigleaf maple, oak, Pacific dogwood, and various conifers shade the steep slopes as the road rises above the Trinity. At 7.5 miles our route bears right at a junction; the way left climbs to the ridgeline that the original Denny trail followed on its way from Willow Creek. After crossing a ridge shoulder, the road enters the New River drainage, passing under a flume, mile 12.5, that has long carried water to the

Dailey Ranch, which is then reached at Oak Flat, mile 13.0. A scattering of various-aged structures, along with some pastureland and orchards, marks this sudden opening in the forest. (*See sidebar, next page.*)

Departing the Dailey Ranch, Denny Road returns to the forest, passing through an opening above the narrow gorge of the New River, mile 14.9, before reaching the conifer-sheltered Denny Campground, 17.8 miles. On the left is the foundation of the Denny Guard Station, which was burned during the heated controversy in the 1960s–1980s between the Forest Service and a group of recently arrived local residents. Although the New River newcomers claimed to be miners, the Forest Service believed that their main income derived from marijuana growing. It was not until April of 1971, when one ranger was injured by the effects of a ricocheting bullet and two others were roughed up in a fight, that the outside world learned there were serious difficulties in the Denny area. Complicating the controversy was the Forest Service's use of the phenoxy herbicides 2,4-D and 2,4,5-T on cutover New River timberlands in the 1970s. Claims of miscarriages and reproductive problems related to

Daily Life on the Dailey Ranch

In May 1905 John and Viola Dailey and their young son, Hilton, moved onto the Patterson Ranch at Oak Flat. John had mined for the past 25 years, most recently (with little success) in the upper New River country, and was now ready to try ranching. The spot they chose had been settled by Columbus Patterson way back in 1852, and, over half a century later, it still contained some of the apple trees he had planted. Columbus's nephew, Mose, left the Daileys more than an orchard when he turned the place over to them—a quilt that remained behind was infested with "thousands of bedbugs."

The Daileys burned the quilt and its unwanted occupants, but the eradication was only temporary; the ranch became a stopping place for packers and other travelers, most of whom brought their own crop of bedbugs to replenish the supply. It was, however, a small price to pay for the company of the various visitors, a charming collection of characters that were recalled with great relish years later by one of the Dailey daughters, Jean. In a series of columns appearing in the *Arcata Union* in the late 1970s, she described the locals and outsiders who came by the ranch that lay "Along the old New River Trail."

In 1927, six-year-old Jean met Mr. Tickner, the packer, and his French client, Louis Maire. "Mr. Tick" was packing hydraulic mining equipment in from Salyer to Maire's Upgrade Mine, four miles up the canyon, and while doing so the pair stayed at the ranch. Every evening, after cider and popcorn, one of the men would ask Jean to read to them. Taught, like the rest of the Dailey children, by their former schoolteacher mom, Jean proudly plowed through books written for children twice her age. This was but a prelude for the greatest treat of the evening, one of Mr. Tick's tales of his stagecoach driving days. Jean's favorite involved alcohol and dynamite, a dangerous combination. According to Mr. Tick,

> I'd been drinkin' pretty heavy for a week an' had a real buzz on that day. I came around a bend an' a fellow ran out wavin' his arms for me to stop because they was doin' some blastin' along the road. But I'd had couple of snorts too many, an' I yelled, "Ya' can't stop the United States mail" an' went on through. All the harm the blast done was I lost one back wheel an' some spokes out o' the other one—but the team an' the two lady-passengers was kinda' spooked all the rest o' the day.

Mr. Tick eventually switched to a motorized stage, but, as he told it, "I yelled 'Whoa!' twice at that Model T, but the darned thing kept going right over the bluff, so I quit an' got me a pack train."

Entirely different but equally interesting was Louis Maire, a "remittance man" who claimed to be the illegitimate son of a member of the erstwhile French royal family. As was required in such cases, he was forced to leave France when he turned 12, but was sent a monthly emolument of $35. To supplement this he became a cabin boy on a ship and then graduated to being a sailor. Maire saved his money, bought the Upgrade Mine, and then went into debt upgrading it, so that he had to go back to sea to raise more funds. His time at the Dailey Ranch remained frozen fondly in his memory, for when he returned for a visit 13 years later and met Jean, now a grown woman, he was taken by surprise. "Not Jean, the little girl who used to sit in my lap and read to me!" he exclaimed, as tears came to his eyes.

Another sometime sailor who stopped at the ranch was Charley Schwedler, a German immigrant who, like Maire, had a mining claim upstream from the Daileys'. During his first years on the New River, Charley was a bachelor—but a neat one. When he headed for the city he always left in a suit and starched shirt. On one such occasion, Jean's father remarked, "Charley don't look like he's walked out from East Fork—he looks like he was just ready to have supper—with the governor."

Then Charley, at age 63, got married. His new wife, Millie, came from the city, but she soon adapted to her new home—with one exception. When packing in goods to their mine and ranch in the summer, Millie would declare that the weather was too hot for the "poor animals" and insist that she and Charley transfer the mules' loads onto their own backs. For the hardworking Charley this was of little consequence—he was known to arrive at the Daileys' at 8:00 A.M. (after having earlier had breakfast at the Irving Ranch 12 miles down the trail), visit for an hour, and then hike the remaining four miles to his ranch, where he was still able to put in a full day's work.

In 1946, 81-year-old Charley fell off the trail near his ranch and landed on a ledge below, breaking *(continued next page)*

168

Daily Life...

many bones. After a trip to the hospital in a pickup truck "ambulance" Charley returned for another ten years on the river. Following his death Millie lived alone on the remote ranch until failing health forced her to move to a place on Denny Road. Even then, at age 91, she walked all the way out.

Louis Maire and Captain Tick, the Schwedlers, and also John P. Harrington and Sally Noble—perhaps the most intriguing pair of the lot. When Harrington arrived in the summer of 1921 to interview Sally Noble, she was his last, best hope for transmitting the language of her New River tribe. Born in the river's upper drainage about 1855, Sally had survived the attacks that had killed most of her kinfolk. She had married a miner, Steve Noble, who had died several years earlier, and now resided at an old Indian village site about a mile down the river trail from the Dailey Ranch.

Harrington, a linguist with the United States Department of Ethnology, was racing against time to record the languages of western tribes before their last fluent speakers died. For six weeks he lived with the Daileys, going daily down to Noble's house for a "lesson" in her language. Soon she learned that when he returned from the Denny store he always brought treats for Jean Dailey; Sally would then wait for Harrington on the trail to demand her share, or, she threatened, "no lesson tomorrow!" At other times she refused to work with him until he had worked for her—by picking two gunnysacks full of the acorns that were one of her main foods. This the complaisant linguist was quick to do, even though his office was already paying Sally an "unheard-of" hourly rate.

At last Harrington had recorded all he needed. He boxed up his thousands of sheets of notes, gave them to Jean's mother, Viola Dailey, to keep, and left.

Twelve years passed without a word from Harrington. Finally, Viola wrote the Smithsonian Institution in search of him. In due course a letter arrived from him about his Sally Noble notes: "I wasn't concerned—I knew you'd take care of it."

Which was something that Viola Dailey, who had bore her nine children at home without a midwife or doctor and had then taught them through the eighth grade, always did.

Pack train bound for Old Denny after leaving Tener Camp, c. 1915-20. Willard Ladd at front of train; brother Grover one of two gents at rear. (TCHS photo, courtesy Lowrie Gifford)

Ladd's Store (left) at New Denny, early 1930s. Willard Ladd is standing in front of car. (TCHS photo, courtesy Lowrie Gifford)

herbicide exposure resulted in an inconclusive EPA investigation and an out-of-court settlement with four of the alleged victims.

Another opening at mile 18.6 announces the environs of Denny, which consists of fields, a few houses, and the now-closed Ladd's Store, a striking log and stone structure embellished by a nearby "Fire Chief" gravity-flow gas pump.

Frank Ladd originally had a store, post office, and hotel at "Old" Denny, far up the New River drainage, but as that town neared its end, he relocated the post office 23 miles downriver to what had been called Quimby but now became "New" Denny. Here his sons Willard and Grover—the Ladd lads—had already opened a store and hotel of their own. Frank continued

to operate the post office at the new location until his death in 1932, the year the road from Hawkins Bar reached Denny.

Denny Road continues up the New River canyon for several miles, ending at the trailhead to the upper New River mining district. This remote high country, which rises up to the Trinity-Salmon divide, is more often written about than visited, and all but the most dedicated backpackers will reach the region only by way of this—or another—printed page. (*Note: check with the Forest Service for current trail and camping information.*)

A Captain Bess and his mining party came into the area in the middle of 1851, followed promptly by another group of gold-seekers. The two factions first talked, then fought, then made up and pooled their resources. The New River mining boom had begun. Before it was over it had busted thrice, revived twice, and left little on the landscape to mark its final passing.

The early mining was placer, where gold-seekers washed through streamside gravel deposits in search of paydirt. Accordingly, the early communities—Hoboken, Quimby, Forks, and Lake City—developed along the alluvium-rich lower and middle sections of the New and its tributaries. In 1859 "Uncle Billy" Kirkham, mining on Virgin Creek, described his claim as being "25 miles from anywhere," and it was certainly farther than that from most other places. Lengthy trails made their way into the New River country from Willow Creek, Cecilville (over the mountains to the north in

Siskiyou County), and North Fork (Helena). Later routes from Hawkins Bar shortened the trip, including the cliff-clinging trail up the lower New River that was completed in 1915.

The mining camps that developed in the upper end of the drainage during the hard-rock boom (c. 1870–1910) were never reached by roads, although one was built to connect the three towns of that era—Marysville, White Rock (Couer), and New River City (Old Denny). The self-contained route was used by two wagons and, later, a pickup truck, all of which had been disassembled, packed into the area, and then reconstructed for short hauling between the towns. Some residents hardly needed the road and seemingly had little use for even the trails: when Frank Ladd, who kept the store at Old Denny, came to Weaverville in 1915 for a lawsuit, it was the first time he'd visited the county seat in 25 years. "He made the trip from North Fork [Helena] in an auto," the *Trinity Journal* informed its readers, "this being his first glimpse of a motor car."

Shortly thereafter, Lucy Young, a candidate for county office, braved the rigors of the New River mining country trip in search of a lode of votes. (*See sidebar, next page.*)

Young's visit to Denny came in the middle of its second bust. During the 1930s it boomed once again, albeit briefly, as a wave of Depression-era miners sought a minimal income. A little gold dust bought them staples to supplement their favorite recipe, poached venison, and they somehow hung on, often living in "the awfulest shanties you ever saw."

The third bust that followed was to be the upper New River's last. The old mining district, now part of the Trinity Alps Wilderness, is gradually returning to its natural state, helped along by the heavy winter snows and a severe forest fire that burned through the region in the fall of 1999. Backpackers who visit the nearly vanished townsites will find nary a saloon or stamp mill, nor even—Lucy Young's successors take note—any votes.

Old Denny Post Office. (Gay Holland Berrien drawing)

When Going up Got out the Vote: The High-Elevation Electioneering of Lucy Young

In 1914 Lucy Young lost the election for Trinity County Superintendent of Schools. When she ran again in 1918, she decided that her canvassing of the county should leave no corner, however remote, unvisited. Accordingly, she set out one July day with a guide and her niece, Blanche, to a location where the number of voters was inversely proportional to the difficulty of reaching them. In other words, she was bound for Denny.

Blanche, a novice rider, provided certain distractions near the start of the trip. In quick succession she dropped the pillow she was using to soften her saddle and then lost her gloves. All went well for the next few hours until, during the heat of the summer day, she lost her sun hat. With a bareheaded Blanche courting sunburn, the party continued on "over a narrow, twisting trail, over one high mountain after another" until, bone-weary, they reached Denny at 9:30 that night.

The next day, Young canvassed Denny's electorate, which consisted of "one lady and four men." Since this didn't take long, her party was soon off on its return trip, but not before Blanche, more mindful of the comfort of her upper, rather than lower, regions, had traded her pillow for a replacement hat.

Their trip now took them down the rapidly descending New River drainage. According to Young:

> Nothing eventful happened that day with the exception of a continuation of chills and thrills as we wound over the tortuous, shoestring trail and gazed down hundreds of feet to the waters below. Blanche also lost her saddle blanket, but I, being behind her, picked it up.

This was but a prelude for the next day, when they came down to the Trinity where

> ...we came upon our first mountain swinging bridge. A little bridge swung high in the air by cables, over a rocky river gorge, and just wide enough for a pedestrian. Crossing a swinging bridge of this kind cannot be adequately described, but I had the sensation of being utterly at sea, the bridge wobbling and swinging under me, and at each step I took the bridge came up to meet me. This sensation increased until I reached the center, where I seemingly bounced up and down like a rubber ball, completely at the mercy of this little swinging bridge. Gradually this sensation subsided as I neared the other end....

If Young thought their trail-bound travails were over, she hadn't counted on the following day's event, crossing the infamous China Slide:

> Picture this narrow trail carved in the rock, about one-half mile in length; not even a tree or bush to break the fall, in case one became dizzy and slipped over the bank. It just meant that one would keep on sliding and sliding until one reached the treacherous water below and then—oblivion.

> As I dismounted my horse (for no one but an expert would stay with his horse), I gave one long look around which completely took in the yawning abyss, the dizzying heights, the glassy mountain side and the sublime beauty and horror of it all, then I glued my eyes steadfastly to the narrow little trail and kept them there until I landed safely on the other side, after what seemed an eternity of time.

> It was a thrilling experience and one that I would not have missed for worlds, nor yet would I wish to repeat it.

Blanche had apparently created little trouble during these last, dangerous phases of the trip, but once on safer ground she resumed her old habits and, one by one, proceeded to lose all her hairpins, so that she entered Hayfork looking, according to Young, like "Lady Godiva herself" with her "long, luxuriant golden tresses...floating gracefully to the breeze."

Then it was August, time for the primary election. When the votes were tallied, Young found she had won: 518 to 513. Her margin of victory was provided by—where else?— Denny, which she carried in a 5 to 0 landslide. The results probably made a little bit of bridge crossing—and a few lost hairpins—all seem worth it.

The Scattered Dream Town of Marshall Salyer

After following Highway 299 high above the Trinity Gorge from Cedar Flat to Hawkins Bar, travelers can breathe more freely as they pass the Safety Rest Area and cross the Carpenter Bridge into Salyer, at the western end of Trinity County. The population/elevation sign claims 250 residents for the town, but its only really salient feature is the Six Rivers National Forest Work Center. In 1949, a *Humboldt Times* reporter described the station as if it were the town—"an attractive community with its own post office and school, as well as stores." The squat brown buildings and the light green vehicles of the Salyer Work Center, completed by Civilian Conservation Corps crews in the mid-1930s and complemented by the nearby Community Wayside Chapel, give the place the appearance of a cozy company town. That's especially true on Sunday mornings when the church parking lot fills up. But the impression of compactness belies the dispersion that has characterized the community since its ambitious founder arrived from the North Coast in 1913.

Born in Kentucky in 1888, C. Marshall Salyer spent much of his youth rambling across the country before finally landing in Arcata, where he met and married a cook named Tessie. They soon decided that their future lay inland among the scattered mines and ranches of the lower Trinity. The young couple caught a stage in Blue Lake on July 24, at 4:00 A.M. They had lunch at Berry's Redwood House, near the crossing of Redwood Creek, and arrived in Willow Creek at dusk. According to an account he wrote in1938, Marshall soon set out for a New River mining camp with a pack train that passed through the future site of Salyer, then "a wild woods except for a tiny school house of rough lumber with a shake roof." For two years he worked as a hired hand, first for the Corona De Oro Mining Company and later on a ranch. With his savings the Salyers soon acquired property on the Trinity about a mile upstream from the mouth of the South Fork.

When construction began on the long-awaited road to link the Willow Creek area with Burnt Ranch, work crews swelled the local population. Young Salyer seized the chance to establish himself (and his name). After his small peach orchard matured, he supplied fresh fruit to road builders. His fortunes, along with his trees, blossomed nicely. He scraped up enough capital to start a small riverside canning operation that for awhile supplied the Del Monte Company.

The "live wire" on the Trinity, as an *Arcata Union* reporter labeled Salyer, scored another success when the emerging community had to choose a name for its new post office in 1917. A number of possibilities were submitted to the postmaster, but a five-dollar bribe supposedly clinched Marshall's bid for the honor.

The fruit business sustained the Salyers and others through the 1920s and even the depressed 1930s. Marshall bought a Cletrac tractor so he and a partner could expand their orchard to 14 acres and 1,000 trees in the spring of 1923. The lower Trinity above Willow Creek flourished as "the pick and shovel men" followed by "the steam and shovel crew"—all headquartered at the Work Center—labored to finish the final section of Highway 299. By then the (lower) Trinity Valley Farm Bureau had enough members, under the leadership of Eleanor I. Brizard from Hawkins Bar, to fund a "Civic Center" with a big dance hall down the road, half a mile past the chapel that was then a café.

When skyrocketing tin and sugar prices put his cannery out of business at the onset of World War II, Salyer already had his hand in another promising enterprise. Although the glory days of Trinity mining had passed, Marshall acted on the prevalent notion that ancient river gravels in the lower South Fork area held gold. Like other operators, he faced two obstacles to profitable recovery of the elusive mineral. He needed a source of water to work the steep slopes above the river. And he had to develop an efficient method of extraction in an era of slim profits.

Salyer solved both problems in grand style. First he constructed a flume across the South Fork to tap Madden Creek (now named once again Campbell Creek) on the west bank. He then ran the water through a penstock, generating electricity for "booster" pumps that provided ample pressure in the monitors used to work his claim. A double recovery system, of his own devising, extracted much of the fine gold normally washed through the sluices into the river. The system, adopted elsewhere in California, allowed Salyer's mines to produce for many years.

Alas, Marshall's fortunes took a downturn in the late 1940s when legal disputes forced Salyer Consolidated Mines into bankruptcy. The humbled promoter went back to work as a hired hand at a local mill. Now in his 50s, he needed yet another enterprise to see him through till retirement. During his misfortunes, he had held on to his properties. One of them was an old homestead high on the north side of the Trinity that had no road access until 1932. By subdividing the land and selling it off lot by lot, he regained financial security. Marshall and Tessie organized a cooperative of landowners in Salyer Heights. The suburb secured its own water supply by building low concrete dams on two creeks above the area. The "live wire" and his wife lived out their lives in the Heights, high above the dispersed dream town that still bears his name.

A right turn in Salyer onto the Campbell Ridge Road, at the abandoned gas station, leads across one of the newest bridges spanning the Trinity. The next road right follows along the edge of the Fountain Ranch, one of the few homesteads in the area when the Salyers arrived. Thomas G. Campbell, a Border South rambler like Marshall, had settled this large flat in 1871 with his Hupa wife Maryann. He set up a general store and a blacksmith shop on the ranch to serve the mule trail traffic. Soon he hired out two 30-mule pack trains in addition to raising stock and running a sawmill. In 1891, shortly before his death, the *Blue Lake Advocate* reported that "Mr. Campbell has everything nearly that could be wished for in the line of fruits, also a large amount of land devoted to grain."

Dr. Matthew Fountain, a Blue Lake/Arcata dentist, acquired the 240-acre Campbell ranch in 1911 to raise walnuts. Unable to drive his automobile across the Trinity on the Campbells' "tiny wiggly mule bridge" that carried only one mule at a time, he hired two Eureka engineers to design and build a more serviceable structure. He later turned it over to the county, which maintained it until 1936, when the bridge-building Forest Service replaced it with a one-lane wooden span that lasted until 1995.

Highway 299 motorists should reduce their speed west of the junction with Campbell Ridge Road, if only to see Salyer's most salient feature. On the left, the Salyer Work Center is imposing enough to indicate the agency's importance as the town's major employer. The Forest Service located its first Salyer Station near the old South Fork bridge and then gradually increased its involvement in road building. By 1913, when a steel bridge finally spanned the South Fork, officials were convinced that "Nothing would create favor for the United States Forest Service as much as this project" to forge a road through the Trinity Gorge. As the USFS gained influence, if not always favor, it acquired its central role in Salyer. Past the work center stands the less imposing Community Wayside Chapel. Built in 1923 as a cafe and converted by the Assembly of God into a church by 1933, it has passed through numerous hands but still functions as an active place of worship.

Tessie Salyer, left, and husband Marshall, right, flank a young relative outside their Salyer Heights home. (Salyer family photo)

Beyond the chapel the highway makes a long left curve, leaving the rest of the town behind. As the road straightens out, one last structure appears on the left, almost as an afterthought. This oblong brown building long served as Salyer's Civic or "Pumpkin" Center. From the 1970s until the late 1990s, it housed both a restaurant and the Lower Trinity Redbud Theatre, which produced a variety of shows—usually four per year—with local talent well worth the modest price of admission. The plain exterior of the theater belies the comfort and bright interior of the old town hall. As long as it remains all but abandoned, locals will likely continue to call it the "morgue," symbolic perhaps of the passing of an era.

Right after leaving Salyer, the Scenic Byway reaches the South Fork Trinity River and the boundary with Humboldt County. Travelers wanting to linger at the border to explore the South Fork should prepare themselves for yet another long twisting road and a short but steep trail that takes them down through Hell's Half Acre to the river. Those who elect to stay on safer ground and Highway 299 will have to face Bigfoot, warily waiting for them in the Humboldt gateway town of Willow Creek.

Hlel-Din to Hell's Half Acre: South Fork Road & Trail

Starting just across the mouth of the South Fork Trinity from the Tsnungwe village site of Hlel-Din, paved South Fork Road, some 13 miles long, runs roughly parallel to but high above the river and dead-ends in a large turnaround. Along the winding route, one can spot remnants of old ranches homesteaded in the late 19th century, often by refugees from the Hoopa Valley Indian Reservation or by ex-miners who married Native American women. For instance, the flat covered by Ozzie Bussel's "truck garden" or car collection (at 2.5 miles, right) originally belonged to a gold-hunter named John Coon, whose wife had survived a massacre of Indians in the Mattole Valley.

The many forks along South Fork Road can cause confusion, even consternation, if one takes a wrong turn. When no sign says otherwise, stay to the left. But don't be misled when, on the left (at 3.4 and 4.0 miles), you see not one but two old roads ascending Hennessey Ridge, logged over on a large scale in the 1940s–1960s. The one constructed first, mostly by generous John Hennessey for his mother

Maria, actually comes second. Because it was never paved, it has fewer potholes than the newer one. (*Warning: the first part of unmarked Hennessey Road is narrow and cliff-hugging, and is not maintained in winter. Check with the Forest Service for current road conditions.*)

In 1922, the *Trinity Journal* announced that the Limestairs post office of the scattered South Fork community "is now connected with the outside world by wagon road" after completion of a three-mile stretch south of Hennessey Road. The only public service that South Fork's poor and scattered families never had was a school, forcing them to send their children up to "several miles on foot" to the small Lower Trinity school down near the bridge.

The Trinity's South Fork has "wild and scenic" status, making it a popular destination for rafters and kayakers, who usually put in at the convenient Todd Ranch River Access near where the road surface turns from pavement to gravel. Neither the river access site nor the end of the road, about three miles farther, has a campsite or picnic table. (*Warning: the trail is narrow, sometimes slippery, and crosses steep mountain slopes. Hikers may encounter poison oak and ticks. There is no bridge crossing at the South Fork, and fording the river can be hazardous. On the west bank a poorly maintained trail continues upstream for about four miles to a swinging bridge at Underwood Creek. Contact the Forest Service's Lower Trinity Ranger District office in Willow Creek for information about trail and river conditions.*)

The trail begins with a steep but short climb into thick stands of grand fir, Pacific madrone, pine, and black oak. The path to the river via Hell's Half Acre curves up and down, paved—so-to-speak—with the good intentions of a Forest Service crew constructing a "good mail route" from Salyer to Hyampom along the South Fork in 1920. As the trail bends around the wet and dry sides of the alternating ridges, sharp contrasts in vegetation become apparent, ranging from mixed forests to sun-loving lace ferns. The variation becomes even more visible when viewed directly across the 1,000-foot canyon cut by the South Fork. One ravine, half a mile from the bottom, presumably got the name Hell's Half Acre for good reason, courtesy of livestock herders or miners who had to hike the upper slope during the hot and dry summer. Paradoxically, the creek, where the trail crosses it, is choked with vegetation. The South Fork itself slips and splashes below but remains virtually inaudible until one passes this point.

Eventually the trail dissolves into jumbled boulders and Indian rhubarb strung along the South Fork. Until the 1964 flood swept it away, a swinging mule bridge, built 50 feet above low water, made it easy to reach the other side. According to the *Blue Lake Advocate* (Sept. 18, 1920), the bridge-building crew caught "many hundreds of fish" at this "splendid camping place which is well supplied with cold mountain water." Unfortunately, anyone who reaches Dry Camp now will find neither fish nor potable water, thanks to all the mining, logging, and flooding that have occurred since then. But on the stream's sandy beaches or in its rocky pools, hikers can heat up and cool down—imitating in a human way the lounging lizards that shift from sun to shade along the trail.

The Busy Little Bird

The lower reaches of the South Fork Trinity were the homeland of the Tsnungwe Indians. Like other tribes in the area, they suffered terribly during the incursion of white miners in the 1850s and 1860s. When ethnographer Stephen Powers observed the surviving Tsnungwes in the 1870s, he found only fragments of their earlier culture, but enough remained to provide him with some sense of what pre-white life had been like on the South Fork.

Powers called the tribe the "Kelta," after the name "bestowed on them by the Hupa." He noted that the Kelta-Tsnungwes were "per force polyglots," and that one elderly, half-blind inter-tribal interpreter had "one eye and six languages in his head."

The effects of mining had greatly diminished the salmon stocks that the Tsnungwes had formerly relied on as a main source of food, but Powers found members of the tribe still gathering both huckleberries and manzanita berries, as well as two root crops:

...they eat soap-root (*chlorogal-um* [*sic*] *pomeridianum*) when they are hard-pushed in the spring. They extract the poisonous quality from it by roasting, which they do by heaping a large quantity of it on the ground, covering it over with green leaves, and building a fire over it. This is allowed to burn many hours until the poison is thoroughly roasted out, when the root is said to be quite sweet and palatable. They also find a root growing in moist places, of which they make much account, and which is probably cammas [*sic*], and is called the wild potato, which when roasted and peeled is sweetish and toothsome.

Near the end of his account Powers related what he'd learned of the tribe's spiritual beliefs:

When a Kelta dies...a little bird flies away with his soul to the spirit-land. If he was a bad Indian, a hawk will catch the little bird and eat him up, soul and feathers; but if he was good, he will reach the spirit-land.

When Powers wrote this, more than 20 years had passed since the miners began wreaking destruction upon the Indians. During those long days of darkness the little bird had, sadly, all too often taken flight.

177

Willow Creek: Bigfoot's "Bordertown Hub"

The South Fork Bridge marks the county line, but Trinity County's influence—including its area code—spills over into Willow Creek, the largest town by far between Weaverville and Blue Lake. For various reasons this place, called China Flat until 1912, is one of those towns that's hard to pin down. Its geography and history have made it almost as elusive as its best-known resident, Bigfoot (also spelled Big Foot). While linked by the same river and the same mining history as many Trinity County settlements, Willow Creek lies within Humboldt County's jurisdiction. This border location makes its ties with equidistant Weaverville and Eureka tenuous, since both county seats sometimes seem to ignore this isolated, poorly delineated outpost.

As a North Coast reporter observed in 1949: "The town [of 400] is not incorporated, hence its limits are more or less optional," reaching roughly from the South Fork bridge to four miles down "Hoopa Road" (Highway 96). Willow Creek has quadrupled its population since then but, at the same time, has extended its

sphere of influence to coincide with the Trinity Recreation Area that it, the Forest Service, and the Hupa Tribal Council recently created to promote "River Fun in the Mountain Sun." The TRA reaches all the way from Burnt Ranch to Berry Summit along Highway 299 and also takes in the long South Fork-lower Trinity axis.

Willow Creek's center, consisting of the mile-long strip of gas stations, restaurants, and sundry stores that slow highway traffic down to 35 mph, is more easily defined than its outer limits. But the town's hub has shifted several times over the past 150 years. Not until the precursor to Highway 299 replaced the Three Creeks–Brannan Mountain Road as the main route over Berry Summit in the early 1900s did "downtown" move to its present site.

As if to increase the difficulty of "fixing" Willow Creek as a place, its residents have spread out and up in all directions to occupy every habitable, often hidden, niche they could find for farming, mining, recreation, or simply subsistence. Moreover, some of the town's settlers, striving to improve their position, have

shown a strong tendency to change occupations and relocate within the region. The Thomas G. Campbell whom we met in Salyer, where he "finally settled down" on "one of the finest ranches on the river," homesteaded in Hoopa in the late 1850s and then owned several farms and businesses in Willow Creek before moving into Trinity County. Conversely, James A. Patterson started out as a lumberman/farmer/butcher in Hawkins Bar but eventually ended up as a rancher and "barbecue king" on Patterson Road and Lane at the north end of Willow Creek. (*See sidebar, next page.*)

The Forest Service itself matched the mobility of ranchers like Patterson and Campbell in locating their lower Trinity district headquarters. The first office was next to the Brizard's store at the mouth of Willow Creek. At a later date the ranger station was shifted to a site near the South Fork ferry/bridge on the Humboldt County side. The facility built by the CCC at Salyer during the Depression proved much more satisfactory. Yet another change in location occurred when Brizard's built the present compound on Highway 96, close to the original site, and leased it to the Forest Service.

Perhaps a local meter-reader's description of Willow Creek as a "Bordertown hub" best captures its basic character as a Trinity Highway place. It serves both sides of the county line from Burnt Ranch to Berry Summit and reaches north to several Klamath River towns. The community also finds itself tightly intertwined with the sovereign Hoopa Valley Indian Reservation, which borders it just a few miles to the north on Highway 96. Since about 1960 Willow Creek has touted itself as the gateway to Bigfoot Country, but for many decades before then it served as a second gateway (after Blue Lake) to the Klamath-Trinity mining country and as a summer mountain resort for fogged-in denizens of the North Coast.

The town's early history is muddled by the intermixing of the names Willow Creek and China Flat, which actually refer to two distinct sites two miles apart. The store and hotel that serviced miners were located at the mouth of Willow Creek, where the Brannan Mountain Road from the west now meets the road to Hoopa. The China Flat area to the southeast attracted a sizable number of Chinese miners who successfully employed their "wing-dam method of gravel washing along the lower bars of the [Trinity] river." Even after Humboldt

Willow Creek's Barbecue King

Blue Lake's *Advocate* reported on March 2, 1907, that James A. Patterson, much to everyone's surprise, had just married the former wife of a Judge Belcher in San Francisco. The paper failed to point out that the newlyweds had met when the Belchers vacationed on the lower Trinity the year before and went on a hunting trip led by Patterson. A few years after the marriage, the *Advocate* recorded Jim's return home from Arcata, "where he [had] delivered 117 head of beef cattle to the Bull[s'] Meat Market" located on the Plaza. The *Trinity Journal* soon added that he "has just set out a splendid orchard on his [Hawkins Bar] homestead....Patterson made a trip to Quimby this week, where he did some butchering for the New River Mining Co." And a year later Marshall Salyer found him busy cutting lumber for a flume being constructed by a different mining company.

Patterson apparently gave up milling when James Marshall and Sons bought his small sawmill and moved it from Hawkins Bar to Hoopa. Perhaps Patterson used the proceeds of the sale to buy a ranch in Willow Creek from John Douglas. There, well before dawn on December 19, 1922, Jim killed a 300-pound black bear and "hauled him fifty miles over mountain roads to Arcata, in time to ship him [to San Francisco] on the night express." The bear stayed in cold storage until January 6, 1923, "when it was served roasted at a banquet given by the Alameda Elks, which was attended by more than 450 guests." The previous summer Patterson had promised a few Bay Area sportsmen camping with him in the mountains that he would provide them with a bear. The *San Francisco Chronicle* as well as the *Arcata Union* featured Patterson's feat of feeding nearly 500 Elk with a single Bear. To cap the evening, generous Jim presented the bear's tanned hide to the Alamedans as a souvenir.

By the early 1950s, the Pattersons, owners of the Circle-P Ranch in Willow Creek, had occupied a new "U-shaped home" on a knoll next to their forest park. The *Advocate* announced that Jim was in charge of a big fundraising barbecue on behalf of a new Emergency Center that Willow Creek wanted to build now that it finally had phones and electricity. "Patterson's private barbecue pit is located in the grove near the ranchhouse and Jim will barbecue the meat [with his "private-formulae sauce"] and cook the beans...and take the food to the dinner which will be served at Gambi's [resort] on open-air tables."

The barbecue fed more than 600 people, a big success for the new center's ground-breaking ceremony, at which Mrs. Eleanor I. Holcomb, former resident of Hawkins Bar, turned the first shovel. But for the "Barbecue King" the feed must have been small potatoes. The year before he had fed 5,000 guests in 35 minutes at the annual Labor Day barbecue in the Pacific Lumber Company town of Scotia; this year (1954) he planned to serve 19 or 20 beeves to 6,000 in 30 minutes!

County's 1880s purge of Asians, China Flat persisted as the name of the increasingly white community until 1912. In that year, confusion caused by another California town with the same name prompted the United States Postal Service to adopt Willow Creek as a new name. Fittingly, the popular local museum founded in 1988 has adopted both the town's two names as its own—Willow Creek-China Flat.

The Willow Creek area functioned as a major trail hub long before either whites or Chinese entered the region. The Chimariko Indians lived along the Trinity River above its South Fork while the Tsnungwe or southern Hupa occupied the area surrounding the confluence of the two streams. Located at this site, Hlel-Din became the Tsnungwes' largest village because of its pivotal position for trade. The Hlel-Din Memorial Bridge across the South Fork and the Hlel-Din river trail on the Trinity County side represent a belated effort to recognize the import of this vanished village.

The Willow Creek Hotel, a quarter mile down Highway 96 from its junction with Highway 299, became the area's center of activity during the latter half of the 19th century. Built in 1877 by Charles Brown, the original hotel burned in 1894 but was rebuilt at its present site, directly across the road from where Brizard's of Arcata located a branch store. The hotel has undergone remodeling by many owners, but the five strangely asymmetrical front windows that identify the building in old photos are still visible from the highway.

A pair of autos and a row of pines obscure the second Willow Creek Hotel, c. 1912. (HSU photo)

Across the street from the motel, Brannan Mountain Road begins its long ascent from the valley floor to the top of the ridge. This route, once connected to Old Three Creeks Road after it crossed the ridgeline, saw many weary wayfarers when it served as the main link between the Trinity River and the North Coast. Among them were Thomas G. Campbell, who told the *Arcata Union* before leaving town one day in 1889 (at age 63), after buying "a good spring wagon," that "he had made his last trip over the mountains mule back…As he tips the beam at 260 pounds this is good for the mule," the newspaper wryly noted. Today's travelers are mainly residents of the assorted dwellings scattered along this mountain road. Lots of gnarled white oak and red-barked madrone test gravity as they lean out from the slope to shade the pavement. Taller stands of Douglas-fir, with tips of bright green buds in the late spring, and western red-cedar spread out through gullies and over spur ridges.

This is the kind of wooded, isolated setting that many Willow Creekers seem to prefer. Driveways marked with a cherub birdbath or a rusted-out truck chassis lead to mini-ranches complete with orchard or vineyard, to silver Airstream trailers on dirt plots, or to modern redwood-decked homes. Where turnouts and thinner vegetation allow, the winding road offers splendid vistas of Willow Creek, both town and stream. Like most secondary roads in the

Trinity Recreation Area, Brannan Mountain Road is narrow and neglected. Visitors should use extreme caution when driving along any such routes, even if they are as resourceful as Doctors Eugene Fountain and C. N. Mooney were when, in September 1910, their "steering gear broke" near the top of Brannan Mountain Road. They were returning to Blue Lake from Hoopa after responding to a medical emergency. According to the *Advocate*,

They managed to go as far as Senator Haas'[s] residence [just below Three Creeks Summit], where they engineered a gearing apparatus consisting of a pole tied to the front wheels of the auto with baile [sic] rope, steering it by hand. It fell Dr. Mooney's lot to operate the steering gear by walking in front of the machine and steering it over the road where sharp curves are quite numerous....Dr. Fountain was chauffeur and controlled the power, which had to be at the very lowest possible speed. From Three Creeks to Berry's, a distance of about 11 miles, Dr. Mooney steered the machine in two hours and a half, which is remarkably good time considering the task of walking in the dust and sweating like a steamed potato. At Berry's Dr. Mooney was relieved by young Tripp, and the two changed shift about until Blue Lake was reached at 12 o'clock at night. The party left Hoopa that morning at 5 o'clock.

China Flat's (or Willow Creek's) position at the center of a far-flung road and trail network enabled it to market one of its first and most enduring products—fruit. In 1890 a *Blue Lake Advocate* reporter remarked:

After looking over correspondence from Willow Creek and vicinity I am at a loss to know which they prize the higher, the fruit they raise or the road over which they carry it to market [via Brannan Mountain]. They may well be proud of their fruit for in quality it is unsurpassed by any in the state. They may well be proud of their new road for without it the surplus fruit which they raise would rot under the trees.

By the time of World War I, with a new and lower roadway connecting Willow Creek and Redwood Creek, more and more fruit and tourists moved between the mountain basins and the coast. The two kinds of "commodities" were more closely linked than one might think. Arcata grocer G. Gambi, a Florentine, established a resort on Willow Creek's China Flat in 1919 and eventually developed a fish farm, a fine peach orchard, and Humboldt County's first bonded winery. The fruits and nuts raised on the warm flats of the lower Trinity supplied not only the Humboldt Bay area but also many a mining camp. (And a Gambi Motel is still in business at China Flat.)

Today the North Coast remains the main market for Willow Creek produce. The 30-odd farms in the area are all small-scale operations, some of them specializing in organic crops. One of the largest (with only five acres) occupies a good portion of Flower's Flat, located near the heart of town.

Country Club Drive, one block east of the Highway 96 turnoff, crosses a low ridge to reach the horseshoe bend where Flower's Flat stretches along the Trinity River. Named after Andy and Delphia Flower, who bought the property in 1909, the area attracts sun-seekers from the summer-cool coast as well as overheated drivers from the Central Valley. Just before the organic farm, a right turn onto Kimtu Road leads to shady Veterans' Park, a pleasant place for a picnic. Farther down the same road, signs direct drivers to the Kimtu Recreation Area. Here, below a steep bluff at the bend of the horseshoe, a popular beach tempts swimmers and waders to take a dip in the water. In the spring season, water-lovers should judge their ability and the river carefully, since high flows and chilly temperatures make a dangerous combination.

Country Club Drive continues north across the Trinity and then ends where Patterson Road starts to the left and Seely-McIntosh Road to the right. Except for the upscale subdivision that surrounds the Bigfoot Golf Course off of Patterson, both roads wind through the same patchwork of homes, orchards, and wood lots described earlier for Brannan Mountain Road, although the slopes are gentler and the population denser.

While summer water shortages were once chronic problems for both farmers and miners, occasional floods have provided more dramatic events for Willow Creek. The disastrous "Christmas Flood" of 1964 wiped out all the area's major roads and bridges, and three people lost their lives in a landslide five miles to the west. Another slide, dubbed "Mount Slipmore," destroyed the western end of town. The regenerating forest above the south side of Highway 299 still reminds residents of the size of that slide.

After World War II, the Willow Creek area experienced a logging boom that lasted about 20 years. When timber companies began pulling out in the late 1960s, the exodus of jobs dealt the economy a heavy blow. The region's last mill, at Burnt Ranch, closed in 1990. With the decline in timber production, Willow Creek has turned increasingly to its recreation resources for economic support, quite in keeping with its long tradition as a mountain summer resort. Those who want to savor Willow Creek's blue-sky summer days should add Big Rock to their itinerary. This Forest Service recreation site, just half a mile north on Highway 96, is named for an island of bedrock that rises out of the river like a breaching whale.

Many Willow Creek visitors come to see the region's most famous resident—Bigfoot! (*See sidebar, next page.*) At the "Gateway to Bigfoot Country," two life-size statues of the creature stand watch over the Trinity Scenic Byway. More than any other town, Willow Creek has adopted the furry primate as its mascot since the flurry of publicity he (or she?) received in the late 1950s. An hour's drive from the Bluff Creek site north of Hoopa where Jerry Crew sighted his tracks, Willow Creek was then home to most of the loggers working there. Perhaps because precious little of the town has survived so many fires and floods, Willow Creekers have adopted Big Foot as their primary icon. They host an annual "Big Foot Days" as a Labor Day weekend ritual. Started in 1960 to raise money for the creation of Flower's Park, the three-day festival features softball games, dances, a short but colorful parade, and…barbecues.

Until the spring of 2000, the Willow Creek-China Flat Museum had a modest but popular Bigfoot corner of artifacts, secondary to a set of attractive exhibits related to the homes and lives of the town's early settlers. Now, thanks to a much larger collection of Bigfoot memorabilia and research materials donated by the late Bob

Workers remove portions of "Mount Slipmore," which obliterated the southwestern end of Willow Creek during the Christmas 1964 flood. The photo shows the junction of highways 96 and 299. (HCHS photo)

Bigfoot's Roots

Mike Gordon pulled his dusty brown Ford van into the Grays Falls campground late one summer night in 1974. He had just drifted off to sleep when his van began to sway and then rock. He rubbed the sleep from his eyes, struggling to focus as fingernails scratched along one side of the vehicle. Someone was trying to get in. Assuming it was just another camper playing a trick on him, Gordon peered through the van's curtains. What he saw was no camper!

Mike stared, then blinked, hoping he was dreaming. Just outside stood a giant animal. Seven feet tall and covered with hair, it looked like a human crossed with a gorilla. The creature circled the van as if trying to find out what it held. In the moonlight, Gordon could make out a big torso, broad shoulders, and a flat face. By this time, he felt like a big bowl of Jell-O during an earthquake. When the figure jostled the van a few more times, Mike knew he had to do something. He fumbled with the ignition key and,

after a few tries, managed to start the engine and begin blowing the horn. Looking as startled as Gordon felt, the animal fled into the tangled forest below the campground. Grinding gears, Mike headed for the nearby Salyer Ranger Station with his unbelievable story.

Did some Trinity County prankster play a joke on Mike Gordon? Did he lie about what he saw? Or did Bigfoot, the most mysterious denizen of the Pacific Northwest, actually visit him?

Logger Jerry Crew coined the name Bigfoot in August 1958 while cutting roads with a bulldozer near Bluff Creek, a Klamath River tributary 20 miles north of Willow Creek. Crew's crew started seeing footprints in the freshly dug earth of the new road. They had the shape of a human foot but measured 16 inches long and 7 inches wide. Whatever made them had a stride that varied from 4 to 10 feet and made impressions 2 inches deep in the hard soil that barely showed the mark of a logger's heavy boot. The footprints, appearing almost nightly and in widely separated areas, baffled the normally reserved road builders enough that they went to the Eureka newspaper with their tale. Wire services soon picked up the story and passed it on, making Bigfoot a national household name.

The first written account of giant human-beasts in California appeared in Crescent City's *Del Norte Record* in 1886. Several men reported seeing a "wild man" seven feet tall with "a bulldog head" near Happy Camp, 60 miles north of Willow Creek. One of them refused to shoot because it looked so human.

While most reported sightings have occurred in Klamath country, Bigfoot has raised its hairy head now and then all along the Trinity, especially in more remote areas. Willow Creek alone has enough tales to back its claim to being the "Gateway to Bigfoot Country." In 1967, a visitor from Ventura, California saw a Bigfoot along Highway 299 just half a mile west of town. While seeking shade from the afternoon sun, the startled man watched a creature 8 or 9 feet tall stroll along the road for 50 feet before it vanished into the forest.

Although skeptics write off Bigfoot stories as publicity stunts, others point out that those who first reported them—loggers and road builders—were unlikely to seek such attention. Some Bigfoot enthusiasts suspect that loggers have told fewer stories in recent years because the reports of the 1950s and '60s brought too many curious outsiders into the

woods. Of course many more men worked in the woods then than now. Whatever the reasons, Bigfoot has kept a low profile in Northwest California since the early '70s.

Today, Bigfoot prints on the Trinity landscape are more likely to take the form of business names than giant tracks. The name and likeness appear on storefronts and billboards all along the lower Trinity, luring travelers into everything from campgrounds to produce farms. In Willow Creek alone, one can play a few rounds at the Big Foot Golf and Country Club, buy building supplies at Big Foot Lumber, or get gas at Big Foot Chevron. In perhaps the most appropriate use of the name, Big Foot Podiatry can take care of the biggest foot problems!

It is easy to scoff at the Bigfoot mystery in the bright light of midday. The shadows retreat into deep draws far from the river as the sun illuminates the landscape. But as night falls, vision fails. With a moonless sky and clouds of mist above the treetops, every sound from the forest makes muscles quiver and skin crawl. People stay inside or look over their shoulders as they hurry from one well-lit place to another. In flesh or in fantasy, at night Bigfoot walks!

183

Titus of British Columbia, the museum contains an entire two-story detached wing built just for the town's idol. With a commissioned statue outside the main entrance and a diorama inside the addition, the hairy creature has become the museum's main attraction. For a souvenir guaranteed to spark a conversation, pick up a replica of a plaster foot cast sold by the museum (and local businesses). The museum's dedicated volunteer staff hosts special weekend festivities several times a year, including a Wildflower Festival in late April or early May. Each event features a potluck, if not a potlatch, which seems to meet the standard set years ago by the Barbecue King.

At Willow Creek, Highway 299 continues west as it parts company with the Trinity River, which flows north through the Hoopa Valley to join the Klamath. Once out of town, the road starts winding up through Willow Creek Canyon toward Berry Summit. Since it takes about 10 miles to climb 2,000 vertical feet, slower traffic should use turnouts and yield the passing lane to faster drivers. Not far up the road, campers can choose one of two Six Rivers National Forest campgrounds: Boise Creek (right at .75 mile) or East Fork (left at 4.75 miles).

Founder of Marysville in the Old Denny mining district, Frenchman Peter Larcine has been reincarnated as "Cinnabar Sam" by a Willow Creek restaurateur. (TCHS photo, courtesy Lowrie Gifford)

Highway 96 Side Trip: Lower Trinity & Hoopa

California's largest Indian reservation and a lovely river valley are the destinations of this 25-mile round-trip excursion. Attractions along the way include cliffhanging views of the Trinity; a historic, half-hidden ranch; and varied landscapes of steep mountains, tawny fields, and fir-dark forests.

The side trip follows Highway 96 north from its junction with Highway 299 in Willow Creek. The route descends to cross the town's namesake stream, mile 0.2, and then levels as it passes the Lower Trinity Ranger District headquarters, 0.6 mile, left.

After running through mixed forest, the highway reaches the roadside produce stand of Trinity River Farms, mile 2.6, right, one of several places where summer travelers can sample the valley's warm-weather crops. The road re-enters forest, cuts across the hillside above the Trinity River at mile 3.5 and skirts a scattering of canyon live oak, 4.3 miles. A pullout, mile 5.5, right, provides a stunning view far below of the river and the circular valley that contains the Sugar Bowl Ranch. (*See sidebar, next page.*)

The highway circles the rim of the bowl, offering further views of the ranch's tiny red buildings far below. Returning to the hillside above the river, the road passes the turnoff to Tish Tang Campground, mile 8.0, right. A striking mural adorns the retaining wall on the campground's entrance road; dedicated to the Native Americans of Hoopa and the Trinity Valley, the mural mixes Indian designs with colorful pictures of craft works, animals, and plants. At 8.7 miles the highway reaches a pullout, right, for a vista point. Across the river are the low plank houses of age-old Djictoñadiñ ("Tish Tang") village, one of several such Hupa communities that still dot the riversides.

The highway then enters the southernmost residential section in the valley. To the right, beyond the river, oak-covered hills rise, humplike, from the widening plain.

Another ancient Hupa village, Medildiñ, appears above the far riverbank, mile 10.4, right. Located incongruently next to its weathered cedar structures is the Hoopa airport.

The bulky buildings of Hoopa High School stand to the left at mile 11.3. The unsigned road that here departs the highway leads past the school and then traces the northwestern side of the old Fort Gaston square before ending near the mountainside; a left turn continues along the square's perimeter, passing the "Old Adobe," right, in midblock. The boarded-over building is the oldest non-Indian structure in Hoopa, a relic from the days when the fort provided military protection for the valley's white residents. In 1864, after the Hupas and neighboring tribes signed the peace treaty that ended 13 years of Indian-white conflict, the now-former fort became the administrative center for the newly established Hoopa Valley Indian Reservation.

Highway 96 proceeds northward through the valley; at mile 11.8 is the turnoff, left, to the Hoopa Valley Neighborhood Facility and the offices of the Hoopa Tribal Council. The Council is the governing entity for the Hupas, who are one of ten "pioneer" tribes in the nation authorized by the Bureau of Indian Affairs to practice self-governance. Since their days, more than a century ago, as virtual prisoners on the reservation, the Hupas have gradually gained control over their own affairs, building on legal precedents and Congressional action to re-establish their tribal sovereignty; the patterns set by the pioneering Hupas are now used by other tribes as they develop their own governments.

Immediately beyond the Trinity River bridge, 12.3 miles, is the Hoopa business district. In the building containing Ray's Food Place, left, is the Hoopa Tribal Museum, which houses an extensive collection of shell dresses, basketry, and other remarkable objects from the tribe's rich culture. A "living" collection, much of the regalia is periodically reclaimed by the owning families for use at ceremonial events. The museum also offers guided tours of the valley's historic villages, including Takimildiñ, the tribe's spiritual center, which lies close to the river north of town. Takimildiñ still serves

Sweet Times in the Sugar Bowl

In 1876 John Douglas, a Civil War pensioner, purchased a lovely canyon property south of the Hoopa Indian agency. At the time the site served as a hog ranch; earlier it was held as a mining claim. Douglas saw something beyond the pigs and placers, however, and soon sought to make his vision manifest.

He married Nancy Kidd, a Tlohomtahhoi (some say Tsnungwe) Indian described as "a beautiful woman from the New River country," and they began to raise a family. Enlisting the help of his brothers, Abner and James, John built a house of whipsawed lumber, hand splitting the shakes for the roof. The men also cut rails, posts, and timbers for the ranch's storehouse, barns, and outbuildings, and varied their workdays by planting an orchard, a grape vineyard, and a walnut grove. Seeking further diversion, the busy brothers set out honeybees, plowed fields for alfalfa, and tunneled through the ridge to set up a flume from Campbell Creek; Abner and James used the water for mining. When Douglas requested county funds for a spur road to his ranch, the allocation was so small that he built the road himself, relying on a pick and shovel. The route, while functional, later showed its limitations for auto traffic; drivers had to back up their Model T's to negotiate the sharper corners.

In the 1890s a reporter for the Blue Lake Advocate admiringly noted how "it is rather curious that nature would pause long enough in her terrific work of world building to make an ideal farm in these mountains for one family." Douglas, the writer continued, could easily pass his time sitting "on the verandah of his cozy home in the long summer twilight," yet could also, if the spirit moved him, "have access to the outside world over a romantic mountain road."

Douglas had little reason to leave, however, since "[t]here is always plenty of good lard and cured meat in his smoke house," while "the falls on the ranch abound in fine trout." Even the resident deer were only a partial annoyance, for if they sometimes came "into the fields to crop the young corn and clover…[they did] not always go out again." What few items were not grown, caught, or shot on the ranch were purchased at the Korbel store during the family's thrice-yearly supply trips.

The Douglases sold the ranch in the early 1900s. The next owners, George and Annie Hennings, were also hard workers, raising sheep, goats, hogs, and a half dozen or so milk cows, in addition to maintaining the mine. The property continued to change hands, with varying results. One family cut many of the trees to create more grazing land for their cattle; another owner installed a 150-foot-long sawmill. The property was eventually claimed in bankruptcy proceedings and for a time lay nearly idle, patrolled by a caretaker and grazed by but a few head of cattle. Then, in 1960, Robert W. Matthews, the President of A. Brizard Inc., purchased the ranch and began restoring it. The work eventually brought back much of the beauty that John Douglas had beheld over 80 years earlier, when he named the spot the "Sugar Bowl" because it was, in his words, such "a sweet place to live."

Sweet as the Sugar Bowl was as a ranch site, the locale earlier had a different, deeper significance; for the Hupa Indians who traditionally occupied the area, the place was Xaime, where a small boulder (alternately called Mi Rock, Thunder Rock, or Rain Rock) served as home to a spirit-being. Here the early-day Hupas came for feasts and ceremonies meant to please Xaime's powerful resident. Perhaps it was their way of "sugaring up" the spirit.

The White Deerskins and the Great Bird

Some 70 years ago, participants and onlookers at a Hoopa Valley deerskin dance paused to behold a strange sight—a huge, birdlike being was descending onto a nearby field. Various Hupas, some carrying albino deerskins on poles and wearing ceremonial wolf fur headdresses and sea lion tusks, hastened toward the object for a closer look. Staring back at them were the two startled occupants of a biplane, the first aircraft ever to land in the valley. For a marvelous moment, the emissaries of two divergent cultures stared across the centuries at each other in open-mouthed awe. The pilot and his passenger, observing what appeared to be an advancing throng of sea lions, deer, and wolves, were the first to lose their nerve; with a roar of its throttle, the plane sped off across the field and was soon straining its way skyward to safety. In a few moments it had become only a shrinking speck in the firmament, the frightened flyers having escaped from their unexpected encounter with the heretofore unknown world of the Hupas.

as the site for the Jumping Dance, one of the Hupas' two principal ceremonies. Both the Jumping Dance and the White Deerskin Dance, which travels from village to village, are held in the fall of odd-numbered years. The events are open to the public—although, according to one story, a pair of outside observers once wondered if the residents welcomed their presence. (*See sidebar, above.*) Highway 96 bisects the remainder of the reservation on its way north, heading toward such Klamath River hamlets as Weitchpec, Orleans, and Happy Camp. For the traveler on a tight time budget, however, the center of the Hoopa Valley serves as a good turnaround point for a short yet satisfying side trip.

White Deerskin Dance. (HSU photo)

Horse Mountain High Road

South of Willow Creek lies a landscape of rough-hewn ridges and creek-cleft canyons that contains enough scenery for a week's worth of travel. Thanks to a series of well-maintained Forest Service roads, however, adventuresome excursionists can motor a mountainous loop route through the region in but a few hours, sampling several scenic high spots along the way.

The side trip leaves Highway 299 just east of Berry Summit, heading south onto paved, two-lane Titlow Hill Road. The route passes a turnoff, mile 0.5, right, for an abandoned section of the original highway, and then bends left along the ridgeslope above the canyon of Redwood Creek. A trio of oaks—California black, Oregon white, and canyon live—shade the surroundings, along with Pacific madrone, bigleaf maple, and Douglas-fir. At mile 2.0 the summer greenery is speckled by the bright blooms of poison delphinium, crimson columbine, and other colorful wildflowers. The road then winds and climbs through rocky, steep-sloped terrain, coming out onto a grassy opening, 2.9 miles. Across the canyon to the west, a fringe of conifers separates Christmas Prairie from the surrounding clearcuts, while the

ridgeline of Bald Mountain rises skyward in the background.

Ascending sharply on switchbacks to mile 4.0, the road enters Six Rivers National Forest and its Horse Mountain Botanical Area, a small sector of specialized plants growing on serpentine-based soil. Here also is the start of Forest Highway 1, whose sinuous, ridge-running blacktop stretches southward all the way to the Mad River Ranger District office at Highway 36.

The roadbed narrows to a wide single lane, mile 4.6, where two dirt routes depart to the left. The first climbs northward onto Horse Mountain, site of numerous telecommunication relay stations and a wintertime cross-country ski area. The second side road drops to the east, passing through pines and cedars to reach, in about a mile, the remains of the Horse Mountain Copper Company's mine. The site is a mélange of deteriorating foundations, weathered boards, rusty mining relics, two tainted ponds of stream seep, an uninviting mine shaft, and a concrete powder magazine that is the only extant structure. Never successful, but perennially promising, the mine is one of several that have pockmarked the Horse

Mountain hillslopes for nearly a century. (*See sidebar, next page.*)

Forest Highway 1 climbs southward from the mine road turnoff, crests near a vista of Mt. Shasta and the Trinities, left, and then gradually descends through pines and oaks to a junction, mile 6.2, left, with a gravel road (Forest Service route 5N10) that connects to Friday Ridge Road. The highway passes lands belonging to the pioneer Russ family and rises up Titlow Hill, reaching a ridgetop prairie, 7.1 miles, that offers wide-ranging views across the Redwood Creek watershed, right. Just beyond the grassland, mile 7.6, right, a rutted dirt road drops a quarter mile to Cold Springs, a fenced, year-round water source situated above a picturesque outcropping of oak-shaded rock. The surface of the rock bears numerous small indentations called cupules, which were probably created by the Whilkut or Tsnungwe Indians for ceremonial purposes.

In earlier times, the spot was apparently called Oak Springs. Packers favored the area as a campsite, for it featured not only a reliable water supply but also an adjacent grass-filled prairie and proximity to the ridgetop trail that ran from Berry Summit to the South Fork and

Few Bucks from the Horse Mountain Mines

Although over a hundred mining claims were filed in the Horse Mountain area, none of them ever proved successful. Instead of producing industrially important ore (and with it, cash for the claimants), the mines have profited no one, leaving instead a lethal legacy of damaged land, poisoned water, and at least three deaths.

While various speculators filed for Horse Mountain's minerals as early as 1891, not until 1906 did serious work begin, when the Horse Mountain Copper Company started extracting ore for shipment to the Tacoma, Washington, smelter. Because of the distance it had to travel, the ore needed to assay in excess of 20 percent copper to return a profit; when an early sample assayed at 28 percent, the mine owners' enthusiasm was unbounded.

The copper contagion spread to the nearby Humboldt Copper Company's mine. A pair of contractors, Hughes and Duncan, busily burrowed some 500 feet into the mountainside before running an airshaft to the surface. While dynamiting a blockage in the opening, the men were overcome by fumes from the explosives. One after another, three rescuers were lowered into the shaft, but the deadly gas remained overwhelming, and each of the men barely made it out. By then, Hughes and Duncan had been trapped for over two hours—long enough, as would-be rescuer Charlie Blake put it, to be "certainly past all help."

The next day the bodies were raised from the shaft. Blake, an experienced packer, loaded them onto mules for transport to the nearest road. It proved a doubly difficult task, for the effects of the fumes made him ill for some time afterward, producing black blotches on his face and feet. Blake still fared better than Beauchamp, another member of the rescue party, who never recovered from his exposure to the poisonous gas and died within the year.

Perhaps because of the accident, work on the Humboldt Copper Company's claims faltered, but the rival Horse Mountain company soon entered its busiest phase, constructing a set of buildings during 1911–1912 that included a stamp mill, concentrating plant, blacksmith shop, cookhouse, powder magazine, and several cabins. A 1,600-foot shaft was bored into the bowels of Horse Mountain and a pair of lakes south of the mine were utilized as a water supply. Photos from the time show a series of rough-hewn structures clinging to the steep hillslope.

For a brief time the mine appeared to prosper, employing 28 workers from 1914 to 1916 as operations diversified to produce chromium and other minerals needed for World War I. In 1916 the company's treasurer accompanied one of the ore shipments to Tacoma, taking with him all of the business's funds. Neither the treasurer nor the money was ever seen again, and the suddenly insolvent mine closed at the end of the year.

Over the ensuing decades the mine and its many structures moldered on the mountainside, while various entrepreneurs struggled to reopen it. Finally in 1958, several new buildings were constructed and the following year the Emperor Mining Company announced plans to excavate an open pit mine to a depth of 1,000 feet. A newspaper article trumpeting the "million-dollar copper ore plant" indicated that "[u]nder present mining laws, the miner does not have to pay any royalty to the government for the ore taken, nor does he have to pay for the timber used or fees for plant sites. In addition, the laws do not require restoration of the land."

Despite these lucrative land-use conditions, the operation failed to show a profit and soon folded. In the 1970s, beset by insurance and tax costs, the company finally let the mines go.

Today, the long-idle Horse Mountain mine continues its slow disintegration upon the hillslope. The decaying timbers and crumbling concrete have combined with the bits of rust and polluted ponds to form an unwitting monument to the ravages of unrestricted mining. As the Forest Service, at considerable public expense, attempts to repair the damaged landscape, Horse Mountain's mining toll continues to mount.

Mad River drainages. One pack train, when camped here, was attacked at night by Indians and the packers were driven off. The fleeing victims sounded the alarm, and a search party commanded by a Lieutenant Hempfield soon decamped from Blue Lake. Arriving at the camp, the searchers found plenty of plundered cargo, but no pack mules. The missing animals had left ample tracks, however; their trail led

Friday's Unfriendly Ridge

An early-day fixture in the lower Trinity area was an Indian named Friday, described in 1906 as "a well-known character near the Hoopa reservation, half Hupa and half Wintun by birth, but having had close affiliations with the Chimariko many years ago." He had settled, with his wife, east of Willow Creek on what later became the Seeley Ranch. Riding a "little grey horse," his long white hair flowing in the breeze, Friday cut a striking figure as he traveled through the region.

One trip took the couple into the mountains south of their home; their aim was to acquire a bear in the strong steel trap that Friday possessed. Perhaps camping at his namesake site, he then prepared to ascend the higher reaches of the ridge. Friday and his wife set the trap, and he then put the chain over his shoulder and commenced climbing the ridgeslope. All went well for a time, but suddenly, while trudging up the incline, Friday slipped; down he fell, landing upon the open jaws of the trap, which obligingly closed around his backside. Then, according to the story, "[i]n a most uncomfortable position, the old man had to retrace his steps homeward to get his wife's help in removing the trap, a wiser and sadder man in the ways of the bear-trap."

Many years before Friday's em*bear*assing discomfort, others experienced equal unpleasantness in the same surroundings. When, in 1849, the Josiah Gregg Party made its epic trek from the Trinity gold diggings to the coast, the ill-fated expedition climbed the as yet unnamed ridgeline after leaving the Tsnungwe village of Hlel-Din at the mouth of the South Fork. Soon the men ran out of food, so that by the time they camped at Horse Mountain,

> ...[o]ur stock of flour was exhausted; the almost continual rain, however, had saturated our camp equipage—the flour among the rest—and there had formed on the inner surface of the sacks in which it had been carried a kind of paste which the dampness had soured and moulded.

> The paste was carefully peeled off, softened with water and equally divided among the party—...each one...devoured his portion with an avidity that would have astonished and shocked mortals with appetites more delicate than ours.

It was only two days later that Gregg and his men managed to satiate their all-accepting appetites by shooting several deer. Difficult as their situation was, it could have been worse; they might have tried—as Friday did—to use a bear trap.

---

north, eventually ending on a butte above Willow Creek, where some of them had been butchered for meat and the others were found unharmed. The event was commemorated (with twofold imprecision) by naming not the butchering site but a neighboring peak Horse (not mule) Mountain.

Cold (or Oak) Springs' surroundings are especially scenic in spring and summer, when trilliums, violets, and pussy ears add their hues to the various greens of the oaks and conifers. In the pond below the spring attentive observers will find rough-skinned newts swimming through their seasonal breeding sequence.

Back on the highway, mile 8.4, dogwood and blue elderberry soon brighten the forest understory. The route then climbs a ridgetop knob, passing above White Rock Springs, and reaches a junction, mile 10.2. Here the side trip departs Forest Highway 1, turning sharply left onto the Friday Ridge Road, aka Forest Service Road 6N08. This one-lane, paved route winds gently downhill, passing some cliffside Brewer's oak and then entering, mile 11.1, a corridor of seasonally colorful foliage. In autumn the roadside is lined with tinted-leaved trees and shrubs—serviceberry, willow, flowering currant, California hazel, thimbleberry, bigleaf maple, all of them gold or yellow, set off by the pinks, oranges, and scarlets of scattered dogwoods. A side road, mile 11.6, right, offers entry into more of the luminous leafiness.

The road winds its way northward, down the backbone of Friday Ridge, arriving at a junction, mile 13.4, left, with the previously encountered cutoff road that connects with Forest Highway 1. In this vicinity is Friday Camp, named, like the ridge, for an Indian of interesting exploits. (*See sidebar, above.*)

The road continues its gradual descent, winding across the ridgeline while occasionally offering vistas of the oak- and conifer-clad hump of Hogback Ridge, right. At mile 19.2 the route reaches a junction, left, with two dirt roads; the route to the right, 6N17, climbs two and a half miles to the Brush Mountain Look-out. Here a sweeping panorama includes the Trinity River, as it winds past Willow Creek far below, and a host of mountain peaks: Ironside Mountain to the east, the Trinities to the north-east, Big Hill to the north, and Preston Peak far beyond it in the Siskiyous. In summer the look-out is open from 9:30 A.M. to 6:00 P.M.

From the lookout junction, Friday Ridge Road bears east, dropping through mixed woodlands until it reaches Highway 299 just west of the South Fork Trinity bridge. Shortly before the junction it passes a small cemetery, right, that is the resting place of several pioneer settlers. (*See sidebar, below.*)

A Long Way From the Azores

Among the small headstones in the cemetery near the eastern end of Friday Ridge Road are those bearing the names of Flomena Martin and her husband, Frank, Portuguese immigrants from the Azores. They met in the Trinity County town of Indian Creek, which had a substantial Portuguese community in its early years. After a brief courtship the couple was married in Weaverville in June 1868. They then moved to the New River district, where Frank intended to take up a mining claim. It was a difficult transition for Flomena. "We lived in a very primitive way," she recalled, "with only the necessities of life available. Our life was very hard and challenging."

Although most of the local Indians had been killed or driven off by the miners, Flomena feared the few that remained:

...I was so afraid that I de-manded to leave that country. I told Frank that I was leaving even if I had to walk out with the children. Frank finally re-lented and we got ready to leave. We packed up all we owned and tied the boxes on the mules. Mary and Joseph [two of their children] were put in boxes that coal oil had been shipped in, one on each side of a mule and because Joseph was the smallest child, Frank had to put a rock in his box to make the load balance. I was deathly afraid of animals of any kind and would not ride a mule, but Frank insisted and helped me on a tame one. He tied my feet under that mule to keep me from falling or jumping off. The trail was very frightening, it was so narrow and steep. It took us two days to reach the Trinity

River, camping along the way.

Although Frank had intended to travel all the way to Arcata, Flomena, sick from the trip, refused to go any farther than China Flat. The family decided to stay in the area, eventu-ally purchasing the Campbell Ranch at the confluence of the Trinity and the South Fork. The property had a flour mill and other buildings on it, leaving little to show that it had until recently been the Tsnungwe trading center of Hlel-Din.

Now the place became the Mar-tin Ranch, where the family grew to 14 children. Each daughter, while stilll little, chose a cherry tree from the old orchard and named it for herself.

Part of the ranch lay on the far side of the Trinity, and to reach it, Frank constructed a cage that hung from rollers and ran on a cable he'd strung across the river. It served well for several years; then, in January 1899, the cable broke, plunging Frank and the car into the winter-swollen

waters below. Two of Frank's sons and the mail carrier pulled him from the river, dead.

After Frank's death Flomena continued on the ranch with her children, raising vegetables, fruit, and chickens and milking cows. She became a midwife to supplement their income. Her sons found out-side work in addition to their chores on the ranch.

In her later years Flomena lived for a time in Eureka but eventually returned to the South Fork, staying with a son and daughter-in-law at their home above the old ranch. When she died in 1928 she joined Frank and two of their children in the little roadside cemetery. Her of-ten exciting journey, that had taken her across most of the Atlantic and through the deep canyons of New River country, had ended in the peaceful, oak-shaded hills of east-ern Humboldt.

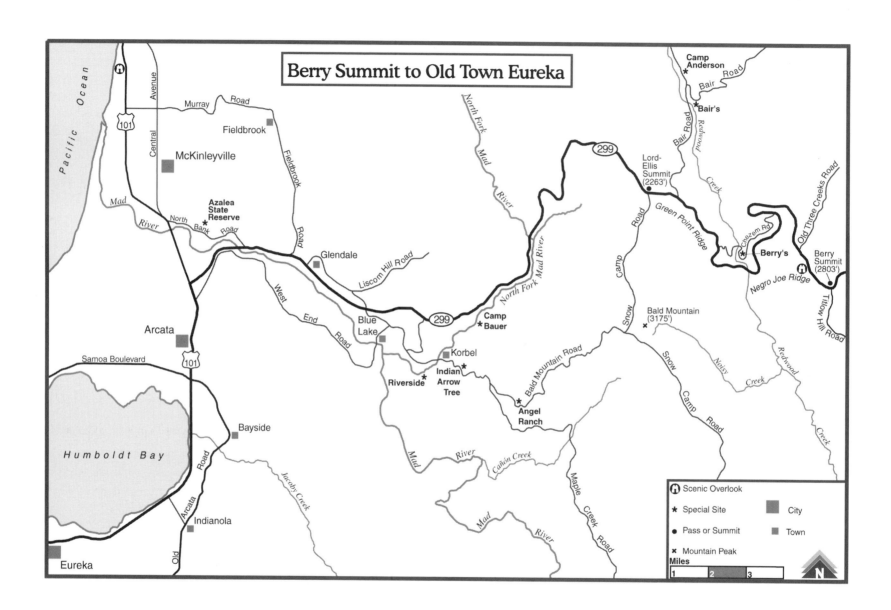

Berry Summit to Old Town Eureka

Pacific Ocean

Camp Anderson

Bair's

Murray Road

Fieldbrook

McKinleyville

North Fork Mad River

299

Lord-Ellis Summit (2263')

Bair Road

Redwood Creek

Central Avenue

101

Mad River

Azalea State Reserve

North Bank Road

Fieldbrook Road

Glendale

Liscom Hill Road

North Fork Mad River

Green Point Ridge

Chezem Rd

Berry's

Berry Summit (2803')

Old Three Creeks Road

Negro Joe Ridge

Titlow Hill Road

West End Road

Blue Lake

299

Camp Bauer

Snow Camp Road

Bald Mountain (3175')

Arcata

101

Samoa Boulevard

Korbel

Riverside

Indian Arrow Tree

Bald Mountain Road

Snow Camp Road

Noisy Creek

Redwood Creek

Angel Ranch

Humboldt Bay

Bayside

Jacoby Creek

Arcata Road

Mad River

Cañon Creek

Maple Creek Road

Indianola

Old

Eureka

Mad River

Scenic Overlook

Special Site

Pass or Summit

Mountain Peak

City

Town

Miles

1   2   3

N

192

VII. Up & Down to Old Town

Berry Summit Vista Point: Vast Views of Upper Redwood Creek

Perched on a grassy hillock just west of Berry Summit, an accommodating vista point offers a panorama of Redwood Creek's upper drainage. The deep stream canyon drops away to the southwest, with conifer-clad slopes in the distance, oaks and grassland on the near hillside. Scattered throughout the scenery is a series of historic sites that the informed observer will delight in identifying.

In the immediate foreground, descending directly below the overlook, is the oak-clad landform known as Negro, or Negro Joe, Ridge. The latter name is probably only half correct, for the site reputedly honors no Joe, but rather one Leroy Watkins, a freed slave from Kentucky. Around 1860 Watkins lived across the valley on the ranch of a Captain Snyder; the ridge that bears his name may commemorate Watkins's bloody encounter with two relatives of his Indian wife. Attacked by the men, Leroy dispatched both of them with his "sheath knife," despite suffering a hatchet wound in his chest.

Three months later, the victims' tribesmen attempted to avenge the deaths by ambushing a pair of packers on the Trinity Trail near Grouse Creek; whites retaliated by mounting a campaign against the local Whilkuts. Watkins eventually relocated to Eureka, where he made his living as a blacksmith.

The remote headwaters of Redwood Creek, far to the south, served as the dwelling place of a slightly later local, Dan Davis, who seldom left his remote habitat unless it happened to be election day. On those occasions, Dan would saddle up his steed and ride to the Bald Mountain precinct's polling place, a half-day trip. Arriving about noon, Davis duly cast his vote for the incumbent sheriff, Thomas McGinnis Brown—and no one else. After visiting around, having dinner, and perhaps partaking in a few election-day libations, Dan would remount his horse and return to his upper Redwood retreat, not to be seen again until either he ran out of tobacco or "Mac" Brown's name again appeared on the ballot.

Across the canyon and a bit to the left of the line of Negro Ridge, keen-eyed viewers can discern a cluster of tall, dark conifers on an intermediate ridge. To the left of the trees, on the reverse ridgeslope, lies Christmas Prairie. The spot gained its name following a December 25th "battle" between white soldiers and the local Indians. A Whilkut village had long occupied the prairie, and in 1863 the tribe fortified the site during their conflict with white settlers, building four log cabins and a stockade. A local resident alerted soldiers from Hoopa's Fort Gaston, who attacked the Indians for two days, finally bringing in a howitzer to shell the structures. At evening on the second day, the troops posted a picket line around the prairie, but it proved to no avail; by the morning of day three the Whilkuts had vanished as completely as Saint Nicholas, much to the post-Christmas chagrin of the military.

Later the prairie served as the improbable

starting point for one of Humboldt County's pioneer phone systems. When, in 1897, the young son of rancher James Henry Blake died because the family couldn't summon a doctor in time, the distraught father decided to improve communication with the outside world. Blake accordingly strung a phone line from their Christmas Prairie homestead to Bald Mountain, on to Angel's Ranch, and thence down the mountain to Blue Lake, where the local physician and pharmacist were the first to be connected. Soon Blake extended the line to Arcata; by 1915 the Blake Telephone Company had some 75 lines and 250 phones, with switchboards in Arcata and Blue Lake.

Rising to the right behind Christmas Prairie is the bulk of Bald Mountain. The low peak, unlike its Russian counterpart, owes its fame to mining rather than Musorgsky; its western slope long supported a way station for the gold-diggings-bound pack trains of Arcata's Brizard & Co.

Below Bald Mountain and to the right is a brightly verdant area suitably named Green Point Ridge. The original pack trail to Willow Creek came down the grassy hillslope here, and a ranch was located on the prairie. The Lupton family settled the property in the 1870s. Lieutenant Lancaster Lupton had been a soldier in Colorado Territory and a fur trader on the South Platte River; he married Thomass, the daughter of a Cheyenne chief, after she had nursed him through an attack of mountain fever. With their six children they took up residence on Green Point, and "Mother" Lupton became known far and wide for her skill as an herbalist. The family started a stopping place for travelers, which they grandly named the Green Point Hotel. When Charles and Elizabeth Marsh bought the property in 1905, it became the Marsh Hotel. It was still called that in the 1940s and 1950s when "Ma" Pollard maintained it as a boarding house. Reinforced by a retinue of pigs, Pollard's place was commonly referred to as "The Hog Ranch."

Today, the canyon shows the effects of decades of change: clearcuts checker the hillslopes, a modern highway slices across the now-obscure remains of its predecessor roads, a vista point replaces a grassy hummock with a flat expanse of pavement. Yet in many places the spring wildflowers still rise beside the grasses and the afternoon wind still whispers among the oaks—as they did for Leroy Watkins and the Whilkuts, and as they still do for all who care enough to look and listen—across the landscape, across the years.

Chezem Road:
A Secluded Section of the
Original Highway

Motorists with time on their hands and history on their minds will enjoy a short, scenic departure from Highway 299 that offers an alternate route across Redwood Creek. Some three miles west of the Berry Summit Vista Point, after rounding a wide hairpin turn, the highway reaches the turnoff, right, for Chezem Road, a four-mile remnant of an earlier, steeper, and more circuitous version of 299.

Two lanes of aging pavement twist downhill through mixed woodlands and prairies. In spring, the bright foliage of bigleaf maple, Oregon white oak, and California black oak contrast with the darker greenery of Douglas-fir, madrone, and California laurel. Douglas's meadowfoam fills a roadside ditch, mile 0.3, right, with its cream-white flowers. At mile 0.7 the twisting road crosses Captain Creek, passing iris, lupine, and fat false Solomon's seal. The route now runs through thicker forest.

(*Note: watch for short sections of one-lane road where small landslides have constricted the route.*)

A break in the vegetation, mile 1.9, right, provides a view of misnamed Princess Rock, a small pinnacle that rises dramatically above Redwood Creek. The landmark is laden with an oft-utilized legend about a distraught Indian "princess" who leaps to her death from the rocky height, but the site actually served a different purpose, that of lookout point for T'chil-kahn´-ting, the Whilkut village located on neighboring Captain Flat. Once, during the white-Indian conflict, the observer stationed on the rock left his post and while he was absent soldiers attacked the unguarded village.

Chezem Road then reaches a wide bend, 2.2 miles, marked by a large, open flat, right. A bright orange windsock recalls the spot's service as a landing strip; much earlier, another Whilkut village, E-nuk´-ka-cheng´-tish-ting, was situated here. The location was later home to Redwood House, a travelers' stop along the route to Willow Creek. The site was owned by the Charlie Berry family, which originally lived farther up on the hillside in the vicinity of Negro Ridge. They moved downslope to this flat, just above the creek, and set up accommodations for travelers; the wagon road from the coast ended here, and only a trail continued east. In the 1890s Redwood House offered a store, saloon, blacksmith shop, hotel, and large barn and stable. Berry also built a small, one-room schoolhouse, which he then filled mostly with his own children. The school district boundaries stretched for miles in every direction to include the requisite number of students. Among the attendees were a few Whilkuts from nearby Captain Flat; they brought such delicacies as dried salmon and venison, hazelnuts, and pine nuts for lunch, which they regularly attempted to swap for the white students' sandwiches.

One morning found the school filled with

a number of new students. Some 15 older Whilkut boys, who as a rule never came to class, had been coerced there by a threat from the government inspector: either go to the Redwood Creek School or return to the reservation at Hoopa. For a few days the boys dutifully sat at their desks, but after the inspector moved on to other schools, their numbers gradually dwindled to none.

The original schoolhouse can still be seen, reconstituted into a trim wooden cabin, near the west side of the flat. Also visible is the original wagon road to Berry Summit, which leaves the east side of Chezem Road at the upper end of the bend, climbing the hillside past a ranch gate. Berry's original house, built about 1880, burned in 1932.

Below the ranch site, mile 2.5, Chezem Road runs directly above Redwood Creek. Across the canyon, a rustic cabin perches on a small flat, its metal roof rusted a deep brown-red, its weathered walls still bearing a covering of spring green paint.

At mile 2.8 is the turnoff, right, for the road to a privately owned summer camp; in spring fawn lilies border the entrance. The campground area is located on Captain Flat, which, along with Captain Creek, was probably named for Redwood Captain, who, along with another noted warrior, Curly-headed Tom, lived here.

Following the 1864 treaty, almost all of the Whilkuts moved to the Hoopa reservation, but eventually many returned to Redwood Creek. In time a new village was established about a mile downstream from Captain Flat, leaving only an elderly couple at what had once been T'chil-kahn´-ting.

Just past the campground entrance, Chezem Road crosses Redwood Creek on a sturdy, green-painted steel bridge. The route rises past a collection of houses, passing at mile 3.0, right, the one-time Green Point business district. A small structure with overhung roof was, from 1931 to 1968, a gas station; its services were at times supplemented by those of several other enterprises—a store, cafe, church, and bordello. Today, as then, the spot provides shaded shelter from the canyon's summer heat, but with the absence of the long-rerouted highway, there is no longer a demand for Green Point's once-varied commerce.

Chezem Road then climbs on switchbacks, passing, mile 3.8, right, the site of the now-vanished Green Point School. The route continues upward to mile 4.4, where it rejoins Highway 299 at the edge of Green Point Ridge.

"Gentleman Jim" Chezem, long-time resident of Chezem Road. (Mark Rounds phtoto)

Reconnoitering Venerable Redwood Valley

In bygone days, the dramatic valley of Redwood Creek played many parts—home to the Whilkut and Chilula tribes, scene of combat in the Indian-white conflict, site of trail crossings for packers and travelers, center for ranches and resorts. A short (nine-mile) side trip will take visitors down 1,300 feet into this deep, history-filled canyon and back more than 130 years in time.

(*Note: private property bounds both sides of the road throughout the side trip. Most of the area is posted, much of it patrolled. During dry months the fire danger in the canyon is extreme.*)

Bair Road, two lanes, paved, departs northward from Highway 299 a mile east of Lord-Ellis Summit at an exit sign marked "Redwood Valley." The route drops rapidly through a mixed forest notable for its many bigleaf maples. Seep-spring monkeyflower, buttercup, and lupine brighten the roadside in spring.

The road levels and then crosses Redwood Creek, mile 3.4. Ahead on the right is the entrance to the Redwood Creek Ranch, a historic property that was one of the first white outposts in the area. Prior to the 1850s, this section of the canyon was the domain of the Chilula Indians, who populated the creeksides with more than a dozen villages. Whites settled here soon after arriving on the North Coast; the fertile valley lent itself to ranching, and the site gained additional importance as a crossing for the pack trail that connected Arcata with the Hoopa Valley and the Klamath and Salmon River mines.

In 1858 Isaac Minor purchased a ranch located at the crossing and delighted trail users by opening, in his words, "a sort of public house." He marketed his ranch products at each end of the trail, selling to both the inland miners and the residents of coastal Arcata. Within a few years, however, the escalating conflict with the Chilulas and Whilkuts forced him to abandon the property; when a detachment of soldiers subsequently left his ranch unattended, the tribesmen burned it to the ground. The soldiers belatedly returned to the ranch site, where, five months later, they engaged in a "desperate fight" with some 80 to 100 Indians that left 10 of the bluecoats wounded.

After the hostilities ended, Minor returned and rebuilt, in time adding to his acreage. Then, in 1882, Tom Bair purchased the property—some 2,700 acres—for $10,000.

Bair was no stranger to the area. From 1855 to 1863 he had ridden bell mare on local pack trains, and a few years later he bought his own string of mules and became the sutler at Fort Gaston, in the Hoopa Valley. The venture soon proved successful, in part because of Bair's habit of sleeping in the middle of the trail at night; this stratagem prevented other packers from passing him en route to Hoopa, thus insuring that his merchandise would reach the valley's eager buyers before his competitors' goods.

After ranching cattle for 15 years Bair switched to sheep. He hired an expert hunter, aptly named D. C. Shotts, to protect his newly established flocks. In his first two months on the job, Shotts did just that, killing eight bears, five panthers, and one wildcat.

By the 1910s, Bair's Redwood Ranch was the largest in Humboldt County. Orchards, hay fields, pastures, and gardens spread along the valley, interrupted here and there by barns, stock corrals, and outbuildings. The ranch also served as a summer resort:

> ...a commodious hotel has been erected where all comforts one may desire can be had. One of the finest packs of [mountain] lion dogs in the country are [sic] maintained here. Mr. Fernall is one of the best pack trainers and most skillful bear and lion hunters on the Pacific Coast. Reliable saddle animals trained to the chase are kept, and a bear or lion hunt at the...Ranch should satisfy the most exacting Nimrod.

A campground with tent platforms, tables, and fireplaces supplemented the hotel. A seasonal dam held back the creek, creating a pool for swimming, and a waterwheel connected to a dynamo provided the ranch with its own electricity. Soon a tanbark extract plant made use of the area's numerous tanoak trees as David D. Peeples, a Eurekan who had just developed a new process for condensing milk, was hired to create a similar technology for the tanbark. The resulting system reduced the bark to a thick liquid, which was then packaged in paper sacks and cooled. Thereafter, instead of shipping multiple muleloads of dried tanbark to the tanneries, only the compactly solidified extract was sent. With the voracious extractor in place, Bair let a contract to cut 3,000 cords of bark.

The Bair family sold the ranch in 1932. One of the later owners, P. C. Merillion, was a diplomat who served in the French delegation during the formation of the United Nations. A local logging family now owns the property.

The road bends left at the ranch entrance, passing a small barn and pasture before reaching a junction at mile 3.9. Here Bair Road branches right, becoming a one-lane gravel route as it climbs the hillside on its 22-mile course to Hoopa. A worthy side trip, the road may prove daunting to macadam-minded motorists, but a springtime ascent of just the first three or four miles will yield such roadside rewards as firecracker flower, blue dicks, crimson columbine, California pinks, iris, clarkia, woolly sunflower, California poppy, and seep-spring monkeyflower—all scattered around and about a stunning, sweeping hillside prairie fringed with oaks, maples, and firs.

A paved route continues left from the junction; it takes the name of Stover Road. After bending up and around the shoulder of a hillslope, the road runs past pastureland that was once home to Camp Anderson, a solitary log cabin that served as a military installation during the white-Indian war. Although strategically located near the Arcata-Hoopa trail, the camp had limited effect. Within its territory was a string of ranches that ran downstream through the valley and then up along the ridgeline of the Bald Hills; each property was several miles from the next. Patrols from Camp Anderson were kept busy chasing after the Chilulas and Whilkuts, who would attack an isolated ranch, burn it, and then discourteously depart before the soldiers could catch up with them. By the summer of 1862, a member of the camp's detachment wrote that "Redwood Creek is now virtually deserted!" He added that except for two ranchers seeking protection near the camp, "only J. P. Albee remains." Soon Albee was dead and his unprotected ranch in ashes.

Camp Anderson's usefulness, already questionable, dropped to nothing following the 1864 peace treaty, and the site was soon abandoned. Today, cattle graze where soldiers once paraded, and the bellowing of a lone bull has replaced the drill sergeant barking his orders.

Before the soldiers came, the grassy flat was home to Ke´-nah´-hung-tah´ch-ting, a large Chilula village. Four house pits were still visible in the 1910s.

Stover Road passes through the flat and crosses Moon Creek, which emerges from a stand of maples, right, on its way to meet Redwood Creek. The stream was named for Charlie Moon, a Chinese immigrant who arrived at Redwood Creek in his early teens to work on the Bair Ranch. (*See sidebar, next page.*)

Moon descendants still own Charlie and his wife Minnie's allotment near the creek. Stover Road continues some six miles northward from the crossing before entering private property at the Stover Ranch. History and scenery seekers can, however, end their exploration at Moon Creek and return to Highway 299, confident they have beheld many of the colorful canyon's most enticing offerings.

The Moon that Shone on Redwood Creek

Charlie Moon came to work for Tom Bair when he was barely a teenager—and stayed on the job for over 60 years. During that time the multitalented Moon filled a variety of functions—cook, companion and teacher for Bair's sons and orphaned grandson, hotel handyman, and, many years later, shepherd for the sheep flocks. He also, with a bit of help from Bair, managed to survive nearly six decades of Sinophobia in a county that persisted in that form of prejudice longer than anywhere else in the state.

Charlie left his home in China when he was 11, traveling in the hold of a ship until he reached San Francisco. He soon headed north with his brother and some other men who planned to work at the Klamath River mines. Believing that he was too young and small to work with them, the group left Charlie in Arcata, where he got a job cleaning up burned houses. Then Tom Bair came along, taking Charlie to his Maple Creek ranch, where he learned to cook, keep a vegetable garden, and do other work.

Charlie had firmly established himself at Bair's second ranch, on Redwood Creek, when, in 1885, a city councilman was shot and killed by a Chinese gambler in Eureka. Angry whites promptly compelled all of the coastal Chinese to depart for San Francisco by boat, leaving only a few of their countrymen remaining in the hill and river country. Soon a pair of Eureka enforcers arrived at the ranch, intent on removing Moon. Bair, by then a widower with two young sons, replied, "Charlie is the only mother my boys have and he is doing a grand job and you are not going to take him." After arguing a while, the disgruntled duo departed, warning Bair that a posse would soon return to "Get that Chink."

Bair posted a guard and waited. In due time a party of about 10 men appeared, announcing they were in search of Moon. Bair met them at the door to his house, a Winchester cradled on his arm, and ordered the riders to stop. The leader of the group responded that they meant to get their man. "All right," Bair replied, "come on, but this rifle is loaded with thirteen shells and you may get me, but there will be more than one of you fellows who will not ride back to town." As the posse wavered, Bair added, "I'm not the only one around here who has a gun and knows how to use it." Epithets, rather than bullets, flew through the air, and then the horsemen departed into the dusk, making, it turned out, a Moon-less night ride back to town.

Moon married Minnie, a Chilula woman; they occupied a small cabin not far from the Bair home and raised a large family. In 1904, a visitor reported that Charlie "has the same number of moons revolving around him as the planet Saturn." For years Charlie would leave work on the Bair Ranch every afternoon at 4:00 P.M. to return home and cook Minnie her dinner.

Late in life Charlie moved to the coast, staying at the house of Tom Bair's daughter-in-law in Bayside. Through the decades, an unwritten code continued to bar Asians from the North Coast, so that when he died in 1943, Charlie was considered "Humboldt County's lone Chinese resident." As the Bair children that he helped raise would attest, he had more than brightened his share of the firmament.

Charlie Moon with his appaloosa, 1919. (HCHS photo)

Blue Lake: "Where Sun & Sea Air Meet"

The Trinity Scenic Byway officially ends just west of Blue Lake—where, as the city's sign says, "Sun and Sea Air Meet." That line, if not the sign, dates back to about 1910, when the town (population: 636) voted for incorporation as a city. For at least a century, Blue Lakers have considered their climate the most salubrious in Humboldt County—neither as cool and foggy as the coast's nor as hot as the interior's. As if to verify the claim, the town's *Advocate* reported (Jan. 1, 1898) that one young doctor "has changed his mind about locating here and will go to Swauger's Station (Loleta) instead. He considers [the] Blue Lake climate too healthy and not conducive to a large and lucrative medical practice."

This city of 1,500 no longer has any hotels, an opera house, or even the lake that became its namesake, but it can claim a famed theater company, a vintage train depot converted into a museum, a microbrewery, easy access to birding and fishing, and a fish hatchery. Moreover, it stands out as the only real burg on the Mad River and as the Scenic Byway's oldest

bona fide timber town. Blue Lake's longevity probably reflects two crucial factors: its ability to avoid being controlled by a single company and its position as a bedroom community, a short distance up the Mad River, for an expanding Arcata. (*See sidebar, next page.*)

The biggest blue lake did not stay blue for long. A mill began using it as a logging pond right after the Arcata & Mad River Railroad crossed Clement Chartin's land en route to a lumber camp at North Fork. Three Korbel brothers had just bought the Arcata & Mad River Railroad as part of the expansion of their Bay Area lumber business. The 1883–84 arrival of the "Annie and Mary," the popular name for the Mad River trains, made Blue Lake less of a resort and more of a timber town. As the 1895–96 Business Directory of Humboldt County tersely put it, "Its industry is lumbering, being situated between the Glendale and Vance [or Essex] mills on one side and Korbel [or North Fork] and Riverside on the other." But Blue Lake also functioned as Humboldt Bay's leading gateway to the Trinity-Klamath interior,

making it an entrepôt like Old Shasta.

Chartin, a true entrepreneur, apparently encouraged the rapid entry of the railroad and the lumber companies into the Mad River Valley. In 1889 he, his wife, and her sister returned to France for the Paris Exposition and stayed long enough to recruit 17 relatives and friends—all "capitalists"—for their growing resort-railroad-timber town. In spite of a shrinking lake, the Chartins' hotel and French restaurant thrived, as did three other hotels in a town renowned as "a sportive place." It claimed a "fine baseball team," a "crack race track," and "Sunday sports." Blue Lake (and North Fork, soon renamed Korbel) hosted grand dances and picnics attended by people from all over Humboldt County who delighted in riding the Eureka and Eel River and the Arcata and Mad River excursion trains.

Railroad Avenue became the main axis of Chartin's burgeoning village, which eventually absorbed two nearby hamlets—Scottsville and Powersville—on the county road (now Blue Lake Boulevard) to the north. William Scott and

A Tale of Two Toponyms: Mad River and Blue Lake

Visitors often wonder how the river and the town got their names. For a river that flows so slowly once it leaves its "narrow trough between the Coast Ranges," the name *Mad* seems like a misnomer. When the exhausted Gregg Party reached the river's mouth in mid-December, 1849, six weeks after leaving Rich Bar above the Trinity's North Fork, most of them wanted to keep pushing south to San Francisco. But Josiah Gregg, geographer that he was, had "to ascertain the latitude" of the area. Infuriated by their leader's attitude, his impatient companions began crossing the rain-swollen river in some Wiyot canoes, forcing the unhappy mapper to gather up his instruments in haste. According to party member L. K. Wood, "he remained silent until the opposite shore was gained, when

Chartins' Blue Lake Hotel, left, and the corner of the A. Brizard Co. store, right. (BLM photo)

he opened upon us...the most withering...abuse." The incident triggered no violence among the eight men, but it gave a new name to a river that rarely rages.

Record rains in the winter of 1861–62 made the Mad rise so high that it left several "blue lakes" in its wake. They eventually vanished, but the name stuck. In the eyes of Clement Chartin, a French *maitre d'hôtel* who reached the North Coast about 10 years later, the shoreline of the largest "lake" looked like an idyllic site for the "pleasure grounds" that he wanted to develop for visitors from Humboldt Bay.

David Powers had begun homesteading the area about the same time as Chartin, but their sites could not compete with his once the railroad ran through Blue Lake and he began promoting the town through the family's *Advocate*. Eventually Chartin's place absorbed both rivals, a fact still reflected in the alignment and naming of the streets. (The Blue Lake Museum's staff has prepared an informative booklet, also available at City Hall, for anyone who desires to explore the place at a leisurely pace.)

For those pressed for time or not wanting to walk, we have designed a two-mile loop drive through town with a few short stops. Leave Highway 299 at the only exit marked Blue Lake and take the second right onto Greenwood Avenue at the elementary school. (***Warning***: *watch out for trucks driving to or from Korbel and Blue Lake's Industrial Park.*) Park in front of the elementary school long enough to look across Greenwood at the high hipped-roof house with the water tower. Then imagine being greeted at the gate by the late Susie Baker Fountain, whose parents bought this home in 1912 after moving from Lincoln, Nebraska (and whose father soon headed the Blue Lake Development Board). Two years later Susie earned the first teaching credential awarded by Arcata's new Humboldt Normal School, now Humboldt State University.

Instead of teaching, Susie soon married into the same Fountain family that had bought the Campbell Ranch in Salyer as a walnut farm. Her husband Eugene set up his dental practice in Arcata, but in 1930 he moved his family into the Baker home. There she gained fame as an avid Humboldt County historian by compiling articles in her "clipping room" for the *Blue Lake Advocate*, the weekly newspaper which members of the Chartin clan published for nearly 60 years of its long life (1888–1969). Back in Blue Lake, Susie gradually settled into a routine that consisted of "mostly gardening when the weather permits, writing letters to the children [and friends], reading and as little housework as I can possibly get by without doing."

If we could get the fast-talking Mrs. Fountain to guide us (preferably in her husband's 1909 Stoddard-Dayton), she would have us stop first at St. Joseph's clapboard Catholic church (340 Greenwood). Built in 1888, it originally stood south of the Chartins' hotel (opposite Chartin Road) on what was then aptly named Water Street. Frequent Mad River flood-

This Christmas card catches Susie Baker Fountain's house, foreground, and the rest of Blue Lake during an infrequent snowstorm. The Blue Lake School is directly behind the Fountains' house. (HSSA photo)

203

A youthful Eugene Fountain with his bride-to-be, Susie Baker, on the Lord-Ellis road. The snapshot was taken with Dr. Fountain's camera by a passing tramp. (HSU photo)

ing finally prompted removal of the church to its present site in 1910. (*See walking tour map, next page.*)

As Greenwood Avenue bends into Railroad Avenue, we pass both City Hall—the best place to inquire about backroads and fishing spots—and Perigot Park, named after Berthe Perigot (a grand-niece of Chartin). His wife's sister, Clemence Deschartes, willed the land to the city in 1914, and a decade later Miss Perigot developed it into a formal French garden. When Blue Lakers lost their baseball field (1947) to the New York-based Grizzly Park Lumber Company, they decided upon a different use for the park than its donor envisioned. Three local Little Leaguers—the Iorg brothers—began their professional baseball careers here, coached by their father, a longtime local mill worker.

Susie would insist that we stop at the Blue Lake Museum if it's open or call a staff member if it's not. (Its May–October hours are limited to 1:00–4:00 P.M. on Sundays, Tuesdays, and Wednesdays.) Only by examining the photos and exhibits neatly arranged in the old railroad station can we begin to visualize the town in its prime—just before the 1911 fire that wiped out a block or two of businesses on both sides of lower H Street. (*See sidebar, page 207.*) The depot itself dates from 1893, when the Korbel brothers built it to handle all the freight shipped to and from a bustling Blue Lake.

The station, which was closed in 1983, persists as a vital part of Blue Lake's townscape, if only because Simpson Timber Company gave

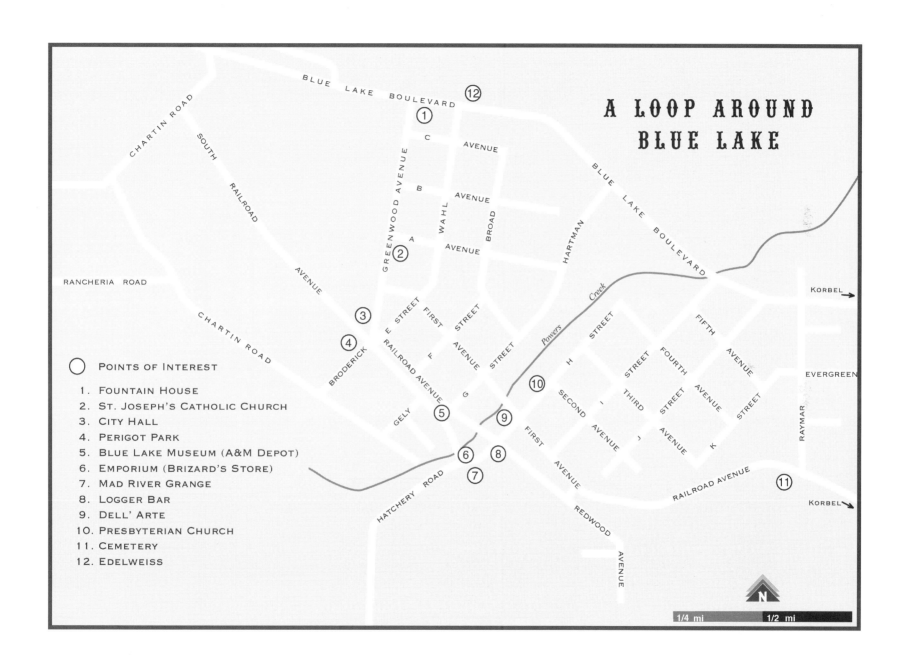

A LOOP AROUND
BLUE LAKE

POINTS OF INTEREST

1. FOUNTAIN HOUSE
2. ST. JOSEPH'S CATHOLIC CHURCH
3. CITY HALL
4. PERIGOT PARK
5. BLUE LAKE MUSEUM (A&M DEPOT)
6. EMPORIUM (BRIZARD'S STORE)
7. MAD RIVER GRANGE
8. LOGGER BAR
9. DELL' ARTE
10. PRESBYTERIAN CHURCH
11. CEMETERY
12. EDELWEISS

BLUE LAKE BOULEVARD

CHARTIN ROAD

SOUTH RAILROAD AVENUE

RANCHERIA ROAD

CHARTIN ROAD

GREENWOOD AVENUE

C AVENUE

B AVENUE

A AVENUE

WAHL AVENUE

BROAD STREET

HARTMAN

BLUE LAKE BOULEVARD

KORBEL →

EVERGREEN

RAYMAR

KORBEL →

RAILROAD AVENUE

FIRST AVENUE

REDWOOD AVENUE

HATCHERY ROAD

GELY

BRODERICK

E STREET

FIRST AVENUE

E STREET

G STREET

Powers Creek

H STREET

SECOND AVENUE

THIRD STREET

FOURTH AVENUE

FIFTH AVENUE

K

RAILROAD AVENUE

N

1/4 mi   1/2 mi

it to the town with the stipulation that it serve as a museum. Each summer, in July or August, the city sponsors "Annie and Mary Days"—a celebration that features a crafts fair, a fiddling contest, an old-timers baseball game, and a parade. The A&M weekend and the Mad River Drama Festival (held in June and July) rank among Humboldt County's most popular annual events. Railroad buffs still dream about restoring a train connection between Arcata and Blue Lake, but it seems more likely that the rail bed—with the tracks already removed—will become part of a Mad River trail system.

Just past the museum, at an odd angle to the right, stands a larger building known as the Blue Lake Emporium. It began in 1883 as a small store operated by the Chartins, but Alexander Brizard, a fellow French merchant in Arcata, replaced it in 1911 with a veritable two-story bazaar. He made it the jumping-off place for his Trinity/Klamath-bound pack trains. The restored emporium now houses Blue Lake's chief purveyor of antiques and collectibles.

From here, Susie would direct us left around the corner to Railroad Avenue and H Street, where she might prefer to bypass the century-old Logger Bar—the only surviving saloon in a town that once had as many as nine (two of them located at this same intersection). However, she would certainly draw our attention to the recently renovated IOOF Hall (at First Avenue and H Street). The same brothers who had built the Baker/Fountain home erected a hall that rivaled Brizard's Emporium in size but

St. Joseph's Catholic Church at its original site on Water Street, near the present Mad River Grange. (BLM photo)

had a much different function. Its upper story housed the Blue Lake lodge of the International Order of Odd Fellows, who had lost their original home across the street in the big fire the year before.

Since 1974, the renovated hall has served as the home of another "odd" but internationally acclaimed group. The Dell'Arte School of Physical Theatre is the only one of its kind in the United States. Its varied and innovative productions—staged throughout Humboldt County and the world—often incorporate local social issues as themes. A sample season (spring 2000) might feature evenings of classic Commedia, improvisational dance, and clown shows, plus outdoor performances for the rural communities of Northern California.

In the same month, June of 1888, that the Catholics completed their church (without a bell) down on Water Street, the Presbyterians dedicated their church (sans spire) near the top of "Nob Hill," at 241 H Street. No one has suggested that the timing of the two projects was anything more than a coincidental part of a general Mad River "cultural explosion" that included two new schools. However, subsequent events and the name Nob Hill imply certain divisions among Blue Lake's diverse citizens. Soon after its dedication, "About 95 persons met at the Presbyterian Church...to organize a Band of Hope..., and all were invited to join a club or lodge to drive out the whiskey sellers from Blue Lake." Apparently the band never became big enough to close any of the town's saloons, but 20 years later the campaign for prohibition seemingly forced a decision on the long-debated issue of incorporation. The *Advocate*, prompted by what its editor had read in a Eureka newspaper, posed the leading question (Dec. 25, 1909) with a long headline:

Will Blue Lake Incorporate?
The Eureka Herald Says We Might
In the Interest of the "Wets"
Thinks the Rural Vote Would Swing Blue Lake
into the Dry Column

According to the Eureka paper, "Blue Lake above all things desires to stay wet, and the town fears that the temperance campaign mounted by Eureka's Good Government League might make the county—except for incorporated places—dry." Whatever the impetus, the following spring Blue Lake finally placed the incorporation question on the ballot, and its "red-nosed" proponents won by a margin of nearly 3:1 over the "blue noses."

Susie Baker moved to Blue Lake soon after the big vote and the disastrous fire. Since she had come from "the largest city in the United

---

Blue Lake's Worst Disaster

In 1908, the Sanborn Map Company of New York City prepared a fire insurance map for Blue Lake, which reported: "Water Facilities Not Good. No Steam & No Hand Engine. No Independent Hose Cart. No Hook & Ladder Truck." Had town leaders heeded the Sanborn report and had enough funds to invest in fire prevention measures, they might have saved their newly incorporated city considerable damage.

The fire began on December 5, 1911, in the tailor shop of Augustus Brand (a German word for *fire*), at 130 H Street. Flames broke out right after he left his store that evening, and within three hours the heart of Blue Lake's business district lay smoldering in ashes. Luckily, a light rain, a shift in the wind, and immediate aid from Korbel, Arcata, and Eureka kept the fire from spreading any farther and spared Brizard's new store. A "continuous line of water-carriers" doused the buildings and fire fighters as best they could. Dawn the next day revealed a downtown reduced to a "mass of charred ruins, twisted pipes and vines, and relics of useful machinery." The *Advocate* and the town found some solace in the fact that no lives were lost. Everyone talked about quickly rebuilding the burned-out section, beginning with Odd Fellows Hall, but few of the same businesses reopened. Dr. Fountain, in a 1937 description of "My Town," stated that "even before the fire the town had started to decay." In his opinion, the automobile had eliminated the need "for a distributing point so near Arcata."

The Arcata & Mad River Railroad's Blue Lake station also served as the city's post office. The building now houses the Blue Lake Museum. (BLM photo)

Blue Lake's "Blue Nose Picnics"

Susie Baker's family settled in Humboldt County soon after the start of the annual 4th of July picnic arranged by Judge Joseph Merriman. In 1911, he invited all of the county's "Blue Noses" to come to Blue Lake for a dinner of "Genuine Eastern mackeral" (only 20 cents per pound at Brizard's in Arcata), cod, dulse (dried seaweed), and beans. The menu catered to the tastes of true Blue Noses—Nova Scotia natives like Judge Merriman, who were used to *cold* winters. He broadened the definition to include other Canadian Maritimers and New Englanders. Judging by the numbers who attended the picnics—as many as several thousand—all Humboldt residents became Blue Noses on July 4th and at least briefly forgot any ethnic or class differences.

States voting dry," namely Lincoln, the staid capital of Nebraska, she could scarcely believe "the whole-hearted merriment over the entire day [and most of the night]" that characterized Blue Lake's celebration of July 4th and other holidays.

Only by perusing past issues of the *Advocate* and mapping early census records could we hope to sort out Blue Lake's social divides, and only a Susie Baker Fountain would undertake such a task. She might propose we make the town cemetery our final official stop and interview those buried there for answers to the questions raised by gaps in her history of Blue Lake. The graveyard lies half a mile past Logger Bar on the right-hand side of Railroad Avenue. Some of the gray and generally flat gravestones record the states or countries where Blue Lake's founders began their lives. Significantly perhaps, some of the French settlers stayed together even after death, notably the dozen or so fenced inside the "French Quarter" around the Chartins at the upper right end of the hill.

From the cemetery, Railroad Avenue takes us a short distance to a stop sign at Blue Lake Boulevard (once Angel's Ranch Road and later part of old Highway 299). We can turn right for a glimpse of the relic company town of Korbel, or we can take a left that will lead us through what was Powersville and back to the Fountains' home in the Scottsville area. Eating places, a gas station, and the elementary school have replaced Scott's hamlet. If we stop at the Edelweiss restaurant on a Thursday-Sunday evening, we can thank the Fountains by treating them to fine Bavarian cuisine—Blue Lake's current alternative to French cooking at the Chartins' restaurant—before bidding them goodbye. If only Blue Lake or Korbel still had a hotel, we could spend a night on the Mad River or its North Fork instead of having to drive to a coastal city.

The A&MRRR wreck on September 13, 1896, claimed 7 lives and seriously injured 23 when the train broke through the bridge west of Blue Lake and dropped to the bed of the Mad River. (BLM photo)

Popping the Cork on Korbel: A Vintage Company Town

Some two miles southeast of Blue Lake, the tiny timber town of Korbel nestles in the narrow canyon of the North Fork Mad River. Half-hidden from Highway 299 by a hillside of regenerating redwood, Humboldt County's Korbel lures visitors not with wine, but with a remnant of vintage buildings, a gray and graceful concrete arch bridge, and its status as one of the county's three remaining company towns (along with Scotia and Samoa). This trio of inducements should tempt Trinity travelers to take a short side trip from Blue Lake, even though they'll find no wineries.

For most Californians, the name *Korbel* evokes images of champagne cellars on the Russian River in Sonoma County. Two hundred miles farther north, after vineyards have given way to redwood forests, the name may trigger debates about "sustainable harvest" and "spotted-owl habitat." Given their different climatic requirements, grapes and redwoods seldom appear in the same environment, but the Korbel brothers from Bohemia made their fortunes by producing both wine and lumber, and, in the process, they created two dissimilar places called Korbel.

Soon after their immigration from Prague to San Francisco (via New York) in the early 1860s, Francis, Anton, and Joseph Korbel developed a cigar box factory. A decade later they (and a fourth brother named Wenzel, who died in 1874) invested in a lumber mill near Guerneville, in Sonoma County, and acquired redwood lands along the Russian River. Not until about 1880, after a terrible fire had destroyed their San Francisco factory and lumberyard (valued at $300,000), did they plant their first vineyard and produce their first wine.

The Korbels' need for a new source of virgin timber coincided with the rebuilding of their Bay Area lumber business and led them to the Mad River forests beyond Blue Lake in the early 1880s. The German-speaking brothers purchased a small mill and George Burg's 160-acre farm on the North Fork and proceeded to build their own "burg" (renamed Korbel when it obtained a post office in 1891). The *Humboldt Times* described the homestead as a "tragic place" for the Burgs. One son had drowned, and "a flood completely destroyed all but the small piece of land their home stood on." The Burgs gladly sold out and moved south to a much higher location at Kneeland.

As a crucial part of their plan to tap the region's old-growth forests, the Korbels acquired the Arcata & Mad River Railroad and extended it from Warren Creek near Arcata to North Fork at a cost of $72,000. The direct rail connection with the coast made the brothers' Humboldt Lumber Company an instant success. Hans Bendixen, Eureka's leading shipbuilder, constructed a steamship—aptly named the *North Fork*—to assist *The Bohemia* schooner in carrying Korbel lumber from Arcata's wharf to San Francisco and other ports along the West Coast. A single shipment may have provided all of the lumber needed to build the Korbels' brick winery upriver from Guerneville.

In spite of a bad fire in 1886 that forced them to rebuild their North Fork sawmill, the Korbels soon transformed their lumber camp into a full-fledged timber town. With a popu-

211

lation of over 300, the booming burg counted 17 houses, 75 cabins, a saloon, a 3-room school-house, and a general store. According to Blue Lake's watchful *Advocate*, "the growth of population exceeded the erection of new houses" for awhile. Not surprisingly, young unmarried males (ages 20–34) accounted for the bulk of the influx, which hailed from a wide range of countries and states. Managers, usually married men from the Korbels' native Bohemia, occupied the houses, while bachelors shared the cabins or bunkhouses on the edge of town or in the scattered logging camps. The woodsmen escaped the isolation of the forests mainly on weekends, via the A&MRRR, when they headed for Blue Lake, Arcata, or—most likely—Eureka. A former employee, lamenting his younger, wilder days as a timber faller, chuckled when asked why he headed for Eureka every other weekend. He simply replied, "to get booze and women, of course! After two weeks in the woods, what would *you* do?"

Blue Lake's Susie Baker Fountain revealed a different side of North Fork life when she described the Christmas Eve celebration of 1888. "Everyone is in high feather anticipating a good time coming…[and] the dispensing of the fruit of the tree; the dainty lunch following; the dance till near daylight—these are as well imagined as told." A depressed timber market resulted in the temporary closing of the sawmill in 1895. But even though "The Humboldt Lumber Company has no force in the woods and the mill is not running, still Korbel is not the quiet place that one would imagine a cessation of operations must make it."

Why wasn't it? Because, as one observer noted as early as 1890, "Nature has endowed this section with far more than ordinary attractions, from a picturesque point of view. The [rail]road, all the way from Arcata, presents to passengers a pleasing picture of well-cultivated fields, willow hedges and forest growth; …at North Fork, the long reaches of maple groves…give an irresistibly enchanting scene that makes one wish to get out at once and wan-

Humboldt County's timber town of North Fork before it became Korbel. (BLM photo)

der through [them]…."

The company provided its employees *and the public* with Camp Bauer—"one of the most beautiful picnic grounds in the state." Named after another Bohemian, mill superintendent Joseph Bauer, the camp included "a fine dance platform shaded by…pretty maple and pepperwood trees, tables for picnickers…, swings for children, and a swimming pool with plenty of water." (*Note: Camp Bauer is still used for company celebrations but, because of liability concerns, now requires prior permission from the Simpson Timber Company for public use.*)

Soon after the death of the youngest brother, Joseph, and just before Francis's return to Prague, the Korbels sold their Humboldt County holdings in 1903. The new owner, the Charles Nelson Company of San Francisco, then merged with the nearby Riverside Mill to form the Northern Redwood Lumber Company. The revitalized business, with 17,000 additional acres of timber, created a self-contained community. Besides the usual cookhouse and general store, the NRLC operated a chicken/turkey ranch, a creamery, and a 40-room hotel—which billed itself as "Humboldt's most modern and up-to-date…summer resort." For a minimum of two dollars per day, summer visitors from foggy Arcata and Eureka could fish, swim, play tennis, ride horses, dance, or simply picnic.

Tourism may have helped cushion a timber-dependent company and town during temporary economic downturns prior to 1930, but

The Riverside Mill and its log pond, located on the south side of the North Fork Mad River a short distance downstream from Korbel. (STC photo)

nothing could have kept the Mad River mills from closing down during the Great Depression. Korbel and even Blue Lake became nearly deserted towns and remained so until a booming World War II economy revived them. By 1949, Korbel's 90 houses were all slated for repainting and its school had 90 pupils. The Firemen's Hall and the Whistle Stop Fountain/Restaurant served as the town's social centers, and the 45-man volunteer fire department supervised all recreational activities at Camp Bauer. The reorganized Northern Redwood Lumber Company even constructed an easier road into town and a standard gauge track for the A&MRRR. Mill capacity reached an all-time high "with a daily average of 125,000 to 150,000 board feet."

Among Korbel's many newcomers during the decade-long postwar boom was Jean Leavitt, current curator of the Blue Lake Museum. Her husband accepted a position with the A&MRRR in 1951, and their move coincided with the arrival of an A. Brizard branch store in Korbel, which replaced the earlier general merchandise store. The Leavitts lived in a company house similar to the few still standing. The town consisted of two neighborhoods—one across the log pond and one across the river. The

213

Northern Redwood Lumber Company camp in the logged-over hills of the Mad River drainage. Note railroad trestle, center left. (BLM photo)

Korbel's Cookhouse Capers

Bill McMillan was barely a teenager when, in 1903, he went to work for "The Company" at Camp 4 in the Korbel woods. At the tender age of 14 his first assignment was not with the logging crew but in the kitchen, where he was expected to wash the dishes of 250 woodsmen daily. It was too big a job for Bill, so he was demoted: his new work was less demanding; he merely supplied wood for the cookstove, swilled the pigs, and waited on tables. He started at 5:00 A.M., took off for a time in the afternoon, and then labored late into the night with the after-dinner cleanup. The pay was a dollar a day, and, more importantly for a growing boy, all the food he could eat. Despite these inducements, Bill was happy to take a job the following year at the nearby Riverside Mill.

Rose Bussier went in the opposite direction with her work, starting in 1919 at Korbel's planing mill at age 16 while many of the men were still away in the service. When the soldiers came home, Rose transferred to Korbel's cookhouse.

Under the supervision of head cook Joe Filgas, Rose rose early each day to mop the dining room floors, load the tables with place settings and condiments, and then help serve 75–85 nearly starved loggers. When many of these men had recently been in the army, their ration was a mere 5,000 calories a day; now that they were back at more demanding work, their caloric needs jumped to about 8,000. Rose's young arms soon grew weary lugging the food-laden platters to the loggers.

Peacetime might have come to the trenches in France, but at the cookhouse hostilities were likely to erupt whenever a logger found his regular place at the table taken by a newcomer. For that reason, Rose and the other waitresses asked the mountain travelers who often stopped for a meal to wait to take a place until the "regulars" were seated.

Rose's pay as a waitress was $45 per month plus room and board. When a job as second cook opened for $75 per month she took it. Here she and Filgas tended five ovens and ranges, all connected to a single huge firebox. Her work now started at 4:00 A.M., when she began preparing the day's desserts and then the lunches that the loggers packed with them, in five-gallon oil cans, to the woods. Those chores finished, Rose could focus on fixing breakfast: rolled oats, pancakes, bacon, boiled or fried eggs, beef steak, fried potatoes, hot biscuits, and fruit.

By lunchtime the loggers were running on empty, so they refueled on a repast that included roast meat or boiled ham, baked or mashed potatoes, dried beans, a vegetable, pie or pudding, and sometimes hot doughnuts. Dinner was similarly sizable, with the net result that Rose might busy herself peeling a hundred pounds of potatoes or slicing 25 pounds of onions at a stretch. On bread baking days Rose continued at the ovens until 10:00 P.M. Although the loggers took off Sundays, Rose's schedule ran seven days a week.

Like Bill McMillan two decades earlier, Rose found the pace of cookhouse work daunting; she moved to Eureka in 1922, took a job there, and that same year married. After three years in the Korbel cookhouse, her new kitchen chores must have seemed like a vacation, although as she stared across the breakfast table at her husband's single serving of victuals, Rose may have wistfully recalled the good old days, when four score of full stomached loggers finally pushed their plates away and waddled towards the woods, content with the knowledge that they would tuck into nine dozen sugar-coated doughnuts, made by you-know-who, at dinner that night.

Of such mealtimes memories are made.

Leavitts lived in the section of smaller homes beyond the pond, but they had three bedrooms and a sun-porch overlooking the water. Jean remembers that her three children never tired of watching the trains dump logs into the pond, and sometimes they sneaked down to play on them. She also recalls how busy she was trying to protect the family's wash from the ash precipitated by the company's slash burners, which incinerated excess wood and bark. Since the 1960s the mill operation has chipped leftover scraps into pulp for paper and used ground-up bark to generate electricity.

Today Korbel's "townscape" reflects the drastic changes that have occurred since 1956, when the Simpson Timber Company purchased Korbel, the A&MRRR, and over 30,000 acres of timber for $10 million. The company showed no interest in assuming "the problems of company-town management." In what seemed like a "sudden" transformation of the town to Leavitt, Simpson removed the stores, most of the houses, and even the handsome hotel to make room for log-sorting decks and lumber-sorting yards. Although most families found good jobs and homes elsewhere, Jean's family felt "on their own" after the move and lamented the loss of "the strong community feeling [that] died along with the mill town."

Simpson's modernization of the mill made most features of the town redundant, including the pond that was no longer needed for log sorting. A cluster of 13 houses, a post office, and an old school house and a gymnasium were the only buildings spared, and then for an ulterior reason. As explained by Tom Richardson, a Simpson employee, "fire insurance is cheaper because the company maintains an all-volunteer fire brigade." Unlike Jean, Tom believes a "strong community feeling" still (or perhaps once again) exists. Casual conversations with mill-workers, many of them third-generation employees, reveal a mutual loyalty between management and labor.

Annual company picnics held at Camp Bauer undoubtedly contribute to this camaraderie. Russell Nelson, a retired employee, has attended these gatherings since 1952. He hears about them through friends or the company paper—*The Barker*. The picnics have enabled him to maintain friendships that might have faded after retiring 15 years ago. He looks forward to swapping stories with friends while feasting at the company barbecue.

Korbel's position in the Mad River Valley has changed greatly since three Bohemian brothers first acquired the site. Now lacking most of the amenities that once made it a bustling place, the town's tiny size conceals its boom-and-bust history. The nearly constant hum of the mill and the steady flow of logging trucks account for most of the activity in Korbel today. Simpson cordially invites visitors to apply for a guided tour of the mill, the town's main attraction, which will show them the milling process from tree to board of second-growth redwood and Douglas-fir.

From the mill, history seekers can continue south on Maple Creek Road, cross over the North Fork Mad River on a 1928 concrete arch bridge, and climb one mile to the Indian Arrow Tree, a roadside redwood snag whose sign states: "Site of treaty between coast [Wiyot] and mountain [Whilkut] Indian tribes."

Northern Redwood Lumber Company loggers with two donkeys (steam) and a mule. (BLM photo)

Korbel town and mill, c. 1956. Hotel to right of bridge and houses next to log pond were later removed. (STC photo)

217

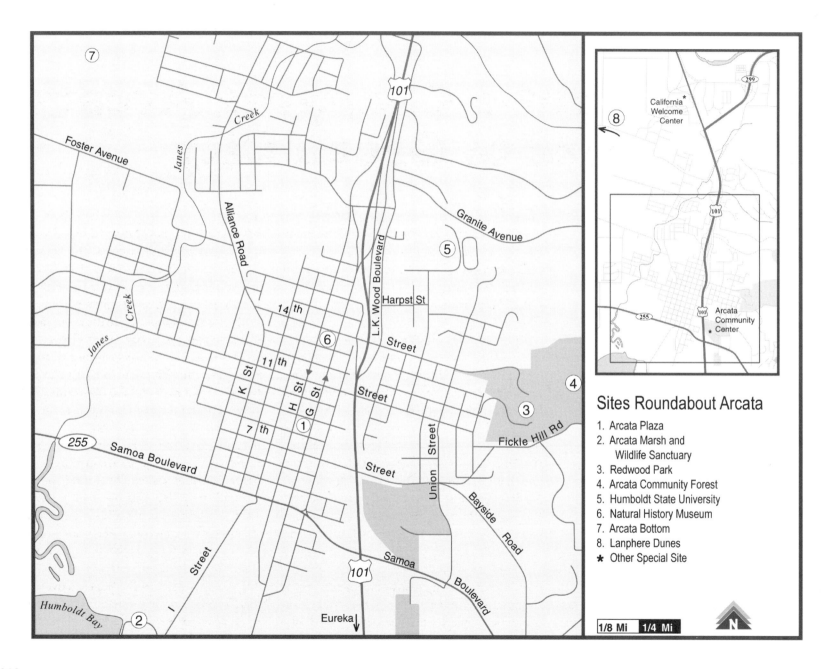

101

Creek

Janes

Foster Avenue

Alliance Road

Janes Creek

Janes Creek

⑦

L.K. Wood Boulevard

Granite Avenue

⑤

Harpst St

14 th

⑥

Street

11 th

K St

H St

G St

Street

⑤

⑦

① 7 th

Street

⑤

255

Samoa Boulevard

Union Street

Fickle Hill Rd

③

④

Bayside Road

Street

Street

Humboldt Bay

②

Samoa

101

Boulevard

Eureka↓

California* Welcome Center

⑧

299

101

255

101

Arcata Community Center

*

Sites Roundabout Arcata

1. Arcata Plaza
2. Arcata Marsh and
   Wildlife Sanctuary
3. Redwood Park
4. Arcata Community Forest
5. Humboldt State University
6. Natural History Museum
7. Arcata Bottom
8. Lanphere Dunes
★ Other Special Site

1/8 Mi 1/4 Mi

N

Roundabout a Changing Arcata: From White to Green City

Where the Redwood spires together
Pierce the mists in stormy weather,
Where the willow's topmost feather
Waves the limpid water o'er;
Where the long and sweeping surges
Sing their melancholy dirges,
There the river just emerges
On the sad Pacific's shore.

—from Bret Harte's "Mad River," 1857

The northwesterly corner of California is a region apart...A marked peculiarity is its sharp slope toward the northwest for its entire length...From an aeroplane the mountains...would suggest an immense drove of sleeping razor-backed hogs nestling against one another to keep warm, most of their snouts pointed northwest.

—Charles A. Murdock, 1921

Outsiders often confuse *Arcata* with Los Angeles County's *Arcadia*, given the similarity of the two names, but no one who knows the two places well would ever mistake one for the other or consider either *arcadian* or pastoral in character. Arcata has become one of the most colorful towns on California's North Coast, if only because of its tendency to change its "color." A century ago it touted itself as "White City;" now it attracts national attention as "Green City."

Whatever the official or perceived color is, it has always varied from one part of town to another. The downtown, centered on the Plaza, has a different hue than hilly Humboldt State University, the Community Forest, the Marsh and Wildlife Sanctuary, the Arcata Bottom, or the Lanphere Dunes Preserve. These distinctive landscapes have emerged within the small area hemmed in between Humboldt Bay and Mad River, close to a surging Pacific Ocean. Before exploring these "scapes," we consider some of the people and events that have shaped or "colored" them.

While the founders of Arcadia dreamed of creating an agrarian colony befitting that name, the Union Company from San Francisco had different motives when they platted a Union Town at the north end of Humboldt Bay in April 1850. The company, led by a few returning members of the Gregg Party, centered the town plat on a plaza not unlike Sonoma's. Above the entrance to Jacoby's Storehouse on the Plaza hangs a small glass plate depicting mules packing supplies into the mountains. The building and the image symbolize the town's origins as a gateway to far-flung mines. Both reflect the fundamental fact that the Trinity-Klamath gold rush, not the redwoods, first triggered serious interest in founding towns around the bay.

Union's position on the 14-mile-long bay put it closer to the mines than Eureka and the other Humboldt sites competing for Trinity-Klamath trade. To enhance that advantage, in 1855 the Union Plank Walk, Rail Track, and Wharf Company constructed an "ambitious pier stretching nearly two miles from Uniontown to deep water." California's first "railroad" consisted of "tracks...covered with planks with...rails of 4x4 inch [pine] timber, the motive power being a single horse" that pulled

A row of ships waiting to load lumber at the Arcata wharf, c. 1895. (HCHS photo)

Union launched the *Northern Californian*, co-owned by Murdock's father. The paper's decision to hire an unknown Harte—"untrained for doing anything that needed doing" on the Humboldt frontier—ultimately backfired. In February 1860, he printed an editorial condemning the massacre of a group of Wiyots, mostly women and children, who were participating in an annual religious ceremony on Indian Island near Eureka. That event, perhaps coupled with the death a month earlier of Lizzie Bull, Harte's first love, prompted his departure for San Francisco, where he would soon gain fame for writings inspired by his early sojourns in the Sierra mines and on the North Coast. Later that year, Union changed its name to Arcata, not to improve its image, but so no one would confuse it with a Uniontown in El Dorado County. The change, however, created lasting confusion over the origin of the new name—a possible corruption of the Yurok name for the Big Lagoon village of Oket'o, meaning perhaps big water. Twenty-six years later Austin Wiley, as publisher of a new weekly, combined both names into the *Arcata Union*.

As an avid promoter of the town's economic interests, the newspaper played a crucial role in preventing Arcata from becoming a backwater. Even if Eureka, about seven times as large by 1900, had emerged as the San Francisco of Humboldt Bay, a progressive Arcata could also make itself "what nature intended—a seaport city" like Oakland. Bret Harte never returned to see this tiny seaport, but when Charles

a wagon with wooden wheels. Primitive as this new "train" must have seemed to young Yankees like Bret Harte and Charles Murdock, who arrived in the mid-1850s to join family members, it reinforced Union's head start as county seat and home of the area's only newspaper— the *Humboldt Times*.

As the distant mines declined and the demand for bayside timber rose, Eureka—with its superior port—eclipsed its north bay rival and captured both the "capital" and its weekly. "In a frantic effort to sustain her failing prestige,"

Humboldt's First Railroad Accident

Saturday last [May 1856], as the car was on its way down, loaded with passengers, express etc. for the Goliah lying at the wharf at the lower end of the road, one of the reins of the horse attached to the car, caught in the wheel, and the locomotive was thrown off the track. It so happened that the car, at the time, was crossing the gulch just below town—over which the road passes, at an elevation, in the centre, of about fifteen feet—and "old gray" was suspended midway between the track and the water and mud beneath until he was "dropped" by cutting the traces. One of the passengers who said he had never seen a railroad before was seized with a panic and jumped off in the opposite direction, and brought up in the brush and mud in the middle of the gulch. The moment he struck he sung out lustily for fear the car and all the passengers were coming on top of him. The horse was led out of the mud on one side, and "greeny" was helped out of the brush and mud on the other. No bones, either horse or human, were broken, and the car was soon on its way again.

Early-day Humboldt Bay commuters took the A&MRRR's ferry "Alta" between Eureka and Arcata. (HCHS photo)

Murdock came back to the Arcata Bay in 1895 after a 30-year absence, he hardly recognized the area. He was most impressed with the "glorious tract of land stretching to the west, and from the bay to the Mad river," recently reclaimed from the salt marshes and covered with "fat cattle [Jerseys and Guernseys] and frequent creameries," "a marked advance over the potato fields of my memory."

Around the Plaza, Murdock found "but one unchanged store"—Jacoby's (albeit with a new owner, A. Brizard)—and only two others that he still recognized despite their being "considerably changed." A terrible fire in 1875, which destroyed Brizard's original business, and a less damaging one in 1889 undoubtedly accounted for many of the changes that had occurred in Murdock's absence. He saved his one criticism

for the plaza itself, "more changed than improved" and "its gateless fence an absurdity... There should be at least a gate at the corner to allow of its being crossed diagonally, and a few well selected trees would soon make it attractive." The *Union* agreed and asked Murdock to find someone in San Francisco who could prepare a plan that would convert the "cow pasture" into a "pleasure ground." In the newspaper's eyes (and ears), the only nuisance worse "than the cows that run in the streets...is the bells the cows wear."

A few years earlier the *Union* had agitated for a city hall:

> Our Board of Trustees and firemen have to meet in a little room in the northwest corner of the primary school building, scantily furnished with no one to either light or keep it clean. The Hook and Ladder Company have their apparatus stored in a 'crack' between a livery stable and restaurant. The library and free reading room is sanwitched [*sic*] by a gin mill and barber shop. The Recorder's office is in the back room of a saddle shop, while the marshal and the police do their business on the street. The town jail stands in the center of a street and is a nuisance in more ways than one.

Pack train preparing to leave the Arcata Bottom for the inland mines. The numerous casks probably contained the miners' mainstay—whiskey. (HCHS photo)

And the best place to put Arcata's city hall? In the mind of the editor, on the Plaza itself! "The plaza would thus be improved and kept green the year around." A year after Murdock's return visit, the town finally brought all of its functions and offices under one roof—on the lower floor of a two-story building shared with two fraternal lodges. City officials chose not to locate the building on the square but close to it, on the northeast corner of the G and 9th Street intersection, the very same site where Murdock's seafaring father had pitched a tent in 1850.

Not until 1901 did a Plaza Improvement Committee finally act on the *Union's* and Murdock's advice and turn the grazing ground into a public park, complete with a bandstand at the center. Ironically, the assassination of President William McKinley later that year prompted a wealthy Arcatan (and ardent Republican), George Zehndner, to honor him by commissioning the statue that replaced the short-lived bandstand. Haig Patigian, a sculptor based in San Francisco, had the bronze ready to ship when the 1906 earthquake struck. Fortunately, workmen managed to rescue it from a burning foundry and send it north. (The new town of McKinleyville, despite having been named for the slain president, had few McKinley supporters and no plaza for a statue on its main street.)

With a handsome city hall and an attractive green graced by palm trees and a statue, Arcata's new Chamber of Commerce began to boast of the city's beauty. " 'White City,' " they called it, "because its houses were painted white and shone bright in the sun from across the Bay." In fact, "It was not a real city...[but] a clean, homey little town with a rustic charm about

George Zehndner and a plethora of young Arcatans pose on the Plaza in front of the McKinley statue's plinth, 1914. (HCHS photo)

it"—almost an Arcadia after all. By the turn of the 20th century, some 1,000 Arcatans, flanked by 15,000 acres of pastureland, shared the general county view that "dairying is the most profitable of all farming pursuits in Humboldt."

Many townsmen, notably Noah Falk and Isaac Minor, had already discovered the profits to be reaped from nearby timber stands—fir and spruce as well as redwood. Those two lumbermen, first partners and later rivals, had the Dolly

Varden and Jolly Giant mills running full blast on the northeast edge of Arcata by the mid-1870s, both connected to the town's depot (where the Post Office now stands) and wharf by iron rails and real, steam-powered trains.

In 1903, when the Korbel brothers pulled out of Humboldt County, the California Barrel Company of San Francisco moved in and established a branch plant in Arcata to lower the costs of processing the fir and spruce bolts needed for making barrel staves. Known for many years as the Humboldt Cooperage Company, Cal Barrel became White City's biggest employer and "as indigenous [until its closing in 1956] as the cows grazing upon the Arcata bottom..."

On the eve of World War I, Arcata finally saw and seized a chance to even its old score with Eureka by securing the northern terminus of the Northwestern Pacific Railroad and, more importantly in the long run, the Humboldt State Normal School. Eureka appeared to have every advantage in the contest for a school to train elementary teachers—size, centrality, and three of the five members of the local board of trustees appointed by Governor Hiram Johnson. One of the three supported Arcata's more generous offer, and although she was later pressured into siding with Eureka, the governor and state superintendent of education cast their decisive votes for the smaller city. Fortunately for Arcata, the governor had close ties with two of the town's most prominent families—the Brizards and the Bulls.

Well before 1914, the owners of the Dolly Varden, Jolly Giant, and other mills had cleared the steep hills east of Arcata of their virgin timber stands. After two years of leasing the downtown Grammar School, where classes were disrupted daily by the noise of trains, the Normal School moved to the quieter 50-acre cutover hilltop donated by William Preston and the Union Water Company. Because the school grew slowly, even after occupying a permanent building and offering a bachelor's degree, Arcata became a bona fide college town surprisingly late. Around 1950, the city still billed itself as the county center of the dairy and lumber industries. Both Cal Barrel and nearby Hammond Redwood Company had payrolls ten times as large as the college's and more employees (1,100) than Humboldt had students (700). No wonder the college then decided to start two-year programs in dairying and lumbering.

Not until the 1960s did Humboldt State experience its own belated boom. During the next decade it emerged as the dominant element in the local economy with the decline of the timber industry. In the process the college on the hill lost some of its "air of aloofness" and became increasingly involved, even when not invited, with the rest of the community. The construction of Highway 101 in the early 1950s and its widening in the early 1970s symbolized the growing rift between the town and gown sides of Arcata. Students and alumni began to seek power in the governing (and "greening") of a city increasingly dependent on HSU. This

trend culminated in 1996 with the election of a Green Party majority to the city council.

Perhaps the best place to begin exploring this "chameleon" of a city and its environs is the new **California Welcome Center**. Unlike the one south of Redding, this WC lies close to the Trinity Highway—just west of the first exit (Giuntoli Lane) north of 299 on Highway 101. The Arcata Chamber of Commerce, with its office there, has produced an "Official Map Guide" that features a fine "Architectural Homes Tour." For our excursion roundabout the area, we highlight the five landscapes already identified (and three additional sites), beginning with Arcata's most important place...

1. The Plaza. Like spokes from the hub of a wagon wheel, four sidewalks radiate outward to the corners and four others to midpoints on each side. President McKinley still stands stolidly in the middle of the green, encircled by a bed of flowers. Two old palm trees grace the square, their fronds keeping rhythm with the breezes blowing in from the coast. On Saturday mornings, from April through October, many Humboldt farmers and gardeners park their vehicles around the Plaza and market a remarkable variety of produce and plants. The Arcata Downtown Business Community supports the town's designation as a Main Street City in two place-minded ways: 1) by promoting special events such as the Migratory Bird Festival known as Godwit Days (April), the three-day Kinetic Sculpture Race (end of May), the Oyster Festival (June), and Pastels on the

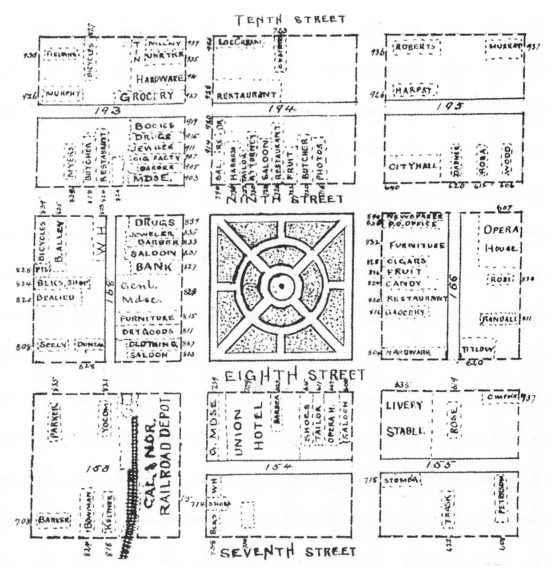

The Arcata Plaza and surrounding businesses, 1903. (HSU map)

Plaza (October); and 2) by encouraging business owners to upgrade their buildings' facades. ADBC plans to erect a bandstand on the square (without displacing McKinley) to foster musical events.

The frequent turnover of buildings and businesses around the Plaza—Arcata's Main Street—will not surprise anyone familiar with the history of urban America. For almost a century two structures in particular have given the town's center some semblance of permanence. First and foremost in every respect is **Jacoby's Storehouse**, which began as a one-story stone and brick "fireproof warehouse" opened by Prussian-born Augustus Jacoby in 1857—the only store still unchanged in 1895. By then, however, it had a new owner—Murdock's old friend, Bordeaux-born Alexander Brizard—who had made it Arcata's leading mercantile. By the time Murdock wrote a 50-year commemorative pamphlet for the company, Brizard's sons had transformed the storehouse into a four-story edifice. Both before and after being enlarged, the store stocked "everything needed by ladies, housekeepers, mechanics, artisans or miners." In addition, "Two heavy freight teams, a thirty-mule pack train and a four-horse express stage [were] maintained for the transportation of goods to the branch stores" on the Klamath and Trinity rivers.

Brizard's, Inc. finally closed in 1974, but the company soon renovated the classic revival storehouse and maintained an office on the fourth floor. More specialized businesses now fill the building, ranging from banking services to beauty and ice cream salons and restaurants. The main floor also houses a small Main Street information office and gift store and a railroad mini-museum.

The Plaza's second anchor is situated diagonally across from Jacoby's (or Brizard's) Storehouse—the **Hotel Arcata**, built in 1915 (a decade before the Eureka and Benbow inns). The aging Union Hotel still stood on the south side of the square, but just the year before, on the west side, Noah Falk and Henry Brizard completed a new neo-classical building for their Bank of Arcata. Never content as a minor operator, Isaac Minor countered with the First National Bank of Arcata and, facing it, the massive Minor Theater, Humboldt County's first true movie theater (and now a restored landmark, located one block north of the Plaza on H Street).

Many Arcatans must have shared the *Union's* view of a modern hotel as another "big boost in a business way" for "the growth and welfare of the White City," even if the owners rejected the paper's proposed name—Plaza Hotel. On the corner next to the Bulls' meat market, and across the street from the town hall and the newspaper's office, a yellow brick "Sportsman's Headquarters" soon filled the empty lot owned by none other than the Brizards. The first manager of the hotel hired by President Falk was a big game hunter from Wyoming's Big Horn Basin. In the main lobby he mounted "two magnificent elk heads, wired for electric lights."

West side of Arcata Plaza, c. 1895–1900, photographed by Dr. Francis Horel from the northeast corner of Ninth and G streets. (HSSA photo)

The banquet room attracted Elks and members of other groups while the two upper stories housed renters, train passengers, and, after G Street became part of the Redwood Highway in 1925, increasing numbers of motorists. Like Jacoby's Storehouse, the Arcata Hotel has received a recent facelift. The elk heads have disappeared, but a new set of specialty stores, a restaurant (with a sushi bar), and refurbished rooms beckon shoppers and travelers.

By now, after walking around the Plaza, place-watchers may have noticed that most of the buildings on the north side have the same function—dispensing drinks. Moreover, the liquor store and the four saloons can claim remarkably long lives (50 years or more) at the same sites. How a town, with a Women's Christian Temperance Union water fountain on its main square (since 1912), can support so many bars in such close proximity remains a mystery that perhaps only loggers, HSU lumberjacks, or bartenders can resolve. The Plaza has always had several cocktail lounges (or "soft drink parlors," as they were known from June "Thirsty First," 1919, to 1933), but until Prohibition ended they were much more evenly spaced.

If Arcatans appear strongly attached to their town, one can begin to understand why by exploring its outer edges. For godwit- and other bird-watchers, the best place to begin is **2. the Arcata Marsh and Wildlife Sanctuary**—75 acres of prime habitat located at the foot of South I Street near the vanished wharf. There you can view the bay and foothills or watch birds while walking or jogging along trails that wind between waving marsh grasses and jutting cattails. The marsh functions as Arcata's renowned wastewater treatment facility. Picnic tables and bird blinds allow visitors to linger and relish the calm of the place, where silence is broken mainly by birdsong.

A short drive up G Street to 11th or 14th, then east to **3. Redwood Park** (Noah Falk's gift to the city in 1904), takes naturalists into a completely different environment—620 acres that comprise **4. the Arcata Community Forest**. After Falks, Minors, and others had cleared the land of most of its old growth, the city gradually acquired and restored it. Ten miles of roads and trails challenge and delight countless mountain bikers, hikers, and equestrians. Fern-lined paths twist around tree trunks and, in the spring, past patches of trilliums; sturdy wooden bridges straddle creeks flowing through narrow gorges.

Return to 11th or 14th Street and turn right on B to reach **5. Humboldt State University**. The campus, having evolved during its first few decades without any master plan, has become an eclectic mix of cottages and buildings of assorted shapes and sizes. As if to compensate for the absence of an overall Humboldt architectural style, the university has spared no expense in landscaping its logged-over hills with redwoods, rhododendrons, roses, and many other ornamentals that thrive along the North Coast. A hidden greenhouse displays scores of species that flourish in a controlled climate. (Off campus, at 13th and G, HSU supports **6. the Natural History Museum**, where visitors can touch dinosaur tails, examine 10-million-year-old insects embedded in amber, and view dazzling displays of butterflies.)

Founders Hall, HSU's first permanent building and the only one with its own "plaza" or courtyard, still crowns the campus and offers some of the best views of the Arcata area's "skyscapes" as well as landscapes. As the sun sets, streams of cirrus clouds may float like pink or purple ribbons high in the deepening sky, even as stars begin to peek through an atmosphere laden with ocean vapor.

To feel and whiff the salty vapors, we can take almost any of the roads that crisscross the dairy pastures of **7. the Arcata Bottom,** or approach **8. the Lanphere Dunes**. To restrict access to a fragile environment famed for its endangered Humboldt wallflower, "Friends of the Dunes" at (707) 444-1397 offer two-hour guided walks on Saturday mornings . Perhaps the easiest way to sample the Bottom, with its distinctive mix of dairies and dunes, is to join the joggers, bicyclists, and others who follow Upper Bay Road to the Mad River County Park or the Hammond Bridge Trail, to gladden their hearts close to "the sad Pacific's shore."

Students at the Humboldt State Normal School stand outside their temporary buildings, awaiting more normal classrooms. (HSU photo)

Old Town Eureka: No Hot Time Tonight

When the sun rose o'er the townsite of Eureka [on May 9, 1850] it was a wilderness, uninhabited by man, and except for the soughing of the wind throughout the timber and the roll of the surf on the beach it was as silent as the dead.

—John T. Young

"But," as settler Young noted, "a change was at hand." He was one of a group of "12 young men, ranging from 20 to 30 years of age, all in the vigor of health and with high hopes for the future," who had just landed on the shore of Humboldt Bay. By nightfall of that May day, Young and his companions had realized a part of those hopes, wresting the beginnings of a city from the waterfront "wilderness." After four days of preliminary work and a Sabbath spent at rest, they commenced surveying the lines for Eureka's first streets (with, it turned out, an inaccurate compass), establishing their initial point at the corner that became First and A. Young's account notwithstanding, the new set-

tlers were not the first to occupy the area; Wiyot villages were scattered along the bay, including one, Toloiaplik, within a block or so of the initial survey point.

The dozen city builders had set themselves a daunting task. The western part of the site was forested all the way down to the bayside marsh, while a low, boggy gulch, "impassable except with an ax to cut your way," slanted southeastward. The northern area, near the water, was mercifully more open, with "only a few scrubby, wind-blown pines . . . and covered with a growth of salal and honeysuckle."

Trying as the topography was, the promise of establishing a lucrative pack train base for the inland gold mines invigorated the settlers' efforts, and a small community gradually took shape. The rosy prospects were, however, slow to materialize. Union (later Arcata), at the head of the bay, garnered much of the initial mine trade and prospered while business-bereft Eureka slumbered. Union added to its advantage in 1853 when it was selected seat of the newly formed Humboldt County.

Yet Eureka gradually gained on its rival. By 1854 the saws of seven mills were cutting logs gathered from the nearby forest; as the tree line receded, the city proceeded, conveniently occupying a series of recently cleared building lots. Then, in May 1856, the state legislature ordered the county seat transferred to Eureka in the aftermath of two inconclusive elections, the second of which was marred by massive voting fraud. A month later Eureka incorporated, and a month after that the infant city opened its own pack trail to the Trinity mines.

The Indian-white conflicts of the 1850s and 1860s that disrupted the pack train trade damaged Union's economy, but Eureka's, by then more diversified, continued to grow. Bucksport, another competing community that lay just south of Eureka, diminished greatly with the abandonment of nearby Fort Humboldt in 1870. Expanding Eureka established an addition on its south side, improved its streets, built redwood sidewalks, and set up both gas and water works. Among the noteworthy new buildings were the Vance House (later called the Vance Hotel), the Young Ladies' Seminary, and the Humboldt County Bank. To protect such symbols of prosperity, the fire department doubled its size by adding a second engine.

The year 1885 saw both the brightest and darkest events in Eureka's early history. On October 25, lumberman John Vance hooked up "an electric machine" at his bayside mill and connected the contrivance to a series of eight lights strung from his wharf up to and along Second Street. A large crowd attended the ensuing illumination. The event occurred eight months too late, however, to prevent Eureka's unfortunate exposure of her shadowy side. (*See sidebar, below.*)

The Kendall shooting was merely the breeze that fanned Eureka's smoldering anti-Chinese sentiment into flame; for some time certain whites had claimed that Chinatown, an area roughly bounded by E, F, Third, and Fifth streets, was a den of opium smoking, gambling,

Eureka's Enforced Chinese Exodus

In February, 1885 a quarrel in Eureka's Chinatown resulted in a fusillade of gunfire that left city councilman David Kendall dead and another white bystander wounded. Kendall had barely drawn his last breath before some 600 angry Eurekans stormed into Centennial Hall, most of them ready to lynch any Chinese on sight. Sinophobes such as writer A. J. Bledsoe railed against the Asian "menace" while Sheriff T. M. Brown and other moderates counseled limited toleration. Finally a committee of 15 leading citizens was appointed to inform the Chinese that they had 24 hours to leave town; they were to assemble at a warehouse near the wharf for transport by ship to San Francisco. To speed them on their way, a makeshift gallows was erected on Fourth Street at the edge of Chinatown.

The Reverend C. A. Huntington described the fate of one of his Chinese parishioners, Charley Way Lum, who tarried on his way to the warehouse the following day:

In the afternoon about two o'clock Charley called at the parsonage on his way to the wharf. I was absent at the time, but my wife and daughters were there. Immediately our back yard was filled with an excited crowd of men and boys. They gave a loud rap at the back door which was opened by Mrs. Huntington, and with a loud voice they inquired, "where's that chinaman?" She said "Charley is here on his way to the wharf; he barely called to say good bye and ask the prayers of the family in his exile." "We want him now!" And they rushed in, seized him by his queue [*sic*], Mrs. Huntington meanwhile pleading with them, "don't hurt him; he's a good boy and on his way to the warehouse." But they dragged him to the gallows, a hundred hoodlums following with jeers and insults. They took him to the gallows and put the noose around his neck in the presence of hundreds of people without a word of remonstrance from the police or anybody else until Rev. Mr. Rich of the Methodist church approached the scaffold and with stentorian voice said, "boys, take that rope off that boy's neck! If you hang him you'll hang him over my dead body!" The effect was like a clap of thunder. They dropped the rope, seized him by his qeue [*sic*] and hauled him five blocks to the warehouse and herded him with the rest of his countrymen under guard.

Upon hearing of Lum's plight, Huntington set off for the warehouse:

As I passed the crowd near the gallows, a loud voice out of the crowd said, "Any man that sympathizes with a chinaman ought to be hung; and I would like to have hold of the rope and help draw him up."

I went to the warehouse and after a long parley with the guard I was allowed to pass in. I found Charley in a remote corner of the room crying, with his classmates around him. As I gave him his things he said, "they scared me almost to death, Mr. Huntington." I comforted him as well as I could. I told him the story of the cross, and the glory there is in bearing the cross in the spirit in which Jesus bore it, and left him with my prayers and benedictions. The next morning they all embarked for San Francisco.

And for nearly 70 years, with but few exceptions, Humboldt's white citizenry kept all Asians out of the county.

The northeast corner of 4ᵗʰ and E streets in Eureka's Chinatown sometime before the Kendall shooting and subsequent Chinese expulsion. The sign to the right of the lamp post states: "WASHING & IRONING. TUNG SING." It is likely Tung himself who appears in front of the building, probably with a load of laundry. (HCHS photo)

and "heathenish disregard of [C]hristian morality." Yet whatever blight the Chinese had visited on Eureka was, in the eyes of the Reverend C. A. Huntington, eclipsed by the activities of Old Town:

> In what was called the lower levels of the city there were half a dozen blocks more or less, densely populated, in which a chaste woman could not be found, and who were employing all the arts and devices known to the trade of harlot, to entice young men into the meshes of destruction. Gambling saloons at every corner stood open night and day. But though their moral effect was evil and only evil and that continually, they were legalized by the government, encouraged and patronized by a numerous class of people, especially by those most loud mouthed in clamoring against the demoralization of Chinatown. . . .

Little had changed by 1909, when a report found the city filled with some 65 saloons, an even greater number of "gambling dens," 32 "houses of shame," and a brewery. Offsetting the iniquitous influences of such enterprises were a mere 13 churches and a public library.

Cultural activities revolved around the Saturday night arrival of the "Whiskey Specials," a series of trains from such logging towns as Korbel, Wrangletown (now Freshwater), and Scotia filled with "freshly scrubbed, bear-greased" loggers whose only aim was to convert their paychecks into pleasure as quickly as possible.

The railcars deposited their cargo along the

This 1902 pictorial "Map of Eureka" shows a growing city with bustling bayside businesses; a towering city hall, center; and a receding forest line in the distance. (HCHS map)

232

First Street tracks, whence the unloaded loggers proceeded south into the glittering Gomorrah that was Old Town. Many were waylaid by the attractions of the Fairwind Bar at First and F or the Louvre on Second Street. Strategically placed balconies at both establishments offered promenading prostitutes a chance to preview their wares for the woodsmen below, who, when tilting back their first schooner of beer, would find their line of sight raised to the exact angle necessary to witness the upstairs exposure of an enticing bit of ankle.

By the 1920s the Louvre was still going strong; now called a "cabaret," it vied with the Woodland as Eureka's premier "dancehall." At either establishment, more than a score of women were available to waltz or foxtrot for a dime a dance. Private lessons, conducted in the women's rooms above Second Street, were not limited to just the slow-footed.

During the Roaring Twenties both bootlegging and prostitution were widely recognized, if not widely respected, contributors to Eureka's commerce. With the advent of Prohibition, carpenters were called to Old Town to construct secret rooms and storage areas for speakeasies. If the beer halls were now hidden, the brothels remained more open in their business; the best of them, the Mission Rooms at Third and E, was conveniently situated above the Splendid Café, thereby encouraging diners to make their way upstairs for a second dessert. Two Eureka physicians examined the town's prostitutes fortnightly; having passed inspection, the women had no trouble assessing an entertainment tax of $2.00 per event. The fee held steady even during the Depression, although a 25 percent discount was then offered to the CCC boys.

Only once during these years were such business activities threatened. Tired of a city government that winked at wrongdoing, Eurekans in 1929 elected Emily Jones mayor on a platform that proclaimed "women have a natural instinct for cleaning up." To that end, Jones fired a police captain and two consecu-

Old Town hot spot: the Splendid Café was situated beneath Eureka's "best brothel," the Mission Rooms. Both businesses came to an end when the building burned in 1959. (HCHS photo)

tive police chiefs for not shutting down Eureka's twin illicit industries. This promptly led to a behind-the-scenes recall attempt by the defenders of the status quo. The recall failed, but despite the distinction of being the first female mayor west of the Mississippi, a frustrated Jones declined to run for reelection.

It took the onset of World War II to succeed where Jones had failed. When the United States Army asked Eureka to shut down its brothels, the city fathers, in a burst of anti-prostitution patriotism, partly complied. Riveting replaced more recumbent pursuits for many of the thus displaced workers, who found new employment nearby at the Chicago Bridge and Iron dry dock plant.

Post-war Eureka found itself almost attaining respectability. As the Whiskey Specials ceased their Saturday runs, Old Town's bars closed up or converted to other activities. Many of the red lights flickered and finally went out. Waterfront warehouses and other redwood-sided residue languished in the damp harborside air, their nails rusting and paint peeling as they awaited a flame-filled finale ignited by an errant match or hobo's fire. Those buildings that survived gradually attained the status of "Victorian relics," visited by vacationers with an eye for slightly scuffed scenery. The Old Town of today is far tamer than in its heyday, but the tattered remnants of its past still titillate or transport those who seek the whiskey-scented soul of early-day Eureka.

Streetcar #21 rattles down the "Duece"—Second Street—in Old Town Eureka during its heyday. The metal sign frame atop the Vance Hotel points skyward in the distance. (HCHS photo)

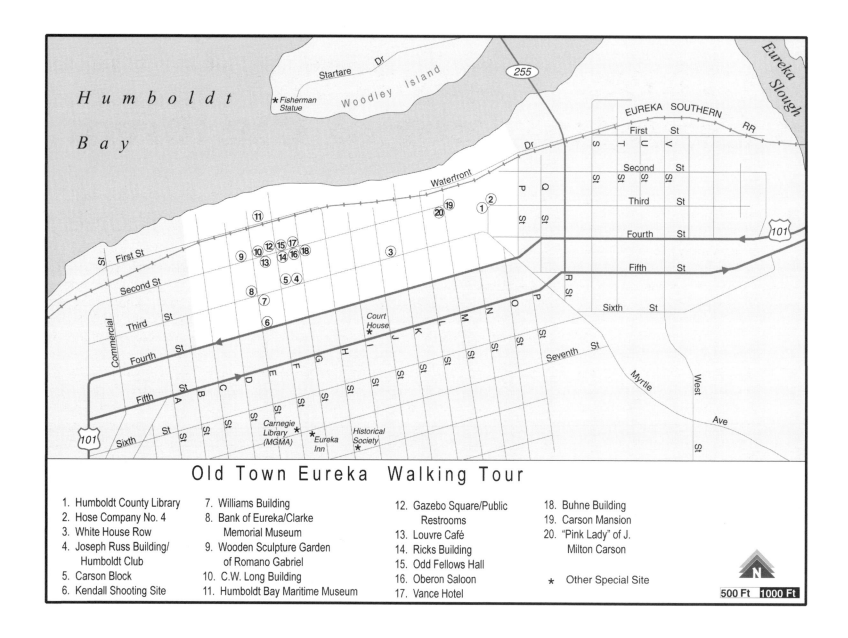

Old Town Eureka Walking Tour

1. Humboldt County Library
2. Hose Company No. 4
3. White House Row
4. Joseph Russ Building/ Humboldt Club
5. Carson Block
6. Kendall Shooting Site
7. Williams Building
8. Bank of Eureka/Clarke Memorial Museum
9. Wooden Sculpture Garden of Romano Gabriel
10. C.W. Long Building
11. Humboldt Bay Maritime Museum
12. Gazebo Square/Public Restrooms
13. Louvre Café
14. Ricks Building
15. Odd Fellows Hall
16. Oberon Saloon
17. Vance Hotel
18. Buhne Building
19. Carson Mansion
20. "Pink Lady" of J. Milton Carson

★ Other Special Site

N

500 Ft 1000 Ft

"Up Three & Down Two": An Essential Tour of Old Town

1. "Redwood redux"—the **Humboldt County Library** at Third and N streets recalls the days when Eureka's signature tree species appeared as part of almost every Old Town emporium. From framing to façade, from wallboard to wainscoting, redwood built Eureka literally as well as figuratively. Figures and facts galore are within easy reach at the library's Humboldt Room, whose collection includes many invaluable documents related to the area's history. Highlights of the holdings are the California Indian Library Collection and a set (with handwritten index) of Susie Baker Fountain's "Papers," the 120-volume gleanings of Humboldt County's most prolific historian.

2. Directly east of the library at 1401 Third Street is **Hose Company No. 4**, the oldest surviving structure used by any of Eureka's seven volunteer fire companies. Recently serving as an antiques gallery, the alarmingly red building housed its first hose cart in 1894.

3. From the firehouse the tour diagonally crosses the library parking lot (and part of William Carson's one-time lumber yard) to reach the junction of Third and N streets. Here the way is west, down Third Street. After passing a duo of modern-day Victorians, the Hotel Carter and Carter House Inn, at Third and L streets, we encounter **"White House Row—the Block of the Half-Dozen Dazzling Dandies"** between K and J streets. A sparkling set of six white-walled, green-roofed Victorians fills the north side of Third Street, all either Queen Anne or Queen Anne/Eastlake in styling except the one-story Classical Revival cottage at 923. The uniformity of coloration also extends to the dark green mudboards but not to the front doors, of which two are green and one each black, red, blue, and yellow.

4. Five blocks west, the second-story slanted bay window of the **Joseph Russ Building/ Humboldt Club** bulges above the sidewalk at 527-31 Third Street. Built in 1883, the Queen Anne style structure was named for early day rancher, politician, and land-fraud indictee Joseph Russ. Notable architectural elements are the "squeezed" pediments over both the outer second-story windows and the slanted bay. Visible through one of the first floor windows is a massive vault that once housed the records of the Belcher & Crane Abstract Company. The Humboldt Club, located upstairs, contained a billiard room frequented by William Carson.

5. Carson had only to go next door to visit his most noteworthy commercial creation, the hulking **Carson Block**, 227 F Street. Constructed in 1891, the three-story structure originally housed offices, businesses, and the 1,400-seat Ingomar Theater. Named for Carson's favorite stage production, *Ingomar the Barbarian*, the theater has fared as poorly as the play; it closed in 1923 and was gutted in 1958. Removed in the process were the brocade-covered seats, which cost a whopping $25 apiece, and a painted backdrop curtain on which was depicted no less than Hadrian's tomb. The building's exterior suffered its own share of architectural abuse, including the removal of much terra cotta ornamentation and most of one corner turret. Indoors, visitors will still find gleaming oak doors and staircases, along with hallway paneling of redwood.

6. The tour then turns south on F Street, skirting the edge of what was once Eureka's Chinatown. The intersection of Fourth and F now displays three banks and an abandoned department store, but it gives no inkling of the impromptu gallows erected in the vicinity in 1885 to intimidate the about-to-be-evicted Chinese. Turning west on Fourth, we proceed one block to the **Site of the Kendall Shooting** at the corner of Fourth and E streets. It was here that the fateful bullet struck and killed Councilman Kendall, precipitating the removal of Eureka's entire Asian population. A right turn on E Street then takes us northward along another edge of Chinatown.

7. Occupying the southeast corner of Third and E is the **Williams Building**, home for over 60 years to a family-run jewelry business. Founder William Williams began as "One-Window Williams," but, as the company's current name attests, the glass has grown tenfold. The Eureka Elks Club met here for a time before moving on to new stomping grounds.

8. Diagonally across the intersection the monumental **Bank of Eureka** now houses the Clarke Memorial Museum. The Classical Revival structure's strange sheen is due to the use of glazed architectural terra cotta on most of the façade. The museum incorporates the bank's teller windows into its exhibits and features a room-high relief map of Humboldt County. An annex houses an extensive collection of basketry from local Indian tribes.

9. From the Clarke, the tour moves north

on E Street to Second. Half a block west (left) at 315 Second is the **Wooden Sculpture Garden of Romano Gabriel**, a collection of vividly painted folk art that challenges easy categorization. Faded by years of exposure, the wooden objects winsomely depict trees, flowers, animals, faces, busts, figures, fences, etc., often arranged in repetitive rows like the targets from some overly extravagant shooting gallery. Gabriel, an Italian immigrant gardener and carpenter, received notice that the California Arts Council designated his garden "an important piece of folk art" on the day he died.

10. Our route then returns to Second and E streets, where the rust-orange bricks of the **C. W. Long Building**, from 403 to 411 Second, are exquisitely complemented by the inky blue coloration of its cast iron storefronts. The striking paint job recalls the structure's service, c. 1900, as E. J. Pulke's paint and wallpaper store.

11. Heading north on E Street, a right turn onto First Street leads to the temporary quarters of the **Humboldt Bay Maritime Museum**, 423 First Street. The frame building, which dates from approximately 1858, became the Buhne Mercantile in the mid-1860s. It currently contains a compact collection of exhibits that depicts the story of seafaring Humboldt. Greeting visitors is the 1913 Fresnel Lens, used for 40 years at the Table Bluff Lighthouse, which provided a 17,000-candlepower illumination visible at 20 miles. Nearby nautical disasters are commemorated by such memorabilia as a life ring from the *Yellowstone* (struck South

Jetty, 2/24/1933), a life preserver from the *Corona* (wrecked on Humboldt Bar, 3/1/1907), and the name boards from the steamer *Bear* (beached in foggy weather at Bear River, 6/14/1916) and the *Brooklyn* (capsized on Humboldt Bar, 11/8/1930). Claiming attention among the other displays is the Whitehall rowing skiff owned by lumber baron William Carson; nearby, the Tubbs Cordage Company's display of nautical knots illustrates the intricacies of not only the "Fancy Turkshead," but also the "Bowline on a Bight" and "French Carrick Bend." The rusting propeller of the tugboat *Ranger* reposes outside, protected from pilferage by its 4,310-pound weight. (*Note: the museum is expected to move from its present location to the corner of First and C streets early in the 21ˢᵗ century. The museum-owned "Madaket," a former passenger ferry, cruises Humboldt Bay from the foot of C Street. Call (707) 445-1910 for additional information.*)

12. We now set a course up First Street a half block to F Street; here a right turn takes us to Old Town's monument to modernity, **Gazebo Square,** located on the northwest corner of Second and F streets, where Schulze's Cigar Factory and R. Duffy's Cigar and Tobacco Shop once held sway. Built with redevelopment monies during the 1970s, the namesake structure's walkway appropriately spirals skyward like a thick curl of tobacco smoke. A fountain decorates the foreground, as does a regiment of parading pigeons that exert themselves upon the square's brick surface. Just beyond the northwestern corner of the square,

across the thin stretch of pavement affectionately known as Snug Alley, lies another recent Old Town addition, the **Public Restrooms**.

13. The central section of the south side of Second Street between E and F contains a quartet of ornately ornamented business buildings. The **Louvre Café**, 426 Second, on the far left, resembles a delicately crafted confection; its mint green and soft yellow paint deceptively conceals another iron storefront. The brothel-beckoning balcony inside now beguiles a less boisterous clientele with its dusty display of used books. Confirmation of the store's earlier identity is found to the rear, in Opera Alley, where the words "Louvre Café" still adorn the aging panel above the door. It was through this entryway on June 3, 1933, that aptly named Tom Slaughter fled after having twice shot Ed Carter, with whom he co-owned the Louvre and adjacent High Lead, to fatal effect. Slaughter was prosecuted for the act but acquitted, a not surprising outcome inasmuch as the main witness who testified against him was blind.

14. The **Ricks Building**, 203–215 F, anchors the intersection's southeast corner. The one-story brick structure was built by developer Casper S. Ricks in 1878. The store closest to the intersection once housed Silverwood and McNamara's men's clothing shop. Silverwood later moved to Los Angeles, where he was credited with writing the song *I Love You California*. Emily Jones, the onetime Eureka mayor, questioned the report, claiming that while in Eureka Silverwood "displayed neither poetic nor musical talents."

15. North across Second Street is the Mansard-roofed **Odd Fellows' Hall**, which displays a striking synthesis of Second Empire and Italianate styling, prettified by its current combination of lilac and purple trim in a manner unimaginable when rough and tumble Two Street was known as "the Deuce." The hall was built in 1882 for $27,000.

16. The entrance to 516 Second Street recalls the building's earlier service as Eureka's premier watering hole, the **Oberon Saloon**, whose name is displayed in blue and white tilework on the sidewalk in front of the door. Upon this threshold two impressive pairs of feet trod one June evening in 1911—those of author Jack London, on his way by horse and buggy up the coast, and collegian Pat Murphy, brother of Stanwood Murphy Sr., president of the nearby Pacific Lumber Company. Jack, an ardent socialist, and Pat, a determined defender of capitalism, commenced a conversation that soon drifted to politics, then escalated to an argument, and finally concluded when London punctuated one of his pro-worker pronouncements with a punch. According to one account, the bartenders locked the doors as London attempted to prove that the fist was mightier than either pen or sword, but youth proved triumphant when one of Murphy's blows dropped the aging author to the ground. Those who now enter the building may observe remnants of the floor upon which London landed.

17. At 525 Second Street, the enormous **Vance Hotel** looms over the intersection of Second and G. A traveler in 1858 reported: "In Eureka we stopped at the old Vance hotel. I remember the dining room was a long room with long, bare tables, with a dirt floor." When lumberman John Vance built the current structure in 1872, it featured numerous improvements. Designed in the Second Empire style, the hotel stood three stories tall, with a central cupola from which Vance reputedly watched his lumber schooners cross Humboldt Bay's bar. The presence of another type of ship was reported by the flying of a flag above the cupola; on days when the passenger steamers *Pomona* and *Humboldt* were expected, "the entire population watched the flagpole at the top of the Vance. All who could get away from their duties went to witness the arrival." In 1902 the original mansard roof and cupola were replaced, the three stories increased to four, and Italianate styling added. The Vance often housed the touring stage companies that played at the nearby Ingomar Theater. One such company went broke while in town to perform *Uncle Tom's Cabin,* stranding its players with an overdue lodging bill. To pay off the debt, the hotel seized the company's only tangible assets, a pair of dogs used to chase Eliza across the ice. The stratagem backfired when the always-hungry canines consumed every edible in sight, often cruising the alleys of Old Town in search of scraps. The Vance itself eventually fell victim of fickle finances and finally closed in the 1970s. A recently initiated remodeling project is con-

The Vance "House" before it became a hotel and before its three stories were remodeled into four. Note the cupola from which ships were sighted. (HCHS print)

verting the structure into a series of office suites.

18. Diagonally across the intersection, at 600 Second Street, the **Buhne Building** displays none of the faded flamboyance of the Vance. Painted a clean, non-committal off-white, its cast-iron storefront reflecting the reserve of Renaissance Revival styling, the structure suggests the substance and dignity required for its early day role as the Humboldt County Bank. The bank's president was none other than the omnipresent William Carson, who would daily make the seven-block stroll down Second Street from his mansion. Owner of the building was former ship captain Hans Henry Buhne, who had the distinction of piloting the first large vessel into Humboldt Bay in 1850.

19.

If I build it poorly, they'll say I'm a damn miser; if I build it expensively, they'll say I'm just trying to show off; so, I guess I'll build it for myself.

—William Carson

So saying, William Carson in 1885 erected the gargantuan, green-hued **Carson Mansion** that still surmounts the eastern end of Second Street at 143 M. Mill owner Carson made his fortune cutting redwoods, but the woods he chose when constructing his dazzling domicile were a collection of species gathered from around the world. Their varied hues and textures invest the house's interior with an impressiveness that is intensified by an overwhelming array of ornamental and decorative devices. Outside, an uneasy eclecticism has combined Italianate, Queen Anne, Eastlake, and Stick architectural elements into a style perhaps best described as Vainglorious Victorian. The building we behold (from the outside only, as it has been a private club since 1950—and only recently open to female members) strikes us with a strange mingling of Gothic gloom and Baroque exuberance—a sort of lumberman's cathedral, dedicated to the celebration of hard-earned secular success. Taken with the Vance Hotel and Buhne Building, the Carson Mansion nearly completes a coda for the stylistic symphony that is Old Town—a trio of enduring monuments to three of Eureka's foremost early entrepreneurs. Only the final cadence remains . . .

20. And it is provided by a glance to the southwest, where the **J. Milton Carson House**, 202 M Street, offers an abrupt change of key, its swelling turret and blush-colored paint justifying the sobriquet "Pink Lady." Built by William Carson in 1889 for his newly wed son, it is everything the somber, sober mansion isn't—bright, not brooding; more curvaceous than chiseled; lighthearted instead of leaden. Finally, our vision freed from the Carson Mansion's imperious pull, it is easy to direct our gaze past the Pink Lady and look westward down the Deuce, where, with the hopefulness of the half-forgotten, Old Town waits, ever so patiently, for another hot time to warm the chill coastal night.

Index

245

Clockwise from upper left:

1. Jerry Rohde in old cabin near Trinity Divide.
2. Ben Bennion beaming through an incense cedar.
3. Robin Stocum satisfying his stomach.
4. July 4th parade, Weaverville.
5. Fishing on the forest-framed Trinity.
6. Traditional Hupa house at Takimildiñ village, Hoopa.
7. Ringtail in Robin Stocum's rafters.

Traveling the Trinity

Clockwise from upper left:

1. Erstwhile Junction City Hotel.
2. Kinetic sculpture racer, near Arcata.
3. Old Town Eureka's "Pink Lady".
4. Trinity Alps from Backbone Ridge.
5. Trinity whitewater above Hell's Hole.
6. "Mr. Museum"—Trinity County's Hal Goodyear.
7. Oregon Mountain hydraulic monitor rusting in peace.
8. Rigdzin Ling stupa near Junction City.
9. Swede Creek fish ladder.
10. Redbud on the Trinity.
11. Middle Falls, Canyon Creek.

Clockwise from upper left:

1. Jacoby Storehouse, Arcata.
2. Founders Hall, Humboldt State University.
3. Trinity Mountains from Whiskeytown Lake.
4. French Gulch IOOF Cemetery.
5. Bigfoot from behind in Willow Creek.